D1706860

It's a Small World

It's a Small World

INTERNATIONAL DEAF SPACES AND ENCOUNTERS

Michele Friedner
and Annelies Kusters,
Editors

Gallaudet University Press
Washington, DC

Gallaudet University Press
Washington, DC 20002
http://gupress.gallaudet.edu

© 2015 by Gallaudet University
All rights reserved. Published 2015
Printed in the United States of America

Library of Congress Cataloging-in-Publication Data

It's a small world : international deaf spaces and encounters / edited by Michele
Friedner, Annelies Kusters.
    pages cm
  ISBN 978-1-56368-652-8 (hardback) -- ISBN 978-1-56368-653-5 (e-book)
1. Deaf culture--Cross-cultural studies. 2. Deaf--Cross-cultural studies. I. Friedner,
Michele Ilana, 1978- editor. II. Kusters, Annelies editor.
  HV2380.I87 2015
  305.9'082--dc23
                        2015026307

∞ This paper meets the requirements of ANSI/NISO Z39.48-1992 (Permanence of Paper).

▌ Contents

Part 3 Projects

Part 4 Networks

Introduction
DEAF-SAME and Difference in International Deaf Spaces and Encounters

Annelies Kusters and Michele Friedner

- Deaf people from all over the world attended the Paris World Fair in 1900. There, a French deaf leader remarked that deaf people around the world "know no borders."
- Andrew Foster, an African American deaf pastor and educator, established more than thirty deaf schools in Africa. His methods inspired deaf Nigerians, who applied Foster's strategies in their voluntary work projects with deaf people in Fiji.
- Expatriates and local Cambodians set up deaf tourism agencies in Cambodia. Previously, local deaf people acted as guides for foreign visitors informally and without financial compensation.
- A deaf American lawyer traveled through Chile and founded a nongovernmental organization to support Chilean deaf advocacy efforts by providing legal services and training.
- Deaf youth from all over the world who attended the World Federation of the Deaf Youth Section camp in Durban commented on how the camp provided opportunities for learning, networking, and empowerment.
- A deaf person from Eritrea traveled to Sweden and was shocked to discover how similar her sign language is to Swedish Sign Language.

While the dynamics in each of these encounters between diverse deaf[1] people around the world vary, they all involve deaf people meeting each other in

---

[1] We write *deaf* with a lowercase "d" because we see *deaf* as more encompassing, less politicized, and less context-dependent than *Deaf*. As readers will note, the chapter authors have made different choices regarding use of *deaf* and *Deaf*.

international spaces. This book's title, "It's a small world," is a phrase often used in such encounters by deaf people who discover mutual connections, often over and across great geographical distances, and these encounters can be seen as examples of this deaf "small world." Indeed, a shared experience of being deaf, which we call "DEAF-SAME," created the conditions of possibility for these encounters to take place.

The phrase "DEAF-SAME," although not extensively researched, is often assumed to be a widespread (if not universal) phenomenon, and in our personal experience in Ghana, India, USA, and Europe it is typically utilized by deaf people coming from around the world. DEAF-SAME or "I am deaf, you are deaf, and so we are the same" emphasizes at the feeling of *deaf similitude* and is one of the most powerful phrases used in and across deaf worlds. DEAF-SAME is grounded in experiential ways of being in the world as deaf people with (what are assumed) to be shared sensorial, social, and moral experiences: it is both a sentiment and a discourse. Thus, as both a launching point and a unifying framework around which the chapters in this book coalesce, the authors use the concept of DEAF-SAME in both affirmative and critical ways.

DEAF-SAME produces feelings and relationships in individual people and groups as they engage in encounters. Enhancing the idea of DEAF-SAME are deaf peoples' communication practices and the fact that many diverse deaf people can communicate across borders and boundaries by using (mixtures of) national signed languages, gesture, and International Sign. DEAF-SAME can create claims of likeness and affiliation between people with very different cultural, racial, class, religious, economic, and geographic backgrounds, thus transcending geography, culture, and history, among other things. In this act of transcendence, it produces a desired and imagined deaf geography in which differences between deaf people are rendered minimal. This deaf geography in turn produces and engenders the discourse of deaf universalism. By *deaf universalism* we mean a (belief in a) deep connection that is felt between deaf people around the globe, grounded in experiential ways of being in the world as deaf people. To be sure, being in the world as deaf people not only includes the shared experience of being deaf sign language users but also shared experiences of oppression, such as the global impact of the Milan 1880 conference, which resulted in a ban on sign language use in deaf education as well as barriers and discrimination experienced by deaf people in everyday life.

We see DEAF-SAME as an experiential and analytical departure point and not an end point. Why is it not an end point? By analyzing such encounters, we see that despite the shared experience of being deaf, there are also substantial differences between deaf people from different backgrounds. These differences include nationality, ethnicity, class, mobility, educational levels, and of course, language, among other things. People also have different expectations, purposes, or intentions in reaching out to deaf people in other countries, including making new friends, wanting to have an "authentic" tourist experience, learning something new, gaining financial profit, and engaging in research, development, or charitable works, among others. There can also easily be combined and competing motivations.

Exploring similarities and differences between deaf people during their encounters is important to clarify for experiential, practical, and theoretical purposes, for both people engaging in such encounters and for people researching them. As the chapters in this book demonstrate, these similarities and differences can create complex and contested dynamics between people. Thus, when initiating this edited volume, we wanted to examine how sameness and difference are actively produced, negotiated, and realized by people in specific times and spaces: we were motivated by the sense that feelings of sameness (DEAF-SAME) are often foregrounded in deaf encounters while differences are ignored or discounted.

STUDYING DEAF WORLDS TRANSNATIONALLY AND INTERNATIONALLY

This book builds upon previous studies of international deaf gatherings and encounters. Transnationalism, or experiences that transcend national borders, has been a topic of significant interest in deaf studies and other disciplines focused on deaf peoples' experiences. Breivik, Haualand, and Solvang (2002) very productively studied international deaf conferences and sports events (and they discuss some of their findings in their chapter in this book). Using multi-sited ethnography in different transnational spaces, they analyzed deaf peoples' experiences in terms of "routes and not roots" (also see Breivik 2005), exploring the ways that deaf people often see themselves as part of a transnational deaf community before they identify with their national or familial communities (hence people who attended such events say that it is like "being with family").

The term *pilgrimage* has been used to describe deaf people's participation in the "ritual" of the Deaf World Games (aka Deaflympics), where deaf people from around the world come together for a "sacred occasion," in which signed language users temporarily constitute a majority (Haualand 2007). Another ideal deaf place is Gallaudet University in Washington, DC, the only liberal arts university for deaf people in the world, a "deaf Mecca" to where deaf people from around the world make pilgrimages (Lane, Hoffmeister, and Bahan 1996). De Clerck (2007) has written about the effect that visits to Gallaudet University and other deaf "ideal places" had on Flemish deaf leaders, theorizing that these people were "asleep" (in that they were unaware of their language, culture, and rights) and then "woke up" during those visits. For deaf people, this experience of a barrier-free environment fascinated, inspired, and recharged them.

As for historical perspectives on deaf transnationalism, Murray (2007) investigated transnational relationships, events, and conferences in the late nineteenth and early twentieth centuries in his dissertation titled "One Touch of Nature Makes the Whole World Kin." The title is tellingly a quote by Amos Draper, a deaf American quoting Shakespeare, implying that shared deafness leads to feelings of kinship in an international context. Additionally, Ladd's (2006) attention to the internationalist discourses used during the Paris banquets (which are discussed by Gulliver, this volume) has been very inspiring and affirmative for deaf people who continue to use these discourses today.

These studies, which constituted the first wave of research on deaf transnationalism, were important not only in laying the groundwork for future studies but also in creating or greatly contributing to *discourses* of deaf transnationalism in academic and nonacademic contexts alike, where such concepts have been enthusiastically embraced. Murray, Haualand, Ladd, and De Clerck are all deaf and have given multiple presentations on the theme of deaf transnationalism in signed language to deaf audiences during World Federation of the Deaf (WFD) congresses and Frontrunners courses for example, which have been instrumental in spreading discourses of deaf people as transnational in nature.[2]

These scholars' historical and ethnographic explorations of deaf transnational spaces tended to focus on those spaces experienced by people who come from the global North (countries in Europe, along with Canada, the United States, Australia, and other nations with access to and control of resources) and who visit "ideal" places (such as Gallaudet University) or events (such as international conferences or sports events), mostly in the global North. These are spaces in which elite, mobile, and connected deaf people can circulate.

This first wave of scholarship has addressed but not explicitly focused on themes that are central in this book: power, (im)mobility, the limits of deaf universalism, and the stakes of international experiences for those not from the global North. Furthermore, research subjects in these studies perform "the right way to be deaf," which can be found (or confirmed) in international encounters, such as learning about discourses about deaf identity at Gallaudet University (challenged by Ruiz-Williams et al., this volume) or discourses about recognition of sign languages (see De Meulder, this volume), which are often disconnected from local or national specificities.

To be sure, an increasing number of journal articles, monographs, and edited volumes have paid attention to contemporary deaf lives around the globe, such as *Many Ways to Be Deaf* (2003), *Deaf around the World* (2011), *The Deaf Way* (1994), and *The Deaf Way II Reader* (2006). A specialized volume on deaf lives in Africa (Cooper and Rashid 2015) has been recently published too. A number of monographs have been published or are in the pipeline, such as Nakamura's (2006) ethnography of deaf identity in Japan, Kusters's (2015) ethnography of deaf spaces in a Ghanaian village, Friedner's (2015) ethnography on valuing deaf worlds in urban India, and Cooper's forthcoming book on the state of signed language and cultural belonging in Việt Nam. In these and other works, scholars have been increasingly attentive to the existence of deaf epistemologies that exist elsewhere in the world.

However, although these works shed light on deaf lives in the global South (countries in Africa, Asia, and Latin America with access to fewer resources than other countries) and examine deaf peoples' experiences in specific places and times, there is a dearth of work critically engaging with questions about international deaf encounters within the context of globalization. We see this book as bridging this gap: the authors bring together increased attention to differences and specificities in deaf worlds with work on deaf international/transnational encounters in a context of globalization. In addition, we, and many of the authors in this volume, explicitly focus on political economic structures and their roles in deaf lives and the creation of deaf worlds. In this sense, we attend to questions of power and inequality in deaf worlds. We see inequality and (cultural, local, national) difference as two different things: inequality should not be glossed over in the name of difference.

Indeed, one of the decisions that we had to make for the title of this book was whether we would write about "transnational" or "international" deaf

---

[2] We thank Hilde Haualand for pointing out how these discourses circulate in nonacademic as well as academic circles.

encounters and spaces. Transnationalism refers to global or cross-border connections that transcend or break down national borders, and recently it has been a widely embraced concept in both activist and academic circles. It is often used in the context of migrants' contacts with people and institutions in their places of origin (Vertovec 2001) but also in the context of feminism (Mohanty 2003), disability politics (Soldatic and Grech 2014), and sexual and queer politics (Povinelli and Chauncey 1999). According to Appadurai (2001), transnational activism can allow for horizontal networking and the ability to leverage cross-border connections to demand changes from international bodies and nation-states. Traditionally, movements have utilized transnational frameworks in strategically essentialized ways to make claims and demand rights (but see Gamson 1995 on the dangers of this).

With the United Nations Convention on the Rights of Persons with Disabilities (CRPD), which has been ratified by many countries, there is a sense that deaf people can go beyond their nation-state to demand rights and entitlements directly from international institutions such as the United Nations. The World Federation of the Deaf (WFD) seems to encourage this by advocating for deaf people around the world to learn about the CRPD and use it as an advocacy tool. However, as Stein stresses in his chapter, it is the nation that actually needs to implement the CRPD by creating national laws. De Meulder shows a similar situation with regard to sweeping definitions of "sign language recognition," which are in tension with differences in national legislation. These and other authors (such as Lockwood, Cooper, and Moges, this volume) argue that there is a danger in focusing solely on what is transnational as such a focus ignores the very real fact that deaf people live in nation-states and that they are members of local, national, religious, ethnic, and race-based deaf and hearing communities, for example. The nation-state is extremely important: it is a guarantor of rights (or not) and it provides a political economic framework. Indeed, deaf people live in specific places and their lives are not only characterized by *routes*: they often have substantial *roots* as well (cf. Breivik 2005).

Thus, as several contributors in our book point out, national borders are often very real, and as such we think that *international* rather than *transnational* is a more suitable framework. Both terms are used throughout the book (depending on the emphasis in particular chapters), but we strategically decided to use the term *international* in the book title to recognize both sameness (using the phrase *it's a small world*) and difference (by using the word *international*). We call on future researchers and scholars to also attend to the stakes of the choices that they might make about whether to refer to transnational or international experiences, encounters, spaces, and relationships.

GLOBALIZATION, ASYMETRY, AMBIVALENCE

Deaf international encounters are happening in a context of globalization, which is a fraught, uneven, and ambivalent process. The authors in this book consider questions about how deaf people negotiate DEAF-SAME and deaf difference. They consider differences in mobility, access to social and economic capital, and differences in ideologies, ontologies, and epistemologies, within a globalized context in which deaf international links, interactions, and encounters are both intensified and regularized. Held et al. (1999, 2) define globalization as the "widening, deepening and speeding up of worldwide interconnectedness in all aspects of contemporary social life." Key to globalization is an increase in flows of people, finance, trade, ideas, ideologies, knowledge, and cultural products (Castles and Miller 2010). Globalization is related to political and ideological changes, such as laissez-faire economic politics and removing international barriers for flows of trade, travel, and capital (Czaika and de Haas 2014). Advances in transport and communication technology have occurred: it is cheaper and easier to travel large distances and to connect with each other through technology.

To be sure, the process of globalization is a highly asymetrical one. Czaika and de Haas (2014, 318) write:

> Although it is often argued that processes of technological progress and growing interconnectivity have "flattened" the world (cf. Friedman, 2005) and made global opportunity structures more egalitarian, in reality, contemporary globalization has been a highly asymmetrical process, which has favored particular countries—or rather cities and agglomerations within countries—and social, ethnic, class, and professional groups within them, while simultaneously excluding or disfavoring others.

In this context of heightened connectivity and increased inequalities, we believe that asking questions about what happens when deaf people (and deaf-authored concepts and discourses) travel (or not) is long overdue, as is an investigation of the stakes of deaf international experiences. We follow Appadurai (2001) in calling for attention to *circulation*: it is important to track how people, ideas, languages, projects, and programs circulate.

Deaf people, at least those in the global North, have become increasingly interested in deaf people in other places.[3] Travelling to international deaf events (documented by Breivik, Haualand, and Solvang 2002) is by no means a new phenomenon (as emphasized in Murray 2007 and in the historical essays in part I of this collection), but it seems that there has been increased mobility in deaf worlds and that ways of being mobile have diversified because both institutional and noninstitutional deaf spaces are increasing in number. Institutional spaces include camps, gatherings, festivals, and educational programs while noninstitutional spaces include informal and impromptu networking and socializing. This volume's chapters give rich description to forms of mobility. Deaf people not only gather and connect in the traditional form of conferences (Gulliver, Zaurov, Haualand et al., Green) and sports events (Haualand et al.), but also during international arts events (Schmitt), camps (Merricks), leadership programs (Green, Rashid, Kusters et al.), academic courses (Ruiz-Williams et al.), development or empowerment initiatives (Boland et al., Kusters et al.), nongovernmental organizations (Moriarty Harrelson, Cooper, Stein), tourism (Cooper, Moriarty Harrelson, Green), research (Boland et al.), and religious missions (Aina and VanGilder).

Circulation does not only take place in geographical space but also in cyberspace. Wellman (2001, 248) argues that a dichotomy between cyberspace and

---

[3] In contrast, Lee (2012) notes that in Tanzania, there were urban deaf people who were adamantly not interested in meeting foreign deaf people.

physical space is a false one: many ties operate in both spaces and physical space and cyberspace interpenetrate as people actively surf their networks online and offline. The Internet has afforded greater involvement in communities of shared interest, and people who connect online have feelings of belonging, share identities, and obtain information and resources. Through the Internet, deaf people keep in touch with their international friends and maintain their networks (Kurz and Cuculick, Schmitt, İlkbaşaran), learn about nongovernmental organizations and tourist opportunities (Cooper and Moriarty Harrelson), and watch videos created by deaf people from other countries (Ilkbasaran, Kurz and Cuculick).

A major theme among many of these essays is relations between deaf people in the global South and the global North. The global South and global North as concepts exist in relation to each other and in critical development studies scholars have argued that conditions in the global North have created those in the global South and consequently the global South is the target of development and humanitarian work (which may or may not be welcomed or helpful). Similarly, deaf people from the global North involved in development work and interventions aim to improve (assumed or perceived) inequalities in the global South (and improving conditions in "developing countries" is a central mission of the World Federation of the Deafs).[4] However, it is not clear how much on the ground actually changes, or whether the changes are those that people in the global South would want (as Boland et al., Kusters et al., and Moges point out).

Seemingly beneficial "development-oriented" programs and practices such as market reforms and humanitarian interventions might not work to everyone's benefit. For example, Cooper's chapter demonstrates that Việt Nam's attempt to include disabled people by giving tax breaks to businesses that hire them means that hearing entrepreneurs in Việt Nam take advantage of these incentives in order to establish deaf tourism businesses in Việt Nam for deaf tourists from the global North (also see Friedner 2015). Moges's chapter reveals that Finnish development efforts in Eritrea, while perhaps guided by good intentions, led to the colonization of Eritrean Sign Language. VanGilder's chapter discusses the complicated dance that American missionaries must engage in to ensure that local people are involved and invested in mission projects.

As several authors note, DEAF-SAME obscures inequalities, which very often remain and are intensified because of globalization. These include the ability to travel, overall socioeconomic status, and access to deaf-related social and linguistic capital (including having social connections, being able to use and understand the more conventional versions of International Sign, having access to the Internet to learn discourses, and being familiar with Western concepts such as "audism" or "sign language recognition," for example). Most authors in the book struggle with how to attend to both sameness and difference while being mindful of inequalities as well. Moriarty Harrelson, for example, calls for a sense of "SAME-SAME but different" and Moges writes about the pitfalls of "excessive sameness."

It is also important to consider ambivalence and ambiguity in deaf worlds in the context of globalization. The role of ambiguity can perhaps best be highlighted in a discussion of Andrew Foster's work in Africa. On one hand, as Aina's chapter

---

[4] See Boland, Kusters, and Friedner (forthcoming) on the history of international development initiatives in deaf communities around the world.

demonstrates, Foster established schools, churches, and educational programs to ameliorate the living and educational conditions of deaf Africans and his work was motivated by a sense of DEAF-SAME; he had a transformative effect on many deaf peoples' lives. On the other hand, many critics of Foster claim that he spread American Sign Language (ASL) and thus engaged in ASL colonialism. However, there are also those who feel deeply grateful to him, and Aina's chapter carves out a space for considering this. In this book we strive to acknowledge these complicated and conflicting feelings and relations. It is clear from the breadth of sites in which international deaf encounters occur that we need a new conceptual vocabulary for describing and analyzing them, as we discuss in the following section.

THEORETICAL CONCEPTS FOR THINKING ABOUT DEAF WORLDS AND INTERNATIONAL DEAF SPACES

Deaf people produce and belong to multiple, distinct, and (sometimes) overlapping worlds, and for this reason we argue for caution with regard to using established deaf studies concepts to describe international deaf encounters. This need for caution emerges from a number of tensions that permeate this book. These tensions exist between certain binaries that appear repeatedly in the different chapters: the binaries between sameness and difference, specificity and generality, local and global, the global North and the global South, developed and un(der)developed, mobility and immobility, roots and routes, and national and international. To be sure, these binaries are extremes, and international deaf encounters are often experienced as a complex interplay of (fluid and constantly shifting) middle points on the continuums created by these different binaries. The goal then is to allow this middle ground to come to the fore and not to become entranced by the binaries. Boellstorff (2005) even pushes anthropologists to examine how the (binary) categories of sameness and difference might no longer be appropriate for understanding increasingly global experiences.

DEAF STUDIES CONCEPTS: A FOCUS ON SAMENESS

The concepts of "Deaf culture" and "Deaf identity" have been extremely productive for deaf studies scholars and lay deaf people. However, these concepts are often uncritically adopted as ideologies rather than as framing concepts, as if there is one way to have a "deaf identity" and as if there is one deaf culture in the world. Indeed, these concepts are often taken for granted and both scholars and lay people often mention "Deaf culture" without qualifying exactly whose Deaf culture or where it exists, assuming that deaf identity or deaf culture is universal (but see Nakamura 2006 on how deaf identity needs to be situated in time and space). Wrigley (1996, 114) notes that "the 'certainty' of 'Deaf culture'—in the singular—hazards a new arrogance: the projection of one certain form of Deaf culture, one experience, and one kind as the model for all." Similarly, Branson and Miller (2002, 244) suggest that the idea of all deaf people having a common, universal, overriding Deaf identity is "a new symbolic violence associated not with the damnation of difference but with the denial of difference," a new but unconscious cultural imperialism not yet recognized as such (Branson and Miller 2002, 243).

Thus, while concepts such as "Deaf identity" or "Deaf culture" have been productive and galvanizing for deaf studies and deaf people, we argue that especially in the context of globalization and increased contact—in person and through social media—between international deaf people, we need to reconsider and qualify what these concepts might obscure in their emphasis on sameness.

In a number of deaf studies concepts, the international dimension of deaf experiences, networks, and signed languages has been explicitly included, although we argue that, similar to the concepts of Deaf culture and Deaf identity, these concepts have focused on how deaf people are similar to each other. Perhaps the most well-known contemporary examples are "Deaf Gain" and "Deafhood" and slightly less well known is "co-equality." Murray (2007) defines co-equality as an understanding of "Deaf lives as being influenced both by Deaf-centered spaces and by larger society," and these deaf-centered spaces are understood as actually or potentially cosmopolitan in nature. Deaf Gain (Bauman and Murray 2014) is a concept that aims to illustrate what deaf people gain from their deafness and how deaf people contribute to society. Being able to connect internationally, through International Sign, is seen as an important example of Deaf Gain.

Similarly, Deafhood theory stresses that deaf people have something in common that goes beyond national or ethnic borders. According to this theory, deaf people share the existential and biological fact of deafness, using signed languages, and experiences of oppression, and they are able to communicate in International Sign across boundaries. In his chapter in this book, Ladd argues that while there is great diversity among deaf people worldwide, they are united in Deafhood, in that they have shared deaf experiences. As such, Ladd seems to privilege sameness over difference. The theory of Deafhood is seemingly essentialist and has a teleological element, implying that deaf people, regardless of where they are, should use signed languages and connect with other deaf people socially (Kusters and De Meulder 2013).

These concepts thus focus on ways that deaf people are the same as each other and they assume that there is one teleological way to be deaf.

DOCUMENTING BOTH SAMENESS AND DIFFERENCE: DEAF WORLDS AND WORLDING

In addition to concepts that focus on and recognize sameness, we argue that we must expand our analytical and conceptual vocabulary to include concepts that represent both sameness and difference. Deaf people in the USA and other places in the global North use the term DEAF-WORLD "to refer to these relationships among themselves, to the social network they have set up, and not to any notion of geographical location" (Lane, Hoffmeister, and Bahan 1996, 5). While the concept of DEAF-WORLD has been productive for deaf people to describe their networks, and for those of us working in deaf studies and at the intersections of Deaf studies and other disciplines, we argue it is important to recognize multiplicity and diversity in deaf worlds, to affirm that there can be more than one deaf world and many ways to be deaf (cf. Monaghan et al. 2003), and to acknowledge that deaf worlds exist in relation to (and often within) other kinds of worlds.

We stress that deaf people *produce* these worlds themselves. In that sense, we find Heidegger's (2008) concept of "worlding" to be especially useful in that it implies agentive action. Through orienting to each other in different kinds of time and space, deaf people create worlds with each other; they move through time and space toward and away from each other. The concept of worlding allows us to consider how deaf worlds might be created anywhere and at any time and that all deaf people are potentially agents in this process; worlding therefore pushes us beyond the concept of the DEAF-WORLD in that it allows us to analyze how particular worlds are made and unmade.

In documenting deaf people's actual production of worlds we derive inspiration from medical anthropologist Arthur Kleinman's concept of "local moral worlds" in which moral experience is created through "local processes (collective, interpersonal, subjective) that realize (enact) values in ordinary living" (Kleinman 1999, 71–72). According to Kleinman, people enact worlds through interaction and shared experiences and in doing so, they determine what is worthy of value. We argue that scholars, activists, and practitioners must attend to deaf local moral worlds, wherever they are, and that in doing so they must locate what is specific about these worlds.

The concept of local moral worlds allows us to examine how deaf worlds are actually created, enacted, and experienced by people. The concepts of worlding and local moral worlds also allow us to see how these worlds are both made and unmade as well as what is specifically local and global about them, even though it is impossible to disentangle local and global (Massey 1994). This is therefore ultimately a more fluid take on the concept of DEAF-WORLD. The concept of local moral worlds also allows us to attend to what is specific about deaf spaces and to deaf peoples' distinct epistemologies, concepts that we discuss in the following two sections.

SPACES AND NETWORKS

Work in human, social, and cultural geography, including deaf geographies is especially productive for analyzing and exploring (local moral) deaf worlds and international deaf encounters, and this is visible in our use of the term *deaf spaces* in the book title and this introduction. Inspired by the conceptual apparatus of geography, deaf geographies looks at how deaf people produce places and spaces through their unique visual modality of being in the world. As Gulliver and Kitzel (2014) state:

> Deaf Geographies describe how, by the simple expedient of living out their lives from within visual bodies, rather than hearing ones, Deaf people produce Deaf spaces. These Deaf spaces might be small and temporary, like the signing space that exists between some Deaf friends who meet by chance in the street. They might be large but temporary, like a regular Deaf pub gathering. They might be small and more permanent, like the home of a Deaf family. Or as large and as permanent as a Deaf university.

Gulliver (this volume) analyzes how deaf French people, together with international visitors, produced deaf spaces by holding deaf banquets in the nineteenth century. Kusters has demonstrated that deaf space can be temporarily and frequently produced on Indian trains (Kusters 2010) and in a Ghanaian village

(Kusters 2015), while Breivik et al. (2002) analyzed how deaf people produce temporary deaf spaces in international deaf gatherings. Another central concept in contemporary geography is "mobilities," which attends to how people, things, and information move through space and time—a framework that is further explored by İlkbaşaran (this volume).

Another concept that we believe to be useful in the description of international deaf spaces is "networks" (see the chapters by Schmitt, İlkbaşaran, and Lockwood). There is a large literature on social networks in sociology; however, in deaf studies the term *networks* has been underused. Hampton and Wellman (2001) argue that northern societies seem to have shifted from a society based on "little boxes" (strongly overlapping and spatially coherent social groups) to a network society with more dispersed connections where membership overlap is smaller. Axhausen (2002) hypothesizes that people have a larger set of active contacts than in the past and that an increasing amount of time is spent in sustaining far-flung contacts. In this respect, İlkbaşaran (this volume) and Kurz and a Cuculick (this volume) demonstrate how deaf people maintain international deaf networks through social media usage.

We argue that the concept of (deaf) networks offers more potential than the concept of the (deaf) community for the academic study of deaf groups. A community typically connotes a group that is more or less closed and to which people do or do not belong in term of membership; it is often unclear whether mainstreamed deaf people, parents of deaf children, children of deaf adults (CODAs), sign language interpreters, and others belong in this community. In contrast, networks are more process-oriented and fluid. They are organized in clusters, people can be more or less connected in networks, and networks overlap and interconnect with other networks; hence we can see a "small world phenomenon" within networks. Indeed, Watts (1999, 495) writes that "almost every element of the network is somehow 'close' to almost every other element, even those that are perceived as likely to be far away." In this book, Schmitt points out how knots can exist within networks and how such knots are entangled during tangible artistic festivals and gatherings.

LOCAL EPISTEMOLOGIES

As we have seen in our research in India and Ghana, concepts such as Deafhood, audism, and a singular deaf community are often put forth by those visiting from the global North (see Friedner and Kusters 2014), something that is addressed in several chapters of this book (such as Kusters et al.). It is important to stress that these concepts and ideas do different things for different people in different places and that there is also two-way process of learning from people in the global South (for examples, see Kusters et al.). While some deaf people find these (northern) concepts to be empowering, others elsewhere might not understand them or find them useful. It is therefore important to examine what ideas and concepts resonate and work in specific places. For example, Friedner (2015) found that the concept of "deaf development" was important in India, and Green (2014b) writes about deaf Nepalis' conception of DEAF SOCIETY. Similarly, De Clerck (2011, 1431), writing about research with members of the Cameroonian deaf community, states that "there is a need for reflections on an integrative epistemological framework and on how African (deaf) indigenous knowledge, local spoken and signed languages, and local cultural practices can be incorporated."

In this respect, too, we emphasize again that the concept DEAF-SAME is very important to analyze: it is used in both local and international contexts. For example, see Kusters (2015) for an investigation of the specific meanings that DEAF-SAME has in Adamorobe, a village in Ghana, and West (2010) for a description of the use of the concept by deaf children when they talk about their deaf teachers. It is not a top-down concept authored by deaf studies scholars to understand deaf interactions and relationships, but a bottom-up concept that is used on the ground by deaf people of different backgrounds in a range of contexts. Scholars and practitioners working in different contexts must attend to what is specific in these contexts (and how concepts are used in specific contexts) and not take certain concepts as given.

Attending to deaf peoples' specific epistemologies and locally authored concepts (such as the example of "deaf development" mentioned previously) allows us to move away from broad teleological narratives of what deaf lives or deaf worlds should be like. When looking at international encounters in which multiple axes of difference are at play, it is important to realize that there may not be a universal deaf epistemology.

INTERNATIONAL SIGN AND ATTENDING TO LANGUAGE

International deaf encounters happen through and are mediated by language, and it is thus important to attend to language use, language choice, language attitudes, and language ideologies. Many of this book's chapters examine the role of different signed languages either implicitly or explicitly and several of them also look at International Sign. The term *International Sign* is used to point at the language used by (deaf) people from different (sign) linguistic backgrounds as they try to communicate with each other and it seems to encompass a continuum of more or less conventionalized language. Several authors in this book argue that International Sign as a category flags ideas about what kinds of communication between diverse deaf people are (im)possible (see the chapters by Green, Crasborn and Hiddinga, and İlkbaşaran).

Questions of unique horizons of linguistic commensuration (Green 2014a) and communication across different linguistic and geographic backgrounds are very much at stake in this volume's concern with deaf people's worlds. As the various chapter authors stress, there are no easy answers, and International Sign both offers possibilities and limits, much like the discourse of DEAF-SAME. This is reflected in the different ways that deaf people refer to International Sign: Green writes that International Sign is signed as "WFD"/INTERNATIONAL SIGN in Nepal, İlkbaşaran writes that International Sign is signed as EUROPEAN SIGN in Turkey, and in Adamorobe (Kusters 2015) International Sign is called AMERICAN or ENGLISH.

In general, we call on researchers to attend to questions of language use and language ideologies among those whom they are studying and we also call on lay deaf people and practitioners working internationally to be attentive to the language that they use in their interactions. As Moges foregrounds in her chapter, choice of language use can have harmful effects as certain sign languages can be seen as hierarchical; also see Cooper's chapter. In addition, there has recently been a proliferation of videos showing deaf people in the global South learning a signed language "for the first time" and there are also accounts, often offered up by development and humanitarian organizations, of deaf people living in the global South who "have no language." Such claims might be political ones, designed to help spur sign language research and the teaching and transmission of national sign languages, but they should not be accepted uncritically (as Moriarty Harrelson points out in her chapter). Such communicable representations of signed languages showcase the need for critical analysis of how signed languages in international encounters (and in international media sources) are represented.

OTHER CONCEPTS

A number of authors have created or used concepts such as "the deaf global" circuit and "moral geography" to describe and frame the quest for deaf spaces in the global South (Moriarty Harrelson), "signed language sovereignties" (Cooper) to describe the desire for authority over and control of signed languages, "Sign Language Peoples" (De Meulder, Ladd) to describe deaf people as collectivities, "informal interpreting" and "moral orientation" (Green) to describe communicative practices in international deaf interactions, "sign language universalism" (Schmitt) as a concept to describe international spaces in which both deaf and hearing people participate, based on a common use of signed language, "deaf globalism" (Ladd) and "deaf internationalism" (Gulliver) as synonyms for "deaf universalism," "crossover" (Kusters et al.) and "mutuality" (VanGilder) to point at (the need for) reciprocity between different actors in international encounters, and "intersectionality" (Ruiz-Williams et al.) to reveal different aspects of people's identities. These concepts all reflect attempts to work through what is specific about deaf worlds as well as issues that emerge when diverse deaf people encounter each other across differences.

THE AUTHORS, THE PROCESS, AND THE BOOK

The call for papers for this book was circulated via email, deaf academics networks, and Facebook, and we received many more abstracts than expected, which demonstrates that this topic resonates with deaf people and deaf studies scholars. Indeed, it was interesting for us to see how the call circulated and how far it went. Friedner received an email from an American hearing friend with a deaf daughter living in Toulouse, France, saying that she had seen the call on a mailing list for parents. Others told us that they had seen people discuss the book at the Deaflympics in Slovakia. The call circulated through colleagues and extended networks and reinforced our ideas of the many levels of connectedness that exist in deaf worlds.

Both editors and the majority of the authors are deaf. To create a nuanced volume, we have recruited a diverse group of contributors: academics and activists, from the global North and South, from various backgrounds and training in disciplines including deaf studies, history, law, economics, international development, anthropology, cultural studies, interpreting, linguistics, language policy, theology, disability studies, education, and human geography. The authors live in the USA, Belgium, the United Kingdom, France, Germany, Norway, Denmark, Finland, the Netherlands, Malaysia, Turkey, and Thailand. The research in the chapters are based on events in, or have been collected in, the USA and Canada, Europe (Denmark, Finland, Sweden, France, Germany, Italy, Spain, Turkey), Asia (Cambodia, Malaysia, Nepal, Thailand, Việt Nam), the Pacific (Fiji), Africa (Eritrea, Ghana, Kenya, Nigeria, South Africa, Tanzania), and South America (Chile and Uruguay).

Many authors are affirmative of international deaf connections, while others emphasize the challenges and disconnects that exist when deaf people meet each other internationally. Our hope is that through placing these voices in conversation, new understandings will come to the fore of deaf similitude and difference, deaf encounters, deaf interventions, and the role of power differentials in determining which bodies, discourses, and concepts travel. At the same time, we acknowledge that this book is limited as we recruited contributors through networks that could be considered elite and contributors have a certain level of (academic) writing skills. Furthermore, while research has been conducted in diverse geographic locations, most of our authors live in northern locations. We hope that in the future more authors living in and/or originating from the global South will write about deaf spaces and encounters in general and international ones in particular. We note the structural issues that exist in relation to writing in (academic) English and we are aware that writing as a process is often deeply ambivalent for deaf people.

Chapters take the form of traditional academic articles, interviews, and personal narratives. While a number of chapters are entirely or mostly based on historical research and/or literature review (Gulliver, Zaurov, Emery, Crasborn and Hiddinga, Ladd), most of the authors draw on ethnography. To investigate international deaf interactions on the ground, ethnography based on observation, participation, informal conversations, and semistructured or unstructured interviews seems to us to be an ideal method. The authors conducted participant observation in a variety of contexts, including long-term ethnography in their own community or in a foreign country (often the global South) (Cooper, Moriarty Harrelson, Lockwood, Moges, Green, Stein, İlkbaşaran, Boland et al.), multi-sited ethnography (Haualand et al., Schmitt), and short-term (repeated) ethnographic research during events, camps, or mission trips (Green, Haualand et al., Schmitt, VanGilder, Merricks). Other chapters utilize data from interviews and conversations (Aina, Kurz and Cuculick, Kusters et al., De Meulder), online research (De Meulder, Schmitt, İlkbaşaran), and autoethnography (Ruiz-Williams et al.). By including a wide range of ethnographic accounts, we hope to demonstrate the importance of ethnography to the discipline of deaf studies.

We also believe ethnographic research must be situated in the context in which it happens. The authors in this book pay attention to their positionality in the research environment and with regard to their research participants or interlocutors. They reflect on their own background and how it might have shaped the research, particularly hearing status, nationality, ethnicity, and language background. The chapters by Ruiz-Williams et al. and Kusters et al. exhort us all to be mindful and critical of how our own positionalities influence our work and the importance of attention to questions of privilege and power. Boland et al., Green, and Schmitt productively question the relative influence of being hearing versus being DEAF-SAME in international deaf spaces: they argue that sometimes it is more important to share the use of a signed language than to share hearing status.

BOOK PARTS

While the book is divided into five parts, there is significant overlap in the themes, approaches, and arguments in each. Indeed, this breakdown by part is organizational and strategic on our part; there are quite a few chapters that would be at home in any of the parts.

Part 1, "Gatherings," begins with Gulliver's inquiry into the French deaf community's attempts to create international deaf banquets in order to influence the French state's policies in relation to deaf people and their institutions in the eighteenth and nineteenth centuries. Gulliver traces the history of deaf spaces in France to argue for the transformational aspects of deaf spaces, both local and international. This argument is taken up by all of the authors in this section: Schmitt explores contemporary international arts festivals in which signed language is celebrated by deaf and hearing people alike; these festivals function as nodes in international sign language arts networks. Similarly, Merricks analyzes how international deaf youth gatherings are spaces where deaf youth from different countries become transformed in their awareness of what it means to be deaf youth camps provide attendees with opportunities for learning about different deaf experiences around the world and deaf youth also become energized and empowered in their connections to a larger internationalist deaf organization. Providing a more somber note, Zaurov argues for the importance of contemporary separate deaf Jewish spaces as he demonstrates that deaf Jews were excluded from deaf worlds in Eastern Europe before and during the Nazi era, after which they increasingly organized their own international associations and conferences. Haualand et al. end this part with a discussion of their groundbreaking work on large-scale institutional deaf events and how their thinking about these has changed as well as how the fabric of social, political, and recreational international deaf events may be becoming more fragmented and based upon specific interests or skills. As such, this part invites us to consider deaf gatherings as spaces in which sameness and difference are negotiated; different identities, affiliations, and positions are performed; and deaf attendees confront (or ignore) questions of political economic inequality.

The first two chapters of Part 2, "Language," continue from and overlap with "Gatherings," as both consider International Sign. Crasborn and Hiddinga provide an overview of studies on International Sign, its limits and its possibilities, and present us with a hypothesis that deaf people are skilled at communicating across different signed languages because of the tools gained from negotiating communication with hearing people. Green argues that deaf people value direct communication and that, because they are morally oriented toward each other and toward communicating across difference, they ask for and offer translations of what other signers have said. These informal interpreters help ensure that understanding happens while not interfering with deaf peoples' direct communication with each other. Green's detailed ethnographic examples are taken from a WFD World Congress and a series of workshops and encounters in Nepal.

The other three chapters in "Language" are concerned with language ideologies; more particularly they describe tensions between the use of national/local/ indigenous signed languages on the one hand and International Sign or foreign signed languages such as Finnish/Swedish Sign Language and American Sign Language on the other hand. Moges discusses the stakes of cross-cultural and cross-national communication as she explores how deaf Eritrean language planners have "demissioned" Eritrean Sign Language from its Finnish/Swedish influences in order to create and codify an indigenous Eritrean Sign Language. She writes about tourism as eye-opening for deaf people from Eritrea who realized, upon visiting Sweden, that they wanted a signed language that is less similar to a Western signed language.

Cooper's chapter continues with this focus on the role of power in the spread of signed languages. She explores tensions that exist between Vietnamese Signed Languages and American Sign Language with the emergence of a tourism industry targeting international deaf travelers who use American Sign Language. Both Moges and Cooper argue that we must be attentive to "signed language sovereignties" in deaf peoples' everyday lives. İlkbaşaran focuses on Turkish deaf people's use of social media networks. She investigates language ideologies with regard to choices made when using International Sign or Turkish Sign Language in Facebook videos and argues that the choice of International Sign is associated with a range of literacies and (potential) mobility. The authors in this part also analyze tensions between specificity and universalism in deaf worlds, specifically in relation to language, and show how signed languages become a complex terrain upon and in which different interests and agendas are produced and negotiated.

The third part, "Projects," explores the work that nongovernmental organizations (NGOs), missionaries, leadership programs, advocates, activists, and technical experts perform. The vagueness of the part title "Projects" is intentional because we are referring to social, moral, economic, religious, and political projects performed by a wide range of stakeholders. Aina begins this part with a discussion of the work of Andrew Foster, an African American minister and teacher who helped to start schools and institutions around Africa. Aina describes how Foster's methods and ideas were also an inspiration for deaf Nigerian missionaries in Fiji, and he demonstrates how both Foster's mission and his results were motivated by feelings of DEAF-SAME. VanGilder follows in the same vein in that he also analyzes faith-based religious volunteerism and mission work by Americans to countries in the global South. However, VanGilder argues that DEAF-SAME is not enough and that project participants must attempt to understand and engage with local cultures, which they can do by establishing mutuality.

Rashid continues by demonstrating how in the fragmented political, economic, religious, and ethnic landscape of Nigeria, establishing a successful international deaf leadership program led by deaf people born in Nigeria but living in the United States and United Kingdom might not be possible, even if the deaf trainers are themselves from the same country and have shared experiences with those who they are training. De Meulder discusses the international deaf agenda for signed language recognition. As she demonstrates, "sign language recognition" means different things in different countries and there are about tensions between universality and specificity in discourses on signed language recognition: there are seemingly universal aspirations exist but legislation is nation-specific. Stein also discusses this tension between universal aspirations and nation-specific legislation, in this case the implementation of the CRPD in Chile. Stein stresses that for any kind of (technical or legal) project to be successful, deaf people living in the country where it is to be implemented must be invested in it. More than this, Stein demonstrates that beyond abstract and "feel-good" leadership or human rights concepts, often what people on the ground need are technical interventions into a country's legal process. The authors in this section highlight the importance of analyzing projects from multiple angles and recognizing the hard work that people must do to make projects successful as well as the extent they need to be tuned in to local and national cultures and politics. Indeed, it is important to look beyond (good) intentions when considering deaf-focused (or any) projects.

The part "Networks" continues to critically interrogate the role of intentions and also evaluates how places come to exist in relation to each other. Emery's chapter invites us to think of deaf people as a diaspora lacking a geographic homeland. In this framework, deaf people are Sign Language Peoples who have much in common with each other regardless of where they currently live. In contrast, in her ethnographic case study in Cambodia, Moriarty Harrelson argues that there is a deaf global circuit that exists whereby and wherein deaf people from the global North travel to the global South both to have so-called "authentic" tourism experiences and to consume differences. Moriarty Harrelson foregrounds the harmful effects that such tourism can have and sheds light on the absence of a universal moral geography (even if some people presume that it exists). Lockwood's chapter demonstrates how deaf Uruguayans eschewed international connections in favor of establishing strong national connections both within the deaf community and with other allies in Uruguay; as she demonstrates, Uruguay's unique political economy meant that intragroup networks were more important for the deaf community to achieve its political goals. Kurz and Cuculick analyze American deaf peoples' social networking practices and explore the role of digital media in their lives. For their interlocutors, social media has resulted in great ease in communication and connectedness.

In the final part, "Visions," authors consider the practices and processes of *doing* international deaf scholarship and interventions. These chapters reflect on how to do research, how to teach in leadership programs or university courses, and how to engage in international interactions. The part also contains reflective pieces about how to manage—and whether it is possible to manage—tensions between "global Deafhood" or "deaf universalism" and intersectional identities and experiences. Boland et al. share their experiences working internationally as deaf researchers and practitioners in the field of international development; they offer advice as well as some cautions. Their chapter demonstrates how deaf researchers and development practitioners can utilize shared deaf experiences to transform and improve the process of conducting research and interventions. However, they caution that shared deaf experiences can also result in the researcher or practitioner making unwarranted assumptions about what is shared and what is not. Kusters et al. continue in this vein. Their chapter is an interactive collaborative discussion of the evolution of the popular Frontrunners international deaf education program; the conversation focused on the program's interactions in the global South. The authors, three of whom are current Frontrunners teachers, and one of whom has been a guest teacher reflect on the practice of organizing international deaf youth programs and are critical of the merits of short-term visits and exchange projects in the global South. They stress the importance of "crossover" but conclude that even if the aim of such interactions is exchange rather than empowerment, it is still hard to reach; and they emphasize the importance of openness and honesty in discussing such interactions.

Ruiz-Williams et al. offer a series of autoethnographies as a method of foregrounding the importance of attending to deaf peoples' intersectional experiences. Their method and process of working and reflecting together proved transformative for each of the authors. Together, they argue that deaf universalism ultimately does not work because it tends to ignore and devalue the experiences of deaf people who do not fit into a single-issue identity politics framework. Ladd ends with a discussion of deaf globalism and argues that Deafhood is a helpful analytic for considering how deaf people, who he regards as forming minority cultures, are both the same and different. Ladd's chapter suggests that there can be a shared global deaf experience or a shared global Deafhood.

Limits and Possibilities of International Deaf Spaces: A Conclusion

While this is a large volume, it is not a complete one. We are missing contributions on deaf peoples' immigration practices and their relationships with deaf people in their new countries, children of deaf adults (including adopted children) in international deaf spaces, international romantic relationships, and the roles of gender, race, and sexuality in the creation of more specific international/transnational deaf communities (such as international deaf queer communities for example). Analyzing international deaf worlds through additional axes of difference, especially in the context of global inequalities, is of utmost importance. We look forward to work on these topics in the near future.

In this book, some authors have highlighted the strength of seemingly universal commonalities between deaf people (such as in the chapters by Gulliver, Haualand et al., Merricks, Crasborn and Hiddinga, Stein, Aina, Ladd, and Emery). Some authors focused on how deaf people come together on the base of a double commonality: being deaf and Christian (Aina, VanGilder), being deaf and Jewish (Zaurov), being deaf and an artist or art lover (Schmitt), or being deaf and a youth (Merricks, Ilkbasaran). Some authors emphasize the need for critical perspectives (such as in the chapters by VanGilder, Zaurov, De Meulder, Moges, Rashid, Moriarty Harrelson, Lockwood, Kusters et al., Ruiz-Williams et al.). Most authors, however, recognize both: they are affirmative of the power of DEAF-SAME and at the same time highlight differences and/or inequalities.

In a number of chapters, the writers emphasize the need to consider what it means to ethically or morally cooperate with local deaf people (see Cooper, Boland et al., Kusters et al., VanGilder), especially in light of inequalities. This question of what it means to be *ethical* in such international contexts is an important one. In our understanding of this, we draw again from Kleinman's concept of "local moral worlds" as it is crucial to note that morality varies across time and space and is not universal. We also want to return to Appadurai's (2001) call for an anthropology of circulation as we see studies of deaf peoples' circulation, studies of circulating discourses, and being a circulating researcher as essential in such fluid contexts.

It is thus important not to look at international deaf experiences through a universalized and decontextualized lens, something that is increasingly difficult with globalization and greater connectivity between certain deaf people. Indeed, globalization creates opportunities not only for making connections (for some people) but also for misunderstanding and misrecognition. We run the risk of obscuring what differentiates deaf experiences around the world. While deaf universalism is an incredibly powerful discourse, it does not mean that a homogenous deaf world exists or should exist. As VanGilder argues in his chapter, "It is possible to overreach across the DEAF-SAME bridge and make our stories everyone else's stories. We run into the 'danger of a single story' as the Nigerian author, Chimamanda Ngozi Adichie, cautions in her TED talk." Indeed, we think that this book provides a needed intervention into understanding how sameness and difference are powerful yet contested categories in deaf worlds.

ACKNOWLEDGMENTS

Thanks to Mara Green, Hilde Haualand, Audrey Cooper, and Joe Murray, for reading and commenting upon earlier versions of this introduction.

REFERENCES

Adichie, C. N. 2009. The Danger of a Single Story. Available from http://www.ted.com/chimamanda_adichie_the_danger_of_a_single_story.

Appadurai, Arjun. 2001. "Deep Democracy: Urban Governmentality and the Horizon of Politics." *Environment and Urbanization* 13 (2): 23–44.

Axhausen, K. 2002. *A Dynamic Understanding of Travel Demand: A Sketch.* Working Paper, Swiss Federal Institute of Technology, Zurich.

Bauman, H.-D., and J. Murray. 2014. *Deaf Gain: Raising the Stakes for Human Diversity.* Minneapolis: University of Minnesota Press.

Boellstorff, T. 2005. *The Gay Archipelago: Sexuality and Nation in Indonesia.* Princeton, NJ: Princeton University Press.

Boland, A., A. Kusters, and M. Friedner. Forthcoming. "Deaf International Development." In *The Deaf Studies Encyclopedia,* edited by G. Gertz and P. Boudreault. Thousand Oaks, CA: SAGE Reference.

Branson, J., and D. Miller. 2002. *Damned for Their Difference: The Cultural Construction of Deaf People as "Disabled."* Washington, DC: Gallaudet University Press.

Breivik, J.-K. 2005. *Deaf Identities in the Making: Local Lives, Transnational Connections.* Washington, DC: Gallaudet University Press.

Breivik, J.-K., H. Haualand, and P. Solvang. 2002. *Rome: A Temporary Deaf City! Deaflympics 2001.* Bergen, Norway: Bergen University. Accessed November 29, 2014. http://www.ub.uib.no/elpub/rokkan/N/N02-02.pdf.

Castles, S., and M. J. Miller. 2010. "Understanding Global Migration: A Social Transformation Perspective." *Journal of Ethnic and Migration Studies* 36 (10): 1565–86.

Cooper, A. 2014. "Signed Languages and Sociopolitical Formation: The Case of 'Contributing to Society' through Hồ Chí Minh City Sign Language." *Language in Society* 43 (3): 311–32.

Cooper, A., and K. Rashid. 2015. *Citizenship, Politics, Difference: Perspectives from Sub-Saharan Signed Language.* Washington, DC: Gallaudet University Press.

————. Forthcoming. *The State of Signed Language and Deaf Cultural Belonging in Việt Nam.* Washington, DC: Gallaudet University Press.

Czaika, M., and H. de Haas. 2014. "The Globalization of Migration: Has the World Become More Migratory?" *International Migration Review* 48 (2): 283–323.

De Clerck, G. 2007. "Meeting Global Deaf Peers, Visiting Ideal Deaf Places: Deaf Ways of Education Leading to Empowerment, an Exploratory Case Study." *American Annals of the Deaf* 152 (1): 6–19.

————. 2011. "Fostering Deaf People's Empowerment: The Cameroonian Deaf Community and Epistemological Equity." *Third World Quarterly* 32 (8): 1419–35. doi:10.1080/01436 597.2011.604516.

Erting, C. J., R. C. Johnson, D. L. Smith, and B. D. Snider. 1994. *The Deaf Way: Perspectives from the International Conference on Deaf Culture.* Washington, DC: Gallaudet University Press.

Friedner, M. 2015. *Valuing Deaf Worlds in Urban India.* New Brunswick, NJ: Rutgers University Press.

Friedner, M., and A. Kusters. 2014. "On the Possibilities and Limits of 'DEAF DEAF SAME': Tourism and Empowerment Camps in Adamorobe (Ghana), Bangalore, and Mumbai (India)." *Disability Studies Quarterly* 34 (3). http://dsq-sds.org/article/view/4246/3649.

Friedman, T. L. 2005. *The World Is Flat: A Brief History of the Twenty-First Century.* New York: Farrar.

Gamson, J. 1995. "Must Identity Movements Self-Destruct? A Queer Dilemma." *Social Problems* 42 (3): 390–407.

Green, E. M. 2014a. "Building the Tower of Babel: International Sign, Linguistic Commensuration, and Moral Orientation." *Language in Society* 43:445–65.

————. 2014b. "The Nature of Signs: Nepal's Deaf Society, Local Sign, and the Production of Communicative Sociality." PhD diss., University of California.

Gulliver, Mike, and Mary Beth Kitzel. 2014. "Deaf Geographies, an Introduction." Accessed March 15, 2015. http://deafgeographies.files.wordpress.com/2014/08/deaf_geographies .pdf.

Hampton, K., and B. Wellman. 2001. "Long-Distance Community in the Network Society: Contact and Support beyond Netville." *American Behavioral Scientist* 45 (3): 477–96.

Haualand, H. 2007. "The Two-Week Village: The Significance of Sacred Occasions for the Deaf Community." In *Disability in Local and Global Worlds,* ed. B. Ingstad and S. R. Whyte, 33–55. Berkeley: University of California Press, 2007.

Heidegger, M. 2008. *Being and Time.* New York: Harper Perennial.

Held, D., A. McGrew, D. Goldblatt, and J. Perraton. 1999. *Global Transformations: Politics, Economics, and Culture.* Cambridge, UK: Polity.

Kleinman, A. 1999. "Moral Experience and Ethical Reflection: Can Ethnography Reconcile Them? A Quandary for 'The New Bioethics.'" *Daedelus* 128 (4): 69–97.

Kusters, A. 2010. "Deaf on the Lifeline of Mumbai." *Sign Language Studies* 10 (1): 36–68.

————. 2015. *Deaf Space in Adamorobe: An Ethnographic Study in a Village in Ghana.* Washington, DC: Gallaudet University Press.

Kusters, A., and M. De Meulder. 2013. "Understanding Deafhood: In Search of Its Meanings." *American Annals of the Deaf* 157 (5): 428–38.

Ladd, P. 2006. "What Is Deafhood and Why Is It Important?" In *The Deaf Way II Reader: Perspectives from the Second International Conference on Deaf Culture,* 245–50. Washington DC: Gallaudet University Press.

Lane, H., R. Hoffmeister, and B. Bahan. 1996. *A Journey into the Deaf-World.* San Diego, CA: DawnSignPress.

Lee, J. C. 2012. "They Have to See Us: An Ethnography of Deaf People in Tanzania." PhD diss., University of Colorado at Boulder.

Massey, D. 1994. *Space, Place, and Gender.* Minneapolis: University of Minnesota Press.

Mohanty, C. T. 2003. *Feminism without Borders: Decolonizing Theory, Practicing Solidarity.* Durham, NC: Duke University Press.

Monaghan, L., C. Schmaling, K. Nakamura, and G. H. Turner. 2003. *Many Ways to Be Deaf: International Variation in Deaf Communities.* Washington, DC: Gallaudet University Press.

Murray, J. 2007. "'One Touch of Nature Makes the Whole World Kin': The Transnational Lives of Deaf Americans, 1870–1924." PhD diss., University of Iowa.

Nakamura, K. 2006. *Deaf in Japan: Signing and the Politics of Identity.* Ithaca, NY: Cornell University Press.

Napoli, D. J., and G. Mathur. 2011. *Deaf around the World: The Impact of Language.* Oxford, UK: Oxford University Press.

Povinelli, E., and G. Chauncey. 1999. "Thinking Sexuality Transnationally: An Introduction." *GLQ: A Journal of Lesbian and Gay Studies* 5 (4): 439–49.

Soldatic, K. M., and S. Grech. 2014. "Transnationalising Disability Studies: Rights, Justice, and Impairment." *Disability Studies Quarterly* 34 (2). http://dsq-sds.org/article/view/4249.

Vertovec, S. 2001. "Transnationalism and Identity." *Journal of Ethnic and Migration Studies* 27 (4): 573–82.

Watts, D. J. 1999. "Networks, Dynamics, and the Small-World Phenomenon." *American Journal of Sociology* 105 (2): 493–527.

Wellman, B. 2001. "Physical Place and Cyberplace: The Rise of Personalized Networking." *International Journal of Urban and Regional Research* 25 (2): 227–52.

West, D. 2010. "We're the Same, I'm Deaf, You're Deaf, Huh!" In *Deaf around the World: The Impact of Language,* edited by D. J. Napoli and G. Mathur, 367–71. Oxford, UK: Oxford University Press.

Wrigley, O. 1996. *The Politics of Deafness.* Washington, DC: Gallaudet University Press.

Part 1

▌ GATHERINGS

1 | The Emergence of International Deaf Spaces in France from Desloges 1779 to the Paris Congress of 1900

Mike Gulliver

On the morning of August 6, 1900, more than four hundred Deaf[1] and hearing people, from places as far flung as Japan, Ecuador, the United States, Russia, and Mexico, descended on the Palais des Congrès for the Paris World Fair. Dressed formally and informally, female and male, signing and speaking, they milled about outside. As they greeted friends and visited the attractions of the Cours La Reine, we can imagine pockets of signed and spoken conversation ebbing and flowing into, across, and around each other.

For many of the French Deaf delegates, the day was one to savor. Deaf community picnics in Paris had drawn sizeable crowds in recent years, but the congress was an exceptionally large gathering. More than two hundred Deaf people from all over the world were drawn to the glittering pavilions of the 1900 World Fair. Most French Deaf people had come simply to be with other Deaf people and to enjoy being a community of visual people in an otherwise predominantly hearing world. Overseas attendance only strengthened that community experience, as did the universality of sign language, which allowed those familiar with different local and national sign languages to rapidly negotiate international communication.

Some French Deaf people, however, had come with an explicitly political aim: to push for urgent change in national policy. Since the 1880s, the lives of France's

---

[1] A variety of terms are used for Deaf people in this chapter. In general discussion, I have used the modern form *Deaf*. Where I have translated historical terms from French, I have stayed close to the original, translating *sourd* as *deaf*, *muet* as *mute*, and distinguishing between *deaf-mute* (the closest nineteenth-century equivalent to *Deaf*) and the more objective *deaf and mute*. Where the French was capitalized, I have retained this. For a contemporary exploration of French terms used in the nineteenth century, see Berthier 1873, 200.

hearing population had been transformed by sweeping aside church control of education and establishing a national system of free, obligatory schooling under the Ministry of Public Instruction. However, the Deaf community had been left under the Ministry of the Interior, the same institution that had been responsible for them since the French Revolution and that also oversaw hospices, almshouses, and lunatic asylums. This ministry saw Deaf people as requiring care, unable to act for themselves, and (powerlessly) represented by experts.

The French Deaf community planned to use the 1900 congress to engineer a transfer of their education to the Ministry of Public Instruction by mobilizing the weight of international Deaf opinion against the Ministry of the Interior. In addition, they also planned to offer the 1900 congress itself as evidence that the Ministry of the Interior did not understand the true nature of Deaf experience: although Deaf people might initially appear to be small marginalized groups living within separate states, the reality was that they formed a single, thriving, international community whose commonality of experience and ability to communicate across and between signed languages challenged the hegemony of a hearing world divided along linguistic and national boundaries. As one leader of the French Deaf community argued, "We are French, Italian, Austrian, American, English, German, etc. . . . United as a community . . . we know no borders, and have but one aim, to complete our social emancipation" (Congress 1900, 258).

The 1900 congress was set up to demonstrate the reality of that Deaf experience. Positioned in the most visible way, at the heart of the Paris World Fair, that international Deaf "reality" would be performed, a "Deaf space" welcoming any hearing person to watch, learn, and realize that Deaf people, far from being isolated by deafness, were in fact the unrecognized heralds of an entirely different but equally valid international form of humanity.

In this chapter I identify the roots of that international Deaf reality in writings of the eighteenth century and chart its development through a century of increasingly international events that culminated in the 1900 congress. I explore the evolving ways in which Deaf people describe themselves through the nineteenth century and discuss why the French Deaf community selected a demonstration of Deaf internationalism to demand policy change. I conclude by looking at the 1900 congress in more detail and use the events of that congress to highlight the potentials and limitations of a Deaf internationalist reality.

POSITIONALITY AND HISTORY

I am a hearing researcher who focuses on Deaf history, mainly in France and the United Kingdom. Much historical work on the Deaf community—particularly on the French Deaf community—uses data collected and translated by others. Because I speak French, I utilize original French documents written by Deaf people themselves, published records of events such as the Paris banquets and international Deaf congresses, and Deaf magazines and newspapers. I own copies of all of the original material and have translated all of the quotes in this chapter myself. Of course, I cannot assume that what I write about Deaf history is accurate or that I have interpreted it correctly. I rely on my experience in making sense of these texts, and I offer a framework that helps us to form the historical data into particular stories.

Deaf Internationalism: Spatial and Linguistic Roots

Deaf internationalism could be defined as the idea that Deaf people, all over the world, have enough in common that they recognize each other as more or less the same. In sign language, this might be described as DEAF DEAF SAME or DEAF, LIKE ME. Although Deaf internationalism (what the editors call "deaf universalism" in the introduction of this book and Ladd calls "deaf globalism" in his chapter) is now being explored as part of modern, western Deaf community's self-understanding, the idea is not new. Historical Deaf communities, particularly in the late eighteenth and early nineteenth century, had a very good understanding of their international connections.

Deaf people today live in a world that is very different from those historical worlds. Nowadays, it is hard to think about identity without envisioning what you *should* be, such as what nation you should be a citizen of, what language you should use, and even local identities such as what football team you should support. Most of these expectations developed in the nineteenth century; before that, people's networks were much less about 'should's, and much more about 'could's: where you *could* work, where you *could* travel, and where others *could* understand you.

For Deaf people living in rural areas in the early nineteenth century, their networks were largely restricted to their immediate surroundings. A Deaf man, Jean Massieu, described his life in a rural part of France in the following words: "We were six deaf-mutes in our family. Three boys and three girls. . . . I expressed ideas by manual signs or by gestures. . . . Strangers didn't understand us when we used signs with them, but our neighbors did" (quoted in Sicard 1808, 636).

Those close to Massieu, and others like him, found ways to meet him on his own visual terms. But others, further from him, were less forgivingly sound biased. We could call Massieu's visual reality an early form of "Deaf space," a way of living that experiences the world from a visual point of view. Deaf spaces emerge from Deaf people's visual experience of the world. The concept of "Deaf space" moves us away from the idea that Deaf people are always a minority in a hearing world toward realizing that the world is neither Deaf nor hearing but becomes Deaf or hearing as we live in it and shape it.

History is full of examples of Deaf people who, like Massieu, inhabited tiny Deaf spaces that allowed them to get by. However, it is also full of examples of Deaf people who lived close enough to others that they were able to connect their individual Deaf spaces to produce a larger shared Deaf space. Within that space, by interacting over a long period, they created and shared natural sign languages and, through them, developed other aspects of what we would now call *Deaf culture*.

One such community was located in Paris, a city which at the turn of the nineteenth century had a population of more than half a million. The Deaf community in Paris was at least two hundred strong by that time and was already well established before de l'Epée began teaching (Epée 1774, 8). The community was old enough to have developed a rich sign language and for other aspects of Deaf culture (such as name signing) to become standard. The community is described by one of its members, Pierre Desloges, who is known as the first French Deaf man to write and publish a book. He states that within the community, a Deaf person might "learn to perfect and combine signs . . . and through the commerce of his comrades, the [easy] art of painting and expressing all ideas, even those most independent of the senses, by means of natural signs" (Desloges 1779, 14).

Desloges's community is important because it is the first suggestion that Deaf people's natural sign language offered a way to communicate that gave their Deaf space a different "shape" from the space of the hearing world that surrounded them. This meant that although Deaf people remained involved in the hearing world, they experienced the Deaf community and the shape of its interactive spaces as an *alternative* to hearing-world boundaries of language and country:

> They [Deaf people] have a natural language, which they use to communicate amongst themselves. This language is none other than the language of signs . . . among them, one is like a man transplanted suddenly into the midst of a foreign nation. (Desloges 1779, 7–8)
>
> I have at my disposition a wealth of signs that I can combine, one with the other, in the blink of an eye. . . . A Deaf person from Peking, as well as a Deaf person from France would understand the object that I'm describing. (56–57)

Desloges's book was not specifically designed to argue this point so it would be inappropriate to read too much into it. However, this is clear evidence that—as early as the eighteenth century and in a Deaf community that had come about quite spontaneously (i.e., without being centered on a school or other form of structure that might have lent it an international network)—the idea that Deaf people are international in some form was already important.

Note that universality, as understood in the periods and places of this chapter, does not deny the existence of different local and national sign languages, but rather suggests that Deaf people are more able than hearing people to quickly construct mutually intelligible, visual communication. This is by no means the only Deaf shared experience and is part of the ideology of sign language, as other chapters in this book demonstrate.

DEAF INTERNATIONALISM: THE DEAF NATION

We now look at the first explicitly political use of internationalism by the Deaf community in the mid-nineteenth century. Before we move on, however, it is helpful to discuss two examples that demonstrate the differences in the ways that Deaf people saw the hearing world and their own Deaf reality. These will also help us to fill in the gap between Desloges's writing in 1779 and texts from the mid-1900s.

Both the following examples are from the life of Laurent Clerc, a Deaf man who spent his formative years within the walls of the Parisian Deaf school originally founded by the Abbé de l'Epée. Clerc is the first Deaf Parisian that we know of to travel extensively, and both his life and his written words clearly show the fundamental reality of his membership in an international Deaf community. The first example is from a trip that Clerc took to London in 1815. He visited the London school for Deaf children, where he met some young English Deaf children. This is the description of his visit by the Paris Deaf school administrator:

> As soon as Clerc beheld them, his face lit up; he was as agitated as a traveller would be who, in regions far from home, suddenly chanced upon a colony of his own countrymen.
>
> For their part, the hundred and fifty [English] deaf-mutes immediately recognised Clerc as one of their own. . . . Clerc approached them, he made some signs, and they responded with other signs. This unexpected communication was a cause for wondrous celebration for them. (Ladébat 1815, 170, 172)

In 1818, Clerc was in the United States, where he had helped to establish the first American school for deaf children. This example is ostensibly about language but it also speaks about space. He explains in his own words how Deaf people's specific sensory situation and their consequential inability to acquire the spoken language of a particular people distances them from the spaces of the hearing world around them, while at the same time making them members of an international Deaf community:

> Nothing can replace their [deaf mute's] natural language (that is of signs). . . . This language, as simple as nature and which is capable of extending itself to describe all of nature has no boundaries other than that in the minds of men. It is universal; and deaf mutes from whatever country they come understand each other. . . . But, they cannot understand you. . . . You understand [don't you?] that the language of a particular people can never be the mother-language of the deaf mutes born in its midst. (Clerc 1818, 15, 18)

By the time Clerc was writing these words in 1818, the Paris Deaf school where he had been a teacher was a well-established Deaf space. It had been founded in 1791 but then virtually abandoned by the state, which left Deaf children in the care of Deaf teachers. The combination of residential schooling, a protective and enclosed environment behind the school's high walls, and Deaf leadership of Deaf children was intoxicating. By the early 1800s, those coming into the school had started to comment on how much it looked like a "foreign country" with its own language, "laws," culture, and customs (Sicard 1803; Paulmier 1820). By the late 1810s, such a rich sign language and culture had developed there that its residents had even begun to suggest the creation of a written form of sign language, *mimographie*, a first step toward establishing the Deaf space of the school as a stand-alone space, uncoupled from the educational policies of surrounding France.

When they learned of the mimographie project, however, the French government was horrified. They immediately replaced the school's management and introduced rules that not only forced the Deaf teachers to leave the premises as soon as they had finished teaching for the day but also separated new pupils from those already having learned to sign. The impact of this was a cruel partitioning of Deaf space.

The shape that Deaf space took was an annual banquet, held each year in November to celebrate the anniversary of the birth of the school's founder, the Abbé de l'Epée. Banquets were a traditional protest event in nineteenth-century France, and the Parisian deaf-mute banquets were no different. They were "reversed," carnivalesque events in which Deaf people became the majority, sign language the norm, hearing people the minority, and spoken French the "foreign" language. The events themselves were subscription-based, black-tie dinners that adhered to a standard format: a sumptuous meal followed by speeches and toasts (Graff, JSM, 25th November 1900: 175; Gulliver 2004). They quickly established themselves as a central feature on the Parisian Deaf calendar. The first, in 1834, attracted fifty guests. By 1845 there were eighty-five guests and by the mid-1850s there were nearly one hundred (see BHR entries for years 1834, 1845, 1855).

For the hearing world, the banquets were a curiosity, the first being covered by no fewer than eleven newspapers. Some carried stories that were plainly sensationalist, such as Maurice's report of the banquets' carnivalesque reversal of the majority-hearing/minority-deaf status, published in *Le Temps* on December 2nd, 1834.

Some, however, were more perceptive in their reporting. One example is Eugene de Monglave's article, published in *La Chronique de Paris* on December 8, 1834: "Last Sunday, the 30th November brought a curious sight. A banquet, the means by which deaf-mutes, ex-pupils of the Paris school, celebrated the one hundred and twenty second anniversary of the birth of the Abbé de l'Epée. . . . At five o'clock, nearly sixty members of this *distinct nation*, came together in the rooms of the restaurant in the Place du Châtelet." (Monglave 1834. italics mine)

The reference to "nation" here is fascinating. Perhaps the hearing author of the article was attempting to capture something of the same dynamic that motivated comments about the Parisian school spaces being "foreign." The foreignness, however, was not that of one hearing-world nation against another; rather, it was the foreignness of the "Deaf nation" compared to the hearing world. This is explored by a young Deaf man named Ryan, who was visiting Paris at the time of the 1835 banquet and invited to attend: "I am English . . . but I come to celebrate with you the memory of our father in common, the Abbé de l'Epée. This is where we see how much better our universal language is than those incomplete languages of speaking humanity, languages that are limited to a greater or lesser territory. Ours covers all nations whatever their particular languages may be—it covers the entire globe" (BSM 1842, 27–28).

Rather than being the exception, Ryan's internationalist understanding of Deaf space appears to have been the rule. The 1835 banquet account reports that "present were deaf-mutes from all countries; for it is a real advantage . . . to only have one language to learn, that is signing, a language that has no words and which, painting only true ideas, is necessarily the same across the whole surface of the globe" (BSM 1842, 19).

If mention of a language in common were not enough to underline the international nature of a Deaf community, then the 1838 statues of the banquet's organizing committee make it clear that the banquets represented something of a focal point for a global reality:

[The organizing committee's] principle aim is to deliberate upon the interests of Deaf-Mutes in general, to gather into a commonly united accord deaf-mute luminaries scattered across the surface of the earth and other learned men who have made a deep study of this speciality, to strengthen the ties that unite this great family, to offer to each of its members a rally-ing point, a place for reciprocal communication and the resources to make themselves known in the world. (Société Centrale 1838)

In fact, the banquets themselves were demonstrable proof of an international Deaf reality. The first, in 1834, welcomed visitors from Prussia, Italy, and Portugal. The second welcomed Deaf people from the United States, Portugal, and Ireland. There-after, each year included at least one foreign representative; 1838 featured at least six: two from the United States, two from Prussia, and one each from Portugal and Ireland. The last of these was John O'Connell, British member of Parliament and son of the celebrated Irish nationalist Daniel O'Connell (BSM 1842, 61). O'Connell's attendance suggests that the idea of an international "Deaf nation" was not just fanciful language. The banquet committee *really did* think that they belonged to a community that was as fundamentally valid as a nation but international in form.

From approximately 1838, the word *nation* crops up repeatedly in Deaf writing. Unfortunately, for most of the wider world, the idea that Deaf people formed an international nation was meaningless. As one of the hearing Paris school teachers argued, if "deaf-mutes were, as they like say, a *nation*, then we would see . . . deaf children learning the language [of signs] on their mothers' knees . . . but almost all are born to hearing mothers who have no knowledge of the language of signs. . . . Do not call yourselves a *nation* and distance yourselves from your hearing breth-ren" (Valade-Rémi, quoted in Palmarès 1855–56, 9, 19).

It was not just hearing people who struggled to see the value of the Deaf nation. Many Deaf people took the concept far too literally and assumed that it would take them away from a hearing French nation that contained their families, friends, homes, and jobs. When they learned that it was a metaphor for an inter-national Deaf reality, they were bemused. Why waste time on a concept that was so idealistic when there was so much to be done to address the very real practical needs of an economically poor, local Deaf community? (see entry for 1844 in *Coup d'œil* document, reproduced in Bernard 1999, following p. 678)

From the 1840s onward, the French Deaf community gradually divided politically. For both sides, the ultimate goal was Deaf emancipation. However, one group believed this could be achieved only as an ideological shift, as the hearing world recognized the validity of Deaf people's extraordinary and unique inter-national reality, while the other viewed ideology as less important than practi-cal improvements to Deaf people's living conditions, employment prospects, and financial security. For the first group, full emancipation hinged on nothing less than the recognition of Deaf internationalist space. For the second, wasting time on an international reality was a luxury they could ill afford

DEAF INTERNATIONALISM: THE "AGENCY" OF DEAF SPACE

Ongoing tensions within the French Deaf community continued from the 1840s until the early 1880s, a sad period in French Deaf history marked by growing gaps in the historical record as those responsible for the society publications found less to celebrate. By the 1860s, the banquets had declined until they were small celebrations aimed primarily at maintaining links with national and Parisian civic dignitaries. Sign language gave up its dominance at the banquets, and calls for the recognition of Deaf internationalism gave way to the recognition of civil rights (BSM 1864: 185). In 1865, only twenty guests attended, and none of them came from outside France (BHR entry for 1865: no page). Apparently, although Deaf space continued to offer the potential for internationalism, in the numbness of internal division, Deaf Parisians had forgotten that such an international reality was theirs.

In 1889, however, that international reality came crashing back into the consciousness of the Parisian Deaf community. This radical change was caused by the first international Deaf congress, an event which was utterly transformative but which—if the record is to be believed—was not originally international in vision. Between 1885 and 1886, the leaders of both opposing factions within the Parisian community died. As a result, the groups found themselves in a scrabble for territory, with neither gaining the upper hand.

Finally, in 1889, the centenaries of both the death of de l'Epée and the French Revolution and the year of the Parisian World Fair coincided to provide an opportunity, which the organization that had previously organized the November banquets seized enthusiastically. Drawing on every element of their banquets, the fame of de l'Epée, and their previous network of connections, they set up a week-long congress consisting of debates, historical visits, and social events, all leading to a final international Deaf-mute banquet (Congress 1889, 7). They invited "Deaf-mutes, in all parts of the world" (letter of February 1, 1889, in Congress 1889, 5).

The 1889 congress was international in that those attending came from overseas. This limited vision of Deaf internationalism failed to account for the spontaneous effect that bringing 179 people together from all over the world would have upon those present. Five German, twenty-four American, eighteen British, eight Austrian, twenty-four Belgian, two Dutch, five Swedish and Norwegian, six Swiss, and two Turkish delegates joined more than eighty French delegates. Discussions covered most familiar subjects from the role of the Deaf community as the home of Deaf people (Congress 1889, 82) to the universality of sign language communication that allowed those present to overcome different national origins (Congress 1889, 83). Even those most committed to the congress's original, local, political aim could not help but be moved. In the words of Brill, one of the Austrian delegates:

> We Deaf-mutes are but one family. . . I find myself in a foreign country, surrounded by foreigners, and yet I find myself surrounded by friends and acquaintances whom I imagine to have known for years and breathe the air of my homeland. To what can I attribute this? It is the unique virtue of sign language that transforms a foreign country into a homeland. (Congress 1889, 86)

The report demonstrates that Deaf internationalism in 1889 had "outgrown" earlier Deaf nation internationalism. Previously, it had been imagined more like a wheel, a series of Deaf spokes that connected the exclusively male alumni of the Paris school to Deaf people of similarly standing in either the New World (e.g., Laurent Clerc) or other European cities. The 1889 congress, on the other hand, uncovered a distribution that was far less centralized and far more diverse. It welcomed twenty-four female delegates and more foreign visitors than French delegates. America dominated the delegates, signalling a shift in focus of the Deaf world away from Paris as the global hub to one that spread across the globe like a net.

This new Deaf internationalism also appears to have accommodated greater variety and was experienced as something that Deaf people could participate in by choice, as they wished. Rather than focus on what made all Deaf people the same, their common gratitude to the Abbé de l'Epée (and by consequence, France) and his gift of sign language education was now less interesting than individuals' own personal experiences (Congress 1889, 87), how each local or national Deaf community's experience differed, and the extent to which those experiences aligned (or not) with each other and with the hearing members of their home nations. The core understanding remained that the Congress represented a unique space that was representative of a much greater "natural, and primordial" (Congress 1889, 29) Deaf reality, the ultimate destiny of Deaf people (86), authored through sign language, gifted to them through time spent with other Deaf people, and potentially transformative for the wider hearing world (83).

Another key to the 1889 congress Deaf space was the way in which participation in an international Deaf reality was itself transformative. The French delegates who originally planned it needed only to look at their own personal experience to see this. In the process of producing a Deaf space along with 178 others, they had been transformed.

The 1889 Congress turned Deaf people away from the issues that divided them toward the greater reality in which they were united. Therefore, in the wake of the 1889 congress, the French Deaf community began to think about how it might challenge its placement in the French asylum system and establish full citizenship within the hearing nation, and it was only logical that they should turn to a solution that reproduced that 1889 congress.

THE 1900 CONGRESS

The solution that the Deaf community adopted was the Congress with which we began this chapter, positioned as centrally as possible at the heart of the 1900 Paris World Fair. It would be a space produced by the Deaf community, unapologetically international and unavoidably transformative. In the opinion of a progressive member of the French government, Republican Paul Deschanel,

> it seems to me that the day when your great family . . . concentrates and converges all its efforts, all its designs, all of its wills upon a single point. That day, your strength will be increased one hundredfold, and no one will be able to act for you without your agreement. . . . Your voices will be heard and you will not only be those protected by the state, but those who collaborate with it. (JSM, August 12, 1896, 247, 248)

From 1896, the Deaf community began to make preparations for the Congress. Within days of writing an official letter of intent to the Paris World Fair organizational committee, however, they were already being undermined. The committee turned down their original request for a Deaf-only congress because any congress likely to debate the future of the Deaf community had to involve "hearing-speaking people" (Congress 1900, 300).

The obligation to involve hearing people in both its preparation and functioning was a serious blow. Three alternatives were debated. The first, to withdraw entirely from the world fair, was rejected on the grounds that the fair offered valuable public visibility. The second, to run the congress as a joint forum, was also rejected on the grounds that a combined Deaf and hearing meeting would be overshadowed by communication problems and could never generate the kind of clear demonstration of an international Deaf space that was desired. The final alternative was to run the congress with both Deaf and hearing participants but to structure it into two separate sections, which would debate separately, and then join together around a final plenary and vote.

In adopting the final alternative, French Deaf community leaders knew that the congress would become a battle fought over the key question, pitched with an international bias but really aimed at changing French national policy: "The organisation of deaf-mute education in different countries. Should institutions for the education of deaf-mutes be establishments for instruction, or welfare?" (Congress 1900, 310).

A vote for welfare would confirm the status quo, maintaining Deaf spaces under the control of the Ministry of the Interior, designated as marginal spaces of asylum. A vote for instruction, however, would trigger a cascade of changes that would oblige the government's Ministry of Public Instruction to consult directly with Deaf people over how to recognize their alternative reality and represent it within the spaces of the state.

French Deaf community leaders failed to note, however, that although this debate format would provide an opportunity to produce an international Deaf space that would not only be produced alongside one that was strongly hearing but would continue to be beholden to the overarching permissions granted by the Paris World Fair organizational committee more generally. Without complete freedom, it was hard to see how the 1900 congress could truly represent the autonomy of an internationalist Deaf space. Instead, what became important was the simple question of numbers. Behind the scenes, the Deaf community (and their opponents in the Ministry of the Interior) began to plot to gain numerical advantage. As the congress opened on August 6, 1900, it appeared as if the Deaf community had won the initial battle. Deaf people and their allies outnumbered representatives of the Ministry of the Interior by nearly two to one.

As the opening speeches ended and the Deaf and hearing sections separated, however, the control of the world fair asserted itself. Deaf delegates found themselves ushered into a closed room away from public sight. Then, as the Deaf delegates were still debating whether to crash the hearing delegates' meeting in the main hall, a representative from the Ministry of the Interior asked for permission to speak, suggesting that because the proposed question regarding the nature of Deaf education "necessarily involves discussion of matters of administration that are internal to specific countries and that are absolutely inadmissible in the context of an International Congress. . . . I would request that this question be removed" (Congress 1900b, 36–38).

After a short debate, which included no Deaf people at all, the question was withdrawn. The hearing delegates then refused to join in a final combined plenary and vote.

CONCLUSION

The only really clear outcome of the 1900 Congress was a lingering stalemate over the reality of Deaf internationalism. The Ministry of the Interior succeeded in preserving the status quo, but they had done so by refusing to listen to the Deaf community and by ignoring the evidence that the Deaf community offered them. The Deaf community had demonstrated that Deaf people could come together from around the world, could communicate across sign language differences, and did—in the commonality of a visual experience of being—share something that united them at an international scale. That demonstration was of little use when those they really needed to convince—the hearing French state—perceived it only as a result of a shared experience of exclusion from the mainstream that was of no universal importance.

This story demonstrates the enormous significance that Deaf internationalist realities played in the nineteenth-century Deaf imagination. However, it also warns of how fragile those realities were in situations where Deaf internationalism was subject to interpretation by an uncomprehending hearing world. On a practical level, it was only too easy for the organizers of the Paris world fair, and then the Ministry of the Interior, to inject hearing control into the 1900 congress Deaf space and then disarm it simply by refusing to acknowledge it. On a more political level, we are faced with the stunning sight of French officials ignoring the potential of Deaf people's internationalist reality, in order to secure and maintain parochial control on a purely national scale.

Perhaps the most shocking aspect of the 1900 congress is that, despite all of the evidence offered by the Deaf community and an explicit attempt by that community to mobilize an internationalist Deaf reality, the Ministry of the Interior was never really confronted with the need to understand Deaf internationalism. The state structures within which they conducted business allowed them to simply sidestep the issue. That something so central to the nineteenth-century Deaf experience (and the core focus of this book) could be dismissed so easily is chilling.

REFERENCES

Bernard, Y. 1999. "Approche de la Gestualité à l'institution des Sourds-Muets de Paris, au XVIIIe et au XIXe siècle." PhD diss., Université de Paris V.

Berthier, F. 1873. L'Abbé Sicard. Paris. C. Douniol.

BHR Banquets des Sourds-Muets. Handwritten accounts (Accounts date from 1834, references are to the annual account by date, no pages in the original). Accounts held by the archives of the Institution Nationale des Jeunes Sourds, Paris.

BSM (1842) *Banquets des sourds-muets réunis pour fêter les anniversaires de la naissance de l'abbé de l'Épée* (1834 to 1848): Published by the Société Centrale des Sourds-Muets de Paris. Paris: Ledoyen.

BSM (1864) *Banquets des sourds-muets réunis pour fêter les anniversaires de la naissance de l'abbé de l'Épée de 1849 à 1863*. Published by the Société Centrale des Sourds-Muets de Paris Second Volume. Lagny: Imprimerie de A. Varigault.

Clerc, L. 1818. *Discours Composé par Clerc et lu par M. Gallaudet à l'Examen des élèves de l'asile établi dans le Connecticut devant M. le Gouverneur et les deux chambres de législature le 28 mai 1818.* Paris: J. J. Paschoud.

Congress. 1880. *Compte Rendu du Congrès International pour l'amélioration du sort des sourds-muets tenu à Milan du 6 au 11 septembre 1880.* Report provided in 1881 to the French Ministry of Public Instruction (Editor, Fornari, P.) Rome: Imprimerie Héritiers Botta.

Congress. 1889. *Congrès International des Sourds-Muets de 1889. Compte Rendu.* Paris: Association Amicale.

Congress. 1900. *Congrès International pour l'Etude des Questions d'Assistance et d'Education des Sourds-Muets. Section des Sourds-Muets. Compte rendu des débats et relations diverses.* Paris: Imprimerie d'Ouvriers Sourds-Muets.

Congress (1900b) *Congrès International pour l'Etude des Questions d'Assistance et d'Education des Sourds-Muets tenu les 6, 7 et 8 Août 1900 au Palais des Congrès de l'Exposition. Compte rendu des travaux de la section des entendants.* Paris: Imprimerie d'Ouvriers Sourds-Muets.

Coup d'œil rétrospectif sur les banquets annuels des sourds-muets a propos de l'anniversaire de la naissance de l'abbé de l'Épée, leur 1er instituteur, 1834–1891. Published without reference in Bernard 1999, following p. 678.

Desloges, P. 1779. *Observations d'un Sourd et Muèt, sur un cours élémentaire d'éducation des sourds et muets; publié en 1779 par M. L'abbé Deschamps, Chapelain de l'Eglise d'Orléans.* Paris: B. Morin.

Epée, C.-M. de l'. 1774. *Institution des Sourds Muets ou Recueil des Exercices Soutenus par les Sourds et Muets pendant les années 1771, 1772, 1773, et 1774.* Paris: L'imprimerie de Butard.

JSM 1896. Passe-Partout. Discours de M. Paul Deschanel. *Le Journal des Sourds-Muets.* 12th August 1896, 247, 248.

JSM 1900. Graff, E. Historique des Banquets de Novembre (Suite 1). *Le Journal des Sourds-Muets.* 25th November 1900, 175.

Gérando, J. M. de. 1827. *De l'Education des sourds-muets de naissance.* Paris: Mequignon.

Gulliver, M. 2004. "Write me a memory." MSc. thesis, University of Bristol.

———. 2008. "Places of Silence." In *Making Sense of Place: Exploring Concepts and Expressions of Place through Different Senses and Lenses*, edited by F. Vanclay, M. Higgins, and A. Blackshaw, 87–94. Canberra: National Museum of Australia.

———. 2009. "DEAF space, a history: The production of DEAF spaces Emergent, Autonomous, Located and Disabled in Eighteenth- and Nineteenth-Century France." PhD diss., University of Bristol. http://deafgeographies.files.wordpress.com/2012/02/mike-gulliver-phd.pdf.

Ladébat, L. de. 1815. *Recueil des définitions et réponses les plus remarquables de Massieu et Clerc sourds-muets aux diverses questions qui leur ont été faites dans les séances publiques de M. L'abbé Sicard à Londres.* London: Cox & Baylis.

Maurice, B. 1834. "Sur le Banquet du 30 November" *Le Temps* 2nd December 1834. – handwritten reproduction in BHR (entry for 1834, no page).

Monglave, E. de. 1834. No title. Article from *La Chronique de Paris* 7th December 1834. Handwritten reproduction in BHR (entry for 1834, no page).

Palmarès. Annual reports of the speeches given and prizes awarded at annual prizegiving ceremonies at the Parisian Deaf school. Reference is by year of delivery.

Paulmier, L. 1820. *Le Sourd-Muet Civilisé ou Coup d'œil sur l'Instruction des Sourds-muets. Second edition.* Paris: de l'Imprimerie d'Ange Clo.

Sicard, R. A. C. 1803. *Cours d'instruction d'un sourd-muet de naissance*, 2nd ed. Paris: le Clère.

———. 1808. *Théorie de Signes pour l'instruction des sourds-muets . . . Suivie d'une notice sur l'enfance de Massieu.* Paris: Imprimerie de l'institution des Sourds-Muets.

Société Centrale. 1838. Master copy of a letter of invitation to membership of the *Société Centrale* containing the statutes of the society, reproduced in its entirety in Bernard (1999: following page 679).

2 | A Global Stage: Sign Language Artistic Production and Festivals in International Contexts

Pierre Schmitt

For the past five years, I have been exploring different spaces of a "global stage." From digital social media to parties at festivals, from backstages to rehearsals, from late-night discussions in apartments to public speeches in theaters, I have followed members of an international signing art community. As an anthropologist, I have utilized a model of multi-sited and itinerant ethnography to figure out how the "net works" and looked at each specific festival as a temporary setting that could bring a better understanding of sign language arts festivals as a global phenomenon. While I have been identifying networks, this community has progressively appeared as a web of relations, with signing festivals as knots where its members gather.

In this chapter I describe artistic festival settings as international deaf spaces and provide an overview of these artistic networks—how they are built and created, how they work, how they are reassembled over time, and how they expand to other networks—and I focus on to what extent both festivals and these networks are intertwined with local organizations and spaces, their pasts and presents. Finally, I argue that because these festivals are attended by a large number of hearing signing individuals too, they provide an opportunity to think about the concept of sign language universalism (as opposed to deaf universalism, the theme of this book). Although my scope is ultimately global, here I mainly focus on French festivals and their social and historical context, especially *Sign'ô* in Toulouse and *Clin d'Oeil* in Reims.

The social life of Deaf and signing artists, professional interpreters, and a few other bilingual hearing workers revolves and evolves around networks of individuals with shared interests or professional activities related to sign language as an artistic medium. This includes movies, theater, television, acting and directing, poetry, and signed songs. In this regard, festivals are spaces where such networks can be described and theorized.

Theorizing Networks

From an image of networks as physical or digital relations among people, places, or other entities, networks emerge as collections of moving social relations, where people themselves appear as knots and their connections as strings. This image is a conceptual tool and a metaphor. I visualize those networks as constantly changing entities. A specific festival would look like a mess of entangled knots, as many related people are present in a single place at a single time. Then, until the next festival, a net spreads, still with visible knots, such as with constantly active arts communities in Paris and Los Angeles. The next festivals and events pull some strings back. We can imagine that strings are made of rubber, considering that as more people that a given person is connected to attend a particular event, the chances that this person will also attend become greater. Moreover, people do not simply appear or disappear: they are progressively entangled or disentangled. That is how the net works.

Multi-sited and Itinerant Ethnography

Like World Federation of the Deaf (WFD) congresses and Deaflympics, the biggest international signing art festivals bring together Deaf people who fly across world's oceans. This chapter is based on multi-sited and itinerant ethnography (see Marcus 1995), which I argue is a desirable method to study international deaf spaces, such as festivals. As I have progressively become "a member of an international intergenerational community" (Ladd 2003, xiv) between 2009 and 2014, I have met and followed several artists and attendees in diverse places such as *Dövas Nordiska Kulturfestival* (Stockholm, Sweden), Bristol Deaf Festival (Bristol, UK), *Sign'ô* festival (Toulouse, France), and *Clin d'Oeil* (Reims, France). Although I am hearing, throughout my fieldwork as a doctoral student in anthropology interested in sign language and performing arts, I have learned French sign language and have become accustomed to conversations held in international signs and across—or at the crossroads—of several national sign languages.

Sign language arts festivals identified as a specific social and cultural phenomena have no lasting time and space boundaries. Even though they happen in different sites at different times, they are not a collection of unrelated events. What makes them a unique phenomenon is the hypothesis that their very existence and organization rely upon underlying networks and sociocultural phenomena, such as deaf universalism and international networks of mobile artists and public.

My research therefore became itinerant because all sites are steps on an itinerary, or rather variably shared steps on various itineraries. Beyond a diachronic vision, considering that successful festivals such as *Sign'ô* and *Clin d'Oeil* tend to replicate themselves over years and take place in perennially artistic environments, such as Toulouse's active signing community, those sites can also be considered as knots on a web.

In addition to attending festivals and being involved in arts networks in Paris and France, I lived in Los Angeles (LA) from September 2011 to May 2012. I had the opportunity to be hosted at the Center for Language, Interaction, and Culture (CLIC) at the University of California, Los Angeles (UCLA) as a visiting affiliate to work on my research project, "Sign Language Performed: Multi-sited

Ethnography of Signing Artistic Practices in France and the United States." Before my arrival, I found an apartment through Erin Wilkinson, a North American Deaf linguist that I met at an international conference on sign languages in Belgium in 2009. As I let her know my plans, she put me in touch with Tommy Korn, a very active "Deafie," around my age, involved in the LA's signing arts community and who graduated from Gallaudet University. As flatmates, he promptly brought me around LA. Throughout my stay, I followed him from artistic workshops blending young talents and well-known comedians from Deaf West Theatre (DWT), to movie premieres, to official ceremonies, to birthday parties. Step by step, I witnessed what I had already observed in Paris: Deaf artists in LA mingle on both professional and personal levels.

In subsequent years I met many of those people at sign language festivals in Europe—sometimes at large international events, sometimes at much smaller events. I often had the opportunity to participate in improvised reunions with common friends.

Paying close attention to when and where I meet people is a basic and important step to identify a network. Meanwhile, I collect information about how people in the arts networks connect to each other, from direct observation and informal interviews. It is a kind of constant and diachronic process of identifying "who's who" and "who knows whom." Each festival or event is not only an occasion to confirm relationships and to initiate new relationships, but also an occasion to witness how relationships evolve over time and an opportunity to gather more biographical elements about past encounters or future meetings.

Each event makes some connections visible and provides opportunities for people to create new connections. Of course, it is not possible to attend every event—no one in the network does. Each reunion is a partial actualization of some parts of the networks. "Following" people on online social networks, such as Facebook, can provide information about events that could not be attended (see İlkbaşaran, this volume, and Kurz and Cuculick, this volume, for more on the role of social media in deaf networks). Online updates and feeds, pictures, and comments are also complementary sources for ethnographic research at huge festivals with hundreds or thousands of attendees: bigger meetings create more limitations to direct observation, gaps to be fulfilled by other means of documentation.

Digital social media can also provide a way to strengthen identification of networks. Through online social media, such as Facebook and YouTube, I have been connecting to hundreds of individuals already mutually connected. As a knot on the web I am exploring, I have access to information that people leave accessible to other members of their network. Posted group pictures and their comments inform the "online ethnographer" about actual events that bring people together. While personal information is at stake in such enquiry, people's privacy or intimacy are not compromised by the use of such materials: the network is the phenomenon that is under scrutiny, rather than individuals. It is also important to note that information gathered through such online ethnography sheds more light on strings that have been documented through fieldwork. In this sense, I am not interested in online communities but rather in the way the international community I am investigating is making use of online social media to strengthen its continuity.

Arts, Culture, and Local Deaf Communities: Past and Present

Sign language artistic practices are quite recent phenomena. We can trace them back at least to nineteenth-century versions of Don Guzman or Hamlet performed by "deaf and dumb actors" in England or theater plays in French Deaf schools, such as Poitiers or Nantes in the 1920s, with themes related to the history of Deaf education.[1] Throughout the twentieth century, storytelling has also been a common artistic form at Deaf clubs' celebrations.

In the twentieth century, a shift has occurred with the development of professional Deaf theater companies that have gained recognition beyond Deaf communities, such as National Theatre of the Deaf (NTD, created in 1967) in the United States or International Visual Theatre (IVT, 1976) in France. Other professional theatres include *Tyst Teater* in Sweden (1970–), Hand Theatre in the Netherlands (1990), Deaf West Theatre in Los Angeles (1991), *Teater Manu* in Norway (2001), and Deafinitely Theatre in the United Kingdom (2002). Another fairly contemporary shift has been the entrance of sign language as a medium and field of experimentation in contemporary theater, with influential hearing figures such as Pina Bausch, Peter Brook, and Robert Wilson in the 1970s and 1980s using sign. Sign language has also entered mainstream productions. New York's musical lovers and critics remember the US-based Deaf West's most popular production, *Big River*, which held sixty-seven shows on Broadway.

In France, most sign language arts festivals were established after 2000; the main ones are *Clin d'Oeil* (2003), *Sign'ô* (2007), and *Souroupa* (2005). They are less associated with traditional Deaf associations and clubs. Dedicated and specialized associations have emerged such as the French associations *Cinesourd* (2000), Act's (1997), and *Signes* (2003), which respectively organize the previously mentioned festivals *Clin d'Oeil*, *Sign'ô*, and *Souroupa*. In other words, autonomization of arts and culture as a subfield in Deaf community organizations has played an important role in the emergence of festivals.

Documenting artistic festivals thus has to include local recent history of associations. Such history itself is rooted in a set of correlated meaningful social institutions that form a landscape and a solid ground for sign language cultural life to blossom. Toulouse represents a paradigmatic example of such fertile soil. Historically, the city has been part of the avant-garde of the *Reveil Sourd* (Deaf Awakening), the French social and political movement for sign language recognition that started in the mid-1970s.[2] Toulouse displays exemplary accomplishments of this movement's political agenda (Mottez and Markowicz 1980): a sign language interpreter service that is one of the biggest and oldest in France; a sign language bilingual education program that ranges from kindergarten to high school; and sign language courses and degrees inside Toulouse University's walls. Toulouse has no permanent Deaf theatre, as signing arts mainly developed with IVT in Paris during the *Reveil Sourd*. Nonetheless, there is now an active artistic signing community with sign language theater companies and a fair amount of Deaf artists

---

[1] These examples have been chosen among evidence and archives shared by Yves Delaporte through personal correspondence.
[2] Similar and parallel processes happened in other countries such as the Deaf Resurgence in the United Kingdom (Ladd 2003).

known across France. Another vivid example of the connection between festivals and local institutions would be Deaf Way and Deaf Way II, which took place in Washington, DC, in 1989 and 2002. These events cannot be separated from the Deaf community's unique history at Gallaudet University and in Washington, DC.

A conference such as Deaf Way in Washington or festivals such as *Sign'ô* in Toulouse thus invite us to think about a world experienced as small at both local and international levels. Any international gathering can only take place and develop on some local ground, with local associations and professionals holding specific organizing responsibilities and duties, with more attendees from the hosting country, city, or region, and with a local history of sign language artistic and political advocacy.

INTERNATIONAL NETWORKS AND ELITES

From my own observation, international attendees at sign language arts festivals—not necessarily local ones—belong to a transnational elite. Their taste and lust for arts, as much as their timely and economic resources for traveling, display socioeconomic and cultural profiles that prevent them from being representative of the Deaf population across the globe. Deaf artists and festival attendees are a minority among the vast majority of their Deaf peers. They can be considered as an elite among deaf populations, who are statistically disadvantaged compared to their respective average national population in terms of education, incomes, and employment wherever they live. This is also true of Paris and Los Angeles signing arts networks, where higher education degrees are much more common than among the rest of the Deaf population; many American Deaf artists held degrees from California State University, Northridge, or Gallaudet University, for instance, while many French artists went back to university to earn degrees or to get some of their professional skills legitimized by academic credentials.

Deaf artists' networks are created in multiple ways, from acquaintances to long-lasting friendships, from small gigs together to common professional paths, to occasional partnerships to finding a partner for life, from parties to official events. For example, Los Angeles and DWT were already familiar to Ipek Mehlum, a Deaf Norwegian actress, when she went to the United States to perform *Jealousy* in April 2014. Indeed, Ipek was part of the cast for Deaf West's *Cyrano* in 2012. While living in Los Angeles for several months during rehearsals, she had time to mingle with the Southern California signing art community and to take part in other artistic projects. For instance, she appeared in the 2012 Jules Dameron's short *It's My Role*. They collaborated again in 2013 on *Møkkakaffe*, a Deaf Norwegian series, directed by Jules, and starring Ipek as a main character.

To understand such mobilities, it is important to take into account that both Deaf directors and skilled leading role actors (Valley Film Festival 2011) are rare gems in the Deaf world. Hiring a foreign Deaf professional is common practice. *Metroworld*, a French play created by the Lyon-based company On/Off and performed at *Clin d'Oeil* in 2011, had only one French Deaf actor in its main cast of three Deaf actors. Beyond ephemeral professional partnerships, individual itineraries displaying common and crossed paths, as for Ipek and Jules, shed light on specific transnational networks, as the one that connects LA to the Finnish Deaf community.

The successful careers of these two talented artists have made them active members of international sign language networks at many levels. However, when they met again at the *Clin d'Oeil* festival in 2013, they had no current artistic project in common. Jules was invited to direct a professional roundtable and Ipek performed with *Teater Manu*. As such, not only are signing artistic festivals international deaf spaces but they are also among the most visible knots on the web of contemporary Deaf World networks.

FESTIVALS AS OPPORTUNITIES FOR INTERNATIONAL AND LOCAL NETWORKS TO MEET

For many years, *Sign'ô* has organized a party at a local alternative artistic community in Toulouse. Attendees must pay, but they are free to price their participation. In 2014, the party brought together more than a thousand Deaf and hearing people throughout the night, while the festival gathered around three hundred attendees each day, with a French majority but including foreign artists and attendees. At the party, most hearing people were from the area and were not necessarily aware of the festival itself; this was also the case for some local Deaf people at the party. As some of them mentioned during the event, they were accustomed to partying there but quickly became aware that an unusual mass of Deaf people were joining them that night. Such an event appears as a bridge between the festival and the local community at large. The "free" entrance and the focus on the party bring together both hearing people unfamiliar with Deaf culture and local Deaf people who are not as mobile as other international attendees.

Sign'ô is also an open festival in terms of spatial organization: everyone is free to attend the festival venue, its art exhibition, its bar and food court, and even outdoor shows. Theaters and indoor shows are the only parts of the festivals that require tickets and entrance fees.[3] In a similar fashion, public outdoor shows happen in Reims's streets during *Clin d'Oeil* festival. These smaller shows bring public attention to the rest of the festival. Nevertheless, the main *Clin d'Oeil* festival venue is a "closed" space that requires entrance fees. Moreover, the dozens of international shows result in expensive prices for tickets. Many French people mention such prices as a reason for not going, although they regret that they cannot join the thousands of international attendees. The Deaf parties that are organized every night during the *Clin d'Oeil* also bring international performers on stage and have specific fees as well; these are included in the festival pass or can be paid for separately. Therefore, meeting local hearing people who are not specifically interested in sign language arts is unlikely at the festival or at the party. Deaf people from the local community who are not theater patrons or with limited resources also miss the festival but they have the opportunity to mingle around open spaces at *Sign'ô*.

Beyond Deaf parties, artistic representations, shows, and presentation of professional works, festivals are also creative spaces. Indeed, they often feature workshops. The 2014 *Sign'ô* festival included workshops with Giuseppe

---

[3] This is also the case for the Douarnenez film festival, which has a "Deaf World" section and includes interpreters for its roundtables and public discussions with directors, subtitles for international and French movies, and Deaf and signing volunteers in the festival. The local community in Douarnenez can easily take part to the event, which involves encounters with the deaf public.

Giuranna, a well-known Italian Deaf performer, and other workshops open to festival attendees. *Sign'ô* also features sign songs from local amateurs, both deaf and hearing. They are invited to create and rehearse throughout the year in a sign language song group set up by Acts, the association which runs the festival.

Festivals also strengthen international networks by bringing together international professional artists on stage. In 2011, *Clin d'Oeil* presented results from an international theater workshop, hosted at the IVT in Paris with artists from IVT, *Tyst Teater* in Stockholm, and *Teater Manu* in Oslo. Artists communicated through International Sign (IS) and performed in a mix of highly iconic signs and IS. Performers in *Clin d'Oeil* not only bet on IS ability to convey meaning in dialogue-driven plays but they also assume that performances in national sign languages can be understood by an international public. Time, economic, and creative constraints also make it difficult or impossible to ask all theater companies to translate their work into IS. Nevertheless, some companies sometimes do. The French play *Divan Violet*, originally performed in French sign language (*Langue des signes francaise*/LSF) has been presented in a IS version at *Clin d'Oeil*. Other times, works are translated into national sign languages. For instance, *Teater Manu* has translated *Jealousy* into an IS/ASL hybrid to be performed at the DWT in Los Angeles.

Sign Language Universalism: Festivals as Deaf and Hearing Spaces

Through linguistic practices, signing art festivals also represent places where deaf and hearing identities are negotiated in interesting ways. Indeed, in a crowd of hundreds or thousands of signers, it appears that deaf and hearing people are separated by being "signers" and "nonsigners" rather than by being "deaf" and "hearing." In such spaces, ethnic-like terms such as DEAF and HEARING in ASL or SOURD and ENTENDANT in LSF are challenged. At several occasions, I witnessed cases where people joining a conversation assumed that some unknown hearing signer—a Child of Deaf Adults (CODA), interpreter, or some other bilingual hearing individual—was deaf. In these spaces sign languages function as the primary—or ideally preferred and most valued—way of communicating for *everyone*. Some young deaf people that I have mingled with while attending festivals casually said: DEAF HEARING DON'T CARE. This does not mean that deaf and hearing identities are erased. Nevertheless, they are blurred and the deaf-hearing difference is not regarded as significant.

In the end, full access to a festival such as *Clin d'Oeil* is determined by sign language fluency rather than a deaf identity. Indeed, in some cases there were no interpreters for—nonsigning—hearing audiences and plays were performed in sign language-only versions (while they have been performed in bilingual forms in other contexts), and most informal conversations in IS and various sign languages were not intended for beginners. Nonetheless, this does not mean that hearing people were not welcome. Moreover, at some festivals, like *Sign'ô*, encounters between hearing (signers or not) and deaf people through sign language artistic practices are an aim (as discussed in the forewords of the 2012 and 2014 programs).

For a short time, in a small world of interaction, when deaf and hearing sign together, emphasis can be put on what is shared and on what make people gather, on what precisely brings those *deaf* and *hearing* people together: sign language performed, by the public and by artists. By definition, these festivals are artistic reunions, promoting sign language as an artistic medium: *Clin d'Oeil* defines itself as "an artistic pluridisciplinary event" (a visual art exhibition is also presented onsite, which is also the case at *Sign'ô*), and *Souroupa*, another festival in southern France, is born from a will "to share a passion for performing arts" (Association Signes 2014).

I coin these events "Sign language art festivals." What motivates this conceptual label, rather than "Deaf art festivals," is that a noticeable amount of them use a variety of names and expressions that do not explicitly or exclusively define them as "Deaf," especially in France. While *Clin d'oeil* presents itself on the 2013 edition's main webpage as a "European panorama of Deaf culture," it also claims to "aim at shedding light on the richness of the signing community." In my opinion, this expression goes beyond traditional equations such as "sign language = language of the Deaf community," which would lead to "signing community = Deaf community." This is evidence of a "sign language universalism" ideology. Through the concept of a signing community, sign language does not cease to be the *language of Deaf people* and sign language arts do not cease to be an expression of Deaf cultures. Nonetheless, deaf people potentially cease to be the only guests and hosts of events celebrating these languages and their artistic expressions. Through the idea of a single community of signers, organizers may invite hearing signers in.

In a similar fashion, *Sign'ô* names itself *Rencontre des Arts en Langue des Signes*, literally "meeting of arts in sign language" (or "sign language arts meeting" with more English word order). This definition is probably as close as possible to the category that I suggest. Moreover, the festival presents itself as the rendezvous of the "*amoureux des Arts en Langue des Signes*" ("lovers of arts in sign language/sign language arts' lovers") on the 2014 edition's website, a presentation page where the word *s/Sourd* (*d/Deaf*) does not appear (Association Act's 2014).

What is more, in 1997, when the association that runs the festival was created, its acronym, Act's, initially stood for *Association Culturelle et Théâtrale pour les Sourds* ("Cultural and Theatrical Association for the Deaf "). In 2002, with a new board, Acts changed what this acronym stands for, switching its full name to *Ateliers et Compagnie Théâtrale en Signes* ("Workshops and Theatre Company in Signs") (Assocation Act's 2013).

Finally, the southern France festival *Souroupa* is named after a contraction of *Sourd ou pas*—("Deaf or not").

CONCLUSION

Throughout this chapter, I have described what appears to me as a *signing* art world (Becker 1982), rather than a *Deaf art world*. This is neither an attempt to legitimate my own position as a hearing researcher nor a denial of Deaf people's achievements and talents in the arts. It does not intend to minimize or put aside differences between Deaf and hearing as social, cultural, and linguistic categories. Rather, it advocates for a frame of analysis that does not separate individuals— Deaf and hearing (Schmitt 2013)—who are working and living together, who collectively participate in artistic processes, who organize or attend the same shows and events, and who share common values about sign language as the most appropriate language not only for Deaf people to express themselves but also for direct Deaf-hearing interactions.

Focusing attention on hearing attendees and hearing signers, who have long belonged to an analytical blind spot in Deaf studies (except perhaps for CODAs and interpreters), and their participation in a sign language universalism, I aim to point out some shifts in the deaf world, where sign language festivals, for people who are deaf or not, have appeared beside deaf festivals such as *Dövas Nordiska Kulturfestival*. Such festivals as open international deaf spaces are also critical responses to the challenge of developing access to artistic practices for the largest number in the deaf community. For instance, beside (future) interpreters and students in sign language classes, hearing attendees, organizers, and volunteers include not only children of deaf adults but also hearing parents of deaf children. Their involvement, participation, and support is a key element for ensuring artistic and cultural blossoming for the next generation of deaf children and adults.

From a hearing perspective, documenting deaf-hearing interaction in sign language in artistic spaces allows the ethnographer to shed light on human based, rather than technologically or eugenically driven, solutions to the "issue of deafness" in a society that is eager to "integrate" deaf people. In which ways should/could deaf and hearing people interact? What should/could be the role of sign language and vocal language—written and/or spoken—in these relations? Festival settings, theater venues, and shows as shared spaces and as multimodal and multilingual environments foreground new norms of communication among deaf and hearing people. These settings also push us, scholars and participants, to think about other kinds of desired universalisms beyond deaf universalism. Perhaps the concept of sign language universalism holds some answers to this.

REFERENCES

Association Act's. 2014. "Un peu d'histoire." Association Act's. Accessed May 12, 2015. http://www.festival-signo.fr/un-peu-histoire.

Association Act's. 2013. "Historique." Association Act's. Accessed June 25, 2014. http://www.acts31.fr/a-propos/historique/.

Association Signes. 2014. "Présentation." Association Signes. Accessed May 12, 2015. http://www.signes-roya.org/fr/presentation/association.html.

Becker, H. S. 1982. *Arts Worlds*. Berkeley: University of California Press.

Ladd, P. 2003. *Understanding Deaf Culture: In Search of Deafhood*. Clevedon, UK: Multilingual Matters.

Marcus, G. E. 1995. "Ethnography in/of the World System: The Emergence of Multi-Sited Ethnography." *Annual Review of Anthropology* 24:95–117.

Mottez, B., and H. Markowicz. 1980. "The Social Movement Surrounding French Sign Language." In *Sign Language and the Deaf Community. Essays in Honor of William C. Stokoe*, edited by C. Baker and R. Battison. Silver Spring, MD: National Association of the Deaf.

Schmitt, P. 2013. "New Directions in the Study of Deaf/Hearing Interaction in a Deaf World." In *Cartographies of Deafness: Communities, Languages, Practices, and Pedagogies*, edited by O. Coelho and M. Klein, 365–74. Porto, Portugal: Editora Livpsic.

Valley Film Festival. 2011. "Jules Dameron on Deaf Women in Film," Valley Film Festival, Accessed May 12, 2015. http://valleyfilmfest.blogspot.fr/2011/05/jules-dameron-on-deaf-women-in-film_21.html.

3 | The World Federation of the Deaf Youth Camp in Durban: An Opportunity for Learning, Networking, and Empowerment

Philippa Merricks

In the twenty-first century young Deaf people have many opportunities to become involved in Deaf community events on local and global levels. This chapter draws on empirical research on the experiences of young Deaf people attending the Fifth World Federation of the Deaf (WFD) Youth Camp in Durban, South Africa, in July 2011. The research investigated how the WFD youth camp impacted young people's identities and cultural and social interactions and how they were influenced by this transnational experience. There is no existing research about international Deaf camps and therefore this chapter provides important initial insights into the experience and impact of attending a youth camp.

The WFD was established in 1951 during its first World Congress. It organizes quadrennial WFD World Congresses that have always attracted attendees of various ages from all over the world. However, it was not until the 1987 WFD World Congress, held in Finland, that there was a first gathering of Deaf youth who established a youth working group (WFDYS 2011). The consecutive WFD World Congress in Japan in 1991 saw the development of the youth group through discussion forums, and the youth group proceeded to organize the first World Deaf Youth Camp in Austria in 1995. The first World Deaf Youth Camp involved ninety-seven participants from twenty-three countries (WFDYS 2011). The first election of new committee members in the youth section of WFD took place at the WFD World Congress in 1995, hence the name World Federation of the Deaf Youth Section (WFDYS). The WFD youth camps are now organized to coincide with the WFD quadrennial congress; the camp takes place one week before the congress, so that the camp participants can attend the congress when the camp ends.

In addition to the youth camp organized for youth aged eighteen to thirty, the WFDYS hosts quadrennial camps for other age groups: a camp for juniors aged thirteen to seventeen years old was started in Ireland in 1997 and a camp for children aged nine to twelve years old was started in Denmark in 2006. The Deaf young people involved in these camps are selected via their national Deaf association or national Deaf youth associations to represent their countries. The junior and children camps are normally held for approximately one week in a host country that is selected by the WFDYS General Assembly, which is a two-day event that takes place after the youth camps have finished. All of the candidates' countries have to present their bids for hosting the junior and children camps, and the delegate members in the assembly then vote for the most preferred host country. The one-week camps typically include a balance of educational workshops addressing the themes of Deaf identity, culture, history, and politics, along with social and fun activities and opportunities to explore the host countries.

The WFD youth camps have successfully increased the number of participants and countries involved since the first camp in 1995 in Austria. The camp in Durban, in 2011, involved 120 young Deaf people from forty countries. The average number of participants to represent each country is between three and four campers, depending on the venue and the camp capacity. The camp selection varies in each country, as some countries select their youth by interviewing the candidates, or offering spots according to gender and background, or deciding on the most suitable person to represent their country. The camp participants are expected to pay for the camp fees, approximately $550, which includes accommodation, travel expenses within the host country, and activity and presenter fees; the camp fee does not include the travel expenses to the host country. The majority of the camp participants either pay the full cost or half of the expenses and their national Deaf youth association covers the other half. There are some initiatives by various groups, such as Frontrunners 3 (Frontrunn3rs) (www.fr3.frontrunners.dk), which aim to help fund the camps. Frontrunn3rs, in which I took part, spent two days planning, filming, and editing three different videos to raise awareness of the camps. These three videos were made into a DVD, which Frontrunn3rs decided to sell to raise money for WFDYS after spending a few days observing the WFD and WFDYS board meetings.

The findings from this study of the real-life experiences of the young Deaf camp participants provide insights into their motivations for attending the camp, the networking opportunities, and their feelings of empowerment. Overall, the WFD camp was viewed as a positive experience for all study participants as it enabled them to learn about different cultures and to meet and identify with other Deaf people. They shared these experiences in their native countries afterward.

RESEARCHING THE CAMP

The research method consisted of semistructured interviews with five camp participants during the Fifth World Federation of the Deaf Youth Camp in Durban, South Africa, in July 2011. I advertised the research at the start of the camp to make people aware and to promote interest amongst the camp participants. In addition to being a researcher, I was the president of the European Union of the Deaf Youth (EUDY) and represented EUDY at the camp. I stressed to the participants that I was wearing a different hat as a researcher and that my research was not related to the EUDY. The recruitment then took place at the end of the camp week, when I asked for volunteers, and the interviews were conducted during the WFD congress in the week following the end of the camp. This gave the participants time to reflect on their camp experience.

More than five people volunteered to participate and I selected one person per continent: Europe, Australasia, North America, Central America, and South America. All participants were between eighteen and thirty years old (as this is the official age criteria for the youth camp). Four of the participants were female and the fifth was male, and all preferred to conduct their interview in International Sign (IS). The duration of each interview was approximately fifteen minutes in total. The interviews explored how camp participants perceived the camp, their reasons for attending, the impact of the camp on the individual's identity, culture, and social interaction, and their views on the continuity of the organization of the camps throughout the years. All of the interviews were video recorded and I transcribed the recording into written English. The data were then analyzed to identify similarities and differences across the five interviews.

My previous experience of attending the WFDYS junior camp in 2001 and the EUDY youth camp in 2006 formed part of my motivation for researching this topic. I felt at home when I attended the WFDYS camp and these experiences led to my belief that global encounters can benefit an individual's identity and confidence. The advantage of being an "insider"—I was in the same age group as the participants and I am fluent in International Sign, was one of the participants in the camp, and had previously attended other camps—was that I could engage with the participants through shared experiences. In this, I follow Lapan, Quartarolli, and Riemer (2012, 25–26), who state that "the more closely researchers are involved with the researched, the more likely it is they can be responsive and adaptable. . . . Hearing researchers cannot really learn what it means to be deaf" (also see Boland et al., this volume). However, this could potentially have also been a disadvantage, as the camp participants might not have fully expressed their views if they assumed that I knew what they meant and particular responses might have been "expected" by me.

It must be noted that the five participants involved in this study already had connections with Deaf relatives, Deaf organizations, or Deaf peers, all of whom have previously been involved in international Deaf events. For example, Alexandra Kotsaki, from Greece, and Drisana Levitzke-Gray, from Australia, both attended the WFD Madrid congress in 2007; also, both of them have Deaf family members. Irene Coen, from Costa Rica, had participated in the WFDYS Madrid camp in 2007 and was also involved in the Deaf community in Costa Rica. Rodrigo Araújo, from Brazil, and Bregitt Jimenez, from the USA, were both involved in the Deaf community in their countries before they participated in the camp. It is possible that those who were first timers at the camp, or those who did not have any connections to Deaf peers or organizations, may have been less likely to volunteer to take part in the interviews and thus the perspectives in this chapter may not be as recognizable for them.

Camp Activities

As the camp participants arrived with various levels of International Sign, or without any knowledge at all, the WFD youth camp provided a one-hour International Sign workshop for all of the participants on the first day; this allowed the participants to become used to International Sign in order to communicate and develop throughout the week.

The WFDYS camp in Durban organized a variety of activities and presentations. For example, Anna Mothapo, the chairperson of Deaf South Africa, gave a presentation about her organization. The WFDYS provided a whole-day presentation about the WFD and the history of WFDYS. Other presenters included Braam Jordaan, a South African Deaf person who is highly skilled in the field of animation; he is a three-dimensional (3D) visual artist, director, illustrator, and an advocate for the Deaf community. Megan Young presented on her work within villages in Kenya. Ambrose Murangira focused on deaf youth leadership in Uganda, speaking about how it was important to involve young deaf people in deaf associations. John Meletse, a Deaf gay activist working on lesbian, gay, bisexual, and transgender (LGBT) issues and peer education, presented on his life with human immunodeficiency virus (HIV) and how he now supports other people going through similar experiences.

The camp participants also attended different types of workshops in which they discussed cases provided by the WFDYS, such as the closure of Deaf schools, children being sent to day schools rather than residential schools, and what their youth organization could do with a donation of €50,000. In each group there were about ten participants, all from different countries. The workshops were designed to encourage collaborative critical thinking.

Furthermore, several team-bonding activities were organized to encourage leadership, teamwork, and communication skills. For example, throughout the camp, the participants were split into teams named after iconic African animals such as buffalo, elephant, lion, shark, and springbok. The activities included building the highest tower made out of balloons, straw, and tape. Each of the materials cost a certain amount of money and the aim of this activity was to create the highest tower with the lowest budget possible.

Motivation for Attending the WFD Youth Camp and the Continuity of the Camps

The majority of participants stated that they learned about the WFDYS camp during former global encounters such as WFD congress or from their Deaf peers, parents, or Deaf youth groups, who encouraged them to go. Drisana, who attended the WFD congress in 2007 and the WFDYS junior camp in 2009, has Deaf parents who were involved in international deaf gatherings:

> Especially my mum was always involved in international things, and she always informed me what was available out there, so if it was not for her then I probably would have not known anything. Because of that, it made me get involved.

Alexandra had also attended the WFD congress in 2007:

> I knew about WFDYS before, throughout my five years' experience within a Deaf organization [Hellenic Deaf Youth Association]. I went to WFD congress in Madrid, Spain, I didn't participate in the camp but was in the congress and I knew at that time that in four years there would be another camp. And now I am the president of my Deaf youth organization and I must be a delegate for the [WFDYS General Assembly], so at the same time I was very eager to be in the youth camp.

Another important factor in promoting the youth camp is the use of technology, including social networks. Three of the five interview participants became aware of the WFDYS camp via their Deaf organization's website and social network sites. For example, Bregitt explained:

> I found out through Facebook. My national Deaf association was publicizing the application and information but I do not check the national Deaf association website, I probably check one a month, whereas via Facebook I get updated information, so really thanks to Facebook as it is a really vital network.

Previous camp participants played an important role in the promotion of the WFDYS camp and motivating others. Bregitt Jimenez from the USA said of a previous camp participant: "I understood her [a previous participant's] reason but it was not until I participated in the camp myself, I completely empathized with her experiences." The majority of the participants felt motivated to ensure that their Deaf peers of the same nationality will have the opportunity to experience the international Deaf youth camps in the future. Drisana explains:

> I definitely hope that all the next camps for three age groups—children, junior, and youth camps—will always have Australian participants going. If this means that I have to promote, I don't care as I will do it and make sure that someone is going as it is an awesome experience and just too invaluable to miss this opportunity. This experience was very important for me and I want other Deaf people to have the same opportunity.

Rodrigo expresses a similar concern:

> I want to make sure that more young Deaf people go to the future camps as it is important, I do not want to be the only one who has been to such a camp, as this camp was a positive experience for me.

Thus, all of the camp participants were inspired to (in Drisana's signs) "encourage [signed as elbow prod] other friends that they should go to the next one and spread the word because it is always a thrill to meet people from all over the world." Bregitt believed that spreading information about the camp ensured its continuity: "because many people over time continued to spread the positivity about the camp, which allows the camp to continue strongly."

NETWORKING OPPORTUNITIES AND CULTURAL LEARNING

Rodrigo felt strongly that the international Deaf camp ensures that Deaf young people are not isolated and promotes empowerment and bonding among Deaf young people:

> I want more youth camps in the future and Deaf youth should have the opportunity to be involved as this is an important way to mix with other Deaf peers and to unite with them to make the Deaf world stronger. If there is no camp, then I feel that we won't be strong and Deaf people will be isolated and more spread out. It is important to be strongly united, to be able to make changes in the future.

Transnational connections allow Deaf people to develop contacts and networks on a global scale, whereby Deaf people can collect information from the international Deaf event and bring it home to their native country (De Clerck 2007). The WFD youth camp in Durban provided the opportunity for the camp participants to network with others and to share aspects of their home cultures and Deaf cultures with each other. Traditionally, youth camps also host a cultural themed night where every country brings their flag and introduces themselves and their country. They dress up in their country's clothes, show some dances, and explain some features of their national culture, as well as bringing their countries' traditional food to share with other camp participants. One of the Irish camp participants stated in an online report: "Jason was in charge of this and he did a good job on the sweets! We had Viscount, Rowntree, Smarties, bon-bons, clove rock and barley sweets and we attempted to do some Irish dancing, Riverdance style! We didn't do a good job but we tried! After that, it was time to mingle and taste the other countries sweets!" (IDYA 2014). Drisana comments:

> The camp gives me more knowledge of culture, the different cultures, as well as Deaf cultures. Every time I go to different international events, I always gather and learn more about a person's life experience or a country, or association or board, or whatever. I am always learning more and more about cultures.

During the second day of the camp, each country had to share their country's report, which focused on the youth association/organization and how they received funding and support for the association. One of the Irish camp participants, Caroline, was "amazed to see that most of the youth associations have paid staff whereas Ireland, a 'first world' country doesn't" and that "I was amazed at one country; Reunion Island. They said they had a population of 840,000 people and 5,000 of them were Deaf! Of course it includes those who were deafened or hard of hearing but for such a small population, the youth association had over 200 members! WOW!" (IDYA 2014).

Feeling Empowered

Another important factor of social interaction at the camp involves meeting Deaf peers and Deaf leaders who are positive role models, such as fellow participants and presenters. This corresponds with what De Clerck (2007, 17) writes: Deaf community gatherings "are crucial to the transmission of deaf cultural information to young deaf people, as well as to their identification with deaf role models." He (2007, 17) also states that global Deaf encounters "contribute to the empowerment of young deaf people and the deaf community; advocacy and information sharing will also inform the majority society about deaf ways of life." Similarly, Kamm-Larew and Lamkin (2008, 62) discovered in their American survey of deaf leadership programs that "empowerment through role models from within a strong cultural identity" was vital to promote individual deaf rights. Jankowski (1997) defines the term *empowerment* in terms of a social movement, where the movement is a process through which a marginalized group—in this case the Deaf community—develops the need for a stronger community and a strong positive identity.

Similarly, the WFD youth camp played an important role in empowering the Deaf individuals who participated in the international Deaf youth camp. Through interacting with Deaf peers from all over the world, and the sharing of culture and knowledge, participants are encouraged to see their future more positively. Alexandra signed: "I feel that I will appreciate more when I am back in my country and will not take . . . things for granted." Drisana also commented how learning about various countries encouraged her to become more ambitious and active:

> Learning information about their countries, their youth associations, whether or not their countries have signed the United Nations Conventions CRPD. This made me realize that the world is not the same and all have their unique differences and also I think that various presentations inspired me to do something more [signed as pull up sleeves].

As she commented afterward in her online blog (Deaf Odyssey of Drisana), she wanted to change the fact that her native country did not have a Deaf youth association:

> With all that we've learnt and experienced from the WFDYS Youth Camp, the WFDYS General Assembly and the WFD Congress, we have one particular area that we really would like to focus on and that is the Deaf Youth of Australia. This is a particularly big topic as after all, we were representatives of Australia for the youth camp and the General Assembly and it was disappointing to admit that we did not have a Deaf Youth Association in Australia. Several of the developed countries present had a Youth Association but that was not all, even several of the developing countries had

fantastically-run [*sic*] Youth Associations and that made us realise that we need to roll up our sleeves as a nation and do something.

Similarly, Bregitt said the camp triggered an interest in Deaf national politics:

> Before I was not really interested in Deaf national politics but during my stay here I have learnt a lot and am eager to go back to America and fight [signed as to pull up my sleeves], research in politics.

De Clerk's (2007) study recounted similar "wake up" experiences, where some Deaf people attended international events and noted a comparison between the provision for Deaf people in Belgium and other countries, which empowered them to be proactive about improving the provision in their country.

This empowerment had both direct and indirect impacts on the Deaf community. The direct impact occurred when the camp participants further developed an understanding of their identity, culture, and social interactions. The indirect impact occurred when the camp participants, who had gained experiences from the camp, felt a sense of importance to empower their Deaf peers within their national Deaf community. Drisana commented:

> I have met so many inspiring people who presented at the camp and some are very successful in their life and this made me want to gather this information and inform young Deaf people in Australia.

Bregitt agreed: "I really want to give lectures on different countries and their challenges, perspectives and understanding, and work in the [next] WFDYS children's camp in America." The concept of information sharing was vital as part of the empowerment that the camp participants gathered from their experience within the WFD Youth camp in South Africa.

CHALLENGES IN INTERNATIONAL INTERACTIONS DURING THE CAMP

Alexandra points out that the social interaction is not always smooth from the first day of the camp, as there are accounts of regional bonding and segregation due to cultural and language differences:

> Throughout the week there was a big group difference linking to continents such as Africa and Asia, as I noticed that they tend to stick together in continent groups and have their own trend of international signing, . . . such as Latin America due to [their shared knowledge of] Spanish language, which helps them to bond.

Irene also commented on how Deaf participants from European countries interacted together and that South America, North America, and the Asia Pacific areas each had unity among the countries.

However, as the week progressed the language and cultural barriers improved (also see Haualand et al., this volume). Alexandra comments:

> It was not easy, as throughout the week it was challenging to try to discuss and engage with participants from different regions, but it was achieved and this is very positive as we have learnt so much from each other.

The participants were eager to face these challenges and eliminate the barriers to ensure social interaction among the camp participants: "Everyone fits in together because we all are Deaf and we 'understand each other,'" commented Bregitt. She is not referring to understanding each other in the same language, but instead she is referring to an understanding based on the connection because of their deaf sameness.

While there is an understanding based on shared deafness, Bregitt also observed that some campers struggled to use and understand International Sign during the lectures and group activities and did not participate fully. Some camp participants told Bregitt that other camp participants did not make an effort to ensure that they understood, whereas other participants felt that it was their own responsibility to ask for clarification if they did not understand. Bregitt felt it was really important to make sure that everyone had a certain level of International Sign so they could fit in and learn the most from the camp. She also suggested that rather than having a one-hour workshop, the camp could offer a full one-day workshop where they can focus on International Sign; this would include more practical exercises and interaction.

Final Thoughts

In October 2014, I contacted the research participants again to ask them to look back on how the WFD camp experience in Durban had impacted them. Drisana explained that she had helped to establish the new Deaf Youth Australia and was one of the first board members (before resigning due to too many voluntary commitments); she also interned for WFDYS between June to August 2013 and gave a presentation "Frontrunners: An International Deaf Youth Leadership Training Program" at the WFD Conference in Australia in October 2013. After returning to Brazil, Rodrigo decided not to be involved with any of the Deaf organizations in Brazil. Instead, he focused on the Deaf church and he felt that the leadership experiences gained at the camp helped him with his work. Alexandra confirmed that her decision to apply to be involved in the EUDY board was influenced by participating in the WFDYS camp, and she was involved with the EUDY board for two years. Also, she became an intern for WFDYS for a few months in 2014, during which she travelled around Central and South America to share her experiences with Deaf communities. Alexandra went to Costa Rica for part of her internship with WFDYS, where she worked with Irene to set up a one-day workshop for Costa Rican Deaf youth, which focused on WFDYS, leadership development, and project management. Also, Irene was elected to the board of the Costa Rica National Association of the Deaf for nearly two years.

This empirical research was a small-scale study for a bachelor's thesis, which only involved five people, and it is possible that the participants were inclined to stress mostly positive experiences. If I had the opportunity to repeat the research, I would gather more in-depth experiences from a wider range of people (such as including people who experienced their first international deaf interactions during the camp), and I would make more field notes on observations, in order to gain a greater understanding of the camp participants' interactions with each other and their learning during the camp.

This small-scale research has demonstrated that the participants felt that the camp positively influenced their lives and they were empowered by their peers and Deaf leaders. Although some communication barriers initially existed, these barriers were (partially) broken down throughout the week, when people rapidly improved their command of International Sign. The experience of attending the camp seems to motivate some Deaf youth to get more involved in activities and associations in their own countries and to encourage their peers to attend an international camp to gain similar experiences.

REFERENCES

Deaf Odyssey of Drisana. 2014. "WFDYS Youth Camp Durban, South Africa." Accessed September 28, 2014. http://www.drisanalg.com/?p=243.

De Clerck, G. 2007. "Meeting Global Deaf Peers Visiting Ideal Deaf Places: Deaf Ways of Education Leading to Empowerment, an Exploratory Case Study." *American Annals of the Deaf* 152 (1): 5–19.

Irish Deaf Youth Association. 2014. "WFDYS Camp Day 1." Accessed September 28, 2014. http://irishdeafyouth.com/blog/wfdys-camp-day-1.

Jankowski, K. 1997. *Deaf Empowerment: Emergence, Struggle, and Rhetoric.* Washington, DC: Gallaudet University Press.

Kamm-Larew, D., and M. Lamkin. 2008. "Survey of Leadership Programs: Valued Characteristics of Leadership within the Deaf Community."*Journal of American Deafness and Rehabilitation Association* 42 (1): 48-69.

Lapan, S., M. Quartarolli, and F. Riemer. 2012. *Qualitative Research: An Introduction to Methods and Designs.* San Francisco: Jossey-Bass.

World Federation of the Deaf. 2011. "Fact Sheet." Accessed April 12, 2011. http://www.wfdeaf.org/databank/fact-sheet.

World Federation of the Deaf Youth Section. 2011. Accessed April 12, 2011. http://www.wfdys.org.

4 | Deaf Jewish Space and DEAF-SAME: The International Conferences of Deaf Jews in the Twentieth Century

Mark Zaurov

Nobody is able to deny seriously that due to anti-Semitism prevailing in many countries, Jewish Deaf-mutes have it far more difficult to make a career comparing to their non-Jewish fellows.

— Erwin Kaiser and A. Birnbach, Weltbund der jüdischen Gehörlosen (World Association of Deaf Jews),[1] Berlin, 1931

I recall my happiness when getting together with Deaf people at social events. This immediate feeling of belonging and familiarity, based on a shared sense of a Deaf "being-in-the-world" (Ladd 2003, xviii) and a shared visual language, put me at ease. Once, after some initial chatting, someone suggested I buy a beer for everyone. After all, "I was a Jew and therefore had to be rich. Or was I stingy?" he added. There was no way out of the stereotype. At that moment, happiness gave way to bitterness. DEAF-SAME was not for me. DEAF-SAME is not for Jews. What exactly was it that expelled me from this common ground? Anti-Semitism may have been at its peak in the Nazi regime, but is still prevalent today.

During the Fifth World Organization of Jewish Deaf (WOJD) Congress, held in 1995 in London, the British Deaf psychologist Sharon Ridgeway, from a Deaf family, talked about anti-Semitic attitudes in the Deaf community and started with a personal incident. She had gone to a church to meet with Deaf people and was told

---

[1] Erwin Kaiser was president and A. Birnhack was secretary of the organization. The Deaf German newspaper *Die Stimme* misspelled his name (Kaiser and Birnbach 1931, 74). E. Kaiser was deported to Auschwitz 1943 and killed there.

that entering a church as a Jew was shameful. She outlined common stereotypes: Deaf Jews are "seen as thieves, money mad, witches, thinking about profits." Deaf people themselves have labeled Jewish Deaf as being mean (Ridgeway 1995, 38). She also foregrounded the prevalence of audism within the Jewish community: Hearing Jewish parents do not recognize the problems of their Deaf children and want them to "just to become Jewish and not deaf." Ridgeway means here that deliberate hybridity is denied such children and makes a strong case for claiming it: "Many of us have problems, are we Jewish or are we deaf? We do not have to choose, we can have both and it is our responsibility to allow people to become both" (39).

This London conference was my first encounter with the international Deaf Jewish intelligentsia. I was too young yet to commit myself to anything, and the discourse seemed confining rather than freeing. However, it was an incisive moment: Germany felt repressive to me because anti-Semitism was threatening each and every human interaction. In this Deaf Jewish transnational space outside of Germany, however, I was able to encounter other interesting people without the threat of anti-Semitism. Six years later, after my third US-Jewish Deaf Congress (JDC) conference in 2001, I was ready to commit myself to re-establish Deaf Jewish space in today's Germany: the Association for Deaf Jews and Their Descendants in Germany (Interessengemeinschaft Gehörloser jüdischer Abstammung in Deutschland e.V., IGJAD).

In this chapter, I explore the limits of the concept of DEAF-SAME through the experiences of Deaf Jews, particularly in international associations and their conferences in Europe and the United States. I claim that Deaf Jews, who have always been very diverse, get together in transnational spaces to share and celebrate two often oppressed aspects of their identities: being Deaf and Jewish. I see Judaism as both a religion and ethnicity. In varying practices and with varying attitudes, Jews follow religious traditions and celebrate the rites of the temple. Because Jewish religion is part of Jewish ethnicity, the religious context is not the only reason for them to get together (see also Gitelman 2009). In this chapter I demonstrate how distinctly separate Jewish Deaf spaces such as national and international associations were established, especially at times when they have to practice religion secretly and hide their ethnicity. I conclude that at least for Deaf Jews in Europe, the idea of a border-crossing universal DEAF-SAME that disregards religious and ethnic differences is but a myth.

DEAF JEWS AS A TRANSNATIONAL HYBRID COMMUNITY

I argue for the importance of exploring Deaf Jews as a transnational hybrid community. This community contains a discursive space in which many conflicts around strongly opposing identities, whether they be Deaf or Jewish identities, are negotiated (see also Murray 2008).

Wherever they find themselves in the diaspora, Deaf Jews bridge cultures that, by virtue of audism from the Jewish side and anti-Semitism on the Deaf side, seem to mutually exclude each other. Deaf Jews typically do not effectively take part in (hearing) Jewish tradition. They are not encouraged to sign because signed languages are hardly present in the diasporic nations of residence and thus not part of the multilingualism so typical for Jewish history. However, there are more factors that lead to the rejection of signed languages in Jewish culture. First is the nonvocal modality of signed languages within a religious universe that is based on the creative speaking voice, much like the Christian tradition (Bauman 2004). Second, in the hierarchy of identities for hearing Jews, Jewishness always comes first. There is very little tolerance for Deaf Jews who see themselves as Deaf as well or even Deaf first (Ridgeway 1995, 38; Tzukerman 1995, 54). Last the traditional Jewish idea of deafness as divine punishment forecloses any kind of positive approaches to deafness (Ridgeway 1995, 37).

The low social status of signed languages and Deaf culture leads to the fact that many Jewish Deaf children grow up orally and in isolation. Even if interpretation is provided in Jewish religious services, which is only common in the United States, the community members involved are very reserved towards Deaf participants outside of the United States (WOJD 1995, 45). This rejection, in turn, leads to the fact that many Deaf Jewish children grow up knowing nothing about their Jewish heritage and identity (WOJD 1995, 61). At the same time, they grow up in social environments, mixing with non-Jewish children for lack of Jewish institutions tailored to their needs. At Deaf schools they can experience brutal anti-Semitism (Brojer 1995, 42). Social bonds, negative as well as positive, develop within these mixed environments via signed languages. Experiences during the formative years of a person, caused by essentialist social environments, strongly contribute to the competition of self-ascribed labels of identity mentioned previously: Jewish first or Deaf first?

This is where Homi Bhabha's concept of hybridity (1994) comes into play. Hybridity marks a continuum between two mutually exclusive terms and does not allow for an "either/or." A third world between the two opens up. Ladd stated that "minority cultural members contend with what Bhabha has termed hybridity, an existential condition containing a mixture of characteristics of both cultures without a clear understanding of how these processes work upon us and within us" (2008, 51). While Deaf Jews form a transnational group, we can have differing expectations of Jewish behavior depending on factors such as the country of residence, our generation, and religion. An example of the latter is that orthodox and secular Jews are both Jews, but they value and practice their heritage differently. Within this wide continuum of hybridity, American, German, or Russian (as examples) Deaf Jews share their Deaf-Jewish parts of their identity. Because of their hybridity, the Jewish element does not keep them from identifying with the country and culture of their residence as yet further aspects of their identity.

Constituting Deaf-Jewish Identity in Europe

Before the Deaf Jewish international conferences (discussed in the next section) were organized, strong Deaf-Jewish identities had sprouted in particular institutions in Europe, particularly in Germany, Poland, Czechoslovakia, Latvia, Lithuania, England, France, Belgium, the Netherlands, and Austria-Hungary's Habsburg monarchy. Especially in Berlin, Vienna, and Budapest, Jewish Deaf life had been flourishing between 1840 and 1944. Local Deaf Jewish associations existed in several European countries. Among them was the Association of Deaf Zionists

in Vienna (Verein der zionistischen Gehörlosen in Wien; Zaurov 2013). Local Deaf
Jewish organizations, institutions, and occasions produced a Deaf Jewish space
(Zaurov 2009; Zaurov and Günther 2009) where Jews celebrated their religious
rituals and common cultural values, for example, gathering for holidays such as
Hanukkah or Purim.

In many European countries, elementary and secondary Jewish schools for
the deaf were established by Jewish individuals (mostly religiously inspired by
De l'Epée in Paris) in the 1840–1920s. Their curricula included Jewish education
and Jewish holiday celebrations. At the same time, most of the national schools
for the Deaf in Europe were led by Christian organizations or individuals who
denied Deaf Jewish pupils access to proper Jewish education. In general, these
schools used the oral approach.[2] During breaks, in associations, and at sports
events, however, the students communicated in sign language. There also was a
home for elderly Deaf Jews in Berlin that started in 1912, which was partly funded
by the Deaf Jewish Association in Berlin (Verein zur Förderung der Interessen der
israelitischen Taubstummen in Deutschland, 1896–1937).

All over Europe, there were Deaf Jewish sports clubs such as the Jugend-
abteilung des Vereins der ehemaligen ITA-Zöglinge (Youth Section of the Alumni
Association of ITA, est. 1928), affiliated with Verein der ehemaligen Zöglinge der
ITA (Alumni Association of ITA, est. 1908). Deaf Jewish youngsters spent time
together in the sports hall, had meals together, and hung out (Zaurov 2009). In
their own clubs, Deaf Jews enthusiastically celebrated every Jewish event and got
together for sports. Many Deaf Jews were also members of their national Deaf
clubs before the Nazi regime.

Deaf Jewish conferences on the national and international level were not yet
organized until 1930 (national) and 1931 (international). Instead, Deaf Jews participated in general Deaf national and international conferences, even though they
were sponsored by Christian organizations or were organized during Christian
festivals. For example, in 1873, the first German Deaf-Mute Conference (Erster
Deutscher Taubstummen-Kongress) was organized in Berlin together with the
European Deaf-Mute Conference and the annual Deaf Christian festival. The conference was not organized by the Christian Church but by Eduard Fürstenberg,
who was Deaf and president of the Berlin Deaf association, the very first worldwide Deaf association established in 1848, and editor of a Deaf newsletter titled *Der
Taubstummenfreund* (*The Deaf-Mute's Friend*). He also presided over the nationwide
Central Association for Well-Being of Deaf-Mutes (Zentralverein für das Wohl
der Taubstummen), established in 1849. The Central Association, a secular body,
was the organizer of the conference and festival. There were many social events.
Thanks to an 1872 decree by the Prussian emperor, Deaf persons from the German
Reich were granted free train rides (Fürstenberg 1873, 84) and many made sure
they were there. At the opening ceremony of the conference, fourteen hundred
visitors were counted (82).

This festival had been celebrated since 1855 in Germany (Brill 1874a, 52).
Similar national and international conferences happened in other European

---

[2] This requires further research because some sources reveal that there was support of sign
language use such as Signing Exact English (SEE), finger spelling, and use of gestures
(Meyer 1923; Schott 1999).

countries, particularly in France (see Gulliver, this volume). In Europe, most Deaf schools were established by Christian missionaries such as the Abbé de l'Epée (1712–89) in Paris, who was a Catholic priest, or Samuel Heinicke (1727–90), who was a cantor in the Church of St. Johannis in Eppendorf (Hamburg, Germany). Neither the investment of Christian organizations nor the occasion of Christian festivities, however, kept Deaf Jews from participating in the events. There were converted or assimilated Deaf Jews such as Salomon N. Loew from Vienna, who visited the first German Deaf-mute congress (Fürstenberg 1873, 89). He worked together with its Deaf organizer Eduard Fürstenberg and presided over the second Deaf-mute conference in Vienna 1874 (Brill 1874c, 55). Another Deaf Jew, Jaques Loew, was endearingly called "the soul" of the Viennese congress committee (Brill 1874b, 55).

Deaf Jews Facing a Rise of Anti-Semitism in Europe

However, things changed: anti-Semitism within the Deaf communities in many European countries increased before the Nazi regime and reached its peak during 1933–45. Because of this, Deaf Jews had to get together outside of regular all-Deaf events and organizations. There is no doubt that anti-Semitism had a substantial impact on Deaf Jewish history and everyday life, as Erwin Kaiser and Adolf Birnhack unapologetically stated in the quote with which I opened this essay (Kaiser and Birnbach 1931, 74). Deaf Jews were kicked out of local Deaf associations, their own Jewish associations and institutions were destroyed, they could not obtain Jewish religious education among Deaf peers, and they experienced brutal anti-Semitism.

The Deaf Jewish newsletter written in Germany, *Das Band*, reported on anti-Semitic incidents, for example, in Berlin and in Krakow in 1928–30, when there were motions to drive away all Deaf Jewish members from the general Deaf Association of Krakow. Although not all members supported these motions, these incidents explain why national Deaf Jewish associations were set up and followed by international ones. Deaf Jewish associations on a much smaller level have always been around to celebrate Jewish culture and religious rituals. However, Deaf Jewish organizations on national and international levels had not been regarded necessary until massive anti-Semitism was experienced. In Germany, an umbrella organization of the local Jewish Deaf associations, Verband der jüdischen Gehörlosen-Vereine Deutschlands, was founded in 1931, when the first international Deaf Jewish Conference was being planned. The ambitious goal to create national and international organizations of Deaf Jews was encouraged by the national Deaf Jewish Conference in Kracow, 1930, and the international conference in Prague, 1931.

The First Deaf-Jewish Conference and Its Aftermath

The first national Deaf Jewish congresses took place in Kracow, Poland, in 1930 and the first international congress took place in Prague, Czechoslovakia, in 1931. A close look at the agendas of these conferences and the issues in their preparatory meetings reveals a desire to create a Deaf Jewish space free from anti-Semitism, a safe space in which anti-Semitic issues in the general Deaf community could openly be addressed and dealt with. They discussed, for example, the exclusion and ignorance of Deaf Jews within non-Jewish Deaf Schools (such as that kosher food and Jewish education were not provided) and Deaf associations. According to the Prague congress's statute, the purpose was "1. Mutual advice and exchange of experiences, 2. Help and support in all matters, 3. Provision of accommodation for peers in need in proper institutions and homes, 4. Legal protection, 5. Help and support in advice and action for immigrating and emigrating peers, 6. Representation in the Jewish public" (Kaiser and Birnbach 1931, 74). "The idea of a Jewish . . . idiosyncrasy" was stressed as well as the "responsibility to educate the entire Jewish public about the situation of deaf-and-mute Jews." Participants came from Austria, Czechoslovakia, Belgium, Germany, Hungary and Poland, a clear signal of the transnationalism of Deaf Jews, as anti-Semitism was not limited to one country.

The background to the national congress in Cracow is the following: Bogumil Liban was president of the Polish Deaf Jewish Association and elected as annual auditor to the board of the International Deaf League in 1928. At the end of 1928, the Polish Deaf sports association put Liban under pressure: He was to resign as first auditor of the league. His Jewish deaf countrymen, however, asked him not to give in (Verein zur Förderung *Das Band* 1929). Liban initiated a meeting on July 12–13, 1930, to establish the Bund der israelitischen Gehörlosen Europas (Union of European Jewish Deaf) in Krakow, Poland, in 1930 according to the model of the International Deaf League[3] (Zaurov 2009, 189; Verein zur Förderung *Das Band* 1930). His reasons included incidents of abuse of Deaf Jewish children in the main Deaf non-Jewish school in Krakow (Verein zur Förderung *Das Band* 1930). In the wake of these anti-Semitic incidents in Krakow, a complaint by the European Deaf Jews against the International League of the Deaf was filed about their neglect.

As one consequence and role model of the International League for Liban, the first Deaf Jewish international Congress was held in Prague in 1931 on the occasion of the tenth anniversary of the Central Association of Deaf-Mute and hard of hearing Jews in Prague (see Zaurov 2009, 189; Verein zur Förderung *Das Band* 1931).

Erwin Kaiser from Berlin had, at first, objected to the founding of the European confederacy (Bund der israelitischen Gehörlosen Europas) by Liban in 1930; he had feared allegations of competing with the (Deaf) International League. However, he realized why it was necessary, both in relation to the Deaf community and in relation to the Jewish community. Many Deaf Jews felt that the Jewish communities treated blind Jews better than Deaf Jews. Jewish organizations provided support for blind Jews in many ways but failed to support Deaf Jews. One of the decisions of the conference in Prague was to send a protest to the Zionist executive in Palestine about their indifference to the needs of Deaf Jewish children. In the end, Kaiser accepted the presidency of the Union of European Jewish Deaf. He founded and presided over the World Union of Jewish Deaf (Weltbund der jüdischen Gehörlosen) in Prague one year later in 1931. Bogumil Liban became its vice president (Zaurov 2009, 183).

---

[3] The International League was similar to the present-day European Union of the Deaf (EUD) and their conference was held in Prague in 1928. The next conference was planned for Berlin in 1931. See also Meyer 1928.

CRITICISMS AND THE DESTRUCTION OF DEAF JEW ASSOCIATIONS

The developments described in the previous section were criticized by Deaf non-Jews. For example, in 1931, an article in *Die Stimme* was signed with the pseudonym "Pegasus." It claims that world congresses like those of Deaf Jews in Prague were unnecessary (Pegasus 1931, 58). Curt Laschinsky, editor-in-chief of Die Stimme, criticized the founding of the Weltbund, claiming that Deaf Jews were already represented within the REGEDE (Reichsverband der Gehörlosen Deutschlands, the German Reich's association of the Deaf, est. 1927): "That's all we needed in Germany, that the Deaf Jews mess with the Reichsverband der Gehörlosen Deutschlands (REGEDE) with their 'Weltbund' just after the Catholics got special treatment with their association. Why pronounce these religious oppositions? Aren't we all companions suffering the same fate and don't we all suffer the same sorrows and the same affliction?" (Laschinsky 1931, 62). As a consequence, Kaiser had to officially declare his loyalty to the REGEDE (Kaiser 1931, 83). Just like Kaiser had to officially proclaim that his Deaf identity came first and his Jewish identity second, many Deaf Jews were bullied by their Deaf peers to prefer their Deaf identity over other identities in a hierarchy. The congress to be hosted in Berlin in 1934 fell through: The National Socialists had taken over.

During the forcible coordination known as Gleichschaltung (the Nazi term) in 1933, the Association for the Promotion of the Interests of Israelite Deaf-and-Mute in Germany (Verein zur Förderung der Interessen der israelitischen Taubstummen in Deutschland,[4] est. 1896) was merged with other associations such as the alumni association of the ITA and forcibly grouped under the newly founded Reichsbund, Reich's Confederation of Deaf Jews (Reichsbund der jüdischen Gehörlosen) under the lead of Felix London (1890–1956) (Zaurov 2009, 178). The Reichsbund was dissolved in 1934 and continued as a self-help group of Deaf Jews (Selbsthilfegruppe der jüdischen Gehörlosen) under Erwin Kaiser. A forced merger with the Self-Help Community of Physically Disabled Jews in Germany (Selbsthilfegemeinschaft der jüdischen Körperbeschädigten in Deutschland)—which in turn became part of the Central Welfare Office of German Jews (Zentralwohlfahrtstelle der deutschen Juden)—meant that the Deaf-Jewish association gradually lost its autonomy (Festschrift 1936, 10).

Furthermore, Aryan law excluded Deaf Jews from Deaf associations, which also happened in Hungary. From the membership fees they had paid, they were not allowed to claim their pension entitlement. Deaf Nazi enthusiasts betrayed their Jewish peers, and in Hungary, the Deaf Arrow Cross Militia systematically targeted Deaf Jews (Schuchman 2002, 193). At the end of the Nazi regime, all German Deaf Jewish organizations were destroyed and most of its members murdered. Recent research shows that three Deaf Arrow Cross members were tried in court in Hungary. Of the two who were sentenced in 1946 and 1947, one was given seventeen years in prison for compiling a list of Deaf Jews and their addresses, looting their homes, and their involvement in the shooting of (Deaf) Jews in the Danube River. After decades of silence, the fragments of Deaf Jewish

---

[4] At this location, in the center of Berlin (Rosenstr. 2–3), I have initiated a free-standing digital information plaque about the association including German Sign Language and International Sign; see http://www.igjad.de.

history were collected by research (e.g., Ryan and Schuchman 2002; Zaurov 2009) and exhibited. The massive experience of anti-Semitism from Deaf non-Jewish peers all over Europe shows that border-crossing universalist DEAF-SAME does not apply for Deaf Jews in Europe, perhaps even for the entire Jewish Deaf diaspora in general.

DEAF JEWISH REVIVAL AFTER WWII

The former alumni of the Israelite Institution for Deaf-Mutes (Israelitische Taubstummen-Anstalt, ITA) Chaim Apter had emigrated in 1939 from Nazi Germany to the formerly called Palestine (today Israel). From there, he was looking to continue the conferences. He was the executive secretary of the Association of Deaf and Mutes in Israel (Fleischmann 2001, 26). During the Fourth Conference on Deafness in Tel Aviv, Chaim Apter, Moshe Bamberger and Moshe Shem-Tov from Israel, Alexander Fleischmann from the USA, and Bernard Baran and Maurice Sebban from France planned to "upgrade the educational, social welfare, communication and religious needs of the Jewish Deaf people and foster Judaism world-wide" (WOJD 1995, 4; see also Meyenn, Plotzki, and Zaurov 1995). According to the World Organization of Jewish Deaf report's passage about its history, Emil Stryker inspired its foundation (ibid. WOJD). Fleischmann considered Apter aggressive enough to be involved with the World Federation of Deaf (WFD) (Fleischmann 2001, 26); however, support from the WFD and other Deaf organizations was denied.

It took a while until the World Organization of Jewish Deaf was established in Tel Aviv, 1973, and had its first conference there in 1977. Fleischmann concluded that "the Congress encouraged the spirit of Zionism and Jewish traditions and the need to pull together in an increased effort to unite all Jewish deaf" (2001). The second congress took place in Jerusalem in 1981, the third in Tel Aviv in 1988, and the fourth in Paris in 1992. The fifth and final one took place in London in 1995, before the usual four-year interval had ended. In the USA, an international audience, including representatives of foreign Deaf Jewish associations, attended the biennial Jewish Deaf Congress, the former National Congress of Jewish Deaf (NCJD), first established in 1956.[5] The most recent one had a panel with participants from France, Israel, and other countries and took place in Washington, DC in 2013. The conference theme was "Reenergizing the Jewish Deaf Community." A major difference between the topics at the WOJD and the American conferences is that the American conferences did not discuss anti-Semitism. This perhaps is because of the American view of Jewry as a religion rather than ethnicity.

During the Fifth World organization of Jewish Deaf Congress, July 24–27, 1995, in London, the conference's Deaf Jewish presenters covered fields such as psychology, sociology, history, religion, social work, education, and networking for an audience of about two hundred people. High priority was given to cooperation among Deaf Jewish institutions and between Deaf Jewish associations and all-Deaf associations, and to the education of Jewish institutions about Deaf Jews and the education and social welfare of their own members. Last but not

---

[5] The NCJD coexisted with the JDC from 1992 to 1998.

least the conference was a protected space in which to exchange experiences of anti-Semitism and learn strategies from professionals about how to deal with this kind of permanent stress.

Present-Day Anti-Semitism in Deaf Communities

The Deaf and multiply disabled Canadian sociologist Tanis Doe writes that Deaf people treat "multiple minorities in much the same way as deaf people are treated by the hearing majority—by discriminating against them. It is important to see how the general deaf community reacted to this type of discrimination from hearing people" (Doe 1989, 467; also see Bauman 2008, 11–12). There is increasing research on diversity within the Deaf community (Erting et al. 1989).[6] Deaf Jews, however, have rarely been discussed as double minorities. If at all, they are mentioned in religious contexts (Zaurov 2013).

The agendas of contemporary Deaf Jewish conferences reveal that Deaf Jews clearly understand themselves as a double minority. However, at all-Deaf conferences and events, Deaf Jews are not included in individual groups for "multiple minorities" such as "black," "gay," or "women." In 1997, the motto of the Deaf Studies V conference proclaimed "Toward 2000: Unity and Diversity" (see also Lemcke, Weinmeister, and Zaurov 1997). How much diversity, however, does DEAF-SAME or Deaf universalism in fact tolerate? At the Deaf Studies Conference III in 1993, Carolyn McCaskill-Emerson listed the following groups as members of the American Deaf community in her lecture about multicultural/minority issues in Deaf studies: "African American, Native American, Hispanic American, Asian American and European American." The underlying ideas of the omission of the Jewish minority within the Deaf minority is first a construction of Jews as "white" (Sznaider 2012, 191), and second, many American scholars view Judaism as a religion, not an ethnicity. As a consequence, Jews are not listed with other minorities. However, key aspects of Jewish, in particular Deaf Jewish reality, can be grasped only in terms of ethnicity: "In modern times, several modes of Jewishness were devised. . . . Secularization need not mean the abandonment of faith, though it can include it, but a process wherein religion no longer is the primary driving force of thinking and acting" (Gitelman 2009, 242). Paddy Ladd pointed out that "the only Deaf ethnic minority group to be organized on an international basis is the Jewish Deaf Community" (2003, 61).

Hence, for the Madrid conference in 2007, the IGJAD sent a petition to the WFD to introduce a special interest group for Deaf Jews on the basis of ethnicity and anti-Semitism, supported by several Deaf scholars and political leaders (Zaurov 2007). However, the WFD board rejected the petition without official explanation. With respect to the WFD's history of disregard for Jewish issues, this can be considered another act of anti-Semitism, especially because the WFD claims to be open to diversity.

As I explained earlier, anti-Semitism within the Deaf community also prevails today. It is necessary to cultivate and safeguard Deaf Jewish space where we can celebrate Jewish culture and religious rituals. Deaf Jews are very diverse in their

---

[6] See also Aramburo and Kane in the same proceedings.

expression and attitude toward their identity and the practice of their religion. However, as David Jackson points out, observance is stereotyped via the philosophy of ultraorthodox Jews (Mottez 1993b, 95). General public ignorance of Jewish culture, particularly severe among the Deaf population, fuels existing stereotypes and propaganda. According to the retired Baltimore-based Deaf Rabbi Fred Friedman, 95 percent of Deaf Jews hide their Jewishness to escape anti-Semitism. This denial of their identity contributes to the problem, especially if they are among the many Deaf Jewish leaders in the Deaf community (Zaurov 2003, 116). These leaders could serve as role models if they insisted on scheduling events on days other than Jewish holidays and educated their peers about Jewish culture (Mottez 1993b, 96).

Thanks to outreach campaigns toward hearing Jewish associations to educate them about Deaf Jews, more Jewish communities are opening up to Deaf ways of "being-in-the-world" so that Deaf persons can become rabbis, such as Rabbi Friedman. He argues that to develop large-scale Jewish awareness among the Deaf population, Deaf Jews with good standing in the Deaf community need to affirm their own Deaf Jewish identity and act as role models (Mottez 1993b; also Zaurov 2003, 116). In 2013 and 2014, Jewish religious celebrations such as Hanukkah and Sukkoth were hosted at the campus of Gallaudet University, in the presence of the Deaf Jewish president of the university, Alan Hurwitz. A further step toward opening up both cultures would be to consider the Sabbath when scheduling NAD gatherings. Any gatherings on Friday evenings and Saturdays lead ultraorthodox and reform Deaf Jews into a cultural dilemma, although Deaf Jews such as Fred Schreiber, Roslyn Rosen, and Howard Rosenblum have had key roles in the NAD.

deaf-same: A Myth?

Just as DEAF-SAME seems to produce a space without audism, Deaf Jewish space is a space imagined without audism and without anti-Semitism, where Jewish culture and ritual can be openly celebrated. However, I argue that as long as there are Deaf persons who feel excluded from this Deaf space for having the "wrong" gender, skin color, disability, religion, or ethnicity, DEAF-SAME remains a myth, a privilege for people who are similar enough to claim this sameness. Paddy Ladd (2003, 59ff) pointed out the tensions Deaf blacks and Deaf Asians experience within the British Deaf community. He stresses that the establishment of their own associations goes back to the fact that identities could not be openly negotiated because of stereotypes. The stereotypes reign because the discrimination the Deaf community experiences from hearing oppressors is passed on to other members instead of being dealt with. Another layer of labeling as multiple minorities is not enough: let us reapproach Deaf identities from the perspective of transnationalism and hybridity in an open dialog. Categories of identification are dynamic instead of rigid and resist the essentialism inherent in any stereotypes, be they audist, sexist, racist, ableist, or anti-Semitic.

In the face of the recent bombardments in Israel and Gaza 2014, anti-Semitism has risen dramatically. Social media is one platform where Deaf community members post well-trodden anti-Semitic accusations. The Facebook group "Deaf World love Sign Language" kept pro-Palestinian posts but deleted posts by Deaf Israelis and others in support of Israel. As a consequence, another group was founded: "One World love Sign Language." Yet another group was set up as a closed one for Jewish Deaf participants only to avoid anti-Semitism: "JEAF—Deaf Jewish People of Europe" in the United Kingdom. In the light of these current events I repeated my petition from 2007 to the WFD's upcoming conference in Istanbul in 2015 under the slogan "Strengthening Human Diversity," in the hope that the response will be positive this time.

REFERENCES

Anderson, B. 1991. *Imagined Communities*. London: Verso.
Aramburo, A. 1989. "Black Deaf Community." In Erting et al. 1989, 474–82.
Bauman, H. L. Dirksen, ed. 2008. *Open Your Eyes: Deaf Studies Talking*. Minneapolis: University of Minnesota Press.
———. 2004. "Audism: Exploring the Metaphysics of Oppression."*Journal of Deaf Studies and Deaf Education* 9 (2): 239–46.
Ben-Rafael, E., and Y. Sternberg. 2009. *Transnationalism: Diasporas and the Advent of a New (Dis)order*. Leiden: Brill.
Bhabha, H. 1994. *The Location of Culture*. London: Routledge.
Brill, B. 1873a. "Das große Kirchenfest in Berlin." In Fürstenberg 1873, 7–9: 52–53.
———. 1873b. "Der zweite Taubstummenkongress in Wien 1874." In Fürstenberg, 7–9: 53–55.
———. 1874c. "Protokoll." In *Der Taubstummenfreund. Mittheilungen des Central-Vereins für das Wohl der Taubstummen in Berlin*, ed. E. Fürstenberg, 7–9: 55–58.
Brojer, M. 1995. In *Towards a Freer World: Report of the Fifth World Organization of Jewish Deaf Congress 24th to 27th of July 1995* by WOJD, 42–43. London: Author.
Doe, T. 1989. "Multiple Minorities: Communities within the Deaf Community." In *The Deaf Way: Perspectives from the International Conference on Deaf Culture*, ed. C. J. Erting et al., 464–69. Washington, DC: Gallaudet University Press.
Eickman, J. 2006. "Tracing Deafhood: Exploring the Origins and Spread of Deaf Cultural Identity." In Zaurov and Günther 2009, 79–91.
Erting, C., R. C. Johnson, D. L. Smith, B. D. Snider, eds. 1989. *The Deaf Way: Perspectives from the International Conference on Deaf Culture*. Washington, DC: Gallaudet University Press.
Fleischman, A. 2001. "Chaim Apter, Israeli Activist, Dies." *JDC Quarterly Newsletter* 3: 26.
Fürstenberg, E. 1873. "Kirchenfest der Taubstummen im Jahre 1873." In. *Der Taubstummenfreund Mittheilungen des Central-Vereins für das Wohl der Taubstummen in Berlin* , ed. E. Fürstenberg, 9–10: 82–84.
Fürstenberg, E., et al. 1873. "Vereinswesen." In *Der Taubstummenfreund. Mittheilungen des Central-Vereins für das Wohl der Taubstummen in Berlin* , ed. E. Fürstenberg 1873, 9–10: 88–95.
Gitelman, Zvi. 2009. "Jewish Identity and Secularism in Post-Soviet Russia and Ukraine." In *Religion or Ethnicity: Jewish Identities in Evolution,* edited by Z. Gitelman. New Brunswick, NJ: Rutgers University Press.
IGJAD Interessengemeinschaft Gehörloser jüdischer Abstammung in Deutschland. n.d. Accessed July 15, 2004. http://www.igjad.de.
Kaiser, E. 1930. "Auszug aus dem Protokoll [. . .] zur Gründung eines Bundes der isr. Taubstummen in Europa [. . .]." *Das Band* 8: 59.
Kaiser, E., and A. Birnbach. 1931. "Der Weltbund der jüdischen Gehörlosen." In *Die Stimme* 14: 74.
———. 1931. "Erklärung." In *Die Stimme* 17:83.

Kane, T. 1989. "Deaf Gay Men's Culture." In Erting et al., 483–85.

Ladd, P. 2009. "Deafhood and Deaf History." In Zaurov and Günther 2009, 71–78.

_____. 2008. "Colonialism and Resistance: A Brief History of Deafhood." In *Open Your Eyes: Deaf Studies Talking*, ed. H. Bauman, 42–59. Minneapolis: University of Minnesota Press.

_____. 2003. *Understanding Deaf Culture: In Search of Deafhood*. Clevedon, UK: Multilingual Matters Press.

Lane, H., R. Hoffmeister, and B. Bahan. 1996. *A Journey into the DEAF-WORLD*. San Diego: Dawn Sign.

Laschinsky, C. 1931. [no title]. In *Die Stimme* 12:62.

Lemcke, S., K. Weinmeister, and M. Zaurov. 1997. "Deaf Studies V 'Toward 2000: Unity and Diversity.'" *Das Zeichen* 40:278–79.

McCaskill-Emerson, C. 1993. "Multicultural/Minority Issues in Deaf Studies." In *Deaf Studies III: Bridging Cultures in the Twenty-First Century*, 45–52.Washington, DC: Gallaudet University Press.

Meyenn, A., T. Plotzki, and M. Zaurov. 1995. "'Sie sollen wissen, was die Juden früher erlitten haben ... ': Interview mit Moshe Bamberger." *Das Zeichen* 31:30–39.

Meyer, M. 1923. "Markus Reich als Direktor." In F. Reich, *50 Jahre Israelitische Taubstummenanstalt und ihr Gründer Direktor M. Reich*, Berlin, 9–15.

Meyer, R. 1928. "Der international Kongreß in Prag." *Das Band* 5:39–40.

Mottez, B. 1993a. "Gehörlose und Hörende, Juden und Nichtjuden: Eine soziologische Betrachtung." *Das Zeichen* 23:47–50.

_____. 1993b. "Vierter Kongreß der Weltorganisation der jüdischen Gehörlosen, Paris, 12.–17. Juli 1992." *Das Zeichen* 23:94–97.

Murray, J. 2008. "Coequality and Transnational Studies: Understanding Deaf Lives." In Bauman 2008, 42–59.

Pegasus. 1931. "Randbemerkungen." *Die Stimme* 12:58.

Ridgeway, S. 1995. In WOJD 1995, 37–39.

Ryan, D. F., and J. S. Schuchman, eds. 2002. *Deaf People in Hitler's Europe*. Washington, DC: Gallaudet University Press.

Schott, W. 1999. *Das Allgemeine Österreichische Israelitische Taubstummen-Institut in Wien 1844–1926*. Wien: Eigenverlag.

Schuchman, J. S. 2002. "Hungarian Deaf Jews and the Holocaust." In Ryan and Schuchman 2002, 169–201.

Sznaider, N. 2012. "Diaspora-Nationalismus: Jüdische Erfahrungen und universale Lehren." In *Lebensmodell Diaspora*, edited by I. Charim et al., 185–93. Bielefeld, Germany: Transcript.

Tzukerman, I. 1995. In WOJD 1995, 53–54.

Vereins zur Förderung der Interessen der israelitischen Taubstummen in Deutschland. 1936. *Festschrift zum 40-jährigen Bestehen des Vereins zur Förderung der Interessen der israelitischen Taubstummen in Deutschland e.V.* Berlin.

Verein zur Förderung der Interessen der israelitischen Taubstummen Deutschlands e.V. and Verein der ehemaligen Zöglinge der ITA, Israelitische Taubstummen-Anstalt zu Berlin-Weißensee. 1928. *Das Band: Zeitschrift der jüdischen Gehörlosen* 6:54–55.

_____. 1929. *Das Band* 1:7.

_____. 1930. *Das Band* 4:30–31.

_____. 1930. *Das Band* 8:59.

_____. 1931. *Das Band* 6:50.

WOJD. 1995. *Towards a Freer World: Report of the Fifth World Organization of Jewish Deaf Congress 24th to 27th of July 1995*. London/UK: Author.

Zaurov, M. 2003. *Gehörlose Juden: eine doppelte kulturelle Minderheit*. Frankfurt am Main: Peter Lang.

_____. 2007. "Petition for SIG Deaf Jews in WFD Madrid." Accessed July 15, 2014. http://www.hagalil.com/01/de/Europa.php?itemid=819.

_____. 2009. "Deaf Holokaust." In Zaurov and Günther 2009, 173–97.

_____. 2013. *"Taube Juden als transnationale* "hybrid imagined community":*Ein Forschungsgegenstand im Spannungsfeld von* Deaf History *und* Deaf Studies." *Das Zeichen* 94:246–55.

_____. In press. "A Postcolonial Approach to Deaf Jews as a Cultural Minority in the Field of Deaf Studies." In *Conference Proceedings of "Deaf Studies Today! 2010: Beyond Talk."* Orem: Utah Valley University Press.

Zaurov, M., and K. B. Günther, eds. 2009. *Overcoming the Past, Determining its Consequences, and Finding Solutions for the Present.* Seedorf, Germany: Signum Press.

5 | Deaf Transnational Gatherings at the Turn of the Twenty-First Century and Some Afterthoughts

Hilde Haualand, Per Koren Solvang, and Jan-Kåre Breivik

At the turn of the twenty-first century, when we investigated the quadrennial Deaflympics and the world congresses of the World Federation of the Deaf, these gatherings stood out among the numerous international and regional events and gatherings organized by and for deaf people. These megaevents have been organized with steady regularity since the first World Games of the Deaf in 1924 and the first World Congress of the World Federation of the Deaf (WFD) in 1951. They explicitly aim to attract participants from as many countries as possible. The gatherings have been important arenas for the development of social relations and manifestations of ideas about deaf culture and deaf identity politics. To the participants who attend or are involved in the official program as well as the social life surrounding the events, the sense of sharing a common experience may become quite intense during the course of the events. An experienced deaf traveler said in an interview, "Deaf people are the same at heart. But background, culture, habits, and traditions are different." The South African swimmer Terrence Parkin said in an interview with the daily video bulletin broadcast by DeafNation that attending the Deaflympics in Rome in 2001 was like "being with my family" (cited from field notes).

More than a decade after our research at the turn of the century (Breivik, Haualand, and Solvang 2002; Haualand 2007; Solvang, Breivik, and Haualand 2005), these gatherings have continued to be important meeting places for deaf people from all over the world. However, today, the participants are not only from more countries than ever but they also have increasingly diverse backgrounds, in terms of education, technological and material resources, linguistic preferences, and professional status, for example. In this chapter, we first discuss certain ritual elements during the events that staged them as manifestations of an imagined global deaf community at the turn of the twenty-first century. To understand the significance of these events today, we need theoretical, methodological, and thematic innovation compared to the approach we had to these events 1999–2003, and we identify some of these in this chapter.

Studying Global Deaf Connections in 2001–2003

Many deaf people have their prime sites for belonging and connectedness at other places than their birthplace or where their (mainly hearing) families live. These places could be at permanent locations such as schools or clubs for deaf people or transient meeting places such as regional, national, or international events for and by deaf people who use sign language. To Breivik's (2005) deaf Norwegian informants, transnational megaevents such as the Deaflympics and the world congresses of the WFD stood out as meeting places and arenas for potential self-realization, new personal friendships, and network building (Breivik 2005).

To learn more about these megaevents, their significance, and how they could have such lasting impact, we carried out fieldwork at four large events: the Summer Games for the Deaf (Rome, Italy, 2001), the Deaf Way II Festival (Washington, DC, 2002), the Winter Games for the Deaf (Sundsvall, Sweden, 2003), and the WFD World Congress for the Deaf (Montreal, Canada, 2003). The way our informants referred to and talked about these events made them stand out as nodes or junctions in a wide network of deaf people. To our interlocutors, the events were, in spite of their limited temporality and transience, tangible manifestations of a deaf community that transcended national borders. While the athletes in the Deaflympics competed under their national flags and the delegates to the world congresses represented national states, individual nationality was not prominent when we talked to the participants or observed the social life at the events. The experience of a shared communication modality, similar experiences, and a sense of sameness across national origin gave these events a strong transnational appearance. The concept of *transnationalism* as used in this essay refers to this feature: national differences are downplayed or diminish in importance and the similarities across nations and cultures are emphasized.

The research team consisted two social anthropologists and one sociologist, of which one was deaf and two were hearing. The deaf social anthropologist (Haualand) is a fluent signer of Norwegian, Swedish, and American Sign Languages and International Sign. The hearing social anthropologist (Breivik) could engage in one-to-one conversations in Norwegian Sign Language and had previous research experience with Norwegian deaf people. The hearing sociologist (Solvang) did not know sign language but, through previous cooperation with Breivik and an interest in disability studies, had some theoretical knowledge about deaf people and the discussions related to deaf people as disabled and/or as belonging to a linguistic and cultural minority. As such, the team consisted of an "insider" (Haualand), an "outsider" (Solvang), and one researcher that was both or neither (Breivik). We shared field notes and gave comments on each other's observations. We organized the field notes thematically and analytical categories were then developed.

Having distinct positions and perspectives with regard to the phenomena to be studied enabled a multiangled approach to and insight into the intense lives at these short events. Working in a team like this is a very effective methodological strategy for building up a rich body of ethnographic data, where significant social events tend to move around and appear spontaneously at different places simultaneously (Senghas and Monaghan 2002). In addition to participant observation, we interviewed informants approached at these events, following up contacts with them by means of information and communications technologies (text messages and e-mail) whenever possible, and monitored relevant websites to capture how these events affected the lives of both those physically present and physically absent.

The triple pairs of eyes, feet, and hands notwithstanding, there were still some limitations in our observations: our analysis is based on the experiences of informants who belonged to a global deaf elite. They had the money and resources to travel and a strong drive or interest in networking and connecting with deaf people from other countries. The research team mostly attended official programs with competitions or presentations (depending on type of event) and planned or spontaneous social meeting places in the evenings, often located at local pubs, restaurants, or night clubs. All these activities required money, and thus a group of people who fell below our radar were deaf people (many of non-Western origin) who went to the events with a very tight budget and hence avoided meeting points where they would have to spend money on drinks or food. Their experience of the events would most likely be very different from our informants' experience, and the events may have appeared as exclusive and limiting to them.

It is hence crucial to notice that the events that we discuss in this chapter have been and are reflections of an existing and continued global inequality. A disproportionate share of the participants (registered delegates or athletes as well as unregistered tourists) are from North America and northwestern Europe. Although the number of participating countries at the WFD world congresses and the Deaf World Games continues to increase, these "new" countries are often only represented with a handful delegates or athletes and do not have the number of observers, interpreters, and tourists one can see from more financially affluent nations. The dominance of a few regions at the events implies that the identity work, the assertion of deaf unity and network consolidation, is less global (in terms of scope and degree of participation) than our informants tend to express. There is a need for further research to understand other perspectives and experiences of these events, and we discuss some methodological, theoretical, and thematic implications in the last part of this article.

THE RITUAL STRUCTURE OF DEAF EVENTS

The ritual aspect of deaf events was obvious from the very beginning, with four ritual phases more or less visible at all megaevents. The first stage, *arrival*, is marked by a gradual process of coming together. To search for quickly moving hands in the crowds of people (i.e., "deaf-spotting") is a very effective way to catch other deaf persons because of the visibility of sign languages. During the first days, the researchers observed signers about three to four times a day, which is more than usual, but nothing compared to what was to come. Within a few days of arrival in Rome for the Deaflympics for example, signing people could be seen everywhere in the city all the time.

The second ritual phase is the more formal *opening ceremony* (at the sports events) or a first section with opening addresses and welcome speeches (at the conferences) when the international deaf community is confirmed and celebrated formally. This can be through speeches (at the conferences), but it can also be very visual (i.e., with flags etc.), often with explicit references to the different nations present, and sometimes with a local folkloristic dance or so from the nation where the event happens (typically at the sports events). In the opening ceremony in Rome, the international feature of the official program was prominent, with the national delegations marching in more or less neatly ordered groups behind flags carried by an athlete in the front of the national groups. Athletes are expected to compete against other nations and spectators are expected to show support of their national teams and athletes. (Note that at the more politically oriented events such as the WFD congresses, nationalism is less visible.)

The increasing presence of deaf people in the urban space introduced the third stage, the establishment of a temporary *deaf place*: the streets, cafés, and restaurants are full of people using sign language. The effect was most observable at the surrounding areas of the main sites of the event and/or in a popular area of the city where deaf people gather. Hearing people providing regular service to sign language users, such as waiters, shop assistants, and hotel personnel, use gestures and quickly pull out their pens and paper. They develop an orientation where deaf people become part of the ordinary. Deaf people get accustomed to this and begin to expect service on their own terms. In certain instances, some bars and cafés can be completely taken over by deaf people for the duration of the event. This often starts with a few people who gather at a pub or café one evening in the beginning of the event. The site may be accidental or suggested by the local deaf community. As the information about the meeting place spreads and the people tell stories about the fun or networking opportunities that happen here, the number of deaf guests rises every night. Eventually, it becomes a major informal social meeting place not only for registered attendees but also for unregistered crowd of tourists and locals who do not attend the organized event itself.

At the sports events, the transformation from an international event to a transnational community is highly visible. There was an observable gradual withering away of the visibility of national supporter teams and growth of one mixed transnational deaf community. This was visible at the social gatherings in the evenings and during the closing ceremony in Rome: different nationalities mingled behind other nations' banners in a colorful mix and the national spectator groups in the bleachers were far more diffuse than they were during the opening ceremony. So while the athletes, supporters, or delegates represent their national home countries during megaevents, at the same time these transnational meeting places are arenas for being at home among strangers. After a few days, a sense of *communitas* (Turner 1967) evolves and a stage of in-betweenness where the place is "made deaf" appears and where a joint community of sign language people is strengthened.

The fourth and last part of the ritual is the *departure* when "the temporary deaf place" is virtually emptied of deaf life and the international-turning-transnational temporary deaf community disintegrates. The sense of a withering community was particularly palpable for a few days after the events had ceased, when deaf people face the communication demands of a hearing majority after becoming accustomed to an all-visual environment. One begins to wonder whether *home* actually was the transnational deaf space (cf. Emery's article, this volume, on the meaning of *home* in the deaf diaspora). A unique experience has taken place: one has felt a sense of how a community based on communication in sign language could be.

CELEBRATIONS AND NEGOTIATIONS

The sense of communality and shared experiences were highlighted in public discourse about these events. In the next two sections, we will discuss two aspects of the gatherings that reveal internal tensions and differences. These are translation/interpreter arrangements and the construction of images of "the other," those who are perceived not to belong to the deaf community. In the next two sections we discuss two aspects of the gatherings: translation/interpreter arrangements and the construction of images of "the other," those who are perceived not to belong to the deaf community. As we discuss, these two aspects are cause for both celebration and negotiation. In the conclusion we link these discussions to the increasing diversity in deaf communities.

During the plenary sessions of the WFD 2003 congress in Montreal, only deaf interpreters worked on the stage. They took their inputs from hearing interpreters who worked as so-called feeders; they only provided a translation to the deaf interpreters on the stage of what was said in the oral or sign language presentation. Deaf interpreters have in general more understanding of sign language nuances than hearing interpreters, which strengthens the linguistic quality and the cultural adjustments of the interpreting on stage (Adam et al. 2014; Boudreault 2005). One deaf participant told us she was glad to avoid "interpreter faces," referring to what she saw as a lesser visual quality of hearing interpreters. The congresses are sites where excellence in communication and accessibility is demonstrated. One of the participants pointed out to us that "Deaf people don't come to the WFD congress to have more of the frustrations they experience at home." By this, she referred to lack of communication access and subpar interpreter solutions experienced at home. Access for hearing people was also well arranged: the organizers provided headsets with translations to English and French, which also was a key resource for the numerous hearing interpreters translating to the numerous sign languages used by deaf attendees.

However, a number of deaf attendees had a strong preference for national interpreters even if International Sign translation was provided. Far from all attendees felt that IS translation was sufficient (also see Green, this volume). First, the status of IS was discussed at the general assembly during the Montreal congress. Representatives from the Scandinavian countries were strong proponents of an increased status given to IS in WFD gatherings, but representatives from other parts of the world, with the Chinese being most active, argued that a rise in the status of IS could weaken the political pressure worldwide to increase the status of local sign languages. Second, on the flat floor of the conference hall used for plenary sessions, deaf people gathered around their accompanying interpreters in the national or regional sign languages represented. Some attendees told us they were fully reliant upon the translation into the sign language they practiced on a daily basis and other attendees told us they combined watching the International Sign presentation and the interpreter using their national or regional sign language.

This conference floor was also a highly visible demonstration of inequality in deaf worlds. Large groups of deaf people gathered around the several turn-taking interpreters from the northern European countries, who had to stand on a chair to be visible to all. In stark contrast, participants from the global South typically were one to three persons in front of one interpreter sitting on his or her chair interpreting without any breaks. Some countries also had interpreter teams at several parallel sessions simultaneously, which further strengthened the freedom of the participants from more affluent countries.

Deaf "Right" and "Wrong"

Identity is never only about an imagined "us" but also about an imagined "them," the interplay between "us" and "them," the more or less solid borders that separate "us" and "them," and the relative power of the one in defining (or restricting) the other. The politics of identity is both about creating images of self and one's own group, and it is about creating images of "the other" (Anderson 1983; Barth 1969). In the quest for recognition of individual and collective identities by others, an image of what is "right" and "good" (Sicakkan and Lithman 2006) is also involved.

The dynamics at several of the events did in various ways also create a contrast between "right" and "wrong" ways of being deaf, such as by bringing up the contentious issue of oralism and its historical roots. For example, during the 2003 Winter Games in Sundsvall, it became evident that the players in the US ice hockey team did not use sign language among themselves and that the team thus displayed a somewhat oral public image. In a match between the United States team and Finland, a huge and easily visible banner was hung up, declaring "Orals don't belong here! ASL does!" Heated arguing started beneath the banner, and it was removed only minutes after it had been attached to the wall. One of the initiators (they were all from Scandinavian countries) of the banner expressed disappointment: "Why do they react with censorship?" We asked him about the motives for hanging the banner.

> Dammit! Deaflympics is more than sports; it is deaf culture and social life, and sign language! There were many of us from Sweden and Finland, and also a few Americans and others, who reacted to the behaviour of the American ice hockey team; they only communicated verbally. Well, this is ok if it is occasional and just a few doing so. On the basketball team, where I am involved, for instance, we have seven or eight players who use sign language, and then there are a few that mostly talk. But in the sports arena, everything is communicated in sign language, and SDI [the Swedish deaf sports organization] supports sign language. This seems not to be the case with the Americans; no one masters sign language on their team.

The match started but the commotion continued. The spectators struck up conversations and made statements that represented the present match as a confrontation between oralism and sign language, not as a game between Finland and the United States. This struggle was not confined to the grandstands, as we witnessed that several Finnish players employed "signs of abuse" toward their opponents, with unconcealed references to their oral orientation.

The ice hockey match instigated discussions about core deaf values. We observed people referring to the Second International Congress of Education of the Deaf in Milan 1880 when hearing professionals involved in teaching deaf people decided that the oral method was preferred. The reactions during and after this intense incident were mixed. Some held that taking a clear stance on this issue would strengthen the global signing community. Others took a critical stance and argued that this could demotivate potential American Sign Language (ASL) users among the oral players on the US ice hockey team. A few days after the banner incident, we spotted the president of the international sports federation, Donalda Ammons, and took the opportunity to talk to her about the incident. She pointed out how the games are an arena for inclusion:

> Sports are not politics. At games we are all deaf. That is what we have in common, and the oral versus sign thing does not belong here. I did not appreciate the banner, and I was further provoked by the fact that they highlighted ASL. At least they should have referred to sign language in general. . . . Deaflympics is a unique possibility for more people learning sign language and to be included in the community of the deaf. For young people growing up orally, when they meet with the society of the deaf through sports, most often they find a place in the society of the deaf, even if their hearing parents actively work against it.

In this perspective, the banner incident would be counterproductive in terms of recruiting and welcoming new members to the deaf community.

This incident flagged tensions around normative ways of being deaf. A challenging aspect of deaf identification is the establishment and promotion of an idea of a correct kind of deaf life, paralleling an opposition of an idea of a deviant kind of deaf life. The anticipated "right" way to be deaf is to take pride in and accept being deaf, use sign language, refrain from using hearing aids and/or cochlear implants at least during a deaf event and spend time on deaf culture and deaf politics. Deaf people who want to have a go with the hearing world, to try out the possibilities of oral communication and hearing aids are deemed "wrong," as pointed out by the banner instigator cited earlier.

While the transnational events are strong manifestations of unity and the collectivist traits of deaf lives worldwide, the events are not without internal tensions. These tensions may be especially noticeable to newcomers, who may meet, and eventually become part of a deaf, signing space for the first time at these events. The dispute around the US ice hockey players revealed that there is a fine balance between welcoming newcomers who have a background that is deemed as "wrong" for the well-being of a deaf person and at the same time the importance of holding onto ideas of "right" ways of being deaf.

IMPROVING QUESTIONS, THEORIES, AND METHODS

The events we followed took place at a certain time in history and we followed them from a certain perspective. Around 2000, the transnational meeting places discussed here appeared as gatherings of utmost importance as manifestations of deaf cultural practices, deaf spaces, sites for critical discussion of what being deaf is about, and sites where deaf epistemologies are exchanged, created, and strengthened (Paul and Moores 2014). They were preceded by decades of political and linguistic awakening in many deaf communities. The linguistic recognition of sign languages as natural languages had resulted in increased research in sign language and subsequently its users. During the 1970s and 1980s, deaf people in Europe and North America started to take pride in their deafness (through Deaf Power and Deaf Awareness movements). The Deaf President Now! revolution at Gallaudet University in 1988 had a symbolic effect far beyond the United States, since it showed that deaf people were ultimately able to take any professional position and were not inferior to hearing people. The interest in and awareness about deafness as a possible positive asset in terms of linguistic and cultural identification had reached a peak at the turn of the twenty-first century, and the informants we followed at the large events had grown up with these trends.

There are a number of issues that we believe of particular importance at this point in time (and many of these issues are addressed in this volume). First, it is important to pay attention to North-South differences in understanding of deaf worlds. One example mentioned in this chapter is that people from the North were well provided with interpreters and eager to develop IS as a language practiced in WFD, whereas people from the South were few in number, poorly equipped with interpreters, and hesitant about and unfamiliar with the use of IS. When we applied for funding for our study of the transnational connections in deaf worlds, we wanted to include a stay at a site in the South but were not successful in securing this funding. Today, we would not have given up so easily. To study transnational connections among deaf people, the inclusion of diverse viewpoints is mandatory to gain understanding about what it is to be deaf worldwide.

Second, the decline of the traditional meeting places like the deaf schools and the deaf clubs has been under way for some time (cf. Emery in this volume). The parallel increase in digital communication technologies resulted in the establishment of new meeting places that often are far more transitory and temporary than the older meeting places (cf. İlkbaşaran in this volume). Deaf individuals all over the world increasingly engage in world travel, pay visits to transnational deaf gatherings and sites, and use the Internet. These meeting places contribute, as far as we can observe, to creating a common ground for deaf people to come together. We believe that researchers paying attention to both physical and virtual arenas and how these interact are important to capture how transnational connections unfold in deaf people's lives and how deaf spaces are formed.

Third, the diversity among deaf people, in terms of geographic background, class, education, ideologies on deafness, and interests, for example, may have consequences for the ways deaf people meet in the future. The example of the clash during the ice hockey match suggests that significant commonalities are challenged by experiences of diversity. During the past decades there has been an even further diversification of (1) educational backgrounds because of the rise of inclusion philosophy and the decline of deaf boarding schools; (2) age of onset of sign language learning; (3) use of hearing technologies such as cochlear implants, and (4) use of sign language interpreters in higher education and a corresponding increase of highly educated signing deaf people. Also, there seems to be an increase in specific conferences or gatherings such as gatherings of deaf interpreters, deaf teachers, deaf academics, deaf tattoo artists, deaf lesbian, gay, bisexual, and transgender people, deaf Methodists (van Gilder, this volume), and so on.

It is not obvious if and how the increased diversity will affect the structure and functions of the transnational megagatherings. Another question is how diversification results in new kinds of gatherings and what will this mean for the deaf identity work we have discussed. One of the most distinctive social trends in the 1990s, the decade that led up to our fieldwork period, was social action around identities and the power of identity. This stood out as important at the gatherings that we observed, with participants repeatedly praising the community of deaf people and the use of sign language exclusively. These identities were geographical, ascribed, and actively rooted in a defined history, or newly established in search of novel meanings. With a plurality of deaf experiences, interests, and epistemologies, the borders between "us" and "them" that have been important for identity negotiations in deaf communities have blurred, and there seems to be a shift from identity politics to a process of more fluid identifications and diversified networking. We may ask if there is a possible future where the traditional deaf communities become destabilized and come to lack a distinct common identity project. Perhaps there is a move toward a scenario where deaf people may become active as participants in networks of a more temporary and special-interest-driven character. Consequently, there is a need for a diligent analysis of diversity, widened theoretical perspectives, and renewed research methods in our studies of deaf worlds.

REFERENCES

Adam, R., C. Stone, S. Collins, and M. Metzger. 2014. "Deaf Interpreters: An Introduction." In *Deaf Interpreters at Work*, edited by R. Adam, C. Stone, S. Collins, and M. Metzger, 1–18. Washington, DC: Gallaudet University Press.

Anderson, B. 1983. *Imagined Communities: Reflections on the Origin and Spread of Nationalism.* London: Verso.

Barth, F. 1969. *Ethnic Groups and Boundaries: The Social Organization of Culture Difference.* Oslo, Norway: Universitetsforlaget.

Boudreault, P. 2005. "Deaf Interpreters." In *Topics in Signed Language Interpreting*, edited by T. Janzen, 323–56. Amsterdam: Benjamins.

Breivik, J.-K. 2005. *Deaf Identities in the Making: Local Lives, Transnational Connections.* Washington, DC: Gallaudet University Press.

Breivik, J.-K., H. Haualand, and P. Solvang. 2002. *Rome: A Temporary Deaf City!*, vol. 2. Bergen, Norway: Stein Rokkan Centre for Social Studies.

Haualand, H. 2007. "The Two-Week Village: The Significance of Sacred Occasions for the Deaf Community." In *Disability in Local and Global Worlds*, edited by B. Ingstad and S. Whyte, 33-55. Berkeley: University of California Press.

Paul, P. V., and D. F. Moores (eds.). 2014. *Deaf Epistemologies: Multiple Perspectives on the Acquisition of Knowledge.* Washington, DC: Gallaudet University Press.

Senghas, R. J., and L. Monaghan. 2002. "Signs of Their Times: Deaf Communities and the Culture of Language." *Annual Review of Anthropology* 31: 69–97.

Sicakkan, H., and Y. Lithman. 2006. "Politics of Identity, Modes of Belonging, and Citizenship: An Overview of Conceptual and Theoretical Challenges." In *Changing the Basis of Citizenship in the Modern State: Political Theory and the Politics of Diversity*, edited by H. Sicakkan and Y. Lithman. Lewiston, NY: Edwin Mellen.

Solvang, P., J.-K. Breivik, and H. Haualand. 2005. Minority politics and disability discourse at global deaf events. In *Resistance, Reflections, and Change: Nordic Disability Research*, edited by A. Gustavsson, 177–89. Lund, Sweden: Studentlitteratur.

Turner, V. W. 1967. *The Forest of Symbols: Aspects of Ndembu Ritual*. Ithaca, NY: Cornell University Press.

Part 2

▌ LANGUAGE

6 | The Paradox of
International Sign:
The Importance of
Deaf-Hearing Encounters
for Deaf-Deaf Communication
across Sign Language Borders

Onno Crasborn and Anja Hiddinga

Standing in the lobby of a hotel in Washington, DC, waiting to check in among a crowd of deaf people from many different countries, Anja Hiddinga's ten-year-old deaf son became friendly with a man from Egypt. They chatted along, although the little one did not know any Egyptian Sign Language or American Sign Language (ASL), and it was not Sign Language of the Netherlands they were conversing in either. In communicating back and forth, the conversation seemed to develop quite easily. Other interactions across sign language borders in that lobby were similar, with deaf people arriving from all over the world to attend the Deaf Way II conference and festival. The week of performances, lectures, and other events that followed was impressive for many reasons but particularly because of this very circumstance, the relative ease with which deaf people from different countries seemed to interact with one another in international sign. Equally impressive is the process of interpretation to and from international sign for the benefit of multilingual deaf audiences at other international (deaf) conferences.

In contradiction to the well-known misunderstanding of many hearing people that there is only one sign language, international sign, a construct bridging different signed languages, is an enigmatic phenomenon. How can one communicate without a shared language? The actual form of international sign (IS) depends on the shared context at large, which includes not only shared experiences and shared knowledge of the surroundings but also shared knowledge of any spoken and signed languages (including English and American Sign Language, but depending on the region it may also be Sign Language of the Netherlands or British

Sign Language, to name but two languages, and shared fingerspelling alphabets). For reasons of clarity, we use the capitals IS as a shorthand to refer to international sign, but we want to refrain from using capitals when naming it in full because we use it to refer to spontaneous contact forms rather than more conventionalized forms. Of course this is not a binary distinction but rather a continuum, something we revisit later. Not a language, or a pidgin, Creole, or koine (Woll 1990; Supalla and Webb 1995; Allsop, Woll, and Brauti 1995), IS merits close scrutiny from linguists as well as from social scientists interested in the workings of communication (Hiddinga and Crasborn 2011; Green 2014). Although international sign may be a construct specific to the communication between deaf people, questions about its nature, the contexts in which it is used, the characteristics of signer and respondent, the quality of the resulting interaction, and the conditions under which it is possible and effective pertain to communication more broadly. Indeed, we claim that the questions arising in the study of international sign are germane to all human communication.

In this chapter, we build on an argument we developed in a previous article on international sign (Hiddinga and Crasborn 2011). There we characterized international sign as a form of visual communication between deaf people who do not have a shared sign language and we focused on its functional properties (enabling social relations) instead of structural features such as morphology or syntax. Here we use a similar starting point and hope to raise a number of interesting questions as we go along. Our argument is of a theoretical nature and draws on secondary literature rather than empirical material. However, our own practical experiences, as regular visitors at deaf conferences and as colleagues, friends, certified sign language interpreter (Crasborn), and family member (Hiddinga) of deaf people in the Netherlands, are constitutive to our questions. Given the enigmatic and variable nature of IS, we are curious about its role in the characterization of deaf people's relationships to and with each other. In line with our earlier inquiries, we want to investigate if and to what extent the possibility of communication in IS is a result of the communicative flexibility and creativity of deaf signers and therefore also a core feature of deaf communities.[1] In this chapter, we focus on shared characteristics in communication of deaf people and explore the relation between the local and the global with respect to communication. What is the relation between the local communicative settings where communication between and with hearing people is often the norm, and communication between deaf people across community and across language boundaries? To what extent is the use of IS enabled by such variety in settings and modes of communication? To what extent is this construct and the implied skill in practicing it characteristic of the shared experience of being deaf?

These are complex questions requiring empirical research. This is not what we aim at here. Rather, we raise a challenging hypothesis for such work by discussing what is known from the literature in a new way. We first sketch a picture of some characteristics of communicative practices deaf people are involved in, focusing particularly on deaf-hearing interactions. Subsequently we try to motivate our

---

[1] We are aware of the many discussions around notions such as deaf community, deaf world, and d/Deaf. See Friedner (2010) for a discussion of classificatory terminology in relation to deaf people.

hypothesis taking the situation of deaf people in settings where the majority of people are hearing nonsigners as a frame of reference.

DEAF-HEARING INTERACTION: WHAT DO WE KNOW?

While hearing people can go through life without ever interacting with a deaf person, the reverse is unimaginable. Although we expect substantial variation from individual to individual, it may well be that the majority of interactions deaf people have in life are with hearing people. Parents are typically hearing, neighbors will be hearing, and playmates in the family and in the initial vicinity will be as well. For adults, most work settings will predominantly feature hearing colleagues, staff in shops, bars, and public transport will be hearing, et cetera.

Although deaf people may choose to avoid actual interactions with hearing people, it is likely that the majority of interactions in an average day are still with hearing people, even though the duration of these interactions may be very brief in comparison with deaf-deaf interactions. The use of speaking and speechreading (a shared spoken language), pointing to the immediate visual context, gesture, and pantomime will all be combined to achieve a specific communicative goal. In addition to this rich repertory of strategies, the flexibility in actually using these strategies is shared deaf-deaf and deaf-hearing interactions. These phenomena are well known and have been described in the literature (e.g., Boyes Braem et al. 1987; Rosenstock 2008). Our hypothesis is that these deaf-hearing encounters feature the exact same communication strategies that deaf people use in first-time encounters with deaf people from other sign language backgrounds and that these encounters thus constitute a founding feature for one of the core elements in the experience of being deaf.

For forty years, since the groundbreaking work of Tervoort (1953) and Stokoe (1960), sign language researchers have studied foremost the linguistic properties of these languages analogous to those in spoken languages. More recently, the differences in sign languages and the sociolinguistic conditions in which they are used have gained attention. While it has always been clear to sign linguists that sign language is not a universal language, little attention has been paid to explicit comparison of their different lexicons and grammars. Rather, with the two decades of research on American Sign Language (ASL) predating research in most other parts of the world, many studies on European sign languages in the 1980s and 1990s were implicitly aimed at establishing that these languages showed similar degrees of complexity and similar grammatical phenomena to those found in ASL.

The growing number of different sign languages that are studied (cf. the regional surveys in Brentari 2010) together with explicit typological comparisons of sign languages (Zeshan 2004a, 2004b) made clear that there are also other contexts in which sign languages are used in addition to the national deaf communities in Western countries. For example, a number of shared signing communities have been documented (see Zeshan and De Vos 2012 for an edited collection on such communities). In such small, local communities, there is a relatively high incidence of deafness (although deaf people are still a small minority), but more hearing people can sign than in typical national deaf communities or a city context. Both linguistic anthropologists and linguists have argued that (village) sign languages evolve from gesture (Le Guen 2012). Studies of home signers have made claims to the same effect (Goldin-Meadow 2003, 2012). Home signers are deaf people who have not grown up with exposure to an existing sign language and within their hearing environment have developed an elaborate gesture system through interaction with hearing people. In such contexts, interactions between signers and hearing nonsigners will differ from those of deaf signers in a country like the Netherlands, for instance. In the latter context, hearing people are not only nonsigners; they are often not even aware of sign language as a means of communication. We come back to this difference at the end of the chapter.

International Sign: What Do We Know?

Many deaf people both within the Netherlands and outside have told us that it is easier to communicate with deaf people using another sign language than it is to communicate with hearing people using another spoken language. A Dutch deaf person going on holiday to Turkey will typically have less difficulties interacting with a deaf local than with a hearing local, when no shared sign language is available to communicate with the former and no shared spoken language is available to communicate with the latter. That is, if there is no shared language, deaf-deaf communication is typically more fruitful than deaf-hearing or hearing-hearing communication. In fact, this is an understatement: deaf communication across language boundaries, often called *international sign* but sometimes called *cross-signing* to distinguish it from more conventional or planned contact language varieties that are more like Esperanto (Zeshan, Sagara, and Bradford 2013), seems to take place with remarkable success. International deaf events, which are frequently held, provide ready evidence of this. International sign interpreting is offered at many large events. While it is not always seen as equivalent to interpreting in an established (national) sign language (see Green, this volume, and Haualand, Solvang, and Breivik, this volume), it succeeds at bringing across at least parts of very complex messages in oral and signed presentations.

Very little empirical research has been performed on international sign so far. The largest study we know of dealt not so much with spontaneous international interactions but looked at the communicative setting at Gallaudet University, where deaf people from all over the world study and gradually learn more ASL (Rosenstock 2004). In fact, Rosenstock (2007) describes the international interactions at Gallaudet as the "emergence of a communication *system*" (from the title; italics ours). Other authors have looked at other instances of international deaf communication, which could be conceptualized as placed on a continuum from first-time interactions between deaf signers who do not share a language (which Zeshan termed "cross-signing"; see, e.g., Allsop et al. 1995; McKee and Napier 2002) to a top-down created and published variety such as Gestuno (WFD 1975; Supalla and Webb 1995).

Deaf signers we have consulted in the Netherlands differ about the amount of exercise and experience that are needed to sign across language boundaries as well as about the level of communicative success one can achieve. A current European Union (EU) project called "Signs2Cross" highlights that some training is at least beneficial (http://signs2cross.eu): it is developing localized courses for different deaf communities on how to successfully communicate with deaf people from other countries.

Elsewhere (2011), we argued that this skill of communicating across language boundaries is a core element of the experience that comes with being deaf. We came to this conclusion in comparing the world language system outlined by De Swaan (2001) for spoken languages with the situation for sign languages. For hearing speakers, English has a dominant role as a global language, with a smaller international role for one of twelve regional languages including Spanish or Hindi that enable communication between speakers of different language "families" across large geographical areas. While ASL would appear to be the most learned foreign sign language, it clearly does not fulfil the global role that English has for hearing people. The reason for this, we argued, is that the apparent success of international sign in enabling deaf-deaf interaction mitigates the need for an actual shared sign language. However, these interactions will typically be temporary, such as at conferences and other (cultural) gatherings or in chance encounters between deaf people with different sign languages. When situations of interaction are more permanent (as when moving to another country, e.g., to study at Gallaudet University, or marrying someone who uses another sign language), the local (or dominant) sign language will often be learned.

COMMUNICATION AS A SKILL: MUTUAL INTELLIGIBILITY OF RELATED LANGUAGES

Little is known about the way in which deaf people acquire the ability to use international sign. In our experience (the first author in international academic circles, the second author in observing her deaf children and their friends for more than twenty years), deaf people, even if they are very young, are able to communicate somehow with deaf people with another sign language. This happens by trial and error, and in some cases is guided by a more experienced deaf signer as counterpart. This presupposes, of course, a mutual intention to communicate and an expectation that this could indeed work. This, and the pleasure it evokes, is what Green (2014, 460) terms *moral orientation*, arguing that it is "embedded in deaf notions and practices of sameness, and experienced as both good and right."

Such situations are not unique to deaf people. Hearing people will likewise mobilize similar communicative intentions to make themselves understood or try to understand the other. Our point is that deaf people make use of different modalities in their communication and thus manage greater communicative repertoires. Thus, they do not only exploit the iconic nature of sign language lexicon and grammar (as observed by many earlier authors; see, e.g., Supalla and Webb 1995; McKee and Napier, 2002), but they also profit from their continuous existence in nonsigning, speaking environments. We suggest that this adds to the available communicative strategies they have at their disposal. Second, cultural, emotional, geographic, and linguistic distances are mitigated to a certain extent by the shared experience of living a deaf life among a hearing majority. This in turn may contribute to the mutual intention to make interaction work. It is thus not just the shared variety of communicative repertoires as such, but also the experience of being deaf (DEAF-SAME) that constitutes the particular outside condition (cf. Gumperz 1982) in which strategies for understanding and being understood can persistently be worked out.

The skill in question consists of combining iconic elements from the native language, lexicon, and grammar from any shared languages (including shared fingerspelling alphabets), the shared visible context such as objects one can point to, and the shared social context ("what is the relationship between us and why are we interacting here?") in flexible ways (see also Sáfár et al., 2015). This communicative content in turn is combined with interactive strategies that are more prominent than when communicating with speakers of the native language. It is an empirical question of how exactly all the elements that are important in deaf-deaf communication (linguistic elements, signs, mouthing, everyday gestures, pantomime, facial expressions) interact with social knowledge and with cultural experiences to create successful communication in IS. There will be considerable individual differences in the use of various strategies and the way in which meaning is negotiated.

Where deaf people have international sign skills at their disposal, hearing people tend to master multiple spoken languages. It is often estimated that more than 50 percent of the world population speaks more than one language regularly, although hard data is lacking (Grosjean 2010). This high number might be expected given that there are fewer than two hundred countries and about seven thousand languages. Language endangerment often comes with the transition of a community to a larger language, leading to a period of a few generations that are bilingual. As De Swaan (2001) argues, people are likely to learn additional languages if this brings them economic success, and in many areas of the world it is vital to not just use the language of your parents but to learn additional languages. This holds for learning English in the Netherlands, but equally for learning English by Mexican immigrants in the USA, for instance. As Myers-Scotton (2006, 9) puts it, "bilingualism is a natural outcome of the socio-political forces that create groups and their boundaries."

Where some authors focus on situations where people are bilingual in the sense of speaking more than one unrelated languages (such as English and Hindi), others have looked more at mutual intelligibility of more closely related languages. Research on communication in Scandinavia, for instance, has demonstrated that people speaking Norwegian and Swedish can understand each other's language relatively well when used in cross-language interaction (e.g., Gooskens 2007). That is, without using a shared (third) language, speakers use their native tongue and rely on the listener's perceptive skills to match the input to their own native language, without explicit training. This has been called *semi-communication* (Haugen 1966) and *receptive multilingualism* (Zeevaert and Ten Thije 2007). These authors have likewise emphasized the importance of being understood rather than speaking exactly like one's interlocutor (Ten Thije 2013).

Because most sign languages have developed with minimal language contact to other sign languages, we see less family relationships than for spoken languages. For some family relationships that have been argued for on the basis of old texts, few data sources are actually available. The relationship between ASL and French Sign Language (LSF), for instance, is argued for on the basis of the comparison of present-day lexicons and the few older dictionaries that are available (e.g., Frishberg 1975). The strongest evidence for family relationships is perhaps the case of British Sign Language (BSL)–Australian Sign Language (Auslan)–New Zealand Sign Language (NZSL) (McKee and Kennedy 2000). While there may be few similarities between sign languages due to family relationships, there are many correspondences and similarities in both lexicon and grammar due to other factors.

The limited time-depth of sign languages (typically going back to not more than three hundred years, compared to many thousands of years for spoken languages) in combination with iconic, pantomimic, and gestural strategies employed in the development of sign languages leads to similarities that can easily be explained. For instance, most sign languages appear to map time onto space to talk about temporal concepts. The fact that there may be cultural differences in how such a mapping takes place (e.g., De Vos 2012) leads to some variation, but all mappings appear iconic in nature, which makes them more suitable for use in cross-language interaction than fully arbitrary expressions.

From the perspective of international communication among hearing speakers and listeners, communication across language boundaries as witnessed among deaf people of various backgrounds is not so unique. What does remain unique, though, is that it appears to be possible to some extent across any language or language family boundary and that an organization like the WFD chooses international sign even at worldwide international meetings, as Green (2014) observes. In what follows, we try to relate deaf peoples' language skills to the composition of deaf communities in terms of their communicative interactions.

DEAF-HEARING INTERACTION AS A FOUNDATION FOR THE PARTICULARS OF DEAF-DEAF COMMUNICATIVE CREATIVITY

Irrespective of the preferred manner of interaction with hearing people, deaf people have grown up learning how to handle such encounters. Signers will constantly need to appeal to their communication skills that go beyond the linguistic and interactive resources offered by conventionalized sign languages. How exactly this is learned we know little about: whether by formal or informal instruction at school, by parents or peers, or by mimicking the behavior of other deaf or hearing people. Variation between individuals is expected. It is clear, however, that these embodied practices are part and parcel of the experience of being deaf.

Many authors looking at deaf communities from a sociological or anthropological perspective have emphasized the similarities rather than the differences between diverse settings. The shared difference in communicative mode with the large majority of the surrounding hearing population in almost any context is an important part of that similarity. Moreover, the shared orientation to and involvement with visuality also unites deaf people, hence the focus on deaf people as "visual people," as some scholars stress (Bahan 2008; Baynton, Gannon, and Bergey 2007; Haualand 2008). Discussing the implications of such a focus on visuality, Hilde Haualand (2008, 112) points out its potential analytical gain: "Like studies of sign language have altered the understanding of what language is, studies of communities that establish connections through vision or other channels than the audible may challenge the understanding of what a community is." Deaf communities are usually not only dispersed within a larger hearing society, but even in a village context with a high proportion of hearing signers, they are at the same time similar to each other in this very respect. This similarity is not just located in deaf people's visuality but also in shared experiences, histories, orientations, ways of "being in the world." Some refer to this as DEAF-SAME (e.g., Friedner and Kusters 2014).

Various authors have emphasized the existence of a global deaf community. Breivik argued that "Deaf people are . . . potentially and actually members of a transnational and trans-local framework that overrides any local or national loyalty they may additionally possess" (Breivik 2005, 12). However, this notion should be used prudently. As Haualand (2007, 45) shows, the international visitors of the Deaflympics in Rome in 2001 could only move effortlessly within the transnational Deaf network "without being locked to a certain nationality or one specific sign language" because "they possessed the linguistic and cultural knowledge to move effortlessly within [it]." Access to such knowledge will vary widely within and between different communities. Indeed, there is a growing unease with unifying concepts such as "the deaf community" or "deaf identity" in which differences in socioeconomic background, cultural environment, class, race, religious orientation, and gender are easily overlooked, not to mention the (often) enormous differences between deaf people in the global North as compared to those in the rest of the world (see, e.g., Monaghan et al. 2003; Kisch 2008; Friedner 2010). Any analysis of global shared experiences of deaf people should thus take into account widely differing "localities."

Our hypothesis, that deaf-hearing encounters feature the exact same communication strategies that deaf people use in first-time encounters with deaf people from other sign language backgrounds, leads us to better understand how the seemingly miraculous cross-signing skill is possible in the first place. If it is an elaboration of embodied practices, of something that deaf people have (implicitly and explicitly) learned to do on a daily basis throughout their lives, then communicating across sign language boundaries is not such an incredible task.

The perhaps surprising conclusion is then that something that may be seen as a core feature of deaf-deaf communication is in fact made possible by the fact that deaf people spend a significant amount of time interacting with nonsigning, hearing people. Deaf people's experience and skill in dealing with a large variety of communicative settings are not necessarily unique or unparalleled by hearing people. However, it is certainly better developed at the group level in most countries.

Concluding Remarks

With the little work that has been done both on international deaf interactions and local or national deaf-hearing interactions, our hypothesis outlined remains just that: a hypothesis in need of testing. One possible way to do this would be to compare signers from Western deaf communities such as the Netherlands with signers from shared signing communities with little interaction with hearing nonsigners: the former will have more experience in interacting with hearing nonsigners and would thus be predicted to bring more interactive skills to the table than deaf signers who are used to the average hearing person knowing how to converse with deaf people. Also, both the qualification and the quantification of different types of interactions and social relations of deaf signers is something that appears to be underexplored. The same holds for the intensity of these different contacts: insofar that the variety of topics or semantic domains of interactions are similar, what is the difference in length of the interactions and how does the emotional engagement of signers differ in both contexts? We have tried to motivate the hypothesis by highlighting the minority status of deaf people within society and the minority status of deaf native signers within the whole community of signers. It is thus plausible that most deaf people interact more frequently with nonsigners than with other signers. Moreover, we have suggested that similar communicative strategies are used in interacting with different groups with whom a signer does not share a sign language, having to resort to more pantomimic expressions, a shared spoken language (if any), and increased use of (visible, shared) context. But most of all, we have suggested that the experience of being deaf, reaching further than just communicative strategies and extending into shared visual practices, shared history, a sense of kinship, and other practices of sameness, provides for the space in which IS works to communicate with deaf others across language borders.

REFERENCES

Allsop, L., B. Woll, and J. M. Brauti. 1995. "International Sign: The Creation of an International Deaf Community and Sign Language." In *Sign Language Research 1994*, edited by H. Bos and T. Schermer, 171–88. Hamburg, Germany: Signum.

Bahan, B. 2008. Upon the Formation of a Visual Variety of the Human Race. In *Open Your Eyes: Deaf Studies Talking*, edited by H.-D.L. Bauman, 83–99. London: University of Minnesota Press.

Baynton, D. C., J. R. Gannon, & J. L. Bergey 2007. *Through Deaf Eyes: A Photographic History of an American Community*. Washington D.C.: Gallaudet University Press.

Boyes Braem, P., M.-L. Fournier, F. Rickli, S. Corazza, M.-L. Franchi, and V. Volterra. 1987. A Comparison of Techniques or Expressing Semantic Roles and Locative Relations in Two Different Sign Languages. In *SLR'87*, edited by W. Edmondson and F. Karlsson, 14–120. Hamburg: Signum Press.

Breivik, J.-K. 2005. Deaf Identities in the Making. Local Lives, Transnational Connections. Washington D.C.: Gallaudet University Press.

Brentari, D., ed. 2010.*Sign Languages*. Cambridge, UK: Cambridge University Press.

De Swaan, A. 2001. *Words of the World: The Global Language System.* Cambridge, UK: Cambridge University Press.

De Vos, C. 2012. Sign-Spatiality in Kata Kolok. How a Village Sign Language of Bali Inscribes Its Signing Space. PhD thesis, Radboud University Nijmegen.

Friedner, M. 2010. "Bio-power, Biosociality, and Community Formation: How Bio-power Is Constitutive of the Deaf Community." *Sign Language Studies* 10 (3): 336–47.

Friedner, M., and A. Kusters. 2014. "On the Possibilities and Limits of DEAF DEAF SAME: Tourism and Empowerment Camps in Adamorobe (Ghana), Bangalore, and Mumbai (India)." *Disability Studies Quarterly* 34 (3). http://dsq-sds.org/article/view/4246/3649.

Frishberg, N. 1975. "Arbitrariness and Iconicity: Historical change in ASL." *Language* 51: 696–719.

Goldin-Meadow, S. 2003. The Resilience of Language. What Gesture Creation in Deaf Children Can Tell Us About How All Children Learn Language. New York: Psychology Press.

———. 2012. "Homesign: Gesture to Language." In *Sign Language: An International Handbook*, edited by R. Pfau, M. Steinbach, and B. Woll, 601–25. Berlin, Germany: De Gruyter Mouton.

Gooskens, C. 2007. "The Contribution of Linguistic Factors to Intelligibility of Closely Related Languages."*Journal of Multilingual and Multicultural Development* 28 (6): 445–67.

Green, E. M. 2014. "Building the Tower of Babel: International Sign, Linguistic Commensuration, and Moral Orientation."*Language in Society* 43 (4): 445–65. doi:10.1017/S0047404514000396.

Grosjean, F. 2010. *Bilingual Life and Reality*. Cambridge, MA: Harvard University Press.

Gumperz, J. J. 1982. *Discourse Strategies*. Cambridge, UK: Cambridge University Press.

Haualand, H. 2007. The Two Week Village. The Significance of Sacred Occasions for the Deaf Community. In *Disability in Local and Global Worlds*, edited by B. Ingstad and S. R. Whyte, 33–55. Berkeley: University of California Press.

Haualand, H. 2008. Sound and Belonging: What is a Community? In *Open Your Eyes. Deaf Studies Talking*, edited by H.-D.L. Bauman, 111–23. London: University of Minnesota Press.

Haugen, E. 1966. "Dialect, Language, Nation." *American Anthropologist* 68 (4): 922–35.

Hiddinga, A., and O. Crasborn. 2011. "Signed Languages and Globalization." *Language in Society* 40 (4): 483–505.

Higgins, P. C. 1980. *Outsiders in a Hearing World: A Sociology of Deafness*. Newbury Park: SAGE.

Kisch, S. 2008. Deaf Discourse. The Social Construction of Deafness in a Bedouin Community. *Medical Anthropology* 27 (3): 283–313.

Lane, H. 1992. *The Mask of Benevolence: Disabling the Deaf Community*. New York: Knopf.

Lawson, L. 1992. "The Role of Sign in the Structure of the Deaf Community." In *Constructing Deafness*, edited by S. Gregory and G. M. Hartley, 31–35. London: Pinter.

Le Guen, O. 2012. "Exploration in the Domain of Time: From Yucatec Maya Time Gestures to Yucatec Maya Sign Language Time Signs." In *Endangered Sign Languages in Village Communities: Anthropological and Linguistic Insights*, edited by U. Zeshan and C. de Vos, 209–50. Berlin: Mouton de Gruyter.

McKee, D., and G. Kennedy. 2000. Lexical Comparison of Signs from American, Australian, British and New Zealand Sign Languages. In *The Signs of Language Revisited*, edited by K. Emmorey and H. Lane, 49–76. Mahwah, NJ: Lawrence Erlbaum Associates.

McKee, R. L., and J. Napier. 2002. "Interpreting into International Sign Pidgin: An Analysis." *Sign Language and Linguistics* 5 (1): 27–54.

Monaghan, L. F., C. Schmaling, K. Nakamura, and G. H. Turner, eds. 2003. *Many Ways to Be Deaf: International Variation in Deaf Communities*. Washington, DC: Gallaudet University Press.

Myers-Scotton, C. 2006. *Multiple Voices: An Introduction to Bilingualism*. Malden: Blackwell.

Rosenstock, R. 2004. "An Investigation of International Sign: Analyzing Structure and Comprehension." PhD diss., Gallaudet University.

———. 2007. "Emergence of a Communication System: International Sign." In *Emergence of Communication and Language*, edited by C. Lyon, C. L. Nehaniv, and A. Cangelosi, 87–103. London: Springer.

———. 2008. "The Role of Iconicity in International Sign." *Sign Language Studies* 8 (2): 131–59.

Sáfár, A., L. Meurant, T. Haesenne, Y. E. Nauta, D. De Weerdt, and E. Ormel. 2015. "Mutual Intelligibility among the Sign Languages of Belgium and the Netherlands." *Linguistics* 53 (2): 353–74.

Stokoe, W. C. 1993 [1960]. *Sign Language Structure: An Outline of the Visual Communication Systems of the American Deaf* Buffalo, NY: Department of Anthropology and Linguistics.

Supalla, T., and R. A. Webb. 1995. "The Grammar of International Sign: A New Look at Pidgin Languages." In *Sign, Gesture, and Space*, edited by K. Emmorey and J. S. Reilly, 333–51. Mahwah, NJ: Lawrence Erlbaum Associates.

Ten Thije, J. D. 2013. "Lingua Receptiva (LaRa)." *International Journal of Multilingualism* 10 (2): 137–39.

Ten Thije, J. D., and L. Zeevaert, eds. 2007. *Receptive Multilingualism: Linguistic Analyses, Language Policies, and Didactic Concepts*. Amsterdam: John Benjamins.

Tervoort, B. Th. M. 1953. "Structurele analyse van visueel taalgebruik binnen een groep dove kinderen." PhD diss., Universiteit van Amsterdam.

Woll, B. 1990. "International Perspectives on Sign Language Communication." *International Journal of Sign Linguistics* 1 (2): 107–20.

World Federation of the Deaf. 1975. *Gestuno: International Sign Language of the Deaf.* Carlisle, UK: British Deaf Association.

Zeevaert, L. and J. D. ten Thije. 2007. "Introduction." In *Receptive Multilingualism. Linguistic Analyses, Language Policies and Didactic Concepts,* ed. J. D. ten Thije and L. Zeevaert, 1–25. Amsterdam: John Benjamins.

Zeshan, U. 2004a. "Hand, Head, and Face: Negative Constructions in Sign Languages." *Linguistic Typology* 8:1–58.

_____. 2004b. "Interrogative Constructions in Signed Languages: Cross-linguistic Perspectives." *Language* 80 (1): 7–39.

Zeshan, U., and C. De Vos, eds. 2012. *Sign Languages in Village Communities: Anthropological and Linguistic Insights.* Berlin: Mouton de Gruyter.

Zeshan, U., K. Sagara, and A. Bradford. 2013. "Multilingual and Multimodal Aspects of "Cross-signing": A Study of Emerging Communication in the Domain of Numerals." Poster presented at the Theoretical Issues in Sign Language Research 12, London, July 11.

7 | One Language, or Maybe Two: Direct Communication, Understanding, and Informal Interpreting in International Deaf Encounters

E. Mara Green

In July 2007 I was sitting in a cavernous auditorium in a convention center in Madrid watching the opening ceremonies of the World Federation of the Deaf's (WFD's) quadrennial World Congress. At the conclusion of a visually sumptuous theatrical production, the actors on stage chanted, "SIGN LANGUAGE RIGHTS!" using International Sign (IS) vocabulary, and encouraged the audience to sign along with them. Dinakar,[1] a Nepali delegate to the WFD with whom I was sitting, gamely joined in the chant, then turned to me and asked what the sign RIGHTS meant. I had understood because the sign articulated by the actors was identical to that used in American Sign Language (ASL). Although at the time I did not know the Nepali Sign Language (NSL) sign RIGHTS, I did my best to explain the meaning.

I use the term *informal interpreting* to refer to how, as in the scene just described, signers at international deaf events ask for and offer translations or rewordings to facilitate their own and others' understanding.[2] The word "informal" emphasizes that the individuals providing these translations are not formally designated interpreters but instead are present in some other capacity, e.g., as board members,

---

[1] Institutional names are all real; personal names are all pseudonyms.
[2] In this chapter, I write *deaf* rather than *Deaf* or *d/Deaf* because the big D/little d distinction and its orthographic representation are grounded in the histories and cultural contexts of the United States and other Western countries. In international settings, this distinction may be relevant to or used by some participants but not to or by others; applying it to such settings thus risks positioning Western cultural logics as if they were—or should be—universal. I have chosen the term *deaf* as the least marked option available in written English; it is not intended to carry the meanings it takes on when used in contrast with *Deaf*.

organizers, delegates, and/or audience members. In most cases, moreover, the interpretation is not continuous but rather given as the need arises or is thought to arise. This chapter argues that in the context of international deaf encounters in which signers use either IS or a sign language that is quite new for some participants, informal interpreting negotiates between two strongly valued practices: (1) communicating directly with other signers across linguistic differences and (2) achieving mutual understanding.

Previously (Green 2014a), I suggested that many deaf signers value direct communication because it both arises from and helps to produce a profound sense that deaf people are similar to each other—and different from hearing people—because they communicate in sign.[3] The ability to communicate not only with deaf people who sign the same language but also with deaf people from other linguistic and national backgrounds is for many deaf people central to their sense of what it is to be deaf (see also Moody 1989, Ladd 2003, Murray 2007, Hiddinga and Crasborn 2011, and Crasborn and Hiddinga, this volume). In general, deaf people also deeply value understanding, perhaps because in non-deaf spaces they frequently must engage in hard and often asymmetrical work to understand (see Crasborn and Hiddinga, this volume). To be sure, these two valued practices—direct communication and understanding—are not always in conflict. Deaf signers expect to understand each other across linguistic differences in part because of their collective and individual experiences of easily communicating in IS and/or easily learning other sign languages. My focus in this chapter on moments of interpretation should not be taken to imply that such mediation is always necessary.

The term *International Sign (IS)* is used in writing and sign to cover a very wide range of signing practices, from a fairly conventional set of lexical items, syntactic patterns, and pragmatic strategies used by regular participants at WFD meetings to any communication that occurs between deaf signers who do not share—and are not trying to learn—a mutual language. In Nepal, I have seen NSL signers use two distinct terms for cross-linguistic signed communication. One is the sign phrase INTERNATIONAL SIGN as signed in IS, where the first sign (INTERNATIONAL) is identical to the second sign in the IS phrase WORLD FEDERATION DEAF, a sign that can be used on its own to denote the WFD. Although further research is needed, my sense is that INTERNATIONAL SIGN in NSL thus connotes IS in relation to the WFD. Cross-linguistic interactions between deaf Nepalis and foreigners are also referred to with the NSL sign NATURAL-SIGN,[4] which does not suggest any relationship to the WFD.

In an academic context, Zeshan, Sagara, and Bradford (n.d.) have introduced a distinction between IS, which they define as "semi-conventionalised," and what they call *cross-signing*, which they define as "ad hoc contact signing" with a "minimal level of conventionalisation." Crasborn and Hiddinga (this volume) use the term *international sign*, without capitals, to refer to "spontaneous contact forms rather than more conventionalized forms." While these distinctions are productive, I have found that the line between categories is hard to draw. In fact, what counts as IS in a particular social context may be contested by the participants

---

[3] Of course, there are deaf people who do not communicate in sign.
[4] The hyphen indicates that two English words are required to translate a single sign; see Green 2014b for more on NATURAL-SIGN as a metalinguistic category.

themselves (see Green 2014a). In this chapter, therefore, I use the term *International Sign* in the broadest sense, to mean communication between signers who do not share a common language, whether in the context of the WFD or not.

Most scholarly literature frames the ability of deaf signers to communicate in IS in terms of the unique affordances of the signed modality for the visual representation of meaning. In Green (2014a) I argued that the actual practice of using IS also involves a critical moral dimension. That is to say, when deaf signers interact through IS, they are able to do so in part because they *want* to (see also Moody 1989, 10). Moreover, they consider the work involved to be valuable—and it often does take work; communicating in IS is not always effortless, especially at first. Engaging in such communication both requires and produces a "heightened relationship" (Moody 1989, 7) between signers that involves the bodily, linguistic, and cognitive turning of one's self toward one's interlocutor(s). I have called this turning *moral orientation* because it is moral in the sense of relational as well as moral in the sense of socially valued and expected (Green 2014a).

While my prior work on cross-linguistic communication focuses on IS, the material in this chapter also includes situations where signers are working to express themselves in a newly learned sign language or, complementarily, to understand foreign signers who are using the addressees' own language. Bringing IS and such cases together makes sense because both are shaped by powerful social norms around the importance of direct communication. In fact, as suggested above, the experience of communicating in IS, or in a sign language that is new to some participants, and the expectation that such communication is possible mutually reinforce each other. Nevertheless, understanding is not inevitably or always achieved in such situations. Both in cases involving IS and in those involving a newly learned sign language, I have found that signers work to facilitate their own and other signers' understanding by requesting and providing informal interpreting.

Informal interpreting, in other words, is one of several concrete practices through which signers morally orient to each other and to the task of communicating across difference. The informal quality of the interpreting allows it to be incorporated into the process or practice of direct communication rather than experienced as antithetical to it. In the opening vignette of this chapter, for instance, the actors addressed the audience in IS, without using national sign language interpreters, and the audience members worked to understand them. By attentively watching the actors, participating in the chant, and then soliciting a translation from me, Dinakar sought to fulfill both the desire to communicate directly and the desire to understand. While my translation was inexact (I explained the IS sign RIGHTS with the NSL sign EQUALITY), it did not disrupt the sense that the actors and Dinakar had directly communicated, whereas formal interpreting would have.

The remainder of this chapter is organized as follows. In the next section, I discuss my research methods, as well as how my national, audiological, and linguistic positions have shaped my fieldwork and analysis. In the following three sections, I analyze informal interpreting practices in three distinct scenes: (1) the WFD's General Assembly in Madrid, Spain, in July 2007, attended by delegates and observers from around the world; (2) a Women's Day program put on by British and Nepali participants in an exchange program in Kathmandu, Nepal, in March 2010, with an audience of mostly Nepali women; and (3) a dinner party in Kathmandu in April 2010, spontaneously organized by old and new acquaintances from North America and Nepal. These scenes vary in terms of the events' relationship to formal institutions and in terms of language policies and practices; what they share is an explicit or implicit commitment on the part of participants to direct communication and understanding as well as the use of informal interpreting. Analyzing informal interpreting across these three contexts allows us to consider how potentially competing values get negotiated in on-the-ground communication. In the final section, I conclude by showing how informal interpreting articulates with a tension between deaf people's understanding of sign as a shared form of language and sign languages as distinct languages, or, put more broadly, between sameness and difference.

METHODS AND POSITION

My training is in linguistic anthropology, and my primary research focus for many years has been deaf communicative and social practices in Nepal. This chapter draws on several events in Nepal that I took part in during long-term fieldwork as well as on short-term fieldwork I conducted at the WFD's 2007 General Assembly and World Congress in Madrid. Grounded in my disciplinary background, the methodology I employed in both sites makes use of shifting positions on a continuum of participating and observing. I took notes on what I saw and experienced, sometimes during the fact and sometimes afterward. I also video-recorded several open-ended interviews with some of my interlocutors at the WFD.[5]

As with all ethnographic research, my methods and findings have been inextricably shaped by who I am, how my interlocutors perceive me, and what linguistic and communicative resources I am able (or unable) to use to make sense of and to others. I am a hearing white woman from the United States, and in the social spaces analyzed here, my interlocutors generally read me easily as a white Westerner, if not necessarily specifically as American. At times, I was also quickly identified as hearing, while at other times, my interlocutors did not realize I was hearing unless or until the topic came up, such as during personal introductions. Particularly at the World Congress, I found that people from Europe and North America tended to know I was hearing as soon as I signed, whereas people from Asia, Africa, and South America were more likely not to know until I said so. Although beyond the scope of this chapter, the reasons for this dynamic are undoubtedly complex and worth thinking about more closely.

In relation to the questions at hand, this dynamic contributes to the difficulty of specifying exactly how being hearing has affected my research. On the one hand, I am sure that there are important forms of deaf sociality that I am unaware of, do not understand, or cannot experience because I am not deaf, and on infrequent occasions deaf interlocutors have said as much. On the other hand, I have never felt excluded from interactions in international deaf contexts, and my being hearing sometimes has been ignored or treated as unimportant in comparison to some other quality. During a casual conversation at the WFD, for example, a deaf man from Mexico told me that in his experience most Americans were uninterested

---

[5] In this chapter, all fieldwork-based quotations were recorded by me in English-language field notes that I wrote after the communicative event had occurred.

in talking with non-Americans and that I was an exception, since I had listened respectfully to him. This example reveals how in international spaces, particular axes of difference get thematized or backgrounded according to the context. Here what seemed to matter to my interlocutor was that I could sign and that, despite being an American, I was interested in doing so with people from other countries. Ladd (2003) notes that the sign DEAF often functions as a first-person plural pronoun, and I have observed that among NSL users, a hearing person who is part of a larger deaf group—such as a hearing interpreter traveling with a deaf sports team or a hearing friend joining a deaf organization's picnic—may be incorporated into the "we" indexed by DEAF. These patterns, like the Mexican man's comments just mentioned, suggest that in certain spaces hearing signers may be rendered at least partly commensurable with, and expected to engage in the same forms of social and linguistic labor as, deaf signers. In sum, deaf people themselves may or may not attend to deaf-hearing distinctions, and may prioritize other differences or similarities instead.

Along with my nationality and hearing status, the linguistic resources that I use to express myself and to understand others have strongly, and perhaps more obviously, affected the process and findings of my research. These linguistic resources include spoken, or mouthed, and written English (which is my first and primary language) and, in degrees of competency that vary across the times and places described, ASL, NSL, and IS (all of which I have learned in adolescence or adulthood and none of which I use as a primary language). Knowing English, for example, helped me to make sense of British signers' NSL, which was sometimes accompanied by mouthed English words, while knowing NSL enabled me to notice and understand when Nepali women translated for each other. Although the relationship between IS and ASL is contested, I also have the strong sense that my familiarity with ASL aided my (partial) understanding of IS in several of the contexts analyzed here. At the same time, I am very much aware that many deaf signers are exponentially more skilled than I am at communicating not only in sign languages but also between and across them, and deaf informal interpreters have helped me to understand other signers on countless occasions. In this chapter, therefore, I try to be careful not to equate what I do and do not understand with others' understanding.

The World Federation of the Deaf General Assembly[6]

In July 2007 the WFD held its Fifteenth World Congress, an international extravaganza attended by several thousand people, mostly deaf, from more than 125 countries. At the World Congress, the WFD provided teams of interpreters who signed in International Sign and Lengua de Signos Española (Spanish Sign Language). Plenary lectures were also voice translated and captioned in English and Spanish. Along with these institutionally sponsored interpreters, I often saw, seated in the audience, national sign language interpreters around whom signers of a given language would cluster.

The congress was preceded by a meeting of the general assembly (GA), the WFD's governing body, composed of up to two deaf delegates from each of the

---

[6] This section's material and argument overlap with Green 2014a.

WFD's "Ordinary Members," the official term for national members. In stark contrast to congress events, the meeting of the GA neither provided nor allowed IS or national sign language interpreters. Instead, the delegates were expected to communicate with each other directly, using IS to the best of their abilities. To help facilitate this process, a workshop held the day before the two-day GA meeting included a brief introduction to IS vocabulary relevant to the GA's work. At this event, interpreters were permitted, and I witnessed some participants turn repeatedly to watch interpreters.

During the meeting itself, delegates sat in alphabetical order by country toward the front of a spacious auditorium, while observers sat at the back. Board members facilitated from the stage, where delegates also sometimes stood to ask questions or offer commentary. Given the number of delegates, their diverse linguistic backgrounds, and their varied experiences at WFD-sponsored and other international events, it is unsurprising that I observed delegates produce very different forms of sign (there was less variation among board members). Both board members and other delegates were conscious of these differences. On occasion, signers were asked to repeat what they said. Several times, signers were advised, either during the meeting or afterwards, not to use signing that looked (too much) like ASL and not (enough) like an expected form of IS. As discussed in Green (2014a), these exchanges reveal how a single utterance might be evaluated by some people as an appropriate instantiation of IS and by others as belonging to a national sign language and thus not to IS. For my purposes here, these kinds of judgments provide evidence that participants were keenly attuned to the forms that other participants produced. While from one vantage point we might think of such judgments as forms of linguistic monitoring or control, from another we can consider them to be part of the process of jointly working to produce signs that were likely to be widely understood. Despite this process, the intention was not always achieved; some delegates and observers directly told me that they did not fully understand IS.

Occasionally, board members went beyond asking delegates to repeat themselves and actually re-signed what a delegate had said. While not especially frequent, the presence of informal interpreting in this most formal/institutional of settings shows how engrained it is in deaf practices and processes of negotiating cross-linguistic communication. A board member, Kamal, later told me that at board meetings, another board member, Niklas, was able to understand what everyone present said and also to translate what they said into a form of IS that everyone—or at the least Kamal himself—could easily understand. In fact, Kamal said that while he only understood about half of what some other board members said, he could understand all of what Niklas said. When the board dealt with documents written in English, Niklas also translated into IS for the members who were not proficient English readers. It is worth mentioning that I also found Niklas very easy to understand. Kamal's and my different linguistic and cultural backgrounds combined with our shared sense that Niklas was not only consistently comprehensible but also mesmerizing to watch hints at the level of skill involved in using IS in a way that is clear and compelling to diverse audience members.

The way that Kamal and I could understand some IS utterances more than others also suggests that at the GA, informal interpreters were translating not from one language to another, which is how we tend to think of interpreting, but rather within IS, from one version or instantiation of it to another. We see a similar pattern in the following example, as deaf Nepalis translate from foreign signers' novice NSL into expert NSL. Before moving to the first of two scenes based in Nepal, however, I question why the GA does not employ a team of IS interpreters or allow national sign language interpreters.

As I have shown, delegates did not always understand each other and sometimes had to repeat themselves or re-sign what others said. What is more, not all delegates supported the policy of IS/direct communication (see Green 2014a). In general, I observed that participants from Western nations were more able to understand IS than their non-Western counterparts (there were exceptions of course, and I met delegates from non-Western countries who quickly learned IS). This pattern, arising from the relationship of (some forms of) IS to Western sign languages and/or from more frequent opportunities for Western than non-Western deaf people to participate in international events where more institutional forms of IS are used, articulates in troubling ways with broader geopolitical disparities in both deaf and hearing worlds. I think it is important both to acknowledge this and to consider what social dynamics are at stake other than, or in addition to, entrenched global inequalities. Put another way, what is specifically deaf about the GA's commitment to IS?

Direct communication as a value and a practice is central to both of these questions: why does the GA not use interpreters and what is deaf about this policy? As I have stated elsewhere, my sense is that if the GA employed interpreters, even deaf interpreters, the meeting would no longer be experienced as one that functioned through direct communication (Green 2014a, 458). Directness is especially valued in this space of deaf international governance because it contrasts with deaf people's frequent need for interpreting in hearing spaces and because it affirms that deaf people are unique in their capacity to communicate across difference. After all, the United Nations relies on spoken language interpreting. Moreover, if interpreters were employed, delegates' attention likely would shift toward the interpreters and away from the social process of working to understand and be understood in IS. In other words, delegates would not have to engage in the joint work required to communicate in the absence of a shared language. As suggested above, this work is itself valued and is caught up in—making possible and made possible by—the production of deaf sameness across difference.

DEAF GLOBAL XCHANGE'S WOMEN'S DAY PROGRAM

Several years after the 2007 Congress, I attended a program in Kathmandu put on by the women participants of Deaf Global Xchange (DGX) in celebration of Women's Day. DGX was conducted between Nepal and Britain for six months during 2009–10 and included roughly even numbers of young men and women ages eighteen to twenty-five, nine from each country, plus British and Nepali coordinators.[7] Participants from both countries spent three months in England, followed by three months in Nepal.

Held in March 2010, the Women's Day program was conducted in NSL and consisted of self-introductions by British and Nepali DGX participants, a group

---

[7] These details are taken from field notes and from Voluntary Service Overseas, or VSO (2009).

activity in which we were asked to discuss whether being deaf or being a woman was more important, and three individual presentations. There were about sixty women in the room, which had been rented especially for the occasion. Other than the six or so British DGX participants, I was the only non-Nepali. The Nepali attendees included women with a range of language backgrounds. Some women, for example, were leaders or active members of deaf organizations; they frequently socialized with other NSL signers and some had a great deal of experience communicating with foreigners. Also present were students from a residential vocational training program, some of whom were proficient NSL signers and others of whom were less experienced or had just begun to learn the language. The British women, meanwhile, had been learning NSL for about five months, beginning while the DGX participants were in England, with significantly more exposure since they had come to Nepal seven weeks prior to the Women's Day program.[8]

Following the self-introductions, one of the British women opened the next activity by signing, "Look inside yourself, you are deaf and a woman. Which is more important?" On the chalkboard the question, "Which first?" was written in both English and Nepali, with two other words written underneath, "deaf" and "woman." One of the Nepali leaders briefly re-signed this question and then instructed us to get in groups that included a mix of educational levels. We discussed the issue in our small groups and then came back together as a large group to share our answers.

After the conclusion of the group activity, one of the British DGX participants stood up and gave a short talk about Rosa Parks and the US civil rights movement. Her signing looked very different from fluent NSL, so when she finished her presentation, a Nepali woman re-signed what she had said. Another British DGX participant then gave a presentation about the suffragette movement in England. Several women commented on the clarity of her NSL, which I noticed too, and her presentation was not re-signed (at least not in full; audience members may have interpreted parts of it for each other). Finally, the British coordinator gave a talk about the importance of sharing one's feelings, especially during difficult times, with other deaf women.

This description of the day's activities indicates that the British participants were expected to be able to talk about complex political and social topics after only several months of learning NSL. The Nepali audience, similarly, was expected to understand foreign signers when they used NSL. To a lesser or greater extent, these expectations were fulfilled. At the same time, several practices indicated that understanding was not always achieved. Two British presenters made sure to say that audience members should tell them if they did not understand. My sense, however, is that most Nepalis are unlikely to explicitly stop a speaker during a presentation. I say this not to criticize the British women's communicative strategies (I have no doubt that I have told Nepali audiences the same thing when presenting about my research) but rather to show that signers in international settings are aware that they may not be understood and that how they try to manage this possibility is culturally particular.

Although I did not see anyone directly ask for clarification, Nepali signers certainly recognized potential gaps and sought to bridge them. They occasionally

---

[8] I thank Abigail Gorman for explaining the British participants' learning process and timeline.

offered corrections to the person presenting, and throughout the program I noticed women in the audience interpreting for each other. Several times, as mentioned above, a Nepali woman stood in the presenter's area and re-signed a British signer's NSL into more fluent NSL. As with the interpretation I provided to Dinakar, in the scene with which I opened this chapter, these interpretations were not always exact, at least from my perspective. As an example, I understood a British woman to say that when we make a mistake we should learn from it so as not to do it again, and I understood a Nepali woman's translation to mean that when we make a mistake we should forget it and move on.

These informal interpreting practices—offering corrections, re-signing in the audience, and re-signing for the entire audience—indicate that not everyone was able to understand, or at the least, that those interpreting assumed that others had not understood. At the same time, informal interpreting implies that the people doing the interpreting have understood. Most of the signers I saw informally interpreting were women who frequently socialize with other deaf people, actively attend deaf events, and have at least some experience communicating with foreigners. In other words, understanding across difference is as much a skill as expressing oneself across difference.

When the program ended, I explicitly asked a few Nepali women if they had understood the presentations. While several said yes, two women told me that they had not understood everything and had missed a little because of language issues. These two women often spend time with other deaf signers and have held positions in deaf organizations. At least one has had a great deal of experience signing with foreigners, too. This fact suggests that other attendees, with less such experience, probably also had not understood everything and perhaps had understood even less.

As with the WFD's GA, then, we might wonder why this event did not include a formal interpreter. An initial explanation might be that the presence of a formal interpreter would have been disrespectful of the British participants' earnest efforts to learn NSL. Juxtaposed with the GA's language policy, however, it becomes apparent that the absence of formal interpreters does more than recognize individuals' language-learning efforts. In the context of an exchange program, it also signals the shared expectation that deaf signers can quickly learn a foreign sign language and that users of that language can understand the foreign signers. Of course, the absence of formal interpreters not only signals an expectation, it also creates an opportunity for direct communication to occur. Events like this one serve as social spaces in which deaf signers affirm that they can talk to and understand each other across differences, even if imperfectly. The practice of informal interpreting helps some participants to understand when they might not otherwise have been able to do so. It thus validates the importance of both direct communication and understanding, while simultaneously negotiating the potential conflict between them.

AN INTERNATIONAL DINNER

A month following the DGX Women's Day event, I was invited to attend a leadership program for deaf young adults in Lalitpur, the city adjoining Kathmandu to the south. Partway through the day, Manoj and Abhinas, two Nepali men then in their late thirties/early forties whom I have known since 2002, joined the audience along with a guest, Genevieve, a deafblind Canadian woman in her early thirties who had arrived in Nepal five days earlier. Like many deaf foreigners who come to Nepal, she was staying at a well-known deaf-owned hotel and had met Manoj and Abhinas through the proprietors. Toward the end of the day, the program facilitators invited her to give a brief talk. In International Sign, Genevieve told us a little bit about growing up deaf and learning she would become blind and about her current experiences as a deafblind woman traveling around the world. While I found her signing easy to follow, I talked afterward with my good friend, Purnima, a deaf Nepali woman in her twenties, who said she had not understood much of the presentation. This contrast points again to how even intentionally international forms of signed communication may be differentially understandable to people with different—though in Purnima's and my case, overlapping—sets of linguistic resources. Of course, I do not know how representative either my or my friend's understandings were of other audience members' experiences.

Following the program, six of us decided to go out for dinner: Manoj, Abhinas, Purnima, Genevieve, and me, along with Purnima's and my close friend, Indra, a deaf Nepali man in his mid-twenties whom Manoj and Abhinas had also known for many years. As a group, we asymmetrically shared two languages and two modalities. Genevieve's primary language is ASL, which I could use easily though by no means perfectly (and perhaps it was this shared linguistic background that helped me to understand her IS). Abhinas and Manoj had also picked up a great deal of ASL (and other foreign) vocabulary over several decades of meeting deaf visitors to Nepal and were very accustomed to interacting with foreigners. Indra had also spent time with foreign signers (I remember him telling me, for example, about guiding two deaf people from Spain around the Kathmandu Valley for a day), although significantly less than the older men. He had a good English vocabulary but almost no ASL. Purnima did not frequently spend much time with signing foreigners other than me (we lived near each other, and by the time she and I met I was fairly proficient in NSL) and knew very little English and no ASL. The four deaf Nepalis, meanwhile, were all fluent NSL signers, though of two different generations who sometimes complain about not understanding each other perfectly. At this point in time I was relatively fluent in NSL. Genevieve had picked up what I commented in my field notes was an "impressive amount of NSL vocabulary" in the few days she had been in Nepal, and like Abhinas and Manoj had extensive experience communicating with foreigners. In terms of modality, all of us, including Genevieve, had many years of experience with visual sign. Genevieve's vision was partial, and she used visual as well as tactile reception. With the exception of Genevieve herself, however, none of us had significant previous experience with tactile sign.

As we made our way on foot and in a small three-wheeled bus to Kathmandu's tourist district and then settled in for a meal at a popular Tibetan restaurant, two noteworthy patterns emerged from our interactions. First, Purnima was initially reluctant to engage in direct tactile communication with Genevieve. Instead, she would ask Indra or me to say something to Genevieve: "tell her [this]." At one point, Abhinas literally tried to place Purnima's hand in Genevieve's, and Genevieve told him not to force her. Nevertheless, we encouraged Purnima to try to talk with Genevieve directly, and within ten minutes Purnima was happily chatting with Genevieve as they walked through the crowded streets. In other words, while as a group we requested and provided informal interpreting, we also pushed for an effort to be made toward direct communication, with Genevieve drawing a line between encouraging and physically intervening. This description demonstrates how the social value placed on direct communication across difference, here linguistic as well as sensory, gets reproduced and even explicitly reinforced in specific interactions. It also powerfully shows how when people are *willing* to engage, communication, however imperfect, becomes possible (see Green 2014b).

The second pattern became evident as we sat around the dinner table talking. While our impromptu party was characterized by linguistic, sensory, generational, and national differences, the resources we shared from NSL and ASL, the extensive affordances of signed and gestured communication, and a joint commitment to doing our best enabled us to communicate easily and pleasurably. Our conversation that evening was lively, as we told stories, made jokes, and discussed topics ranging from an HIV/AIDS educational program in the south of Nepal to Genevieve's recent travels in Southeast Asia. I was struck by the degree to which we were able to understand each other, as well as by the flexibility that we exhibited over the course of the evening. Sometimes, for example, either Abhinas (who was sitting next to Genevieve and could therefore use tactile sign) or I (who had the most command of ASL other than Genevieve herself) would interpret for Genevieve (who knew less NSL than anyone else, having been in Nepal only a few days). While at times we all talked together, at other times we had dialogues in ASL or NSL, or across these languages, and there were moments when multiple conversations in multiple codes, and mixtures of codes, proceeded at once. Not everyone was able to follow all the threads of talk at all times, though it felt like a given that if someone asked for an interpretation it would be provided. As we ate, laughed, and signed, I sensed that we were morally oriented to shared time and space, to the experience of being together, as much as to shared reference. This example points to how fully mutual understanding is not always the goal of deaf communication across difference, although to be sure, we also often sought and achieved understanding, both with and without informal interpreting.

CONCLUSION

In this chapter I have shown how signers use informal interpreting while engaging in direct communication across linguistic and other differences. My claim is not that informal interpreting only occurs in international deaf contexts. The practices detailed here are reminiscent of communicative strategies used in other settings (see also Crasborn and Hiddinga, this volume, on the relationship between international deaf communication and strategies deaf people use to communicate with hearing people). For example, I have witnessed and taken part in intranational informal interpreting between sign and speech, such as at English-language events in the US that do not have official ASL interpreters. I also have observed and been told about informal interpreting among signers of a single nationality, both when all the signers are deaf, such as among deaf Nepalis whose language varieties are different, and between hearing and deaf signers, such as when a deaf signer interprets a hearing teacher's Nepali-influenced signing into fluent NSL (see also Forestal 2014, cited in Mindess 2014, on informal interpreting in educational settings).

Nevertheless, I contend, there is something particular about the social value and work of informal interpreting in international deaf spaces because of the importance of direct communication in these contexts. While it is possible to imagine that formal interpreters would have facilitated more consistent understanding for each and every participant, especially in the more institutionally structured settings, I have argued that formal interpreting would be experienced as destructive of the experience of direct communication, an experience that signers find pleasurable and valuable. Informal interpreting, in contrast to formal interpreting, affirms the capacity of deaf people to communicate directly with each other; after all, the person or persons interpreting are themselves participants in the ongoing interactions. Certainly, the act of interpreting acknowledges that not all participants understand each other in the same way or to the same degree. Yet because the interpreting is informal, differences in understanding are incorporated into the process and work of direct communication.

The particularity of informal interpreting in international deaf contexts also can be understood in relation to the sense, mentioned in the introduction, that sign is what unites deaf people, what makes them the same even when they are different. At the DGX event described above, a deaf woman from Britain told the audience, "In here [i.e., in this room] we are all deaf, we all have one language, or maybe two, British [Sign Language] and Nepali Sign Language." This statement reflects a tension in how deaf people think about and experience sign. On the one hand, sign is a modality that unites deaf people and enables them to understand each other across linguistic differences, and on the other hand, sign languages are separate and distinct.[9] The way the signer moves from a declaration of sameness ("we all have one language") to a recognition of difference ("maybe two") articulates with the experiential tension described in this chapter: deaf people can communicate, often with ease, across languages, and yet understanding is not always achieved. In relation to the broader themes of this book, then, looking at informal interpreting enables us to track how sameness and difference are not mutually exclusive. On the contrary, they coexist, and they are both produced and negotiated in signed interactions in spaces where deaf people from different national and linguistic backgrounds come together. In fact, it is the weaving together of sameness and difference that makes direct communication with signers of other languages such an important and pleasurable dimension of international deaf encounters.

---

[9] This tension between "language" and "languages" is not unique to the current historical moment. Focused on the nineteenth century in Western Europe, Ladd (2003, 110) argues that deaf signers "were very well aware that other countries used different sign languages" at the same time that they celebrated the "'universal nature of sign'" (Ladd 2003, 110, citing Mottez 1993, 151; see also Murray 2007, 2). See also Gulliver this volume.

REFERENCES

Forestal, E. M. 2014. "Deaf Interpreters: The Dynamics of Their Interpreting Processes." In *Deaf Interpreters at Work: International Insights*, edited by R. Adam, C. Stone, S. D. Collins, and M. Metzger, 29–50. Washington, DC: Gallaudet University Press.

Green, E. M. 2014a. "Building the Tower of Babel: International Sign, Linguistic Commensuration, and Moral Orientation." *Language in Society* 43: 445–65.

———. 2014b. "The Nature of Signs: Nepal's Deaf Society, Local Sign, and the Production of Communicative Sociality." PhD diss., University of California, Berkeley.

Hiddinga, A., and O. Crasborn. 2011. "Signed Languages and Globalization. *Language in Society* 40:483–505.

Ladd, P. 2003. *Understanding Deaf Culture: In Search of Deafhood*. Clevedon, UK: Multilingual Matters.

Mindess, A. 2014. "Are Hearing Interpreters Responsible to Pave the Way for Deaf Interpreters?" Accessed November 19, 2014. http://www.streetleverage.com/2014/08/are-hearing-interpreters-responsible-to-pave-the-way-for-deaf-interpreters.

Moody, B. 1989. "International Communication among Deaf People." Unpublished manuscript received from the WFD in response to author's request for information on IS.

Mottez, B. 1993. "The Deaf Mute Banquet and the Birth of the Deaf Movement." In *Looking Back*, edited by R. Fischer and H. Lane. Hamburg: Signum.

Murray, J. 2007. "'One Touch of Nature Makes the Whole World Kin': The Transnational Lives of Deaf Americans, 1870–1924." PhD diss., University of Iowa.

VSO. 2009. "World's First Deaf Xchange Volunteer Scheme Launches in Preston." Press Release. Accessed November 5, 2014. http://www.vso.org.uk/news/worlds-first-deaf-xchange-volunteer-scheme-launches-in-preston.

Zeshan, U., K. Sagara, and A. Bradford. n.d. "Multilingual and Multimodal Aspects of 'Cross-signing': A Study of Emerging Communication in the Domain of Numerals." Accessed February 26, 2014. http://www.uclan.ac.uk/research/environment/projects/assets/islands_multisign_cross_signing.pdf.

8 | # Challenging Sign Language Lineages and Geographies: The Case of Eritrean, Finnish, and Swedish Sign Languages

Rezenet Tsegay Moges

When I was signing, they actually understood! I was stunned. I understood all of their signs. My signs were really theirs! I was embarrassed. I already knew that Eritrea and Sweden shared the same sign language but after I saw with my own eyes, I wondered: Where's Eritrean Sign Language? Where is really our language?

A member in a sign language planning group in Eritrea named Nazret Mussa signed this quote. She is a Deaf Eritrean from a Deaf family. She was selected to visit Sweden to learn more about the particular country of her school's supporting missionary and was flabbergasted when she could converse easily with signers there. She knew the history of Eritrean Sign Language (EriSL) previously, but it took a three-thousand-mile flight for her to realize the very close relationship between her language and those of Nordic countries, specifically Finland and Sweden. She felt that she had been robbed of the pride of possessing her own indigenous sign language, instead of just a copy of a deaf European country's language, which led to her realization that it is vital to have one's own culturally identified language.

In this chapter, I present a "multiplicity of language ideologies" (Gal 1993) that are in tension as the result of the incorporation of Finnish signs in EriSL. Finnish Sign Language (FinSL) is closely related to its parental language Swedish Sign Language; hence the similarity between EriSL and Swedish Sign Language in the example. The incorporation of Finnish signs in EriSL happened because of interventions of Finnish and Swedish missionaries using Finnish Sign Language. As I discuss, indigenous Eritrean signs are potentially at risk because of being dominated by a higher status and authoritative language, FinSL. After users realized this, EriSL underwent a process of language purification that I call "demissionization" (Moges 2011), which a group of language planners in Eritrea initiated, removing the foreign signs that did not possess congruity in Eritrean culture. Language planners felt that there was an excessive sameness through a shared language between two very different countries, ethnicities, and customs. Demissionization is one of the enforcements that protects cultural difference and linguistic independence.

I argue that the ideology of DEAF-SAME can go amiss, and I do so by sharing individuals' narratives and discussing the history of linguistic influences and elicited sign similarities. I first present the background of the Deaf Eritrean community and the languages they use. I then discuss methodology, including a consideration of my position as a Deaf Eritrean-American anthropologist. Next, I include narratives from the Deaf Eritrean community describing their thoughts about the history and present of EriSL. I then provide a brief overview of the demissionization process of EriSL through the creation of a dictionary. Subsequently, with several examples, I describe how the language planners decide which incongruent Nordic signs to eradicate and replace with indigenous signs. Finally, this chapter concludes with some discussion of my argument: that the romanticized notion of DEAF-SAME needs to be restricted, especially in terms of language, or else indigenous/native sign languages will perish.

BACKGROUND

Eritrea is located in Africa, between the Red Sea and Ethiopia. The first documented data about sign language in Eritrea, from 1955, was related to the establishment of a school for the deaf in Keren by a missionary group from Sweden, called Deaf African/Dovas Afrikan Mission (DAM). This same missionary group organized several aid projects internationally, such as in Tanzania (Lee 2012) and Nicaragua (Senghas 1997). They sent the first Finnish-signing hearing volunteer, Elsie Roos (Tekleab 1987), to teach English, using FinSL with the Manual Swedish Alphabet.[1] After that, other Finnish volunteers were sent. None of Eritrean native languages (such as Tigrinya, Arabic, or Tigry) were taught until 1979 when the war between Eritrea and Ethiopia intensified; consequently, Finnish volunteers fled and hearing Eritrean natives started teaching in Tigrinya and EriSL. The natives opened a second institution in Asmara as a day school and a safe area at a higher altitude. Today there are still only two deaf schools in Eritrea; the one in Asmara provides less interaction in sign language for the deaf schoolchildren than the first school (in Keren), a residential institution that provides full immersion in a sign language environment.

Because of the involvement of both Swedish and Finnish missionaries in Deaf Eritrean education (the Keren school is still sponsored by Deaf African Mission [DAM] of Sweden), members from the Deaf Eritrean community were often uncertain of whether the signs they used were imported from Sweden or Finland. Further complicating things, Finnish and Swedish sign languages are closely related to each other. Bergman and Engberg-Pedersen (2010) showed that an influential Deaf graduate from the deaf school in Stockholm founded the first Deaf Finnish

---

[1] A manual alphabet is a fingerspelling system that codes each letter for both sign and spoken languages.

school and imported Swedish signs to Finland in 1859. Thus, Swedish Sign Language is the parent language of FinSL. However, because of the history of the first schoolteachers at the Keren school being Finnish, the language contact situation in Eritrea is between EriSL and FinSL. EriSL shares 70 percent of Finnish signs (Moges 2011) and the cognates shared between both languages places EriSL in the same language family as FinSL, yet it is distinctive because of its indigenous lexicon (see Parkhurst and Parkhurst 2003).

The nature of EriSL depends on who is being asked and where they live. My observation of EriSL is that there are at least eight different characteristics that affect each Deaf Eritrean's repertoire of languages: educational attainment, hearing level, area of residence, (multi)language status, language modality, age group, religion, and tribal identity (Moges 2011, 2015). The range of language repertoires can be placed on a continuum roughly summarized as follows: (1) indigenous/village signs, (2) lexicons with the most missionary-imported signs, and (3) codified Tigrinya (and/or Arabic if one is a Muslim). When a deaf individual is from a village and does not have any formal schooling, they most likely use signs that are created and used in villages (closely related to local gestures). Arguably, gestures often are the initial form before incorporation as codified signs in a sign language (Wilcox 2007). These rural dwellers used a different lexicon *and* grammar than urban signers, and a number of their signs were incorporated in the EriSL dictionary during the demissionization process (see further). Not much is known about these gestures/signs used in villages (which I call "indigenous" in this chapter); for example, more research could point out whether there are multiple gesture systems and/or village sign languages in Eritrea and the degree of uniformity of these. If a deaf signer is more than forty-five years old and has been schooled, their language typically contains EriSL in English using the Swedish fingerspelling alphabet. If a person has fluency in both EriSL and spoken Tigrinya (typically late-deafened or hard-of-hearing people), the signed language will be more like Signed Tigrinya (Moges 2011). In sum, EriSL today has a complex language history, due to the past six decades of linguistic changes.

METHODOLOGY

After twenty-five years of listening tirelessly to stories from my Eritrean-born hearing parents in America reminiscing about "back home," I flew to Eritrea for my first time, for a pilot master's study in 2006 to investigate the EriSL documentation process. I had a personal experience of DEAF-SAME during an assembly for Sunday service watching several deaf children, ages ranging between five years old and adolescence, signing songs. When a teacher asked me to introduce myself on the stage, I was completely unprepared for the request. There were some called-out inquiries from the approximately ninety chattering schoolchildren in the audience, guessing that I was a European and a hearing person. Correcting everybody on that stage, I fingerspelled my name in EriSL fingerspelling: RE-ZE-NE-T T-SE-GA-Y. All the children's little flapping arms dropped and their eyes widened. They realized instantly that I was an Eritrean from learning my archaic first name and my father's[2] first name (which counts as a "surname" in Eritrea).

---

[2] *Moges* is technically my paternal grandfather's first name that my siblings and I had to adopt under US immigration law.

When the teacher and pastor communicated with me in sign language, the deaf children saw that I was Deaf too, just like them. Soon after, they swarmed over asking me, YOU DEAF SAME US? I replied with glee, EWE![3] ("yes" in Tigrinya, the majority-spoken language of Eritrea) The next question was, ERITREAN TOO? "EWE!" I experienced this double sameness as an advantage during my field-work. There also were disadvantages of being a native anthropologist in some respects (i.e., sharing the same ethnic group identity/ies; see Jones 1970) and studying my own heritage country (i.e., the difficulty of time management, jug-gling free time between my relatives and my research participants, and keeping a perspective as objective as possible).

During two different periods of stay spanning from two to three months in 2006 and 2009, I traveled alone around Eritrea, which is unusual for any person of Eritrean descent. It is rather a tradition that Eritrean parents would take their child to visit "back home," as my parents said nostalgically. My first Eritrea trip was more of my own personal journey, connecting with my extended relatives while I was exploring if a master's thesis study was feasible. The second visit was better planned anthropological fieldwork to gather specific data for my thesis. My thesis focused on how and who would make the decision on lexicon change in EriSL, in the process of demissionization.

The focal group of my study was Deaf Eritrean urbanites who are members of the Eritrean National Association of the Deaf (EriNAD), which an employee claimed had two thousand members in 2010. There are EriNAD branch offices situated in three major cities: in Asmara (the capital city, where the day school was founded), Keren (where the residential school is), and Menderfera. My reason for focusing on urbanites rather than villagers (or both) was to draw in the voices of those with the most metalinguistic awareness, political consciousness, and a deeper level of understanding of borrowed lexicons. I did qualitative research on the process of the EriSL documentation and dictionary project (and the demission-ization activities in this project), consisting of interviews, lexicostatistics (using archival materials and comparing Eritrean to Finnish signs), and observation of some of the language planning meetings, which happened once a week with seven language planners at the Asmara office of EriNAD.

The Deaf employees at EriNAD, who were my research participants, were multilingual in several languages: Tigrinya, EriSL, and English. The EriNAD employees could also fingerspell using the International Manual Alphabet. I am a native American Sign Language (ASL) / English signer/speaker and never learned Tigrinya while growing up. I learned Manual Ge'ez[4] only by the end of my first stay, but I learned EriSL early enough to have initial conversations with employees. Several Deaf people outside the EriNAD centers would occasionally ask me to reply back in ASL when we first met. In response, I politely declined and explained

---

[3] This sign is also borrowed from FSL that read as KYLLA ("yes" in Finnish). It is signed with one hand opening-closing with fingers shaped as bent-5 to O. On another note, this sign frequently confused me, appearing to be NO in American Sign Language but the number of fingers used is in significance here.

[4] See Moges 2015 for the full description on the manual codes composed with handshapes and movement in the Eritrean fingerspelling system accompanying Tigrinya's syllabic-consonant letter system.

to them that I wanted to sign in their language. There were a few employees who teasingly tested me in front of other Deaf Eritreans by signing some American phrases to see my reaction. My replies would consistently be in Eritrean signs, and they would laugh in admiration and call me SPONGE for absorbing their signs. My fluency in EriSL was intermediate and I used "broken EriSL," since I knew most of the signs but not the proper grammatical structure of the language. All in all, the intelligibility of conversations that I had with Deaf urbanites in general and the sign language planning group in particular was highly functional as opposed to my brief unsuccessful conversations with either villagers or non-schooled Deaf people during which I relied on EriNAD employees for translations.

VOICES FROM THE COMMUNITY

In an interview with Hiruy Gebremeskel, a former chairperson of a branch office of EriNAD in Keren, I asked him, "Can you explain why EriSL is undergoing language changes?" and he replied:

> We were signing and some Swedes visited and signed with us here. We were amazed how similar our signs were! Almost identical! Seldom, we would clarify some slight differences. In Ethiopia, America, Sudan, and Germany, their signs are . . . entirely different! It's great to sign, but . . . other people [foreign visitors] ask if our sign language is actually Eritrean or Swedish. 'Whose sign language is this? Eritrean?' 'No, Swedish.' They [foreign visitors] would say, 'Eritreans should themselves take action with their own signs.' Yes, we must mend and achieve our own EriSL. In the past, we got funding from USAID . . . for new EriSL from our ambition. All Deaf will be happy because all people will applaud after finding out about Eritrean signs. It is extremely important for us, Eritreans.

Another participant during my fieldwork, who preferred to remain anonymous, told me that he traveled in Finland and he shared a book from his travels, which showed basic signs in FinSL. He was grateful for the educational prosperity in Eritrea; however he was embarrassed to sign another country's sign language. He tried to approach this sensitive issue with the first two Eritrean teachers of the Deaf school but they replied discouragingly that "it was already too much work," implying that learning and adopting the missionary language was enough. This resonates with Charles Ferguson's statement about the convenience of teaching in a dominant language:

> The easiest choice for the missionary is to use his own language, teaching it to the people he is dealing with and then proclaiming or explaining his message through it. This choice has often been made, and indeed it has many practical advantages, the chief of which are the immediate utility of written and recorded materials in the missionary's language which do not require translation, the possibility of using additional missionaries

without special language training, and the possibility of more advanced study by promising local individuals at the institutions of the missionary's home country. (Ferguson 1968, 256)

I argue that missionary sign languages function similarly to spoken and written languages: they are another venue for linguistic imperialism in that missionaries use their sign languages instead of the local sign varieties while providing deaf education. The literature on sign language history identifies the historical figures responsible for large impact language transmission: Edward Huet with French Sign Language (Langue des Signes Française, LSF) to Mexico, and Brazil (Lane 1984), and Reverend Andrew Foster for ASL to West Africa (Kiyaga and Moores 2003; Nyst 2010).

The second quote comes from Eden Tareke, one of the language planners, in regards to missionaries that still support their deaf schools financially:

I don't think that the missionaries would be against this dictionary but they still *must accept* this because this [book consists of what is] *traditional* to our language. *Real* Eritrean tradition. This [dictionary] accompanies our culture.

These quotes reveal that Eritreans have a deep investment in demissionizing their language and developing a sign language that is reflective of Eritrean culture.

Language Planning on Demissionizing EriSL

A group called Sign Language Researchers (SLR) was responsible for language planning and the development of an EriSL dictionary. They attempted to engage in "demissionization," which is a purification process of disassociating historical linkage from a parental language by inserting indigenous lexicons from villages and excising foreign terms (Moges 2011). The SLR consisted of seven Eritrean language planners: five were Deaf, four were female, and three were male. The hearing participants were both fluent signers and one of them is a linguist (graduated from the local university with a concentration on linguistics of spoken languages) who trained the rest of the language planners. This group was funded through EriNAD and those planners mostly volunteer their time. They sometimes went in pairs to Eritrean villages to collect various indigenous signs and then returned to their meetings to compare notes and to agree unanimously on the most aesthetic sign for each lexicon. The language planners decided on a general aesthetic in distinguishing signs by how well they flowed phonologically (handshape, movement, and placement), without duplicating any other sign or provoking improper signals. In these discussions, sometimes SLR reached an agreement within five minutes; other times they were stalled for a half hour in a heated discussion over which sign would portray the definition accurately or "more aesthetically" (see Moges 2011 for a more in-depth description). In 2010, after four years of work, they published their first-ever dictionary of Modern EriSL. The dictionary included almost two thousand signs with 20 percent of previously borrowed Finnish signs eliminated and replaced with revived indigenous/village signs or neologisms to reinstate absent translations of Tigrinya terms.

The chairperson of the EriNAD, Okbamichael Tewelde, and the secretary of the EriNAD board, Eden Tareke, were the key language planners. In interviews, they claimed that it was impossible to eliminate every Finnish-Swedish sign or this dictionary project would not be successful, as signers in Eritrea would reject such a radically new dictionary. The language planners focused primarily on those signs that were dramatically incompatible with Eritrean customs and culture such as WATER, BREAD, and FATHER (more explanations later in the section).

The recognition of the shared language provoked many Deaf Eritreans to insist they had no sign language of their own, even though many urbanites already knew about various existing village signs. In addition to that belief, they saw themselves not as an independent linguistic-cultural minority group but as Eritrean-Finnish community members using FinSL. SLR instead prioritized the values of their cultural identity over sharing the linguistic minority property of Deaf Finns. Thus, the SLR attempted to demissionize their imported language in order to gain linguistic ownership of their sign language.

The process of demissionization is not specific to Eritrea. A movement against the ASL-influenced languages in some African countries is also happening (i.e., in Tanzania). I have witnessed fury expressed by Deaf Nigerians claiming that they have their own indigenous signs (not referring to Hausa Sign Language as described by Schmaling 2000), but there is no proper documentation about any attempted indigenization from ASL in Nigeria yet. There have been some similar reports of attempted indigenization in Tanzanian Sign Language (Lee 2012, 100–1) when two deaf and one hearing linguist "cleaned" out foreign words from their dictionary to connect their sign language to their culture. In a similar sense, several Deaf Maori language planners registered all of the foreign concepts from British Sign Language that were not compatible with their native culture (Locker McKee et al. 2007). This group attempted to revive and/or create neologisms, such as proper greetings in Maori culture. In Zambia (Serpell and Mbewe 1990, 283), where Dutch missionaries worked and some other Western European countries and the United States had provided aid, deaf people would sometimes clarify the "etymological origin" of foreign signs and then adopt them if those signs were culturally appropriate and practical. Such examples focus mostly on culturally appropriate signs and not on languages as a whole. It is also important to note that there are broader issues related to language ideologies in relation to native and foreign sign languages. For example, Nyst pointed out that ASL is considered to have higher status and tends to be adopted unless there are "culture-specific" terms when local signs are used (Nyst 2010).

During every interview I conducted with the language planners, the sign for WATER came up as the essential example of the difference between the sign languages of Eritrea and Finland. Figure 1 shows the borrowed sign from FinSL on the left while the right sign (fig. 2) is the replaced sign of a gesture from Eritrean villages.

The demissionized sign no longer carries the incongruous action-movement of taking water from an imaginary water-pump, as is the case in the Finnish sign. This example reveals that Deaf Eritreans and Deaf Finns do not share mutual customs in retrieving water. Similarly in Nigeria, Schmaling (2003) used the ASL sign for APPLE as an example of incoherence as there are no apples in the region in which

FIGURE 1. **Borrowed sign of** VESI **(**WATER **in Finnish) from FinSL.**

FIGURE 2. **Village sign of** MAI **(**WATER **in Tigrinya).**

FIGURE 3. **Village sign of** BANI **(**BREAD **in Tigrinya).**

she studied. Nevertheless, the sign was incorporated into the sign language of the region. This example reveals Western customs infiltrating in a different ecological and cultural environment.

Another example is a village custom of eating (dry) bread, BANI, shown in Figure 3. From her data collection, Eden utilized this sign that she learned from a deaf villager emphasizing the crunchiness of the (stiff) bread. The alternative sign at schools used in Eritrea, as shown by Eden in Figure 4, is done in the same distinctive manner of Westerners putting together sliced bread, such as sandwiches (as shown Figure 5), which are not common as Eritrean meals. That sign resembles BRÖD (bread in Swedish) or LEIPÄ (bread in Finnish) as shown in Figure 5. The handshapes are vaguely different in featuring slightly cupped versus flat positions and the finger orientation is slightly different in a few degrees in the directional angles.

A third example of demissionizing and reviving the Eritrean words of FATHER/ABBO or EGZIABHER indicate the separation of the definitions and improved transliteration. Figure 6 portrays the sign imported from the missionaries,

FIGURE 4. School sign as influenced by the Finnish-Swedish sign of BREAD.

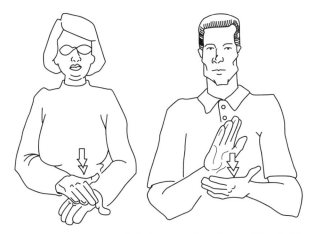

FIGURE 5. BRÖD (Swedish for BREAD) and LEIPÄ (Finnish).

FIGURE 6. Sign of EGZIABHER/FATHER-OF-GOD, now associated only to the religious reference.

Figure 7. Sign from villages, referring to the paternal role, *ABBO/FATHER*.

FATHER/EGZIABHER with its reference to the Christian concept of the Trinity. This was also used in reference to the paternal role, which reads in Tigrinya ABBO. The older school sign contains the prior religious meaning whereas the latter has been accepted by the language planners to revive a village sign referring to the father of the family by indexicalizing the chin area of a beard/goatee. The visual-gestural move of rubbing a beard indicates the wisdom of an elderly man, as shown in Figure 7.

A Concluding Remark on deaf-same

A variety of Deaf African refugees or prosperity seekers came to Eritrea and received assistance (such as advocacy and interpreting services) at the EriNAD. The interaction between Deaf local Eritreans and Africans from neighboring countries is generally unproblematic, regardless of linguistic difference between national sign languages. In this context, the concept of DEAF-SAME naturally seems to exist at the EriNAD centers in Eritrea between deaf Africans of the same racial background struggling with being Deaf, longing to belong, and hungering to communicate. These feelings are not shared with Deaf Finns or Swedes who visit the centers and sign supposedly in EriSL. In such situations, the racial difference between Eritrean and Nordic sign language users illuminated the excessive sameness and the fact that FinSL was a hierarchical language.

It takes an "ethnic awakening" for a Deaf person to realize their identity shared with other Deaf people by "increasingly defin[ing] themselves by the characteristics that lead to creation of relatively *separate and autonomous* communities of Deaf people" from the hearing world (Baker 1999, 130, emphasis added). I want to go further than this definition of ethnic awakening as a Deaf person to a point where ethnic awakening also includes metalinguistic awareness about histories of language development and the articulations of (Deaf) ethnicity and race identity. Excessive sameness imposes the notion of a singular DEAF-WORLD and a hegemonic language seeps into a different country through missioniziation.

In feeling uneasy about the similarities between Eritrean and Nordic missionary signs, Nazret and Hiruy felt that that their language had been colonized. The similarity in sign languages was excessive, and they did not recognize their different national cultures and identities. Such awakening aided the spread of metalinguistic awareness, which encouraged the SLR to inspect the historical linkage of their lexicons and to attempt to transform their language to a more distinct one representing their unique Deaf community, especially as an African group freeing themselves from their colonial history. The SLR in Eritrea imposed their ideology on EriSL through demissionization to move the lexicon of EriSL more towards their own Eritrean roots, by looking to villages for indigenous signs that were closer to those roots than FinSL.

Demissionization can remove the endangering and overpowering monolithic DEAF-SAME effect to promote (lexicon from) indigenous languages, and, in turn, the intersectionality of multiple ethnic identities will emerge (and be protected). As long as Deaf Eritreans experience DEAF-SAME with Deaf foreigners (including Deaf Finns and Swedes), demissionized EriSL embraces the indigenous culture of Eritreans. In other words, demissionization allows Deaf Eritreans to draw the line against excessive DEAF-SAME, manifested in using the same language. I regard DEAF-SAME as an overpowering narrative that risks reducing Deaf people's multiple ethnicities to a singular Deaf ethnicity. Going beyond ethnic awakening, the urban Deaf Eritrean community gained the will-power and capability to finally say with pride and without any doubt, "*Ewe*, this is (indigenous) Eritrean Sign Language!"

References

Baker, C. 1999. "Sign Language and the Deaf Community." In *Handbook of Language and Ethnic Identity*, edited by J. A. Fishman, 122–39. New York: Oxford University Press.

Bergman, B., and E. Engberg-Pedersen. 2010. "Transmission of Sign Languages in the Nordic Countries." In *Sign Languages*, edited by D. Brentari, 74–94. Cambridge, UK: Cambridge University Press.

Ferguson, C. A. 1968. "St. Stefan of Perm and Applied Linguistics." In *Language Problems of Developing Nations*, edited by J. A. Fishman, C. A. Ferguson, and J. Dasgupta, 253–66. New York: Wiley.

———. 1971. "Absence of Copula and the Notion of Simplicity: A Study of Normal Speech, Baby Talk, Foreign Talk, and Pidgins." In *Pidginization and Creolization of Languages*, 141–50. Cambridge, UK: Cambridge University Press.

Gal, S. 1993. "Diversity and Contestation in Linguistic Ideologies: German Speakers in Hungary." *Language in Society* 22 (3): 337–59.

Hall, S. A. 1991. "Door into Deaf Culture: Folklore in an American Deaf Social Club." *Sign Language Studies* 73:421–29.

Jones, D. J. 1970. "Towards a Native Anthropology." *Human Organization* 29 (4): 251–60.

Kiyaga, N., and D. Moores. 2003. "Deafness in Sub-Saharan Africa."*American Annals of the Deaf* 148:18–24.

Lane, H. 1984. *When the Mind Hears: A History of the Deaf.* New York: Random House.

Lee, J. C. 2012. "They Have to See Us: An Ethnography of Deaf People in Tanzania." PhD diss., University of Colorado at Boulder.

Locker McKee, R., D. McKee, K. Smiler, and K. Pointon. 2007. "Māori Sign: The Construction of Indigenous Deaf Identity in New Zealand Sign Language." In *Sign Languages in Contact*, edited by D. Quinto-Pozos, 31–84. Washington, DC: Gallaudet University Press.

Markowicz, H., and J. Woodward. 1978. "Language and the Maintenance of Ethnic Boundaries in the Deaf Community." *Communication and Cognition* 11 (1): 29–38.

Moges, R. 2011. "Demissionization through Sign Language Dictionary-Making Process in Deaf Eritrean Community." MA thesis, California State University, Long Beach.

———. 2015. "'Resistance Is Not Futile': Language Planning and Demissionization of Eritrean Sign Language." In *Citizenship, Politics, Difference: Perspectives from Sub-Saharan Signed Language Communities*, edited by A. Cooper and K. Rashid, 64–80. Washington, DC: Gallaudet University Press.

Nyst, V. 2007. *A Descriptive Analysis of Adamorobe Sign Language (Ghana).* Utrecht: LOT.

———. 2010. "Sign Languages in West Africa." In *Sign Languages*, edited by D. Brentari, 405–32. Cambridge, UK: Cambridge University Press.

Parkhurst, S., and D. Parkhurst. 2003. "Lexical Comparisons of Signed Languages and the Effects of Iconicity." In *Work Papers of the Summer Institute of Linguistics, University of North Dakota Session*, vol. 47. Accessed March 30, 2015. http://arts-sciences.und.edu/summer-institute-of-linguistics/work-papers/2003.cfm.

Schmaling, C. 2000. *Maganar Hannu: Language of the Hands: A Descriptive Analysis of Hausa Sign Language.* Hamburg: Signum.

———. 2003. "A for Apple: The Impact of Western Education and ASL on the Deaf Community in Kano State, Northern Nigeria." In *Many Ways to Be Deaf: International Variation in Deaf Communities*, edited by L. Monaghan, C. Schmaling, K. Nakamura, and G. Turner, 302–10. Washington, DC: Gallaudet University Press.

Senghas, R. J. 1997. "An 'Unspeakable, Unwriteable' Language: Deaf Identity, Language, and Personhood among the First Cohorts of Nicaraguan Signers." PhD diss., Department of Anthropology, University of Rochester, New York.

Serpell, R., and M. Mbewe. 1990. "Dialectal Flexibility in Sign Language in Africa." In *Sign Language Research: Theoretical Issues*, edited by C. Lucas, 275–87. Washington, DC: Gallaudet University Press.

Tekleab, B. 1987. "Mutual Cooperation of the Deaf Churches over Continental Boarder [*sic*]" [unpublished archival document]. School Reports to Deaf African Mission (DAM), Keren, Eritrea.

Wilcox, S. 2007. "Routes from Gesture to Language." In *Verbal and Signed Languages: Comparing Structures, Constructs, and Methodologies*, edited by E. Pizzuto, P. Pietrandrea, and R. Simone, 107–31. Berlin: Mouton de Gruyter.

9 | Signed Language Sovereignties in Việt Nam: Deaf Community Responses to ASL-Based Tourism

Audrey C. Cooper

You know about the WTO [World Trade Organization], right? Việt Nam joined the WTO today. That means Việt Nam is going to be strong, and develop fast! Now we will compete with America! Vietnamese sign languages will develop fast too, and compete with America [ASL] (laughs). I'm just joking. . . . Deaf [people] cooperate. It's not important if you are Vietnamese or American.

After dinner one evening in July 2007, nine people attending a signed-language-based education program for Deaf adults in southern Việt Nam[1] chatted about Vietnamese national development and Deaf people's place in it. Công[2] turned to me and made the comment given in the epigraph, smiling playfully as he marked his attention to transnational relationships between Deaf people. I had been conducting preliminary ethnographic fieldwork in sites of Vietnamese Deaf[3] education and Deaf community organizing, and I had studied Hồ Chí Minh City Sign Language (HCMCSL) with several people in this group. We had also shared long conversations about our two countries, particularly the different historical trajectories of national development and legacies for Deaf education. As we walked along the main road bordering the town's Cao đẳng Sư phạm (Teachers College, now university) that included their education program, two things struck me about Công's commentary: his interest in the status of Việt Nam's petition to join

---

[1] Located about thirty-five kilometers northeast of Hồ Chí Minh City.

[2] All research participant names are pseudonyms, selected by the participants themselves.

[3] In this chapter, I use the capitalized form of *Deaf* (Điếc) according to the preferences of Vietnamese Deaf research participants.

the World Trade Organization and the comparative relationships he drew between national economic power and the power of signed languages.

Công's remarks illustrate the global context of his (and other Vietnamese Deaf people's) linguistic interests, as well as the global lens through which they consider economic development in Việt Nam. Such comments prompted me to focus on the ways Vietnamese Deaf people framed the forces acting on HCMCSL, as well as the ways Vietnamese Deaf and hearing people talked about relationships between HCMCSL and American Sign Language (ASL). In 2008 and 2009, commentary such as Công's were common in sites of Vietnamese Deaf education and Deaf community organizing, describing relationships between HCMCSL and ASL as alternately cooperative and competitive. By contrast, during postdoctoral research in 2012 to 2014, commentaries increasingly critiqued so-called business opportunists whose practices were seen as impinging on Vietnamese signed languages (VSLs) and Vietnamese Deaf cultural integrity.[4]

Such criticism takes place in context of both educational restructuring under Đổi mới—(commonly translated as "renovation"; 1986 to the present), Việt Nam's broad platform of political economic reform—and disability-related development, domains from which VSLs have been excluded, until recently. It also takes place in the context of efforts by Vietnamese Deaf community organizers to address the legacies of nationalized speech-based Deaf education, particularly via efforts to promote VSLs and Deaf cultural recognition.

Tensions between development-related agendas on training and employment of Deaf people are evidenced in Vietnamese Deaf people's responses to the emergence of what I term the *disability marketplace* in Việt Nam. Vietnamese state recognition of persons with disabilities is not new, appearing in the very first constitution of the Democratic Republic of Việt Nam (1945, Chapter 3, Article 32). Following reunification of North and South, the Socialist Republic of Việt Nam further dedicated attention to citizens disabled as a result of the American War, including constitutional articles of protection, passage of preliminary disability laws, national commemoration, participation in international disability-related forums, and ratification of the Convention on the Rights of Persons with Disabilities. However, in 2008 the Vietnamese government enacted the first laws providing tax subsidies to businesses employing or serving persons with disabilities, and this spurred a surge in disability-related business development—particularly that related to producing and selling goods for the tourism sector (Nguyễn, Rahtz, and Schultz 2014, 36) and "new tourist niches" (Suntikul et al. 2008, 68).

"Hearing impaired tourism" was among the first business ventures pursued by hearing Vietnamese entrepreneurs who imported Deaf ASL teachers from Australia to train local Deaf tour guides to communicate with travelers from other countries. Recently, touring companies owned and operated by Deaf people from the United States have entered the Vietnamese tourism market, also offering tours in ASL. Original ethnographic data discussed in this chapter indicate that both of these tourism pathways provoke concerns over cultural and linguistic sovereignty, or "arrangement[s] of authority" (Jackson 2007, 2) that organize decision-making power and access to resources within and between specific language-using groups.

---

[4] An example of a Deaf owned and operated company employing Deaf persons using the local signed language (Hà Nội Sign Language, HNSL) is Deaf Craft 5 Colors (see website: http://www.deafcraft5colors.vn/about-us).

This chapter focuses on the perspectives of Vietnamese Deaf community leaders whose reflections on language and tourism offer insights for practical planning and theorizing in relation to sovereignty, transnational Deaf relationships, and international trade and development. Going forward I discuss my background, research participants, and research methods. In the second section I discuss the rise of the disability marketplace specifically in connection to "hearing impaired" tourism. The third section puts the forces organizing Deaf people's participation in tourism into a broader context of educational and linguistic marginalization. The fourth section then examines commentary by Deaf community leaders in connection to their indexing of cultural and linguistic impacts of ASL-based tourism for VSL communities. Highlighting perceived relationships between VSLs and a "foreign" signed language (ASL), the claims instantiated in signer commentaries suggest a "distinct angle of telling" (Simpson 1993) that include both (1) the potential for linguistic endangerment caused by the spread of ASL and (2) the potential for beneficial partnerships with Deaf persons and organizations that use ASL. Ultimately, the chapter argues that it is in the context of structural conditions limiting Deaf people's access to VSLs that ASL-based tourism poses a threat to the status of VSLs. However, the Vietnamese Deaf persons participating in this research offer an additional possibility: where accountability to individual and group-collective preferences for Deaf sameness are mutually upheld across linguistic traditions, then domestic and global forms of Deaf sameness are enjoyed and desired.

RESEARCHER, RESEARCH PARTICIPANTS, AND RESEARCH METHOD

As noted previously, my interest in signed language sovereignties was sparked by Vietnamese Deaf people's commentaries connecting the expanding market economy with signed language cooperation and competition. I had gone to Việt Nam in 2007 on the invitation of a colleague with whom I was connected through US-based signed language linguistic and interpreter training networks. My purpose then was twofold: to formulate a focus for my doctoral dissertation research in anthropology and to teach an introductory interpreting workshop for three persons working as HCMCSL-Vietnamese interpreters.[5] My days were spent in these activities and my evenings in conversation with my Deaf HCMCSL teachers. Initially, my appreciation for Công's remarks was informed by sociolinguistic and social justice constructs familiar to me from Deaf communities and scholarship in the United States that I had encountered as a nonnative student of ASL and later as an ASL-English interpreter. These included the notion of separate Deaf and hearing cultural frameworks; positive valuation of Deaf-only spaces; sanctioning of spoken English in mixed Deaf and hearing spaces; and an expectation that Deaf organizations, institutions, and educational and political movements will be led by Deaf people.

Once I began ethnographic fieldwork in 2008 in Vietnamese Deaf schools and one Vietnamese Deaf association, my appreciation for the national and cultural heritage features of Công's comments deepened. During that research, introductions by Vietnamese Deaf colleagues facilitated participant observation with one Deaf association and other community-based organizations, while those by

---

[5] This workshop focused on text analysis of texts in HCMCSL and Vietnamese, and application via consecutive interpretation practice.

hearing colleagues facilitated participant observation in special schools and government offices. My ongoing study of HCMCSL (intermediate proficiency) and Vietnamese (conversational level proficiency) supported ongoing research in these settings: I conducted interviews with Deaf people in HCMCSL and after transcribing the data, held follow-up interviews with them to confirm accuracy of my interpretations; for interviews with hearing persons (school personnel, family members, and government officials), I contracted the services of a colleague who is a HCMCSL-Vietnamese interpreter (and thereby familiar with Deaf education and Deaf cultural terms) to provide Vietnamese-English interpretation and assistance with transcription. Conversational proficiency in Vietnamese allowed me to monitor these conversations for key terms, so that I could pursue relevant threads. The latter also indicates that my audiological status and related "hearing privilege" (Ladd 2003) gave me differential access to sites not available to Deaf persons. My known use of ASL constituted another form of privilege—even among hearing people who rejected the linguistic status of signed languages (such as certain special school personnel). Positive commentary about ASL came from both Deaf and hearing people, ideologically marking ASL as a "better" language, both in relation to the United States as a world superpower and/or the perceived success of US Deaf people to achieve social inclusion and equality with hearing counterparts.

The present chapter draws on materials from these data and from postdoctoral research tracing trends in the disability marketplace via online and print-based news reporting; photo-documentation of businesses with reference to disability in their banners; conversations with business owners, managers, and employees; and individual and group interviews with Deaf community leaders. Data examined in the fourth section of the chapter center on commentaries by five Deaf community leaders, collected during one group focus interview conducted in Hà Nội in December 2013; a postscript to the chapter also includes material from a follow-up interview conducted in Hồ Chí Minh City (HCMC) in July 2014.[6]

The Rise of the Disability Marketplace

In April 2008 the Vietnamese government enacted the first national legislation providing tax incentives to businesses that employ and/or assist persons with disabilities.[7] Businesses spotlighting disability sprung up nearly overnight in

---

[6] Interview language was determined by research participants, four of whom use HCMCSL fluently. We also code-switched into HNSL out of respect for the one interviewee most fluent in that language—as well as in recognition, during the initial interview, for the location of that interview (Hà Nội). After transcribing the interviews into English, I met with research participants via webcam and/or in person to confirm accuracy and review points of emphasis.

[7] Decision No. 51/2008/QD-TTg, implementing in April 2008, legislated the "support policy of the State for business and production establishment for the disabled," exempting businesses from paying taxes if they either served or employed people with disabilities. Guidance No.1680/NHCS-TD was then established in July 2008 implementing a new lending protocol requiring the Việt Nam Bank for Social Policies to receive proof from business owners on their mechanisms for "stabilizing jobs for the disabled and attracting more laborers who are disabled" (Section 2, "Project Preparation"). The 2010 passage of national comprehensive disability law provides further legal mandates for employing persons with a disability.

FIGURE 1. *Left*, **Deaf artists making oil paintings and embroidered hangings, near entrance to roadside tourist market (en route to Hạ Long Bay);** *right*, **Vietnamese Red Cross donation box near exit to roadside tourist market with English-language sign: "Helping hand for disadvantaged and disabled people." Photographs taken by the author in January 2013.**

HCMC and throughout the country, with the words *khuyết tật* (disability), *khiếm thính* (hearing-impaired), and occasionally Điếc (Deaf) prominently displayed in their titles and "disabled" workers conspicuously positioned on shop floors (see Figures 1a and 1b). For example, I (2011) described media attention given to Deaf servers working at Café Lang in HCMC (now operating under a new name and management; see also Friedner 2013, which describes a similar phenomenon for Deaf workers in Indian cafes, and Hoffman-Dilloway 2011 on a similar situation in Nepal). In this way, Việt Nam's new business laws created a mechanism enabling the transfer of responsibility for operationalizing "disability inclusion" from the state to the private sector (see also Nguyễn-võ 2008 for discussion of related "socialization" practices).

"HEARING IMPAIRED" TOURISM

Among the first business ventures pursued by Vietnamese (hearing) entrepreneurs was "hearing impaired tourism." In 2008, HCMC-based *Tuổi Trẻ*, one of Việt Nam's leading newspapers, published a story, "Hướng dẫn du lịch cho người khiếm thính" ("Tour Guides for Hearing Impaired People")[8] (see Figure 2). Interviewing the tour company owner Ms. Thi, the article describes how she decided to go into business: she recounts that a Vietnamese-American entrepreneur suggested a partnership to "nối dài tour du lịch dành cho người khiếm thính Mỹ" ("extend tours to hearing impaired Americans"). To prepare prospective Vietnamese Deaf tour guides, Ms. Thi decided to give these trainees a course in "international sign language, tour guide skills, and information on Việt Nam's history, culture

---

[8] Newspapers typically use *hearing impaired* (khiếm thính) as the socially and government preferred form of reference; occasionally, hearing impaired and *Deaf* (Điếc) appear together, used interchangeably. See Cooper 2011 for discussion of government policy regarding print media and everyday forms of language control.

FIGURE 2. "Hướng dẫn du lịch cho người khiếm thính" ("Tour guides for hearing impaired people"). Thái Bình for Tuổi Trẻ, 2008.

and society." Ms. Thi noted that trainees had a difficult time learning "khái niệm quá ư trừu tượng" ("excessively abstract concepts"). Ultimately, the article concludes, training these tour guides was "không dễ nhưng có thể được" ("not easy, but they were able to do the job").[9]

While conducting participant observation in a HCMCSL class taught in a community-based organization run for/by persons with disability, I met a representative from this tour company, who happened to be a student in the class. During the class break the representative approached me, remarking on what she perceived to be my "skill" with HCMCSL. After describing her touring company she then asked if I would teach her trainees ASL. I declined, explaining that, unlike our HCMCSL teacher, I was neither a native signer nor had I been trained to teach ASL as a second language. I then asked why her company decided not to use HCMCSL; she answered that she wanted to attract Deaf tourists from the United States—those with enough money for distant travel—and that these tourists would want to use their language. She added that ASL is used in many other countries either as a first or second language, so her company could attract more Deaf travelers with ASL than with other signed languages. Talking with colleagues the next day I learned that the company owner had invited them to teach her employees ASL as well; these colleagues had also declined her invitation and suggested pursuing HCMCSL–based cultural exchange-type tourism. Some months later, I learned that the company hired several Deaf

_____

[9] Another option—to train hearing people bilingual in a VSL to conduct tours in ASL—was not feasible due to the lack of hearing signers. Educational mandates prominent during this period discouraged hearing teachers in the special schools and families of Deaf children from using VSLs, and VSL-Vietnamese interpreter training was not available in any form.

people from Australia with second-language backgrounds in ASL to train local tour guides.[10]

These events formed the early basis of "hearing impaired tourism" in Hồ Chí Minh City, established according to the interests of local and transnational hearing people, and oriented toward what the latter imagined to be largely US and European Deaf desires. Research participants report that Vietnamese tour companies continue to train Vietnamese Deaf tour guides to use ASL, and videos posted on YouTube show tour guides using ASL.[11]

It is not surprising that tour companies should operate according to a language known to have extensive world-coverage (ASL); this situation parallels the mainstream tourism industry in Việt Nam in which English occupies a dominant position (Nguyễn, Rahtz, and Schultz 2014). That these activities attracted local Deaf people seeking employment is also not surprising, given the widespread marginalization of Deaf people from the job sector.

However, Ms. Thi's characterization (and others like it) of Deaf adults as concrete thinkers with little sociocultural knowledge obscures the actual circumstances of Vietnamese Deaf linguistic marginalization and commonsense notions of signed languages (i.e., as universal) that make businesses like ASL-based tour companies viable undertakings in the first place (and the fact that the article about her tour company did not include Deaf perspectives is not surprising due to the dearth of interpreters at this time).[12] A brief discussion of the sociolinguistic circumstances of VSL varieties, access to VSLs in educational settings, and related Deaf community organizing help contextualize interview data presented in the third section.

SIGNED LANGUAGES, LANGUAGE ACCESS, AND DEAF ORGANIZING IN VIỆT NAM

Woodward (2003) describes three major Vietnamese signed languages corresponding to the areas in and around the cities of Hà Nội, Hải Phòng, and Hồ Chí Minh, reporting that "all show very strong influence from French Sign Language, which was introduced into Vietnamese schools for the deaf" (291). Drawing on earlier lexicostatistical research that found a "61% rate of shared cognates in basic vocabulary" between French Sign Language and American Sign Language (Woodward 1978), he concludes that the three Vietnamese signed languages (along with

---

[10] A 2008 story in *Thanh Niên* newspaper—"Người khiếm thính làm hướng dẫn viên du lịch" ["Hearing-Impaired People Work as Tour Guides"] (staff writer; November 17 edition)— reported that Ms. Thi's tour company had hired two "hearing impaired" persons from Australia as trainers in "international sign language" (ký hiệu quốc tế). While neither the terms of contract nor training content of these Australian consultants are known, what is important here is the evaluation by research participants that the tour company's guides use ASL.

[11] The Smile Tours' website now advertises tours throughout Việt Nam; however, I have not been able to independently verify any further details of the business operation.

[12] VSL-Vietnamese interpreting-related courses and workshops were offered for the first time in 2012 through two international development-related projects: World Concern Development Organization's Intergenerational Deaf Education Outreach Project (with which I worked from 2012 to 2014 as an international trainer) and the Đồng Nai Deaf Education Project.

Modern Thai Sign Language) "have been strongly influenced by one or more sign languages from the French Sign Language Family" (Woodward 2003, 291). Ethnographic evidence also indicates that, following Đổi mới, ASL was directly imported by development organizations, educational personnel, and church-based groups in the form of videotapes and instruction manuals (Cooper 2011).

The Lái Thiêu School for the Mute-Deaf (Trường Câm-Điếc Lái Thiêu),[13] established in 1886 in southern Việt Nam, is among the first places that French Sign Language was reportedly institutionalized in educational practice. Since that time the instructional language at Lái Thiêu has changed a number of times according to ideological movements within and across sites of educational, development-related, and state-level decision making. Notably, late 1980s political economic reform identified education as the primary institution for securing national development and modernization (Phạm 2007); as part of the educational reform agenda, educational leaders established a nationwide system of "special schools" founded on a speech-based method of instruction (Woodward et al. 2004; Woodward and Nguyễn 2012). The institutional turn away from signed language is also clarified by Nguyễn-võ's description of the Vietnamese state's emergent ideological orientation to social problems at this time: "social problems allowed for expert intervention to maximize the health of the population [which] was a new phenomenon symptomatic of a different paradigmatic configuration of governance" (2008, 82). Influential domestic and international experts active in the early reform period advocated speech-based approaches to Deaf education (Cooper 2011; Phạm 1984; Woodward et al. 2004).[14]

Special schools, and the 1990s introduction of inclusive education (Giáo dục hoà nhập), are both founded on use of spoken and written Vietnamese. Depending on resources, schools may provide instruction up to the fifth or ninth grade level; however, Deaf students often take two years to complete one curricular year of content and they typically leave school but do not graduate. Where specialist training is available, such as computer classes, students may obtain training certificates. In general, special school teachers, principals, and educational leaders widely attribute poor educational performance to inferior intelligence or individual motivation, rather than to lack of linguistic access (Cooper 2014; see also Woodward and Nguyễn 2012). However, this situation is changing since passage of the 2010 disability law permitting use of sign language in school.

Responding to these and other circumstances (e.g., social and employment discrimination), Vietnamese Deaf people established regional associations in Hà Nội (late 1990s) and in HCMC (2000; this association soon disbanded). Woodward notes that early Vietnamese organizing efforts were also encouraged by a 1996 meeting involving contact with representatives form the "Japanese Federation of the Deaf (the Asia Pacific regional representative for the World Federation of the

---

[13] Now renamed Trung Tâm Thuận An or the Thuận An Center. According to Pitrois (1914), Lái Thiêu was established by the French-colonial missionary Father Azemar with Nguyễn Văn Trương, a Vietnamese Deaf man whom Azemar had sent for training at the Deaf School in Rodez, France.

[14] In recent years a new wave of speech-based advocates have begun working in Việt Nam in the form of the US-based Global Foundation for Children with Hearing Loss. See http://childrenwithhearingloss.org/projects.shtml.

Deaf) and the National Association of the Deaf in Thailand" (2003, 297). While these initiatives were not officially recognized by Vietnamese state entities (e.g., officially incorporated into educational or rehabilitation programming), they laid the foundation for such developments. The Hà Nội Association of the Deaf also provided support for the establishment of the Đồng Nai Deaf Education Project (DNDEP) in 2000 by publicizing the project and facilitating interviews with prospective students.

Using HCMCSL as the instructional language, the DNDEP teaches the national curriculum in the usual manner, with students completing one curricular year within one academic calendar year (Woodward et al. 2004; Woodward and Nguyễn 2012); over the past fifteen years, more than two hundred students have graduated from ninth and twelfth grades, and Việt Nam's first two cohorts of college graduates have earned degrees in primary education (teaching grades one through five).[15] That the Ministry of Education and Training has modeled an Hà Nội-based project on the DNDEP with classes up to the twelfth grade level is one indication that recognition of signed language is gaining institutional ground in Việt Nam. However, whereas there is limited access to training special school teachers or interpreters in the use of VSLs, efforts by Deaf leaders to teach VSLs and to train VSL(s)-Vietnamese interpreters continue to be limited activities.

Signed Language Sovereignties: Claims from Deaf Community Leaders

Vietnamese Deaf communities' efforts to promote their own languages make certain demands on the nation-state, as citizens and minority language users, for forms of recognition, access to institutions, and opportunities to make social contributions relevant to Deaf cultures and languages (Cooper 2014; see Emery 2011 for a view from the United Kingdom and May 2008 for discussion of minority spoken language rights). Together these demands form a claim to linguistic sovereignty—that is, to authority and control over language policy, programming, and representation in state institutions (such as education and employment), as well as to a determining role in knowledge production and circulation relative to linguistic identities and cultural values (media). However, Jackson argues that the idea of sovereignty "extends across all the religions, civilizations, languages, cultures, ethnic and racial groupings, and other communities and collectivities into which humanity is divided" (Jackson 2007, x). Responding to and constituting such divisions, (re)conceptualizations of sovereignty can be located in ordinary commentaries and reflections on everyday life.

Turning to the interview data in the next section, claims of linguistic sovereignty instantiated by Vietnamese Deaf community leaders index, in particular, classifications according to linguistic, (Deaf) cultural, and national identifications and attributions. These leaders are also keenly attentive to power dynamics constraining their participation in and control over their own everyday concerns—particularly participation in education and work settings, but also increasingly transnational networks and research activities as well. Such concerns have been

---

[15] Cohorts graduated in 2012 and 2014 respectively; seventeen Vietnamese Deaf persons now possess degrees in primary education.

discussed in the Deaf studies literature in terms of "ownership" (see Dively 1991; Jankowski 1997; cf. Harris et al. 2009 for discussion of signed language communities ownership of research; and Emery and O'Brien 2014 for discussion of hearing-dominated Deaf studies academic circles). One key analytic insight developed here is that signer commentaries make a strong political connection between nation-state territories and linguistic sovereignty—much as in the classic model of the liberal democratic state and guiding doctrines of the Socialist Republic of Việt Nam; however, rather than seeking redress at the level of the national state, Vietnamese Deaf community leader commentaries center on local, regional, and transnational negotiation between (international) Deaf communities for securing linguistic sovereignty.[16]

Sovereign Claims to Vietnamese Signed Languages (VSLs)

In this section I draw on data collected during one focus group interview with five Vietnamese Deaf community leaders to examine claims related to linguistic sovereignty. To begin that interview, I inquired about government-subsidized employment opportunities for persons with disabilities and their own employment opportunities. In their responses, tourism emerged as a central concern with extended commentaries addressing hearing-run ASL-based tourism activities in northern and southern Việt Nam, one person's experience with an ASL-based "Deaf Tour" to Cambodia, and upcoming ASL-based tours to Việt Nam organized by Deaf tour operators from the United States. These topics resulted in emotionally charged group-level discussions regarding two issues that interviewees agreed demanded some form of action: (1) how to prevent foreign tour operators from conducting ASL-based tours in Việt Nam, and (2) how to prevent domestic tour operators from using ASL. In these discussions, themes of language displacement overlapped with themes of economic development.

Claims Related to Linguistic Displacement via ASL-Based Tourism

Discussion about preventing use of ASL by domestic and foreign tour operators conducting tours in Việt Nam concentrated on claims to such things as territorial control, boundaries, and rights, as well as less tangible aspects of cultural heritage territorialized via association with Vietnamese Deaf persons and bodies. In their commentaries, signers repeatedly described territorial boundaries distinguishing jurisdictions respectively identified as "belonging to" either Vietnamese Deaf communities or to other entities (Deaf foreign and Vietnamese hearing tour operators, ASL).

Territorial descriptions took the form of, for example, one-handed "C" handshape facing downward to draw a boundary between one referent group (Việt Nam, Vietnamese Deaf people) and another (foreign tour operators); use of the

---

[16] This strategy of addressing language concerns directly with Deaf groups is likely both a reflection of marginalization of VSLs within state institutions (lack of access to state agents and sentiment) and comparatively unconstrained access shared between Deaf people within and across local, regional, and national borders with whom there is an expectation for shared values regarding signed language preservation.

HCMCSL possessive forms MY/OUR and YOUR/THEIR (fingertips of "5" hand contacting the body for MY/OUR, facing outward for YOUR/THEIR); and use of the HNSL possessive form MY/OUR and YOUR/THEIR (isomorphic with ASL possessive forms). One other sign appeared repeatedly, familiar to me from participant observation in adult education classes involving Vietnamese history: the HCMCSL verb form expressing the concept "to colonize" (thuộc địa) or TAKE OVER (see Cooper 2011). Deaf commentaries on colonizing forces are well known to those familiar with the Deaf studies literature, particularly as it relates to hearing-controlled educational systems (Ladd 2003; Lane 1992). Its application not only to domestic hearing-owned touring companies but to foreign Deaf-owned ones is remarkable— which must be viewed in the context of colonial legacies in Việt Nam, among which contemporary racial and aesthetic confrontations with whiteness figure prominently (Carruthers 2002; cf. Wrigley 1996 for the Thai Deaf context).

An example of the concept expressed in what I am glossing as TAKE OVER appears several times in response to the following question, which I posed at about the half-way point of the interview: "What would you all say if [the US Deaf person who co-owns/operates a Deaf touring company in Cambodia] or someone else, wanted to set up the same kind of touring company here in Việt Nam?" With serious expressions, all five participants shook their heads, apparently dismayed; Công responded more forcefully, shaking his head even more emphatically while rapidly waving his right hand from side to side as if to suggest a warning against such action. Thiên then interjected:

> Let me say something. I remember seeing something on Facebook, [Deaf person from United States] signing in ASL . . . "I am preparing to lead a tour to Vietnam" [pauses, looking concerned]. I caught her say that. And it looked like [US-owned Deaf tour company] wants to TAKE OVER the market in Việt Nam. I was really uncomfortable with that so I emailed [friend from the United States now living in Hà Nội] right away and asked if he saw the Facebook posting. He replied that he had not, but then found it and emailed [tour company owner] to tell them not to TAKE OVER Việt Nam, that their activities should end at the border of Cambodia, to stop. This is important: Activities in Việt Nam belong to the Vietnamese. But that company plans to start tours in Việt Nam in 2014.

Thiên's statement provoked startled expressions from the other interviewees, prompting them to open a laptop to pull up some of the webpages he had referred to. Seeing these websites, Su turned to me and signed: "You know [owner of ASL-based tour company in Việt Nam] right? Do you know if they are part of this?"

As that tour owner had US-based partners involved in bringing US Deaf persons to Việt Nam for tourism purposes, this was a reasonable question. It also suggested that whether originating in or outside Việt Nam, tours conducted in ASL contributed to TAKING OVER because tourism (1) positions ASL as an income-generating language against which Deaf persons, and by extension VSLs, have been popularly depicted as burdening the national economy (i.e., a group requiring remediation via speech-only education methods) and (2) facilitates the geographic spread of ASL in Việt Nam, particularly in context of lack of institutional support for VSLs.

However, tours conducted by Deaf tour guides from the United States were apparently especially problematic because of their lack of ethnocultural anchoring (in both Deaf and national heritage aspects), as Su's follow-up question suggests. After replying that I was not aware of any connection between the tour company in Việt Nam and the [US-based tour company], Su asked: "How can [an American Deaf person] give a tour in Việt Nam? . . . Do they know the history and culture?! [Appearing dumbfounded] How could they possibly do a tour?!" Su himself had acted as a tour guide for US Deaf travelers in 2011–12 (which I had played a role in by way of making introductions between Su, then a leader in a Deaf association in Hồ Chí Minh City, and one US-based Deaf touring company).

Criticism of tours led by persons not a member of the linguistic-cultural group extended to tours conducted outside of Việt Nam as well. For example, Thiên related a story about taking a tour to Cambodia. Describing in painstaking detail how he had arranged the Cambodian tour through a third party (a Deaf friend from the United States now living in Việt Nam), Thiên explained that he had expected the tour guide to be a Cambodian Deaf person and to use Khmer Sign Language. As it turned out, the tour guide—who was also a co-owner of the touring company—was a hearing Cambodian ASL user and was not able to introduce the tour group to local Deaf people (see Harrelson this volume for discussion of relationships between Cambodian Deaf perspectives and those of nongovernmental organizations). Thiên continued:

> And I thought to myself, this is a strange situation: I am Deaf. The tour guide is hearing, [signing and] interpreting for me, using ASL. But I am a [implied: Vietnamese] Deaf person. That makes no sense! . . . For me, I must have a [implied: Cambodian] Deaf person as my tour guide. It is important [emphasis] that they be Deaf, that they sign naturally, and are someone who has grown up living in the place that they are telling me about, knows their own culture. That is the best situation.

Here we see a strong value placed on transnational Deaf connection instantiated in relation to cultural and linguistic authenticity and diverse forms of Deaf knowledge. It is not sameness that connects Deaf people and experiences to one another, but appreciation of difference. Su followed Thiên's narrative and, returning to discussion of US Deaf tour companies, asked how they might BLOCK such companies from doing business in Việt Nam. He and another interviewee, Sen, then signed TAKE OVER in its aspectual verb form (repetition, extended space-time features), indicating a viewpoint of repeated occurrences, encroachment, or anticipated encroachment over time. Toward the end of their discussion, Công suggested raising this issue with World Federation of the Deaf President Colin Allen with whom they had plans to meet for Deaf leadership training. Sen then interjected, suggesting they set up their own Vietnamese Deaf tour company. Ultimately, they resolved to discuss the issue within the Hà Nội– and Hồ Chí Minh City–based Deaf associations.

In each of the above examples, Vietnamese signed languages, Deaf cultural sites, and national heritage sites are metaphorized as spatial territories either overtaken or threatened with overtake by an externally located ASL that lays claim to Vietnamese resources. By contrast, in the next example, ASL is represented as already internal to Vietnamese national borders and indeed Vietnamese persons. Describing the language practices he has observed, Công explained how tourism activities have introduced Vietnamese Deaf people to ASL through companies such as Smile Tours. This exchange then followed:

Công: [Vietnamese] Deaf who want to learn ASL also acquire it through webchatting like on Camfrog, so they pick up all kinds of signs from foreigners [mimics ASL]. I meet Deaf people all the time who keep signing in ASL, and when I ask them what they are doing and to sign in VSL, they sign [with facial expression of impertinence] "I like ASL [uses ASL sign for LIKE]" So what am I to say to that? I just leave them alone. But there are many Deaf Vietnamese people who share that idea [whole group nods in agreement].

Su: Oh yes, they say "ASL is so beautiful, VSL is ugly and vulgar" [constructed action showing surprise to an imagined interlocutor making such a statement]

Researcher: Really, many Deaf people say that?!

Su: Yes, many! [Thiên, Sen, and Rồng all sign CÓ, lit. "have," meaning YES]

Here we observe one of the ways ASL achieves higher status in the Vietnamese Deaf context (cf. Schmaling 2003 discussion of impacts of ASL in Kano State, Nigeria). After this exchange, research participants went on to discuss their expectations that Vietnamese Deaf users of ASL might decide on their own to return to using a VSL once the latter had an opportunity to participate in increasingly available regional Deaf association meetings and/or paid employment involving VSLs. Regarding raising their concerns with Vietnamese ASL-based touring companies, two of the Deaf leaders reported that they had already talked with the owner of an ASL-based tour company in Việt Nam and shared their perspectives; their narratives indicated that this was a polite exchange that appropriately avoided direct confrontation on their part (according to mainstream conventions of politeness), but that the owner did not ultimately change the course of her business operations.

While the primary focus of discussion during the initial interview centered on the cultural and linguistic impacts of ASL-based tourism, one segment of the interview relates back to Công's universalist assertion, "Deaf [people] cooperate," described in the chapter introduction. As if in response to naysayers to tourism involving Deaf persons using two mutually unintelligible signed languages, Thiên remarked toward the end of the interview:

Do foreign Deaf travelers have a problem when we take them sightseeing in Hà Nội? Not really—I gesture, point, explain through direct means, and they pick up what I am talking about. They use their sign, and we use our sign, that's it. . . . My recommendation for visitors: first, use gesture and act things out—that is the best. Second, do not write in English—since many [Vietnamese] Deaf people have not had the opportunity to study, or to learn English.

Here we see that grave concerns about displacement of VSLs by ASL, and both Vietnamese and US-based Deaf tour companies TAKING OVER Việt Nam, are not, finally, incompatible with the potentiality of transnational Deaf mutual understanding and support. Thus, it is only in context of Vietnamese Deaf people's highly constrained and contested use of their own signed languages that the disability marketplace's demand for ASL presents a problem. Where mutuality is perceived to exist, direct relationships with ASL users, Deaf persons and organizations associated with the United States, and other "foreign" signed language communities are valued and celebrated as a connection that transcends national boundaries. The observation made by Kusters and Friedner in the introduction to this volume concerning the role that sentiments of sameness play in creating connections and senses of responsibility is clearly evidenced here. In the Vietnamese context, both domestic and global forms of Deaf sameness are enjoyed and desired, as long as accountability to individual and group-collective participation in sameness is mutually upheld.

CONCLUSION

Vietnamese Deaf community leaders' concerns over access to their own languages and the encroachment of ASL offer an important intervention into questions of sovereignty. Seeing economic development through the lens of their concerns, tourism decisions are recast to take into consideration the impact that such decisions have for VSL sovereignties—that is, the "life itself of the linguistic community" (Marazzi 2008, 50). That Vietnamese Deaf communities are keen to lead such efforts is understood in relation to their experiences with and efforts to guide special school education and developments in the disability marketplace. They are also understood in relation to the United Nations World Tourism Organization's (UNWTO's) resolution on Global Code of Ethics for Tourism, which Việt Nam formally accepted in 2004 (UNWTO 2005). According to the analysis pursued here, the disability marketplace in Việt Nam largely benefits hearing conationals and Deaf foreigners rather than the communities and languages upon whose existence that part of the marketplace depends. Deaf community leaders' interests in protecting Vietnamese Deaf cultural and linguistic resources should be, therefore, of great interest to the Vietnamese government, the UNWTO, as well as to domestic and international tourism partners alike.

POSTSCRIPT

When I returned to Việt Nam in July 2014, I conducted a follow-up interview with the five research participants to share my analysis of their interview data and to invite their suggestions and feedback. Politely attentive to my research report— delivered in HCMCSL, accompanied by key concepts and their own interview segments presented in Vietnamese via a Word document on my laptop—they responded that the background context I included (e.g., special schools, Deaf organizing) was key to understanding the language issues involved, and that my interpretations were "correct"; however, they seemed doubtful about the usefulness of reporting these issues to readers of English. "Who will read the chapter?" Rồng asked. Sen followed with a more pointed question—"Will Deaf [people in the United States] read it?" Other related questions were implied here: Will US Deaf touring companies read the chapter? Will they change what they're doing? And how will touring companies in Việt Nam get access to this information?

In response to Sen's question, Thiên proceeded to tell the following story about what he did after the initial interview in December 2013. Incensed by the US Deaf touring company's plans to give an ASL-based tour to Việt Nam, he had contacted a US Deaf friend, who put him in touch with a tour guide working for the company in question. At this point, we all sat forward, our eyes glued to attention. Su looked shocked, took off his glasses, rubbed his eyes and laughed, remarking: "I forgot that we talked about contacting them [US tour company]!" The others had as well. Appearing pleased with their recognition of his initiative, Thiên smiled and continued. He made arrangements to meet the tour guide by Skype video-chat, during which he asked the latter to talk with the company owners about either canceling the tour or making arrangements to partner with Vietnamese Deaf tour guides who would use a VSL and be able to explain Vietnamese national and Deaf cultural history. According to Thiên, after several more conversations with tour company personnel, the company agreed. Thiên went on to describe that he is now in regular contact with the company, working towards creating a partnership for future tours to Việt Nam.

After the group congratulated him and the excitement subsided, I asked: "So what should we do with the chapter? Should I rewrite it based on what Thiên just shared and report that relationships with foreign tour companies are fine now?" Thiên was the first to respond, saying: "No. You should keep it [as is] but include what I just said, emphasizing that foreign companies are welcome but only if they make a commitment to equal business partnerships with Vietnamese Deaf people. They should not come to Việt Nam without contacting us or without our participation." After this, each person took a turn weighing in on the focus of the chapter, all agreeing that the information presented should not be edited to exclude negative experiences with foreign tour companies.

Công commented: "Add Thiên's information, but keep the other parts of the chapter as other Deaf-owned tour companies might have plans to come to Việt Nam—not just US ones but other countries." And Su added: "Keep the chapter—because it makes the point that Vietnamese Deaf people want to prevent those who would come to take Vietnamese Deaf people's jobs and culture." In this final formal interview research participants did not address how the chapter might reach Vietnamese ASL-based tour operators; over the next few weeks, however, the topic did come up in conversations held in social settings. Two of the research participants asked me about having the chapter translated into Vietnamese so they could make use of it in conversations with Vietnamese tour operators, and several large group conversations witnessed the research participants signing with other Vietnamese Deaf persons about raising the issue of ASL-based tourism within the Deaf associations. As in the follow-up interview, these latter discussions highlighted the value of direct communication between Deaf people—whether Vietnamese co-nationals or transnational contacts—as the most effective route for addressing issues of concern. Thus, as indicated by Công's remarks at the beginning of the chapter, nationality was not of utmost importance in these research participants' considerations of Deaf cooperation (deaf sameness), but rather the demonstrated effort to understand and act in accordance with linguistic and sociocultural sovereignty (deaf difference).

Acknowledgments

I am grateful to the five research participants whose perspectives guided the shaping of this chapter, as well as to Vietnamese Deaf community members in both Hà Nội and Hồ Chí Minh City who participated in related conversations. My thanks go to the volume editors and to Bùi Bích Phượng, Paul G. Dudis, Erin Moriarty Harrelson, and Nguyễn Trần, whose feedback contributed greatly to the clarity of the finished essay. Responsibility for errors or omissions is completely my own.

References

Carruthers, A. 2002. "The Accumulation of National Belonging in Transnational Fields: Ways of Being at Home in Vietnam." *Identities: Global Studies in Culture and Power* 9:423–44.

Cooper, A. C. 2011. "Overcoming the 'Backward Body': How State Institutions, Language, and Embodiment Shape Deaf Education in Contemporary Southern Việt Nam." PhD diss., University of Michigan.

———. 2014. "Signed Language and Sociopolitical Formation: The Case of 'Contributing to Society' through Hồ Chí Minh City Sign Language." *Language in Society* 43 (3): 311–32.

Dively, E. 1991. *Keeping Ownership of Deaf Culture in a Hearing World* [DVD-R]. Rochester, NY: Rochester Institute of Technology.

Emery, S. D. 2011. *Citizenship and the Deaf Community*. Nijmegen, Netherlands: Ishara Press.

Emory, S. D., and D. O'Brien. 2014. "The Role of the Intellectual in Minority Group Studies: Reflections on Deaf Studies in Social and Political Contexts."*Qualitative Inquiry* 20 (1): 27–36.

Friedner, M. 2013. "Producing 'Silent Brewmasters': Deaf Workers and Added Value in India's Coffee Cafes." *Anthropology of Work Review* 34 (1): 39–50.

Harris, R., H. M. Holmes, and D. Mertens. 2009. "Research Ethics in Sign Language Communities."*Sign Language Studies* 9 (2): 104–31.

Hoffman-Dilloway, E. 2011. "Ordering Burgers, Reordering Relations: Gestural Interactions between Hearing and d/Deaf Nepalis."*Pragmatics* 21 (3): 373–91.

Jackson, R. 2007. *Sovereignty: The Evolution of an Idea*. Cambridge, UK: Polity Press.

Jankowski, K. A. 1997. *Deaf Empowerment: Emergence, Struggle, and Rhetoric*. Washington, DC: Gallaudet University Press.

Ladd, P. 2003. *Understanding Deaf Culture: In Search of Deafhood*. Clevedon, UK: Multilingual Matters.

Lane, H. 1992. *The Mask of Benevolence: Disabling of the Deaf Community*. New York: Knopf.

Marazzi, C. 2008. *Capital and Language: From the New Economy to the War Economy*. New York: Semiotext(e).

May, S. 2008. *Language and Minority Rights: Ethnicity, Nationalism, and the Politics of Language.* London: Routledge.

Nguyễn, T. T. M., D. R. Rahtz, and C. J. Schultz II. 2014. "Tourism as a Catalyst for Quality of Life in Transitioning Subsistence Marketplaces: Perspectives from Hà Lông, Vietnam ."*Journal of Macromarketing* 34 (1): 28–44.

Nguyễn-võ, T. 2008. *The Ironies of Freedom: Sex, Culture, and Neoliberal Governance in Vietnam.* Seattle: University of Washington Press.

Phạm, K. 1984. *Vấn Đề Phục Hồi Chức Năng Cho Người Điếc* [*Rehabilitation Issues for the Deaf*]. Hà Nội: Nhà Xuất Bản Y học.

Phạm, M. H. 2007. "Twenty Years of the Renewal of Education and Training: Achievements and Challenges." In *Việt Nam: Twenty Years of Renewal.* Hà Nội: Giới.

Pitrois, Y. 1914. "From the Old World." *Silent Worker* 27 (1): 12–13.

Schmaling, C. 2003. "A is for Apple: The Impact of Western Education and ASL on the Deaf Community in Kano State, Nigeria." In *Many Ways to Be Deaf: International Variation in Deaf Communities,* edited by L. F. Monaghan et al., 302–10. Washington, DC: Gallaudet University Press.

Suntikul, W., R. Butler, and D. Aiery. 2008. "A Periodization of the Development of Vietnam's Tourism Accommodation since the Open Door Policy."*Asia Pacific Journal of Tourism Research* 13 (1): 67–80.

Thái, B. 2008. "Hướng dẫn du lịch cho người khiếm thính" ("Tour Guides for Hearing Impaired People"). *Tuổi Trẻ News,* September 20. Accessed May 24, 2014 http://dulich .tuoitre.vn/tin-tuc/279324/huong-dan-du-lich-cho-nguoi-khiem-thinh.html.

Woodward, J. C. 2003. "Sign Languages and Deaf Identities in Thailand and Viet Nam." In *Many Ways to Be Deaf: International Variation in Deaf Communities,* edited by L. F. Monaghan et al., 283–301. Washington, DC: Gallaudet University Press.

Woodward, J. C., Nguyễn, T. H., and Nguyễn T. T. T. 2004. "Providing Higher Educational Opportunities to Deaf Adults in Viet Nam through Vietnamese Sign Languages, 2000–2003."*Deaf Worlds* 20 (3): 232–63.

Woodward, J. C., and T. H. Nguyễn, 2012. "Where Sign Language Studies Has Led Us in Forty Years: Opening High School and University Education for Deaf People in Viet Nam through Sign Language Analysis, Teaching, and Interpretation." *Sign Language Studies* 13 (1): 19–36.

Wrigley, O. 1996. *The Politics of Deafness.* Washington, DC: Gallaudet University Press.

United Nations World Tourism Organization. 2005. *Activities of the World Committee on Tourism Ethics: Report on the WTO Survey on the Global Implementation of the Global Code of Ethics for Tourism.* Dakar, Senegal: WTO.

10 | Social Media Practices of Deaf Youth in Turkey: Emerging Mobilities and Language Choice

Deniz İlkbaşaran

The movement of people across space is . . . never a move across empty spaces. The spaces are always someone's space, and they are filled with norms, expectations, conceptions of what counts as proper and normal (indexical) language use and what does not. Mobility, sociolinguistically speaking, is therefore a trajectory through different spaces—stratified, controlled, and monitored ones—in which language "gives you away." (Blommaert and Dong 2010, 368)

This chapter focuses on mobilities of deaf[1] youth in Turkey, the vernacular strategies they use for engaging with new communication technologies, and emerging trends in their choice of language use on virtual social platforms. I focus on three main themes concerning deaf youth in Turkey: (1) their current media and

---

[1] In my work and throughout this chapter, I use lower case "d" in referring to the larger deaf community of Turkey and to my deaf participants. In Turkey, the prevalent term that the community uses for itself is *işitme engelli*, which can be translated to English as "hearing disabled". While the National Federation of the Deaf in Turkey (*Türkiye Sağırlar Milli Federasyonu* –TSMF) recently changed its name to reflect a political shift from hearing impairment to deafness, the historically situated connotations of the term "Deaf" cannot be automatically assumed for the population at large, especially without more research. Moreover, some of my participants have openly stated affiliating with the hard of hearing or hearing communities. In cases when my participants identified themselves as being what in the US is called "Deaf," showing awareness of and affiliation with this cultural and identity discourse as well as sign language being their dominant language, I use capital "D". I prefer this capitalized spelling also in referring to events and institutions that have traditionally served national and international deaf and Deaf communities as cultural hubs, and on which more social studies have been done.

communication practices, (2) how national and international Deaf events shape their mobilities and sign language exposure, and (3) what the current trends in their language preferences on social media reveal about their past, present, and future mobilities. I discuss the mobilities of deaf youth in Turkey as diversely mediated and socially situated everyday practices. These mobilities are mediated by a collection of bodies, tools, systems, and ideologies that are prevalent in contemporary Turkish society, as well as in the regional and global discourses of which they are a part. The goal of this chapter is thus to explore to what extent various Deaf institutions as well as new digital technologies and social media allow Turkish deaf youth new opportunities for social navigation and participation at different scales. As Blommaert and Dong (2010) point out, language matters to social analysis as its use reveals past social interactions, current affiliations, and future motivations.

In the twenty-first century, more deaf people travel physically and virtually to meet other deaf people around the world and are thus exposed to other national sign languages and International Sign (IS) in a range of social contexts (e.g., international Deaf sports events, travel, and multiuser video chat such as ooVoo). With such increased mobilities of deaf people and growing international deaf contact, questions on the sociopolitical relationships between national sign languages and international contact sign systems have recently been attended to by Deaf Studies scholars, sign linguists, and linguistic anthropologists (Friedner and Kusters 2014; Green 2014; Hiddinga and Crasborn 2011; Lucas 2001). Nevertheless, the notion of *mobility* has been less tackled within Deaf studies. This has been slowly changing in the past years, through the work of a few scholars who explore relations between deaf people and social space around movement (Bauman and Murray 2010; Kusters 2010; Valentine and Skelton 2008). In my work and in this chapter, I predominantly make use of Urry's mobilities paradigm as a critical framework to expand on this relationship.

As a hearing Turkish woman, I spent the first twenty-four years of my life in Istanbul. My involvement with the Turkish deaf community dates back to 2001, when I joined Aslı Özyürek's research project on Turkish Sign Language (TID) as a junior at Koç University. I found out about this project at a time when I was in search for a TID course for myself. Instead, I was fortunate enough to spend the next three years on the documentation of TID. Ever since, I have had many interactions with Turkish deaf community members and organizations, in the context of many academic, governmental, and social events. I have acquired TID mainly in İstanbul via these informal or academic interactions with community members. I began my academic life in the field of psychology but then moved on to educational technology and communication in my graduate studies. Graduate school took me to Montréal in 2004 and then to San Diego in 2007, where I have been living since. Unlike TID, my acquisition of American Sign Language (ASL) was through formal instruction in Montréal, accompanied by frequent interactions with members of both the ASL and Quebec Sign Language (Langue des Signes Québécoise, LSQ) communities there. Currently, I am proficient in both TID and ASL but feel more fluent in the latter. It is also important to point out that both my higher education and my encounter with discourses on Deaf empowerment and culture primarily took place in a Western context. In that sense, my dissertation work, from which this chapter materialized (İlkbaşaran 2015), has been pivotal in grounding my understanding of Turkish deaf people's experiences and social practices, situated in local and global dynamics.

My discussion here is primarily based on in-depth interviews that I conducted in 2012 with thirty-three young deaf and hard of hearing individuals in Istanbul (ages seventeen to forty). Of these participants, eighteen were students at a vocational high school for the deaf[2] and the remaining fifteen were young adults with high school degrees. The interviews followed a script of questions grouped around their linguistic, communicative, social, and media practices. These interviews took between one to four hours each and were conducted in TID, sometimes accompanied by spoken Turkish depending on the participants' language preferences. In addition, I rely on my ethnographic work with the Turkish deaf community since 2010, consisting of online and face to face participant observations. My additional virtual ethnography was conducted largely in the fall of 2014, revealing more recent trends that were not apparent in my 2012 interviews.

MOBILITIES

Our lives are increasingly impacted by digital and mobile technologies that mediate our everyday interactions. These new technologies of information and communication lead to new mobilities: they create new patterns of movement, paths, and relationships among people, objects, and ideas, extending our social practice and experience beyond the physical realm (Latour 1997; Urry 2000, 2007). According to Urry (2000), the concept of *mobility* is critical in understanding late modern individuals and the societies in which they live, as individuals interact with the help of increasingly complex tools that extend further into space and time. Urry (2000) distinguishes between four interdependent modes of human travel: corporeal, imaginative, virtual, and communicative (see Table 1). I use this distinction as a conceptual framework to organize my investigation of deaf Turkish youths' social navigation and networks. Urry's mobilities paradigm can be a productive and pluralistic analytical framework in investigating the many dimensions of deaf people's social life in the twenty-first century, which are diversely mediated and culturally situated. I consider this paradigm to be pluralistic in the sense that it identifies and makes visible the types of social navigation and interaction that would otherwise be overlooked or not considered as interdependent. Through this framework, we get a holistic picture that brings together online and offline interactions of deaf people at the national and international levels, which are made possible through a range of institutions, events, and technologies. The goal of my wider study of Turkish deaf youth mobilities is to understand how the different modes of social navigation experienced by this population are linked to one another (see Ilkbasaran 2015), but in this chapter I mostly foreground communicative travel.

Communicative travel, in this paradigm, refers to the sense of travel we experience by communicating with another person. The technologies that make this

---

[2] The Turkish State uses "Special Education Vocational High School" (Turkish: Özel Eğitim Meslek Lisesi) as an umbrella term for vocational high schools serving students with both "orthopedic disabilities" and "hearing disabilities", while the schools serving these two populations are separate. Currently, there are 18 special education vocational high schools serving deaf and hard of hearing students (MEB 2014).

Table 1 **Modes of Human Travel Based on Urry's (2000, 2007) Mobilities Paradigm**

Mode of Travel	Primary Medium of Interaction	Description
Corporeal	Physical space	People traveling from one physical location to another (for survival, legal reasons, work, pleasure, exploration, etc.)
Imaginative	Cognitive space	The sense of being displaced while interacting with a range of visual media (i.e., text, images, film or one's own memory)
Communicative	Linguistic space	The sense of travel one experiences by communicating with others (via bodies, writing, pigeons, fax, telephone, mobile phones, etc.)
Virtual	Digital space	People traveling in virtual space and interacting with things, people, and places without having to relocate physically (via Internet, social media, gaming, etc.)

happen range from bodies to things, from analog to digital, from stationary to mobile (i.e., telegraphs, letters, pigeons, fax, telephone, mobile phones, text messages). As communication becomes increasingly mobile and mediated by Internet-based technologies in the twenty-first century, communicative travel and virtual travel overlap more with one another. In communicative travel the emphasis is human interaction, whereas virtual travel could also refer to spatial practices that take place in the virtual realm, without having to interact with another person. In that sense, for this chapter, I engage with a smaller subset of virtual travel that has to do with communication.

I find Blommaert's (2010) suggestion to study language repertoires as mobility-bound instead of place-bound to be an accurate response to contemporary communicative practices that are continuously shaped by diversely situated trans-local connections. This means that as individuals and groups move through a range of social spaces, they acquire, produce, and move with them a repertoire of language and literacy varieties, reflecting their particular biographies. This also applies to deaf people's communicative encounters and the language repertoires that they gather on the move. Together, these two complementary frameworks can help us further explore the relations between deaf people's social and language practices.

The Use of Mobile and Internet-Based Technologies

Almost all nonresidential young deaf individuals participating in the study I conducted in İstanbul had access to a computer with Internet connection at home, and many had webcams. Residential students were the most limited in terms of computer and Internet access. Mobile phones are a part of almost all deaf individuals' daily life in Turkey, and smart phones are increasingly prevalent as they become more affordable. With a few exceptions, all my participants had cell phones, most of them being smart phones. There appear to be three main factors that inform their access to and use of text messaging: (1) their own textual literacy abilities, (2) the textual literacy and digital literacy abilities of their interlocutors (deaf friends or hearing parents), and (3) the socioeconomic status of their families. A significant number of my participants used cheaper packages in their smart phones, with limited access to the Internet and multimedia services. They typically keep the 3G services off in these devices and turn it on either when they have more money or if there is a communicative emergency. This is important, as the video chat in TID is not available without 3G. Other strategies used particularly to meet face to face were sharing images of surrounding landmarks or using Whatsapp, a text and multimedia messaging application for iPhone and Android phones, which has a "location share" feature. These vernacular strategies improve their distant communication by helping them overcome their limitations in textual literacy, and allow for more spontaneous Deaf spaces to emerge, freeing deaf people from more traditional meeting spots such as Deaf clubs.

When at home, almost all my informants preferred instant messaging using MSN (prior to 2013) and Skype (when MSN discontinued its services in 2013), accompanied by Facebook for social media. Almost all of my participants had more contacts that they kept in touch via Facebook compared to MSN Messenger, because they perceived the latter as more private. They use MSN and Skype primarily for instant messaging or video chatting with close friends and relatives in TID.

Based on the language measures that I have used in my dissertation work with the same participants, my interactions with the community and my observations of the written Turkish skills of Turkish deaf adults on Facebook, I can say that the majority of (especially profoundly and prelingually) deaf people in Turkey are not skilled enough in standard written Turkish to effectively express their complex thoughts and ideas in text. However, this does not stop them from engaging in regular textual conversation online. E-mail is not a common practice among this group, likely due to textual literacy limitations and the prevalence of online video chat from home computers that allows for direct communication in sign language instead. They prefer text messaging to e-mail, probably because the former is a genre of textual communication that permits the use of simpler sentences and abbreviations to communicate with one another. The majority of written exchanges are either simple or incomplete Turkish sentences, or a string of words that are typed using no punctuation or structures that follow Turkish morphosyntactic rules. Instead, many appear to be using Turkish words to represent TID signs, such that only thinking in TID grammar makes these textual utterances intelligible to others. Also referred to as *glossing*, this is a symbolic manipulation tactic used by many Deaf people around the world, using the written word to represent sign languages (Okuyama 2013).

A few of my participants, especially in the young adult group, also reported using CamFrog (TİD: w-e-b) or ooVoo, which bring deaf people from around the world together virtually. Although some had experienced public chat rooms and the multiuser video chat function of these platforms, many tend to limit their use to password-protected private sessions with close friends. It appears that one of the reasons behind such conservative use of this online platform is the mismatch between their cultural and moral values and the behaviors that they observed in these temporary virtual international Deaf spaces. One of my participants indicated avoiding this platform altogether, due to the "vulgar" or "obscene" things that they encountered in this environment. Another young deaf adult mentioned that because the connections made via ooVoo are not typically followed with face to face meetings, they tend to get boring and not last too long. Apart from a few exceptions, all participants reported that their contacts on online social networking sites and webcam were people that they frequently interact with face to face such as close friends or relatives. This parallels findings in literature on communication and travel practices with respect to the geographical distribution of strong and weak ties within one's social networks (Urry 2003; Larsen et al. 2006).

International Mobilities of Deaf Youth in Turkey

In describing the functioning of mobilities, Urry (2007) refers to "mobility systems" that distribute people, activities, and objects through time and space. This term is primarily used to refer to systems that enable specific means of physical transportation (i.e., the pedestrian system, the road system, the rail system), as well as technologies that organize our imaginative, communicative, and virtual travels (i.e., the telephone system, networked computer systems). In my work, I instead consider Deaf institutions as systems of mobility, organizing the social and spatial distribution of deaf people in particular ways. While the schools for the deaf are the primary institutions that function as systems of mobility at the local and national levels for deaf children and adolescents in Turkey, in this section I focus on institutions that play a large role in creating *international* mobilities and encounters for deaf youth in Turkey.

Both the national and international mobilities of deaf people in Turkey are primarily driven by sports events. While younger students get to travel around Turkey for competitions and festivals, young deaf adults also travel internationally, meeting deaf people from other countries. During these corporeal journeys, they expand their world knowledge, connect with deaf peers from other places, and are exposed to variants of TID or other sign languages. There are almost eight thousand deaf athletes registered with the Turkish Sports Federation of the Deaf (Türkiye İşitme Engelliler Spor Federasyonu [TİESF]), with a 6:1 ratio of men to women. The accomplishments of deaf athletes have been the primary source of success and recognition for deaf people in Turkey.

Turkish deaf individuals' initial encounters with deaf people from around the world seem to primarily take place through their participation in international Deaf sports events such as the *Deaflympics*, or other events organized by the International Committee of Sports for the Deaf (ICSD).[3] Currently there are more than 16,000 "Deaflympians" from 109 countries that are listed with the ICSD. Statistics show a noticeable rise in participation from Turkey especially since 2009, with the number of athletes reaching 169 by 2013.[4] There is a significant asymmetry in

---

[3] For a calendar of upcoming international Deaf sports events organized by ICSD, see http://www.deaflympics.com/calendar.asp

[4] For a breakdown of statistics on Turkish Deaf athletes participating in ICSD, see http://www.deaflympics.com/countries.asp?country=TUR

the gender distribution among Turkish deaf athletes competing internationally, however, with 131 male (mean age 26.9) to 38 female (mean age 23.4) athletes. These are important to keep in mind, with respect to the demographics of Turkish deaf people who have direct access to IS and other sign languages around sports events. In some cases, these short-term encounters lead to more long-term networks through the use of webcams and smart phones. These international events do not typically attract deaf nonathletes from Turkey mostly because of problems obtaining visas.

This international deaf contact sustained through repeated Deaf sports events has led TİESF to become the lead organization creating IS resources for Turkish deaf people.[5] The first TID-IS dictionary with a DVD was published in 2012 by TİESF. This new resource is likely to both increase IS literacy among deaf people in Turkey and possibly lead to more Turkish participation in international Deaf events. Responding to increasing demand, TİESF has also been organizing workshops on IS in several cities. Skills in an internationally accessible sign language are increasing in prestige among young deaf adults in Turkey, following TID. It is important to note here that in Turkey, the majority of the deaf community does not know the globally accepted IS sign for INTERNATIONAL SIGN, however, and instead refer to it as EUROPE SIGN (ES) in TID[6]. This is parallel with the existing and potential mobilities and sign language contact situations available to deaf people in Turkey. Then again, signs referred to as ES signs by Turkish deaf signers may in fact be ASL signs at times, suggesting more of a Western conceptual framing than the signs' actual origins.

Another similar source for Turkish deaf people was a book produced by the Çankaya Deaf Youth Sports Association in Ankara, with TID signs organized thematically in Turkish and presented along with their translations in English, Spanish, Russian, French, and German. It is likely that the choice of these languages reflects Turkish deaf youth's existing international Deaf encounters; however, this needs to be studied before making any claims.

These emerging workshops and resources on IS are partly in preparation for the World Federation of the Deaf World Congress (WFDWC) that Turkey will host in Istanbul in 2015.[7] The Congress is especially of value to deaf people in the host country as they get to interact with deaf people from around the world and are exposed to different sign languages, without travelling to distant destinations. The Congress will likely create a range of communicative mobilities for deaf people in Turkey, perhaps also shaping their virtual and even future corporeal mobilities.

These workshops and resources on IS also reflect an increasing communicative demand among young deaf people in Turkey, who are both corporeally and virtually more mobile beyond national borders compared to older people in their community. As a result of increasing global Deaf events and cheaper travel and communication opportunities, they have more chances to meet deaf people from

---

[5] For the official website of TİESF, see http://sessizler.sgm.gov.tr/

[6] The decision to refer to EUROPE SIGN with the acronym ES in this chapter is mine and for practical purposes only. This is not an acronym that is actually used among TID signers.

[7] The Seventh World Congress of the World Federation of the Deaf will be held in Istanbul July 28–August 1, 2015. For more information, refer to the official website: http://www.wfdcongress2015.org/

other counties. Turkey is also a popular travel destination for many, including deaf people. Many Deaf tourists, especially those from Western countries, seek opportunities to meet Turkish deaf people when they are in Turkey. Then both the national sign languages of the interlocutors and IS become meaningful as they are anchored in shared experience and, depending on the potential of these new connections lasting, worth retaining as a useful communication tool. Similarly, the home countries of these tourists become a part of Turkish deaf people's conceptual map, perceived not only as abstract concepts but also as real places that can be potential future travel destinations

Overall, the international mobilities of Turkish deaf youth are informed by a combination of factors that include but are not limited to the following: (1) the possibility of an initial physical encounter with a deaf person from another country, (2) the communicative success and psychosocial gratification from this shared experience, (3) the conceptualization of these new people and places as destinations that are aligned with one's identity and social goals, (4) the motivation to reconnect, and (5) the socioeconomic and technological factors that inform the ease to communicate and travel to one another.

Online Sign Language Videos

In 2012, when I conducted most of my interviews, TİD videos were not frequently used among deaf people in Turkey on social media. However, this trend of low TID-based authorship on social media has been changing in the past year, particularly on Facebook. One possible explanation could be that the increased frequency of TID videos shared by the leaders or administrators of Deaf organizations in Turkey may have normalized this practice among the community. While deaf individuals initially shared videos concerned with holiday or birthday greetings, these videos are gradually being accompanied by opinion pieces on particular Deaf events (such as national or international Deaf sports events) or other topics concerning deaf people in Turkey (such as nationwide entrance exams for education or employment) or world events (such as the Israel-Palestine conflict).

This eventual normalization of the production and sharing of online sign language videos by deaf people in Turkey has led to several types of D/deaf-authored public pages on Facebook: (1) pages that address deaf people in Turkey, (2) pages that relay international Deaf news to deaf people in Turkey, and (3) pages that aim to reach both Turkish and international D/deaf communities through their videos. My data in this section come from virtual ethnography, consisting of both my virtual participant observations on Facebook and the responses to a small online survey that I conducted in November 2014. This survey consisted of a TID video that I produced and shared on my Facebook wall, through which I asked my deaf contacts in Turkey to post their favorite Turkish D/deaf-authored Facebook pages or groups as comments.

I identified about fifteen public Facebook pages that are authored by D/deaf people in Turkey, where they share original content in TID. Eight of these pages include the words *Deaf* or *TV* in their titles. This appropriation of the English term *Deaf* instead of the commonly used Turkish word *işitme engelli* (meaning *hearing disabled*) could be a political gesture towards the Western Deaf cultural identity and empowerment discourse. It may as well be a reference to a particular genre of Deaf-authored social media channels, a common practice that can be observed internationally. Both on YouTube and on Facebook, a quick search on "Deaf TV" results in many channels from all around the world. In that sense, it could be a shared code among Deaf people worldwide, making pages with sign language content easily searchable and identifiable.

Despite the preference for the English word *Deaf*, the language of choice on these pages is primarily TID. This suggests they are aimed for the Turkish deaf audience and not necessarily the international Deaf audience. The use of the term *TV* suggests their function as similar to that of television channels. One of my hard of hearing informants ties this behavior to the lack of captioning on Turkish broadcast television, stating that this led Turkish deaf and hard of hearing people to make use of Facebook's features so that it functions like a television channel for Turkish D/deaf people. Another feature that many of these Facebook pages share is a page-specific logo that appears both on the profile picture or the cover photo of the page, and sometimes even in the opening or top right corner of the videos produced by the hosts. For all these reasons combined, I use the terms Facebook *pages* and *channels* interchangeably during the remainder of the chapter.

A quick overview and analysis of these fifteen Facebook channels reveal the following: (1) all authors are young D/deaf men from Turkey in their twenties and thirties, except for two pages that are authored by married couples and one hard of hearing woman, (2) half of these pages were launched in 2014, suggesting an increasing or temporary trend, (3) the most popular content appear to be jokes and funny stories, followed by Islamic content and informative videos on a range of topics, (4) some of these authors show advanced skills in video editing, as can be seen from the use of subtitles, photo overlays, transitions, integration of multiple video files, or Skype interviews, and (5) some of the authors use a public YouTube channel in parallel with their Facebook page.

In addition to these Facebook channels, some deaf or hard of hearing people in Turkey use their personal Facebook accounts to occasionally share TID videos, responding to current events or telling their personal stories. However, overall deaf people in Turkey still primarily use a mix of photographs or written Turkish in their status updates. An important technical limitation of Facebook is that one cannot post a "comment" in video, making it impossible for people to carry out sign language conversations directly. That is why even when responding to sign language videos on Facebook, deaf people are restricted to using text and images (e.g., emoticons, animated gifs).

It is intriguing how the exchange of multimedia and especially video content in TID also seems to be changing the nature of deaf people's online textual exchanges in Turkish. By looking at the "comments" feature of Facebook and comparing the threads under photo posts with those under video posts, there seem to be a noticeable qualitative difference between them. It appears that the ability to post more complex ideas in TID by video sharing creates a context in which other deaf people engaging with those videos are motivated to use Turkish in more complex and creative ways. Likewise, the accessibility and content of these videos also trigger responses from other deaf people who post and share sign language videos on their wall. This trend is similar to the interactive practices around YouTube vlogs in ASL that became popular about eight years ago.

Language Choice (TID vs. IS) and Intended Audience

As the practice of sharing self-authored sign language videos on Facebook becomes increasingly popular among deaf people in Turkey, interesting dynamics with respect to language choice develop. Earlier, I mentioned the increasing popularity of IS among deaf people in Turkey. Here, I elaborate on what this could mean in terms of their language ideologies and mobilities, as materialized in their sign language practices on Facebook.

In my 2012 interviews, I found that deaf high school students were typically not interested in watching sign language videos produced by signers from other countries due to language barriers. When asked about what kind of sign language material they tend to watch online, one of the female students from the first study responded: "I watch only Turkish Sign (Language) . . . not those of other countries. . . . I don't know their languages, so I don't watch them." Only a few students reported that they watched videos in other sign languages, because they were fascinated with the sign language song interpretations that Deaf people in other countries were producing. I come back to this genre in the next section.

However, surprisingly, the same students were very interested in learning ASL from me during the time that I spent at this school (also see Moges, this volume). Many times during lunch, students would bombard me with questions, asking me to sign a series of concepts in ASL. They even asked me to spend a night at the dorm, so that I could give them a crash course in ASL. Because of both time limitations and ethical concerns, I had to turn down that invitation. I bring this up because I believe that younger deaf individuals do not watch as many videos in other national sign languages because they do not have the particular linguistic and cultural literacies to make sense of them, not necessarily because of their disinterest in other sign languages or in the lives of other deaf people. When they get older and leave school, however, they seem to find more opportunities to interact with peers who are more competent in IS or other national sign languages. Once they acquire more cultural and linguistic knowledge about other Deaf worlds, have more time and interest in making new connections, and have more access to high-speed Internet, they also seem to be more interested in exploring more sign language videos online. There were several individuals among the high school graduates I interviewed who mentioned watching Deaf vlogs on YouTube or Facebook, for instance, especially those that are tailored to the international Deaf audience, such as interviews with Deaf people from around the world.

There is an increasing tendency among Turkish D/deaf Facebook page hosts to bring foreign signs into their videos. There could be several reasons for this. First, building on the literature discussed previously, one of the appeals of using IS/ES/ASL is its symbolic association with a range of literacies and mobilities. In Turkey, IS or ES symbolizes "mobility" as it (1) reveals one's past physical or virtual international Deaf contact and language exposure, (2) implies a certain social status or mobility by giving reference to one's capability of such travel, (3) offers a form of communicative travel in the moment of its articulation, (4) creates a potential for imaginative travel in the moment of its reception, and (5) suggests one's potential for future corporeal, virtual, or communicative travel outside of Turkish social boundaries.

Second, I believe that this tendency could also be partly the influence of other channels, either on YouTube or Facebook, where Deaf people from around the world publish their original content, primarily in IS. In particular, for many new D/deaf hosts in Turkey, a Romania-based Turkish Deaf man's Facebook page serves as a model. This page has been running since 2011, with close to 165 IS videos to date on a range of topics and more than sixty eight thousand followers from all around the world. Similarly, when it comes to storytelling, song interpretations, or other artistic performances in sign language, American Deaf poets and performers saturate social media. This creates a really interesting case, such that the adoption of the "Deaf TV" genre brings with it elements of IS, while the adoption of "signed performance" as a genre results in the author borrowing from the narrative aesthetics of the American Deaf culture and properties of ASL.

One such example among the videos produced by Turkish Deaf youth is a female host's remake of the Deaf American performance artist Rosa Lee Timm's "It Feels So Good" in ASL. Because the host is not fluent in ASL, the video becomes more of an imitation of Rosa Lee's gestures and body language rather than the actual lyrics. Exactly a year after this video, the host shared another one, this time what appears to be an IS sign poetry authored by herself, based on a French music video that takes place in Paris. In her signing, there are elements of ASL storytelling, and she uses a mix of ASL and European signs. I find these examples valuable as they capture both (1) the appeal that Western and mostly American Deaf performance (poetry, storytelling, and song interpretations) has for Turkish deaf youth and (2) the new generation's growing interest in connecting with the international Deaf audience. It is important to note that this IS influence is often seen in entertainment videos, whereas informative content concerning the Turkish Deaf community, which constitutes the bulk of the self-authored video content produced by the community, is almost strictly in TID.

Although currently the frequency of IS or ES use is not much compared to TID on these Turkey-based Facebook pages overall, this is still an increasing interest and tendency, especially among the younger generation who have international Deaf contacts. These instances are regarded as more disconcerting and threatening by the Turkish deaf community, particularly older members. In fall 2014, several Turkish deaf people made their own videos in TID, criticizing this temptation and explaining why Turkish deaf people should hold on to their own heritage by using TID. These videos and the comments that follow reveal the emergence of TID purists responding to the newly emerging global Deaf citizens from Turkey, who wish to be understood by deaf people beyond their national borders.

However, this anxiety about languages dominating the neoliberal global economy is not unique to sign languages. This is an issue even for Turkish, a well-documented language. Very similar conversations have been taking place about the influence of English on Turkish, which date to before Facebook. In the case of TID, although the language became official and legally recognized in 2005, research on the language is only a little more than a decade old, and it is not yet thoroughly documented. Such underdocumentation makes languages a lot more fragile in the face of established languages, let alone a hypercentral language such as English (de Swaan 2001).

On the other hand, TID interpretations of Turkish songs, which often end up being signed Turkish (as in using TID signs following Turkish word order), are becoming increasingly popular among Turkish children of deaf adults (CODAs) and the hearing TID signer community, along with nonsigner hearing celebrities that are often preferred for public campaigns. These videos appeal to masses of hearing people who then want to learn TID, which creates a faulty image of TID as signed Turkish.

CONCLUSION

This chapter brought together two prominent theoretical frameworks based on the mobilities of twenty-first-century social life as an analytical tool to study contemporary communicative practices of deaf youth in Turkey: Urry's (2000) mobilities paradigm and Blommaert's (2010) sociolinguistics of mobility. Following a description of strategies used by this community to communicate with each other via mobile and Internet-based technologies, I focused on their attitudes and choices with regards to the acquisition and the use of transnationally recognized sign language variants beyond TID (i.e., IS, ES, ASL).

This is a critical point in the history of deaf people in Turkey, where the ubiquity of technologies and social media that legitimize both textual and nontextual forms of expression and exchange creates juxtapositions of symbolic exchange and new routes for empowerment. Within the past few years we have seen the circulation of an unprecedented amount of TID content on Facebook, bringing a range of conversations to a more widely shared public sphere. Similarly, these TID videos seem to elicit more complex textual productions in Turkish, by providing more complex common grounds to deaf people as a starting point. Deaf people in Turkey are in the process of finding their own visibility and voice through social media, both individually and as a group. However, this new wave of Turkish D/deaf authorship is both borrowing from and clashing with Western sensibilities of Deaf performance and visibility.

As I have illustrated throughout the chapter, there appear to be two main incentives for Turkish deaf youth in acquiring and using internationally recognized sign language variants: (1) to participate in international Deaf events such as sports tournaments and (2) to reach a wider Deaf audience via online sign language performances that can be shared globally. However, at least for now, both incentives appear to have an impact on a relatively smaller group of young and advantaged deaf people in Turkey, who are already fluent in TID, live in large cities, and have international D/deaf contacts with whom they can meet in person, even if sporadically. These practices are also situated in existing social divides in the Turkish society (i.e., gender, socioeconomic status). Perhaps more interestingly, such trendy yet infrequent self-authored videos on Facebook that attempt to make use of IS have instead instigated subtle but observable nationalistic reaction and discourse among the Turkish deaf community, on conserving and cherishing TID. Instead of being identified only against Turkish, TID is now also identified and owned against IS or other foreign sign language variants, foregrounding the cultural values and sensibilities that it embodies.

Aligned with Bloammaert and Dong's (2010) quote that I opened this chapter with, I argue that the use of sign language variants on social media gives away not only the past corporeal mobilities and contacts of deaf people but also their conceptual frameworks on the linguistic norms of this virtual social space as well as their communicative motivations and imagined interlocutors. In that sense, as an ever-growing yet relatively unstable communicative archive, social media offers a rich ephemeral space to observe deaf people's changing language ideologies and attitudes.

REFERENCES

AKTİDHK [Akıllı Türk İşaret Dili Hazırlık Kitabı]. 2012. *Ankara Çankaya İşitme Engelliler Gençlik Spor Kulübü Derneği*, Ankara Ticaret, Beyda Ofset, Ankara.

Bauman, H.-D. L., and J. Murray. 2010. "Deaf Studies in the Twenty-First Century: Deaf-Gain and the Future of Human Diversity." In *Oxford Handbook on Deaf Studies, Language, and Education*, edited by M. Marschark and P. Spencer. Oxford, UK: Oxford University Press.

Blommaert, J. 2010. *The Sociolinguistics of Globalization*. Cambridge, UK: Cambridge University Press.

Blommaert, J., and J. Dong. 2010. "Language and Movement in Space." In *Handbook of Language and Globalisation*, edited by N. Coupland. Oxford, UK: Blackwell.

De Swaan, A. 2001. *Words of the World: The Global Language System*. Cambridge, UK: Polity Press.

Friedner, M., and A. Kusters. 2014. "On the Possibilities and Limits of 'DEAF DEAF SAME': Tourism and Empowerment Camps in Adamorobe (Ghana), Bangalore, and Mumbai (India)."*Disability Studies Quarterly* 34 (3). http://dsq-sds.org/article/view/4246/3649.

Green, M. 2014. "Building the Tower of Babel: International Sign, Linguistic Commensuration, and Moral Orientation."*Language in Society* 43:445–65.

Hiddinga, A., and O. Crasborn. 2011. "Sign Language and Globalization."*Language in Society* 40:483–505.

İlkbaşaran, D. 2015. "Literacies, Mobilities, and Agencies of Deaf Youth in Turkey: Constraints and Opportunities in the Twenty-First Century." PhD diss., University of California, San Diego.

Kusters, A. 2010. "Deaf on the Lifeline of Mumbai."*Sign Language Studies* 10 (1): 36–68.

Larsen, J., K. Axhausen, and J. Urry. 2006. "Geographies of Social Networks: Meetings, Travel, and Communications."*Mobilities* 1 (2): 261–83.

Latour, B. 1997. "Where Are the Missing Masses? The Sociology of a Few Mundane Artifacts." In *Shaping Technology / Building Society: Studies in Sociotechnical Change*, edited by W. E. Bijker and J. Law. Cambridge, MA: MIT Press.

Lucas, C., ed. 2001. *The Sociolinguistics of Sign Languages*. New York: Cambridge University Press.

MEB [Turkish Ministry of National Education Strategy Development Presidency]. 2014. *National Education Statistics: Formal Education 2013/'14*. Ankara: MEB. http://sgb.meb .gov.tr/www/milli-egitim-istatistikleri-orgun-egitim-2013-2014/icerik/95.

Okuyama, Y. 2013. "A Case Study of US Deaf Teens' Text Messaging: Their Innovations and Adoption of Textisms."*News Media and Society* 15 (8): 1224–40.

Urry, J. 2000. *Sociology beyond Societies: Mobilities of the Twenty-First Century*. London: Routledge.

———. 2003. "Social Networks, Travel, and Talk." *British Journal of Sociology* 54 (2): 155–75.

———. 2007. *Mobilities*. Cambridge, MA: Polity Press.

Valentine, G., and T. Skelton. 2008. "Changing Spaces: The Role of the Internet in Shaping Deaf Geographies."*Social and Cultural Geography* 9 (5): 469–85.

Part 3

▮ PROJECTS

11 | Andrew Foster Touches Eternity: From Nigeria to Fiji

'Gbenga Aina

Alexander Quaynor, lead instructor in English as a Second Language (ESL) at Gallaudet University's English Language Institute (ELI), was an administrator at Dr. Andrew Foster's Ibadan Mission School for the Deaf in Nigeria. He describes Dr. Foster as a dedicated workaholic who arrived at his office at first light and was often the last to leave, lunching daily on roasted peanuts and bananas. Isaac Agboola, interim dean at Gallaudet's School of Business, Education, and Human Services, has similar recollections (Agboola 2014).

Andrew Foster was born on June 27, 1925 in Ensley, Alabama. Deafened at age eleven by spinal meningitis, he attended the Alabama School for the Negro Deaf in Talladega. In 1954, he became the first African American to graduate from Gallaudet College in Washington, DC, with a degree in education, and in 1957, he was the first to earn a master's degree in education from Eastern Michigan University. Foster then earned another master's in missions and education from Seattle Pacific Christian College. From 1957 to 1987, he established churches and mission schools for the Deaf in thirteen African countries: Ghana, Nigeria, Côte d'Ivoire, Togo, Chad, Senegal, Benin Republic, Cameroon, Central African Republic, Zaire (now Congo Democratic Republic), Burkina Faso, Burundi, and Gabon, plus churches in Kenya, Sierra Leone, Congo, and Guinea. He spent six months each year in Africa establishing schools and the other six months in the United States raising funds to support them through his organization, Christian Mission for Deaf Africans. Consequently, Foster is widely regarded as the "father of Deaf education" in Africa. In 1970 Gallaudet granted him an honorary doctor of humane letters in recognition of his accomplishments. Andrew Foster's life ended in a plane crash in Rwanda on December 3, 1987 (Nicholas n.d.). In October 2004, Gallaudet renamed the Ely Auditorium the Andrew Foster Auditorium, with the honorific "Father of Deaf Education in Africa" on the commemorative plaque beneath his bust. As director of Gallaudet's Office of International Programs and Services (OIPS) at the time, I co-wrote the epitaph on the plaque.

Foster's followers used his methods to bring education to Deaf people in Fiji in the late 1990s. This chapter explores similarities between the cases, based on interviews with two distinct sets of respondents: (i) those who had worked directly with Foster in Africa and (ii) those who worked in Fiji. In the case of the first group, I sought to understand how Foster worked, how he built his relationships, his methods, and his relationship with Deaf Africans. In the case of the second group, I sought any similarities or distinctions between their responses and the responses provided by the first group.

I am Nigerian by birth but now live in the United States. Note that I neither am a Foster protégé nor attended a school established by Foster. The bulk of my education in Nigeria was in hearing settings: at Christ's School, Ado-Ekiti, a prestigious parochial high school, Obafemi Awolowo University, Ile-Ife, and the Nigerian Law School. Nonetheless, as an African of Nigerian heritage, I have connections with Deaf people who are protégés of, or been impacted by, Foster, which helps facilitate my research.

Unless otherwise indicated, all interviewees are deaf. Interviewees in the first group included Innocent Djonthe (Cameroon), Ebenezer Asamoah, the hearing former executive director of the Ghana National Association of the Deaf (GNAD), Isaac Agboola (Nigeria), Stephen Boateng and Joseph Kulego (both Ghana), Alexander Quaynor (Nigeria/Ghana), Ezekiel Sambo (Nigeria), and Elizabeth Tetteh-Ocloo, who is hearing, and her husband,Seth Tetteh-Ocloo (both Ghana), all of whom were Foster protégés during the early years. Matthew Adedeji and 'Wale Alade, both Nigerians, provided illuminating narratives on their strategies in Fiji and the South Pacific, which furnished important material for comparisons to be drawn with Foster's. Finally, Tim Foster, one of Foster's sons who is hearing, supplied insight into his father's motivations in an e-mail exchange. All e-mail conversations were conducted in English and are noted as personal communications in the text.

In addition to the interviews, two notable primary sources were a July 2009 video interview of the late Ezekiel Sambo, one of Foster's first Deaf protégés from Nigeria who later founded the Plateau State School for the Deaf in Jos, Nigeria (interview conducted by Lawrence Musa, coordinator of Immigration Compliance and International Procedures at Gallaudet University's Office of Research Support and International Affairs); and a March 2014 video interview of Seth Tetteh-Ocloo, of the eponymous School for the Deaf in Accra, Ghana, and Foster's first Deaf African protégé. His wife, Elizabeth Tetteh-Ocloo, the second hearing teacher Foster hired to teach in his school at Osu, also participated in the interview (conducted by Mr. Stephen Boateng, Mr. Joseph Kulego, Dr. Kojo Amissah of Gallaudet University's Career Center, and Gallaudet undergraduate student Ms. Jessica Nortey). Both interviews were conducted in the common sign language of West Africa.

THE ANDREW FOSTER MODEL

Andrew Foster's African mission was carried out through the Christian Mission for Deaf Africans, the original name of his international development vehicle, which was incorporated in Detroit, Michigan, in 1956. It is now known as the Christian Mission for the Deaf (CMD) (see http://www.cmdeaf.org/). As the original name suggests, Foster's prime objective was to bring the Christian Gospel to Deaf people in Africa.

Amply demonstrating the point, Tim Foster (personal communication) said:

> I do wish that more people understood the source of my father's passion. Yes—he wanted to help fellow Deaf people advance in the world by education, employment, etc.—but more than this, he cared about the souls of men. He firmly believed that the most important part of a human is not material, but immaterial: his eternal soul. . . . This passion to reach the souls of men is what drove my father to do the things he did.

In that vein, Innocent Djonthe, who was trained by Foster in Cameroon and now runs his own school, Center for Education and Rehabilitation of Deaf and Hard of Hearing children, in Bafoussam, Cameroon, describes Foster as "more of a religious teacher because he preached the Bible so that more deaf people would know God" (personal communication), and Elizabeth Tetteh-Ocloo (video interview) said that "Foster was a very religious man. His original idea of coming to Ghana was to guide Deaf children to God."

In other personal communications, Stephen Boateng, an employee of Foster at Mampong-Akwapim and now a biologist with the US Department of Agriculture, also described him as "a teacher, mentor and spiritual leader" while Joseph Kulego, another employee of Foster in Ghana who now works for the US Postal Service, says that his relationship with Foster was one of "father/son, benefactor, brothers in Christ."

Matthew Adedeji, a former project officer at the Christian Mission for the Deaf in Ibadan and now senior social worker for the Deaf at Croydon Council in Croydon, United Kingdom, expanded on this point by e-mail:

> [Foster's] first mission and vision, when he decided to come to Africa, was to spread the Gospel of Jesus Christ and to prepare Deaf Africans, spiritually. However, he came to realize that there was no education in place for deaf people and whatever literacy skills they possessed were very poor—no reading and writing skills. With this discovery, Foster widened his vision to provide education, vocational training and then added the spiritual aspect of his work to this. He believed that a Deaf man or woman must be prepared spiritually and educationally to face the challenges in life and after then could become an effective leader in the community. [This] established a template that Foster was to use for the next 30 years until his death. This template is still being used by those who he trained and prepared.

Clearly, Foster realized that illiteracy would hinder his primary spiritual mission. Consequently, he went about what had been an ancillary objective but which was now a fundamental mission. He proceeded at a relentless pace—bringing education to Deaf people in sub-Saharan Africa by establishing mission schools where previously there had been no schools whatsoever. He established thirty-two

mission schools in thirteen African countries during thirty years (see http://www
.cmdeaf.org/). This brought about unprecedented access to literacy and, concor-
dantly full access through the educational programs' essential missionary aspect,
to the teachings of Christianity. He also trained Deaf Africans to carry on his
educational, administrative, and ministerial work within their own communities.
Ezekiel Sambo recalled, in a 2009 video interview,

> I met Foster after completing my primary education and he took me to
> Ghana where he trained me as a teacher. I worked with Foster to set up the
> school in Kaduna. He then transferred me to Enugu, where I helped run
> the school. He then transferred me to Ibadan to administrate the school.

According to Alexander Quaynor (personal communication), who is of Ghanaian
parentage but was born in Nigeria,

> He paid for each individual [volunteer] to study for a high school
> equivalency through a correspondence school, the American School
> located on Drexel Avenue in Chicago. Also, he conducted classes on Deaf
> pedagogy in the evenings and gave every volunteer the opportunity to
> gain firsthand experience of teaching deaf children in a self-contained
> classroom. Those who were lucky enough to get this kind of training
> became the vanguard . . . and they trained those who came after them.

In October 1965, Foster established a training center in Mampong-Akwapim,
Ghana, the first African country where he had taught, and his training program
for teachers of Deaf students became formalized. This eliminated the need to train
teachers in England and the United States—which was inadequate—and promoted local staffing of schools for the Deaf (Tetteh-Ocloo 1965). However, Foster
was judicious about whom he selected as leaders and teachers. Adedeji (personal
communication) describes Foster as having a sharp eye for spotting potential deaf
leaders and talented workers who could work with him and the Deaf community.

Engaging the local communities to develop a sense of ownership was fundamental to Foster's method. According to Alex Quaynor, this meant visiting
traditional rulers, homes, and churches in the cities, towns, and villages to look
for potential pupils and build relationships: for example, the board of managers Foster assembled for Ibadan Mission School for the Deaf (IMSD) was composed of local heavyweights and people who could provide needed services. The
proprietor of the Toyobo Printing Press in Ibadan was on the board and often
provided free or discounted printing services for IMSD, such as the printing of
the *Proceedings of the First Conference on the Education of the Deaf in Africa*, convened
by Foster, sponsored by IMSD, and attended by forty-six participants from ten
African and two European countries. This conference opened with a message of
goodwill by the then-governor of Western Nigeria, Sir Odeleye Fadahunsi, and
was held at the University of Ibadan from December 19 to 24, 1965. This convergence of community forces demonstrated the extent of Foster's engagement with
the local community in the pursuit of his mission.

Another example pertains to the donation of land in Mampong-Akwapim by the town's sovereign, Mamponghene Nana Anobaa Sasraku II, in January 1959. This enabled the school to relocate from borrowed premises in Osu, a wealthy Accra suburb, to the more spacious Mampong-Akwapim land, where the Ghana Mission School for the Deaf (GMSD) was established.

Deaf Similitude

This theme of Foster's commitment to training the Deaf populations he met on the ground is echoed by all respondents (personal communications):

Boateng: Yes, Foster did train and prepare most Deaf Africans for leadership roles in their countries. For example, a small country like Ghana today has more than 13 Schools for the Deaf as well as more than 30 Churches for the Deaf. Ghana even has one of the strongest National Associations of the Deaf in Africa. This organization [Ghana National Association of the Deaf, GNAD] was founded by the first deaf person he picked in Ghana to help establish the first School for the Deaf in sub-Saharan Africa, Seth Tetteh-Ocloo.

Kulego: The best thing that could be said of all Deaf Africans who were fortunate to meet and work with Foster is that he did his very best to prepare most of us to assume leadership positions and roles since we were the cream of the crop as well as "eyes of the deaf" in our various countries.

Adedeji: Foster trained and prepared countless Deaf Africans he met to assume leadership roles in their countries. Foster was a great visionary, hardworking and very committed to the cause he believed in.

In his early years in Nigeria, Foster identified Deaf individuals to send to his school in Ghana for a certificate course in Deaf pedagogy. Upon their return to Nigeria, they would then serve as teachers, supervisors, administrators, and office workers. This model was replicated in all the African countries Foster worked in, with many from as close by as Cameroon, Chad, and Niger Republic and as far afield as Ethiopia, going to Ibadan, Nigeria for training once Foster's structures in Nigeria were fully established.

Quaynor (personal communication) corroborates Foster's strategy of growing his manpower quickly by training them himself, and Quaynor is explicit that the majority of people Foster trained were Deaf Africans:

I was only 17 years old when I first met Foster; the fact that I didn't have a secondary education, he made me believe that I was capable of being successful. He instilled in me that I should never say, "I can't" if I hadn't given a shot at whatever task lay before me. *He inspired me to aspire to excel. My association with Foster gave me the confidence to pursue and earn two degrees almost as he had done.*

> *Most of the deaf people in Ghana and Nigeria who had met Foster wanted to be like him. Most of us were so impressed that a deaf man could go to college and earn advanced degrees.* His accomplishments brought hope to those who were formerly helpless because they had become deaf due to some sicknesses. Also, it brought hope that deaf children could be educated too which was formerly thought impossible. (Emphasis mine)

In societies where Deaf people were considered unequal citizens, the notion of Deaf equality and educability was remarkable. Evidence for inequality is provided by Tetteh-Ocloo who, from her vantage point as a hearing person, recalled that

> When men would ask me where I worked and I told them I taught at the School for the Deaf, I would never see them again. People didn't want me to work there for fear that I would become deaf or have deaf children. People were afraid of me. They did not accept deafness. They didn't like it. . . . Deaf couples could be evicted from their rental homes because their children were crying during the night and disturbing the neighbors. . . . People in Ghana need to see Deaf people as human beings who can do anything that hearing people can do. (video interview)

Her husband remembers being unemployed—not unusual for Deaf persons in Ghana at the time—until Foster offered him a job teaching at the school in Osu. Similarly, in her book *Give Them a Name*, Florence Serwaa Oteng, deafened by spinal meningitis and consequently reduced from nurse to laborer, describes the outcast status—even in their own families—and concomitant poverty of Deaf people in Ghana (Oteng 1988).

In those circumstances, a man of Foster's stature, who had graduate degrees and was a preacher, became an inspiration. Quaynor's language underlined the potency of the "deaf-deaf same" mechanism, which was defined to interviewees as "an affinity or kinship arising from shared deafness." Kulego, Boateng, and Adedeji agree:

Kulego: So much has been said and made of the way Foster built relationships with Deaf Africans and for me it is important to note that prior to all of us meeting him, we were treated like second class citizens in our various countries, and *our meeting him made us see the light.* Without doubt, I had the sense of a very special and unique relationship with Foster and I would not trade it for anything else. . . . Yes, *Foster is blessed with a very special and unique way of cultivating that special bond with deaf people.* (Emphasis mine)

Boateng: Yes, *Foster worked to cultivate relationships with deaf children and adults and they were based on Deaf-same.* For example he did not like the way hearing teachers treated deaf children. He always wanted it to be "Deaf like me." (Emphasis mine)

Adedeji: Yes, I observed that Foster's work with Deaf children and adults was clearly based on "Deaf Same", he showed no aloofness or favoritism, his prime ambition, mission and vision was that all Deaf children and adults should attain good education and experience the Gospel of Jesus Christ in their lives and be well prepared spiritually for the future. . . . [He was] *a father figure and leader that Deaf Africans looked up to and aspired to be like.* I have had the privilege of meeting some Deaf Africans. . . . All these people shared the same view of Foster. (Emphasis mine)

An affinity was built between Foster and the Deaf people he met in those African countries, which was based on shared deafness and its attendant existential ramifications that impact their individual and group interface with wider society. Deafness transcended cultural, national, and other differences, undergirded their commonality, and provided for them, through Foster's presence, efforts and example, the possibility of attaining personal excellence.

RIPPLES

By 1987, there were considerably more schools for the Deaf in the various African countries where Foster had worked, including some he did not establish himself. In Nigeria, for example, as of 1985, there were approximately forty-four schools for the Deaf owned, run, and operated by individuals, state governments, and missionary associations (Ojile 1994). The number has increased, as each of Nigeria's thirty-six states and the Federal Capital Territory now own and operate schools for the Deaf. Private individuals and religious and charitable/philanthropic organizations also own and operate schools, and there is at least one school for the Deaf in most large Nigerian cities today. This does not include high school programs, deaf units in mainstream school programs, the Federal College of Education (Special) in Oyo, or various tertiary education programs across Nigeria. The situation is similar in Ghana with, according to Boateng (personal communication), thirteen schools and thirty churches for the Deaf.

SOUTH-SOUTH DEVELOPMENT: FROM NIGERIA TO FIJI

Matthew Adedeji first met Foster as a high school student in 1984 when Foster visited his Deaf Unit program at Methodist Grammar School, in Ibadan, Nigeria, one of the secondary outgrowths of IMSD. Adedeji (personal communication) recalls that the visit was "inspirational and blew everyone away." The experience was an epiphany:

I clicked with him immediately; he had a cheerful demeanor, words of encouragement and inspiration, and he gave a young man like me and my classmates a sense of hope and someone we could look up to or be like in the future. To find a well-educated deaf person who sacrificed all the comfortable things that life offered in the USA, who was prepared to work in Africa to train and prepare future Deaf African leaders was an overwhelming, motivating and humbling experience.

By 1996, Adedeji was working as a project officer at CMD. He recalls the pivotal moment he decided to go to Fiji:

> One morning in early 1996 the CMD director informed us that they were looking for someone to go to Fiji to do some voluntary work with Christian Fellowship for the Deaf and the Deaf community. . . . At that time, the staff had never heard of an island or country called Fiji. We looked for Fiji on the map and discussed the issue of doing voluntary work there. I felt at that time, there were people who were appropriate candidates, I approached them and encouraged them to go but no one was interested. After some reflection and much careful consideration . . . I was inspired and encouraged to go to Fiji, to give something back to the Deaf community there. . . . [Foster] was the inspiration and a good example for influencing my decision to do voluntary work in Fiji.

Adedeji, fluent in Nigerian Sign Language, went to Fiji in 1997 under CMD's auspices with the same clear gospel propagation intention as Foster had nursed when he first journeyed to Africa in 1957. However, just like Foster upon his arrival in Africa, the conditions he met on the ground in Fiji were dismal. Adedeji recalls:

> Throughout one year of travelling/visiting different deaf "special schools" and communities in Fiji, it became apparent that deaf people in Fiji did not have any good schools to meet their educational needs nor any school that could prepare/train them to be able to read and write and support their development in becoming future leaders able to work and contribute to the development of their country. There was also a lack of self-esteem and problems of low expectations among deaf people about themselves and their futures. Of the few deaf people who were employed the majority were in low paid jobs. It appeared that Fijian society's perception of the Deaf community was not a positive one.

This perception was corroborated by Adedeji's colleague, 'Wale Alade, currently employed in England with the National Health Service (NHS). Alade relocated to Fiji to help begin the educational effort in 1999. Prior to this, he had been employed at CMD as a project officer, succeeding Adedeji. Alade (personal communication) recalls:

> By early 1998, correspondence between [Adedeji] and myself had developed around the situation in Fiji. Deaf people in Fiji could neither read nor write. Education of the Deaf was, at best, a mainstreamed arrangement whereby Deaf children are taught with other children with disabilities. So, as soon as Deaf children come of age, they would then be apprenticed with private businesses some of whom were sponsors and supporters of the school—the Hilton Special School.
> Matthew [Adedeji] mooted an idea that a school for the Deaf would be a way to help Deaf Fijian children to acquire better education; he also

mentioned the need for someone skilled in Deaf education, who would lead the school and train teachers capable of working with Deaf children. He asked me to consider the idea of coming to Fiji to help because of my academic qualifications in Special Education from the University of Ilorin.

The conditions on the ground were such that little value was placed on the education of deaf children. The presence of a deaf child in a family inevitably led to family disharmony and separation. Many of the Deaf children we discovered were either living with grandparents or members of the extended family. Deaf Awareness and the recognition of the rights of Deaf people to aspire to, and indeed pursue, higher education beyond elementary school was never a consideration of either the school where deaf students were being taught or of the officials in the ministry of education.

Alade characterizes relocating to Fiji as "not an attractive proposition" as it involved abandoning his offer of admission for Master's degree studies in Special Education at the University of Ibadan. Conversely, there was what he describes as "a special feeling" of having been uniquely equipped for this task at just the right time. He had the academic qualifications, the didactic project-management know-how, and a strong background in strategic planning –based on this propitious convergence of circumstances, he decided that this was meant to be. He arrived in Fiji in October 1999 to take over the reins at Gospel School for the Deaf (GSD), Samabula, Suva, Fiji, which Adedeji had begun in January of that year.

Throughout their time in Fiji, Adedeji and Alade made a conscious effort to learn and communicate using the language in use in Fiji. Aware of the criticism of Foster in relation to ASL use in Africa, they eschewed using Nigerian Sign Language and adhered strictly to Fijian Sign Language. They saw at first a Fijian approximation of Signed Exact English, according to Alade. Later on, they found there was a natural sign language, Fijian Sign Language (FJSL), used by Deaf Fijians.

FOSTER PARALLELS

Adedeji and Alade recall drawing from many of the methods and approaches that Foster had applied in his successful African mission. The Deaf ministry was an affiliate of a larger church, and that church donated the land upon which to build the Fiji school, paralleling the Mamponghene's donation of land to build the Mission School in Mampong-Akwapim in 1959. They were determined to secure the school's independence from government control in order to fully implement their vision and use that latitude to entrench a full Deaf education. Consequently, funding to support the school and cover staff and teacher salaries was a perpetual concern. Adedeji and Alade built critical coalitions of support through their outreach efforts, which included a newsletter direct from the school. The newsletter resulted in donations arriving from as far away as the United States, the United Kingdom, Canada, Australia, and New Zealand from private, corporate, foreign government, and nongovernmental organization donors. These timely donations were applied to staff and interpreter salaries and student sponsorships to cover the costs of tuition, uniforms, food and board, and transportation to and from school for those living in Suva whose families wanted them to live at home. The school buildings—classrooms and dormitory blocks—were eventually constructed with donor support.

Many of Foster's methods and approaches were employed. Adedeji (personal communication) said:

> There were many lessons from Foster's example in Nigeria that guided my work in Fiji—his work ethic, humility, his tendency to set out a clear vision and to reach out to all the people he worked with, were examples I took with me to Fiji. A particularly important example was that of establishing a Deaf school in Fiji—the first of its kind—and that this should be done without having to criticize or "steal" children/teachers from other Special Schools in Fiji, thereby, avoiding confrontations or creating bad feelings/relationships with other professionals or organizations.
>
> Again, the lesson of using public relations and diplomatic ways of working with others, especially in setting up a new project such as a new school in a foreign country, was an invaluable one. Employing these methods enabled me to set up the school, secure land, and gain approval from the government and the necessary funding needed etc. Also, the necessity to use proper strategies to form international partnerships with other organizations was another invaluable lesson learnt from Foster, which guided me in my successful work in Fiji.

Alade concurs:

> Our work in Fiji modelled exactly similar approaches Foster employed in his African missionary work. It was a work based on faith.
>
> I took a great deal of Foster's strategies on board. I built alliances, established networks and entrenched myself within both the Deaf and hearing communities through a systematic process of openness and expression of deep interest in things that concerned and affected their lives. I made home visits a priority. Whenever we were informed of a sighting or known place where a deaf child lives, we would arrange a visit. Talking to, and encouraging parents to bring a deaf child to school was often met with shock and disbelief. Certain people we approached actually believed a deaf child could not learn. Some would . . . point out they couldn't afford to spend money educating a child for whom it was not certain any benefits would accrue. However, our persuasive skills and assurances that we would look for some money to support the child often won over resistant families.
>
> Another key element of Foster's strategy which we adopted was the training and development of leaders, among both Deaf and Hearing

personnel who worked with us. Hitherto, the basic qualification of Deaf Fijians who worked more or less as teachers in the school was elementary education. I took them under my leadership and mentored them, creating a consciousness both of responsibility . . . for their own personal development and of the leadership role that would be expected of them down the road.

Although based in Fiji, Adedeji and Alade embarked on recruitment missions to the surrounding Melanesian island nations such as Tuvalu and Vanuatu and brought pupils to Suva from other Fijian islands, including Kadavu, Savusavu, and Rabbi. These missions were not always successful, but they made efforts wherever news of an unschooled Deaf child was received, and Alade shared this insight:

In late 2001, I took part in an expedition to Kadavu Island. One of my teachers had heard about some Deaf children living on Kadavu. The journey by boat was arduous. We were marooned on Kadavu after our return journey was canceled twice due to the ship's mechanical failure; so I opted to fly back to Suva. It was a terrifying journey by plane . . . nerve wracking. We were about 6 passengers packed like sardines into one of those smaller planes. The prime motivation for the journey was to bring these children education. Out of the three children we were able to meet, only one returned to Suva with us.

Foster's methods were necessarily adapted to fit local customs and conditions:

I remember another village we went to. Our networks told us about this young, unschooled boy of about 7 years old living with his grandparents, helping them out on the farm. We drove to this village in our 32-seater bus donated by the Embassy of Japan—a large entourage of teachers, our deaf pupils and others well versed in the traditional ceremonies these meetings normally entail. Word had gone out that a large group from GSD would visit the village. On arrival we were met by practically the entire village. I think curiosity got the better of some of them. On the one hand, it was inconceivable for them that a deaf child, whom they all knew, would be able to go to school. On the other hand, they were curious to see the Gospel School for the Deaf Head Teacher from Africa, who himself is Deaf. We were ushered into the village hall. We all sat around in a circle on Fijian woven mats, and as was the custom, we brought some gifts for the village Head. Our contact spoke on our behalf and what our mission to the village was. After that I took over, using one of my Fijian teachers as my interpreter. As I introduced myself, my position in the school, where I had come from, my experience and our desire to help the village educate their young boy, I could see tears streaming down the faces of some of the women in the hall. It was an emotionally-charged atmosphere.

Alade and Adedeji's effort also mirrored the Foster paradigm in only concentrating on establishing a primary education program, as they believed that local governments and organizations should take ownership of further education programming efforts beyond primary school. The graduates of Gospel School for the Deaf now transition to the mainstream program, Gospel High School (GHS), which is located adjacent to GSD.

A New Generation of Deaf Leaders in the South Pacific

One feature of the work Adedeji and Alade did in Fiji, just like Foster did in Africa, was the identification and development of potential Deaf leaders who could take over the reins and continue the work not only of education but also advocacy and the training of future leaders.

Alade (personal communication) said:

> I had mobilized Deaf Fijians in Suva, set up the Fiji Deaf Association (FDA), and using the same strategic planning that had worked wonderfully well at GSD, helped FDA prepare a 3-year strategic plan. In Canada [during the 2003 World Federation of the Deaf (WFD) conference], [Adedeji] and I again put our heads together, approached the leadership of Deaf sports, and advocated for the inclusion of Fiji. On my return to Fiji, I met the Fiji Olympic Committee, which was supportive and helpful. The result of all this advocacy was a renewed and energized Deaf community. By January 2004, Fiji would hoist her flag among participants at the Deaflympics held in Australia. Foster's approaches and methods featured prominently in the way we approached the work we did in Fiji.

And from these efforts, there have emerged a new generation of Deaf leaders. Although Adedeji and Alade each spent only about five years in Fiji, their work continues to reverberate across the South Pacific in the same way Foster's work is still felt in Africa. Enrollment at GSD is growing. Students are graduating and transitioning successfully to GHS for secondary studies. Students who succeed in the secondary setting are making the transition to universities and colleges in places as far afield as New Zealand, Hong Kong, and the United States.

Adedeji and Alade have now moved on to new endeavors in England, they continue to contribute to the ongoing work in the South Pacific through their not-for-profit vehicle, the Christian Mission to the Deaf in the Pacific (CMDP).

Conclusion

Intentional or not, Andrew Foster established a template and a model for Deafcentric Christian international development work during his thirty plus years of mission work in sub-Saharan Africa. I define "Deafcentric" as projects or programs conceptualized, designed and implemented by Deaf people and for Deaf people; their importance lies in their inherent transcending of contingent differences between and among Deaf people. A Deaf-Deaf or "Deaf-Same" component was naturally intrinsic to this model. This template was adopted almost in its entirety and with modifications by Adedeji and Alade 40 years after Foster's mission began. Deaf communities in much of sub-Saharan Africa——as in Fiji—are now schooled, although they remain underserved in some ways, such as access to tertiary education.

That Foster succeeded in transforming the bleak landscape he encountered on arrival owed much to his Christian convictions, unwavering resolve, sheer force of personality, and DEAF-SAME, the shared affinity or kinship arising from a common deafness. Similar conclusions can be reached in regard to the much shorter Adedeji-Alade effort in Fiji and the surrounding Melanesian Islands.

ACKNOWLEDGMENTS

This chapter owes a great deal to critical primary sources, all of whom were named in the "Discovering Andrew Foster" section of this chapter. Appreciation also goes to Lawrence Musa, who made his 2009 video interview of the late Foster protégé Ezekiel Sambo available; and Boateng, Kulego, Nortey and Amissah for the video of the Tetteh-Ocloos.

REFERENCES

Agboola, I. 2014. "Andrew Foster: The Man, the Vision, and the Thirty-Year Uphill climb." *Deaf Studies Digital Journal.* Accessed April 4, 2015. http://dsdj.gallaudet.edu/assets/section/section2/entry177/DSDJ_entry177.pdf.

Amissah, K., S. Boateng, J. Kulego, and J. Nortey. 2014. Video Interview of Seth Tetteh-Ocloo and Elizabeth Tetteh-Ocloo.

Musa, L. 2009. Video Interview of Ezekiel Sambo.

Nicholas, D. F. n.d. "Andrew Foster, 'The Deaf Will Hear the Words of the Book.'" Accessed April 4, 2015. http://www.aaregistry.org/historic_events/view/andrew-foster-deaf-will-hear-words-book.

Ojile, E. O. 1994. "Education of the Deaf in Nigeria." In *The Deaf Way: Perspectives from the International Conference on Deaf Culture*, edited by C. J. Erting, R. C. Johnson, D. L. Smith, and B. D. Snider. Washington, DC: Gallaudet University Press.

Oteng, F. S. 1988. *Give Them a Name*. Ashanti, Ghana: Ashanti Regional Association of the Deaf.

Tetteh-Ocloo, S. L. 1965. "Training and Certification of Teachers of the Deaf." In *Proceedings of the First Conference on the Education of the Deaf in Africa*, edited by Andrew Foster. Ibadan: Toyobo Printing Press.

12 | Exploring the Contours of DEAF-SAME Kinship Bonds and Mutuality in United Methodist Short-Term Missions

Kirk VanGilder

In 1997, a group of clergy and laity from Christ United Methodist Church of the Deaf and Asbury United Methodist Church (UMC) in Maryland visited the Kaaga School for the Deaf in Meru, Kenya, to investigate the possibility of a larger mission team visit composed of Deaf and hearing participants. The following year, a team was organized that decided to intentionally highlight Deaf leadership to draw attention to the abilities and leadership qualities of Deaf people. As a white Deaf North American clergyperson on this two-week trip, I found myself teaching, preaching, praying, and playing with Deaf Kenyan children. In this way, the presence of DEAF-SAME identity bonds formed a powerful connection between these children and myself despite the fact that I am a white man from the United States. On the final Sunday, I was invited to officiate over the blessing of the bread and cup at a service of Holy Communion. This happened to also be the first Holy Communion service for a class of Deaf Kenyan students, ages thirteen to fifteen, who were becoming full members in the Methodist Church in Kenya (MCK). The Deaf Kenyan woman who was preparing to train for ministry in the MCK was not yet authorized to preside over Holy Communion, so this community had never encountered a Deaf person with this level of religious authority. My presence, as part of a short-term mission team, allowed for Deaf congregants, and this class of new Deaf members, to take their first Holy Communion from a clergy person who was also Deaf. Suddenly the DEAF-SAME bond became more than simply a kinship bond; it became a bridge to widened horizons of what Deaf people could achieve and become. Kinship in this sense is not a matter of blood relatives but a reflection of the rapidly formed social bonds arising from a sense of sameness that results from our similar experiences as Deaf people in hearing societies. In this sense, DEAF-SAME bonds can form a sense of temporary or longer lasting "family" among people.

This two-week mission trip in 1998 initiated the entry of Deaf ministries in the UMC into a larger movement of short-term missions. Since this trip, productive and lasting mission relationships have been initiated and maintained through short-term mission involvement between Deaf Methodists around the world. This chapter seeks to explore how these short-term mission trips utilize the presence of DEAF-SAME identity bonds that transcend cultural and linguistic differences to mitigate some of the potential pitfalls identified in critiques of short-term missions. In addition, this chapter examines the dangers of overemphasizing DEAF-SAME bonds in ways that occlude the unique and distinct contributions of Deaf people in developing nations to our understanding of being Deaf.

DEAF-LED SHORT-TERM MISSIONS IN A METHODIST CONTEXT

Methodism traces its roots back to the Anglican minister, John Wesley. After being denied a parish appointment in the Church of England, Wesley began an itinerant ministry, preaching in fields and factories in England and a brief overseas trip to the Georgia colony in what would later become the United States of America. In his journal entry dated June 11, 1739, he muses about the criticisms against his travels that took him into other Church of England parishes and declares, "I look upon all the world as my parish" (Wesley [1951] 2014, 65). The spirit of this declaration has echoed throughout the variety of Methodist denominations that have arisen since Wesley's time, including the UMC. One result of this global understanding of the church is that the fastest growing areas of The United Methodist Church are now in sub-Saharan Africa. African delegates to our general conference, where policy and doctrinal standards are decided, constitute 30 percent of delegates at the 2016 General Conference and this number will likely be greater by the 2020 General Conference (United Methodist News Service 2013). In recognition of this demographic shift, plans are being made to potentially have the 2024 General Conference gather in a location outside of the United States for the first time in history (United Methodist Communications 2013).

The United Methodist Church and related Methodist denominations stand apart from other denominations in having a distinctive polity that allows for shared decision making on church policy and doctrinal standards through processes of Christian conferencing. In addition, UMC congregations are related through a connectional and itinerant clergy. This structural relationship means that clergypersons are appointed to serve in churches by area bishops in consultation with congregations rather than directly hired by congregations. In addition, clergypersons are occasionally moved to new churches in order to apply their specific gifts of ministry to other congregations and keep the ultimate leadership and ownership of a congregation in the domain of the laity who are members of that congregation. Sharing these distinctive ways of relating to one another allows various Methodists to bond together quickly and organize mission relationships that seek to implement this shared decision making and a balance between skilled leadership and local ownership true to our common Methodist heritage.

As inheritors of a Methodist way, Deaf people involved with various UMC congregations in the United States began to engage in short-term missions with Deaf people in other countries in the late 1990s. Facilitating these efforts was the United Methodist Congress of the Deaf (UMCD). The UMCD is a special interest caucus of The United Methodist Church where Deaf ministries communicate, coordinate, and advocate for Deaf people throughout the ministry structures of the UMC. From 1997 to 2002, prior to joining the faculty in 2008, I was the United Methodist campus minister at Gallaudet University. This made me a part of the unique international presence of Gallaudet, the only four-year liberal arts school in the world specifically designed to meet the needs of Deaf and hard of hearing students.

My own role in our short-term trips from 1998 to 2002 was as a Deaf clergyperson at of one of the longest standing Deaf churches in the United States, Christ UMC of the Deaf. My involvement in these early trips had a profound impact on my personal and professional development. The experiences of working with Deaf people on short-term mission trips led me to pursue a doctorate in practical theology and missiology in 2002 and join the Gallaudet University faculty in 2008. During mission trips since 2002, my role has been even more multifaceted as I remained a clergyperson but became also an educator and theological researcher. Above all, I find myself experiencing a deep connection as a Deaf person with other Deaf people, both those who travel with me and those we meet in other countries. This DEAF-SAME bond enriches my understanding of others and ability to relate to them. Yet, this sense of being similar also seems to allow me to notice more acutely those moments when cultural differences do arise.

The 1998 mission trip to Kenya became a template for subsequent trips I participated in to Kenya, Zimbabwe, and Turkey. Members of Deaf United Methodist ministries in other parts of the United States participated in these trips and then formed similar mission trips and relationships with Deaf people in Ecuador, Mexico, and Jamaica. These mission relationships eventually led to the formation of the World Federation of Deaf Methodists (WFDM) in 2005, where we were joined by Deaf Methodists in the Korean Methodist Church who have mission relationships with Japan, Guam, and Sri Lanka. The primary purpose of the gatherings the WFDM has been celebration and sharing of ideas and strategies for holistic ministries with Deaf people. We also share presentations on our short-term mission trips, which often lead to important conversations between those who travel to mission sites and those who receive mission teams as we articulate concerns and clarify relationships. What makes the WFDM different than other Deaf global gatherings is that our common bonds are not solely rooted in DEAF-SAME identities but also a shared Christian faith and common Methodist heritage. These multiple ways of being connected with one another shape our celebrations of DEAF-SAME as a grateful recognition of God's grace in our lives. The common bonds we share also shape how we seek to organize ourselves through worship, prayer, mission, and mutual relationships as informed by the shared patterns of Methodist bodies.

As short-term missions, the mission trips organized by US Deaf Methodists are generally two-week visits preceded by a great deal of preparation and communication and followed by continuing communication and financial giving. Teams are often a mix of both Deaf and hearing people with varying degrees of American Sign Language (ASL) fluency. In visits to African countries, we have worked with schools that maintain a relationship with local Methodist churches. In Turkey, the Deaf school we visited was partnered with the United Methodist Committee on Relief (UMCOR) after the 1999 earthquakes. The school requested a continuing relationship to bring Deaf community and education experts together to enliven school morale and explore ways of modernizing the school's pedagogical techniques in teaching Deaf students.

Activities on these short-term mission trips are largely guided by the desires of local Deaf people, school administrators, and ministry leaders working with Deaf people. In all cases, teams seek to learn the local signed language and avoid inserting American Sign Language. In some instances, teams include Christian education in local signed languages. In Turkey, a largely Muslim country, activities were centered on general communication improvement and modeling Deaf achievement and success. Our intention is to lift up local Deaf people, languages, and community as a resource for Deaf people and hearing people alike and not import American Sign Language and American Deaf cultural concepts. Whether working with Deaf children, local Deaf adults, or hearing school and church administrators, our hope is to use our presence to bring attention to the concerns, hopes, and priorities of local Deaf people.

THE SHORT-TERM MISSION MOVEMENT AND ITS CRITICS

The short-term mission efforts initiated by Deaf United Methodists in the United States reflect a growing movement of short-term mission teams organized by hearing church members in Christian denominations since the latter decades of the twentieth century. The short-term mission movement has become a wildly popular way of engaging church members from the United States with those in other areas of the world. However, this movement is not without its critics, who bring very pertinent and valid concerns to the forefront.

Missiologists have begun to question the efficacy of short-term missions and the ethical concerns arising from casual cross-cultural contact motivated by religious impulse by people who may have only minimal preparation for such work. Missiology is the field of theological studies that examines the purposes and methods of how a religion crosses cultural boundaries. As an interdisciplinary field of study, missiology incorporates a variety of academic approaches from theology, anthropology, linguistics, and sociology in its efforts to evaluate and propose effective means for cross-cultural interactions on matters of religious and social concern. Therefore, the critical examination of missions shares an affinity with critiques of cross-cultural contact in these fields.

For example, in *Toxic Charity*, Robert Lupton (2011) argues that while emergency relief efforts are laudable, the short-term mission movement often extends the relief response stage by bringing in teams of volunteers to do work rather than developing local skilled labor and leadership. This leads to the destruction or discouraging of local initiative by fostering a dependency on outside volunteers. "When we do for those in need what they have the capacity to do for themselves, we disempower them" (Lupton 2011, 3). Short-term missions have become a cottage industry with travel brokers, marketing, and facilitators offering package deals to congregations and volunteers to send people all over the globe. Even with

an estimated $2.5 to $5 billion US dollars being spent on these trips, the improvement in the lives of those they visit is often negligible as systemic poverty continues and in some cases deepens as free labor and donations undermine local
economies (Lupton 2011, 6). With a Princeton University study showing that 1.6
million Americans took mission trips abroad in 2005, some have called the short-
term mission movement a form of "religious tourism" that provides more personal benefit for those traveling abroad than those receiving teams and their aid
(Lupton 2011, 15). This concern parallels similar trends within volunteer tourism
that are sometimes pejoratively called "poverty tourism" by critics. The dynamics
of privilege, power, and money make these forms of tourism problematic as the
volunteerism and religious motivations take a back seat to the impulse to simply
peer into the suffering of others without becoming personally engaged.

   This lack of personal engagement is related to inequalities in the dynamics of
mission relationships. In an academic analysis of her experience as a translator for a
short-term mission team, anthropologist Ellen Moodie notes that volunteers often
express an "enchanted internationalism" (Moodie 2013, 148). Such enchantment
locates the benefits of short-term missions in the lives of volunteers who recount
the value of their service trips in how their own lives were changed by meeting
and serving "the poor." Moodie's research reveals an us/them binary in many
short-term mission volunteers' comments that reduce the diversity and complexity of communities in the global South to "not us" (Moodie 2013, 150). Moodie sees
the us/them divide as something that severely limits the social intimacy between
short-term volunteers and those receiving them but a script that makes possible a
relationship that facilitates ordered material and monetary assistance. She argues
that the motivation for such short-term missions is often predicated on the us/
them binary and that "to overcome this distance is to obliterate desire, to rub out
the reason for taking the trips. In mission and service trips particularly, yearning
is inevitably structured on inequality" (Moodie 2013, 158). Therefore she notes
a degree to which short-term missions present a paradox whereby the desire to
meet and know others through service relationships is dependent upon the maintenance of social boundaries of "us" and "them."

Deaf United Methodist Short-Term Missions in Practice

These shortcomings and paradoxes of the short-term mission movement are also
observable among the teams traveling on Deaf United Methodist short-term
missions. Americans who join these mission teams fund themselves either
through personal finances or have the social capital to raise money to support
their participation—resources their Deaf hosts do not enjoy. This disparity along
with linguistic and cultural difference and the experience of long-distance travel
itself creates a strong us/them binary that Moodie (2013) discusses. Yet, the transnational bonds created by the DEAF-SAME impulse seem to provide a very different
relational conduit. Whereas the us/them binary works to create a more one-way
exchange in an unequal relationship, DEAF-SAME means that the relationship can be
more of a kinship bond.

   As a conduit for mission relationships, DEAF-SAME seems to open up different possibilities for the motivations of Deaf people who volunteer for short-term

missions than those observed by Moodie. As Friedner and Kusters (2014) note, Deaf people from North America and Europe often engage in tourism out of a desire to meet other Deaf people and see how they live. Similarly, deaf volunteers on United Methodist short-term missions find their religiously grounded motivations to provide assistance coupled with a curiosity about Deaf lives abroad. Therefore, commixture of a one-way us/them binary with a two-way kinship bond of deaf-same may result in a dynamic of interaction between mission teams and host communities that fosters more mutuality between Deaf people than literature on short-term missions among hearing people suggests. While this mutuality does not eliminate the us/them binary entirely, it seems to mitigate some of its negative aspects and allow for more two-way exchanges.

Mutuality is framed by missiologist Marcus Dean as a way to ameliorate the detrimental social distance created by economic disparity in short-term missions. Dean defines mutuality as action that "leads to mutual benefit, involves reciprocal give and take, is actively pursued by both sides, and a has a common goal or purpose behind the relationship" (Dean 2013, 275). This mutual exchange may not be monetary or material in nature. Often the economic disparity makes the contribution of the receiving community in mission relationships unable to provide equitable material contribution to the common goal. Instead, their contribution to the relationship may be one of a spiritual, emotional, or social nature that, while perhaps less quantifiable, is no less vital to the success of a mission partnership.

For example, on a 2013 short-term mission trip in Kenya, there arose a need for funds to transport a group of children who performed a marching routine commonly done in Kenyan schools for competition from the Kaaga School for the Deaf to the meeting of the WFDM in Nairobi. Those of us leading the mission team from the US had understood this financial cost was to be covered by the Kaaga circuit of churches in the MCK. However, miscommunication led to some confusion as to whether those funds were, in fact, authorized for this specific use or part of the MCK's general financial support to the Kaaga school. It would have been very easy for the US mission team to simply cover the costs of transportation for these children out of funds given to us for mission needs. However, after talking to local Deaf church leadership, it seemed there was a larger issue of communication between Deaf leadership and hearing MCK officials.

Thus, while solving the immediate problem of transporting the children to Nairobi, a simple donation would erode local activity to support Deaf ministry, create dependency on outside funding, and ignore a larger systemic issue regarding communication. At the urging of local Deaf church leadership, we were able to organize a meeting with interpreters where a local Deaf clergywoman was able to articulate her understanding of how the funds were raised and for what purpose they were designated. After some quick investigation, her account of the situation was found to be correct and local funds that had been raised for transporting these children to Nairobi and housing them were released.

During these conversations, I was able to share stories of how miscommunication between myself, as a Deaf clergyperson, and hearing officials in denominational offices of the UMC had sometimes caused misunderstandings that required an additional meeting with a sign language interpreter to clarify. This strategy utilized a deaf-same bond that existed between the Deaf clergywoman and myself as a bridge to address a common issue regarding better communication in ministry and mission. The presence of a short-term mission team that enjoyed a sense of DEAF-SAME bonds seemed to create something out of the ordinary enough that hearing MCK officials took note and modified their way of relating to the Deaf clergywoman in their area.

In discussing my own frustrations with communications back home with this Deaf clergywoman, she told me, "You need friends who will get things going without taking over too!" This comment spurred me to consider how I can coordinate efforts with hearing allies who do have the attention of people I need to communicate with in a manner that "gets things going without taking over." While this gift from a Deaf Kenyan clergywoman did not involve the same monetary value or social impact as what our meeting in Kenya provided for her, it remains an important contribution to how I now approach professional relationships in my own context. While other forms of mutuality can and do arise between hearing people in mission relationships, the bridge of DEAF-SAME seems to have facilitated this exchange in a way that was quick and simple but still very valuable for both of us.

Despite the benefits of a DEAF-SAME kinship bond in short-term missions, the dangers of the „enchanted internationalism" that concerns Moodie remain. Friedner and Kusters (2014) and Moriarty Harrelson (this volume) address this concern as well by questioning the degree to which an easily obtained sense of DEAF-SAME might cause Deaf tourists to overlook or misunderstand the unique features of Deaf life and identity in the global South. I share this concern as a leader of Deaf short-term mission teams working alongside Deaf subaltern communities.

While on a mission trip to Zimbabwe, I met one of the Deaf leaders involved in United Methodist Deaf ministry and a Deaf employment training project. This Deaf man once had a good amount of hearing and could voice in a manner that made himself generally understandable to hearing people and thus would occasionally make use of this ability. However, he generally preferred to use a Zimbabwean Sign Language interpreter or write notes as he was uncertain how he sounded and wanted more control over how he was perceived by hearing people. As my own audiological status provides me with similar options, other American mission team members began to draw quick parallels between how my Deaf identity related to other Deaf identities in American Deaf cultural contexts and how this Deaf Zimbabwean man related to his Deaf Zimbabwean peers.

While some similarities certainly existed, I was a bit concerned that a DEAF-SAME bridge was facilitating a quick move to making direct analogy comparisons between different ways of embodying Deaf identity in American contexts and those in Zimbabwe. Whereas Deaf people in America tend to make a distinction between hard-of-hearing identities and Deaf identities, such distinctions seem to be much less pronounced in Zimbabwe (also see Kusters, Toura-Jensen, Verhelst, and Vestergaard, this volume, who discuss a similar situation in Ghana). While this Deaf Zimbabwean man had some audiological and vocal abilities, he was still seen as a Deaf man by both hearing people and his peers. The unexamined use of a DEAF-SAME bridge could have led to Deaf Americans reading Deaf Zimbabwean identities as basically the same as our own when, in fact, Deaf Zimbabweans may have very different ways of forming their identities, relating to one another, and relating to hearing communities. Yet, for some Deaf mission team members, the DEAF-SAME bridge created a quick leap to noticing similarities that left potentially important differences unexamined until I started to carefully point them out in conversation. One such important difference would be to assume this Deaf Zimbabwean man's identity could be labeled hard-of-hearing as we understand it in the United States when the dynamics of how Deaf people identify themselves and relate to hearing people in Zimbabwe may be quite different.

This is one instance in which the rapidity of a DEAF-SAME kinship type bond might be detrimental to missional relationships. As Deaf communities and scholars in North American and Europe begin to explore the contours of Deaf identity and cultural expression, we often draw on personal and historical community experiences that form our impressions of the world in which we live. While this is a vital and necessary part of Deaf liberation and self-determination in all contexts, it is possible to overreach across the DEAF-SAME bridge and make our stories everyone else's stories. We run into the "danger of a single story" as the Nigerian author, Chimamanda Ngozi Adichie, cautions in her TED talk (Adichie 2009).

Adichie warns that in encountering a single narrative about others, we risk collapsing a wide diversity of experiences and expressions into that single story. The single story often distorts the stories of others into narratives that serve our own goals and interests—even if we are unaware that we are falling into this essentialist trap. While short-term mission trips can introduce Deaf people from Western nations to vastly different Deaf experiences in the global South, the short-term nature of these encounters plus a rapid DEAF-SAME kinship bond needs to be tempered by an awareness that what we see on short-term mission trips is limited and seen through our own eyes. The risk of overwriting the autochthonous, or "home-grown," stories, ideas, and constructions of Deaf identities that spring up from the lives of Deaf communities wherever we encounter them is real. In our desire to explore the benefits of the DEAF-SAME kinship bonds, we should not overlook that even the closest kin retain different experiences, thoughts, and identities. Assumptions of an essential "sameness" should be avoided to allow for local communities to develop their own agency to express and develop their Deaf identities, communities, and languages in ways that they see fit.

STRATEGIES FOR MAINTAINING MUTUALITY IN TRANSNATIONAL MISSIONS

The short-term nature of United Methodist Deaf mission trips could easily lead to ephemeral relationships that wither away, leaving privileged visitors with great memories and experiences and their hosts with an unchanged situation (also see Kusters, Toura-Jensen, Verhelst, and Vestergaard, this volume). Taking advantage of common bonds such as DEAF-SAME identity bonds without overlooking important differences might mitigate some of these dangers. As more Deaf short-term mission groups organize trips and develop missional relationships, further examination may yield helpful insights into how Deaf people use a DEAF-SAME bond to achieve a beneficial mutuality and these insights may lead to strategies that can enhance how everyone does short-term missions.

In *Making Sadza with Deaf Zimbabwean Women* (2012), I discuss three missiological strategies that can engender more mutually beneficial transnational relationships within the field of practical theology. Unlike systemic theology which often begins with categorical questions such as "What is the nature of God?," practical theological research typically begins with a dilemma faced in the daily lives of people. Methodologies in practical theology seek to engage a variety of social sciences in dialogue with religious tradition to develop a more richly nuanced understanding of the dilemma under examination. From this foundation, communities of faith can develop new responses through revised social practices and understandings of their faith to address the dilemmas they face.

On short-term missions in Zimbabwe, Deaf Zimbabwean women often mentioned a variety of complex challenges they faced in raising their children. As a white North American Deaf male, I did not consider the DEAF-SAME bridge sufficient for me to understand the larger cultural context of Deaf Zimbabwean women in a way that would allow me to address their concerns in a practical theological project. I felt my primary methodological commitment had to be to create a process that privileged the Deaf women themselves and created a space for their own agency to guide the development of proposed responses to their situation as mothers.

It was this commitment that led me to identify the strategies of embracing local creativity, allowing for local critique of Western actions, and being intentional in building bridges that left the end result of mission in the hands of local people. Non-Western cultures often have very different ways of interacting and exchanging information. In learning how to make sadza, a traditional corn meal porridge, I discovered powerful Zimbabwean ways of learning and teaching that were very different from Western academic reflection. Embracing such local creativity requires Westerners to set aside assumptions of how things should be done and observe and learn how indigenous cultures discuss dilemmas and create solutions. When solutions arise from the style of discourse and problem solving of local people, these solutions will be much more meaningful and successful.

Westerners engaged in short-term missions also need to intentionally develop ways for those from the global South to critique how their participation in the relationship is being framed. The assumption made by many Westerners that subaltern participants will "speak up" to be heard or correct misperceptions has to be avoided. Westerners would do well to learn and employ how indigenous people offer critique in their own cultures and regularly pause to reflect if they have allowed for such feedback or overlooked it when it occurred.

Lastly, making use of bridges of commonality such as DEAF-SAME kinship bonds or a shared Methodist heritage can enhance mission relationships. While these bonds do introduce certain dangers such as the potential to overlook important differences between Deaf people, they also provide an avenue for relationships that can yield surprising and unexpected results. Lamin Sanneh notes that while the arrival of missionaries in Africa were often entwined with the arrival of colonial administration and exploitation, often missionaries were intentional in learning local languages and cultures as they sought to translate the Christian Bible for evangelistic purposes. What missionaries did not foresee or intend was that this valuation of using local culture and language to talk about spiritual matters, which were seen in African cultural contexts as the most vital matters one could discuss, would undermine colonialist notions of Western superiority (Sanneh 1993, 101). Sanneh argues that the end result of things exchanged by those in cross-cultural relationships will lie in the hands of those receiving them, whether this is intended or not.

An intentional effort to leave the ultimate shape and purpose of a transnational missional relationship making use of kinship bonds in the hands of local people will provide for a more mutual relationship that allows for a rich multiplicity to emerge within our understanding of DEAF-SAME.

REFERENCES

Adichie, C. N. 2009. *The Danger of a Single Story*. Accessed May 15, 2015. http://www.ted .com/chimamanda_adichie_the_danger_of_a_single_story.

Dean, M. 2013. "Mutuality and Missions: The Western Christian in Global Ministry." *Missiology: An International Review* 41 (3): 273–85.

Friedner, M. I., and A. Kusters. 2014. "On the Possibilities and Limits of 'DEAF DEAF SAME' Tourism and Empowerment Camps in Adamorobe (Ghana), Bangalore and Mumbai (India)." *Disability Studies Quarterly* 34 (3). Accessed May 17, 2015. http://dsq-sds.org/ article/view/4246/3649.

Lupton, R. D. 2011. *Toxic Charity: How Churches and Charities Hurt Those They Help (and How to Reverse It)*. New York: HarperCollins.

Moodie, E. 2013. "Inequality and Intimacy between Sister Communities in El Salvador and the United States."*Missiology: An International Review* 41 (2): 146–62.

Sanneh, L. 1993. *Encountering the West: Christianity and the Global Cultural Process: The African Dimension*. Maryknoll, NY: Orbis Books.

United Methodist Communications. 2013. "Minneapolis Chosen as General Conference 2020 Site: The United Methodist Church." *United Methodist Church*, November 15. Accessed May 17, 2015. http://www.umc.org/news-and-media/ minneapolis-chosen-as-general-conference-2020-site.

United Methodist News Service. 2013. "General Conference 2016 Delegates Allotted: UMC Connections." *United Methodist Connections*, November 14. Accessed May 17, 2014. http://umcconnections.org/2013/11/14/general-conference-2016-delegates-allotted.

VanGilder, K. 2012. *Making Sadza with Deaf Zimbabwean Women: A Missiological Reorientation of Practical Theological Method*. Gottingen, Germany: Vandenhoeck and Ruprecht.

Wesley, J. (1951) 2014. *The Journal of John Wesley*, edited by Percy Livingstone Parker. Reprint, Grand Rapids, MI: Christian Classics Ethereal Library. Accessed May 15, 2015. http:// www.ccel.org/ccel/wesley/journal.pdf.

13 | A Deaf Leadership Program in Nigeria: Notes on a Complicated Endeavor

Khadijat Rashid

In December 2005, Gallaudet University sponsored a leadership training program in Jos, Nigeria, which was attended by eighty-four deaf people from Ghana and Nigeria: sixteen Ghanaians and sixty-eight Nigerians. Four trainers originally from different regions and states of Nigeria and from varied ethnic and religious backgrounds conducted and developed the workshop. The four (two women and two men) were deaf signers fluent in Nigerian Sign Language. At the time of the workshop, three of them ('Gbenga Aina, Emilia Chukwuma, and I) lived in the United States and worked at Gallaudet University and one was a social worker in London. The UK-based trainer, Matthew Adedeji, had previously spent years in Fiji as an educator and founder of a school for Deaf youth there (his work in Fiji is discussed by Aina, this volume) and had in-depth experience working with deaf immigrants who came to the United Kingdom from a variety of nations. Our educational backgrounds included law, social work, business, and international relations. We three US-based trainers had worked with deaf individuals from many different countries, and we had experience with a variety of development projects in other countries. As a group, therefore, we had considerable experience in international development issues.

We anticipated that our knowledge of and familiarity with Nigeria would help us avoid communication breakdowns and the cultural misunderstandings that can occur when Westerners without background information visit developing countries. However, during the course of the workshop, sufficient issues arose that, as I argue here, even in a context where DEAF-SAME should have been predominant, there were enough differing and conflicting imperatives that the prevailing ethos might more properly have been known as DEAF-DIFFERENT. Therefore, the concept of DEAF-SAME as an analytic tool should be utilized sparingly, if at all—as even deaf people born in the same country using the same language find it difficult to overcome barriers of culture and worldview.

Planning for the workshop began about a year before it was carried out and involved the four trainers as well as leaders of the Nigerian National Association of the Deaf (NNAD) and later the Ghanaian National Association of the Deaf (GNAD) and the Cameroonian National Association of the Deaf (CANAD). Originally, the workshop was meant to be for Nigerians only, but after consideration of the cost of flying four people from the United Kingdom and the United States to conduct the training, it seemed practical and cost-effective to include participants from nearby Anglophone regions so that the per-capita cost would be less. The written language (English) was regarded as important because the trainers disseminated daily handouts in English to supplement the teaching and also showed movies with English captioning. Accordingly, the number of Nigerian participants was reduced from one hundred to sixty-eight, the scope was widened to include sixteen Cameroonians and sixteen Ghanaians, and the original two-day workshop plan was lengthened to five days.

Because we were based in different countries at a time when videophones and webcams were not as ubiquitous as they are now, the workshop leaders carried out most of our planning sessions through e-mail, supplemented by weekly meetings at Gallaudet University and meetings of NNAD leaders in Nigeria and GNAD leaders in Ghana, the results of which were communicated to the planners at Gallaudet expeditiously.

This chapter reviews the goals, design, and conduct of the workshop and the results of the process viewed after nearly a decade's remove. Although the concept for the workshop was initiated on the premise of DEAF-SAME, over its course it became obvious that there were too many differences between the trainers and the Nigerian participants, and among the Nigerians themselves, for the concept to hold true. Trainers returned to West Africa with a different worldview than that prevailing among the deaf participants, and this affected how participants received their message.

For this chapter, I draw primarily on a trove of documentary evidence from the conduct of the program. The organizers, geographically spread out as we were, established an e-mail list at the commencement of the program to facilitate quick communication across time and space. These e-mails and other correspondence with participants and other parties in Ghana and Nigeria trace the program from its very beginning through its conclusion and include follow-up with program leaders and participants for more than a year afterward. The original proposal for the program by Aina (2005) provided details on the design of the program. The final report (Aina 2006) described actual daily occurrences through the program conclusion. Both documents were not published but are available in the Gallaudet University Office of Research Support and International Affairs. I also draw on conversations and interviews with the other three group leaders and on my own personal experience in this program, as a Nigerian-born woman and Gallaudet professor, and my experience of working on an earlier leadership training program in South Africa.

Background to the Leadership Training Program

The idea for the workshop arose out of discussions between 'Gbenga Aina, the director of Gallaudet University's international services office at the time, and the late Jonathan Tinat, then president of the NNAD.[1] Tinat, a young, dynamic leader, had recently been elected to the position and was eager to unite a fractious NNAD. Prior to his election, NNAD had internal rifts along sectarian and ethnic lines which reflected long-standing cleavages within the greater Nigerian society, and his election had been bitterly contested by deaf people from different ethnic and religious backgrounds.

Tinat was eager to prove the concept of DEAF-SAME or the idea that deaf Nigerians all had common interests despite differences in sect or religion and needed to unite to fight for their common goals. He traveled widely around Nigeria and was careful to appoint NNAD officers from various religions, ethnicities, and regions of the country. Mindful of gender issues, he appointed women to leadership positions within the national NNAD and encouraged state organizations to do the same. This was not the first time women had been in NNAD leadership, but it was the first time there was a sustained effort to ensure the participation of women in anything more than token numbers. The leadership training described in this chapter was not his first venture in this direction: the previous summer another leadership training program organized by Tinat and the other NNAD officers had attracted more than two hundred Nigerian participants. As a result of that event, it was determined that more sophisticated training was needed, and planning for the Gallaudet-sponsored event commenced.

For his part, 'Gbenga Aina was carrying out one of the objectives of the international programs office at Gallaudet as part of that university's worldwide mission. Gallaudet's Center for Global Education had conducted leadership training programs in various European, Asian, and Latin American countries beginning in the 1970s, but had never organized one in sub-Saharan Africa, and Aina set out to rectify that omission.[2] Nigeria seemed a good place to begin—it was the largest country in Africa, had a large deaf population, and the official language, English, presumably made it easier to communicate across the distance in writing with the leaders of the deaf community through e-mails and letters at a time when videophone, Internet, and cell phone use were not yet widespread in Nigeria.

Also, Nigerians were always among the largest groups of international students at Gallaudet, and so a workshop of this kind was considered a beachhead for possible future collaboration with deaf Nigerians. Gallaudet officials gave approval for it to be carried out in December 2005. Because the trainers were all originally Nigerian, the university had to devote less money for start-up costs.

As the world's only liberal arts university exclusively for Deaf students, Gallaudet occupies a unique niche.[3] On the one hand, its largest source of funding

---

[1] This chapter is dedicated to the memory of Jonathan Tinat, who died at age thirty-seven in March 2007, just more than a year after the workshop was held.

[2] Gallaudet did establish World Deaf Leadership programs and leadership training in South Africa from 1997 to 2002—in which this author was also a trainer—but these were organized through a specific grant from the Nippon Foundation and were not part of the mandate of the international programs office.

[3] Although it has always admitted hearing students to the graduate school, the university began accepting a small number of hearing undergraduates in 2001, currently limited to 8 percent of the undergraduate student population.

is the US government, with the clear mandate to provide higher education for Deaf Americans. On the other, Gallaudet is a symbol to Deaf people around the world, and the university administration recognized that it would need to attract more international students to ensure its continued viability.

One danger in working with people in developing countries is outlined by Jackson (2007), who illustrates the processes by which people from Western countries target "developing" countries for political and economic reconstruction in their own images. They ultimately create an international class of development workers (or globalizers) who, while meaning well, actually end up benefitting the multinational organizations that provide funding and further unwittingly subjugate the target community to the whims of more "developed" countries.

In planning projects in developing countries, Gallaudet staff strove—albeit not always successfully—to avoid this trap by enlisting people with an international ethos. The Center for Global Education staff encouraged personnel doing research or leading other work in developing countries to work with people from these countries and give them equal input in setting training agendas. University faculty wrote several treatises on how to work with Deaf people internationally in a manner that empowered these communities, including those by Wilson and Kakiri (2007) and Harris, Holmes, and Mertens (2009). However, the university's primary goal in conducting this work, while not explicitly stated, was name recognition and the development of goodwill around the world rather than international development per se. As I discuss, despite our (and the university's) efforts, it was impossible to entirely avoid issues that arise with development work, even if as in our case, the trainers were all originally from the recipient region.

THE STRUCTURE OF THE PROGRAM

The identified purpose of the leadership training project in Nigeria was to facilitate leadership development among deaf and hard of hearing persons. Five subject areas were covered: strategic planning and problem solving, strategic leadership, accountability and trust development, women and gender issues, and organizational structure and constitutionality.

These five areas addressed in the workshop were developed in cooperation with the NNAD; in fact, NNAD leaders submitted the initial proposal outlining the areas in which they believed they needed training. It was important to all involved in the project that the Deaf communities themselves identified the areas in which they wanted support or training, to avoid paternalism and globalizer-like behavior. GNAD and CANAD leaders also contributed ideas once they joined the project.

To sustain participants' attention and interest in the content, leaders used a variety of methods to conduct the workshop in addition to lectures, which are familiar throughout West Africa. Learning techniques such as games, movies, role play, and daily ice-breaking activities were included. Participants enthusiastically responded to all the new methods.

Involvement in the program was limited to one hundred participants due to funding restrictions. Criteria for enrollment in the program were developed by the NNAD, GNAD, and CANAD leaders and agreed to by the Western-based trainers, with the goal of ensuring that the most qualified people could be selected in a relatively neutral and unbiased manner. Factors determining consideration were that each participant must be deaf; must be a "leader" in the Deaf community and/or Deaf organizations; must be capable of processing the information received during the program (i.e., must be literate and able to read the materials, which were printed in English); and must be willing and able to disseminate what was learned during the five-day program to others who could not attend. "Leaders" were elected members of the organizations they represented, serving in such roles as president, vice president, secretary, and treasurer, and ranged in age from eighteen to mid-fifties. Beyond these basic criteria, all the program leaders were concerned that women should be fairly represented and that participants be drawn from all regions, religions, and ethnic groups of each country and be selected by members from these regions rather than the respective NAD president. Representativeness of any gathering is something that Nigerians are very aware of, given the country's contentious history and rifts over ethnicity, religion, and territory.

Therefore, NNAD leaders determined that selection of the Nigerian attendees would include the nine elected members of the NNAD executive, six regional representatives from each region of Nigeria to be selected by regional members, the chairs of each state's NNAD branch elected by the state's members, and sixteen representatives of Deaf women's groups. Ultimately Nigeria sent twenty female members, as some women occupied other leadership positions within NNAD national and state organizations. CANAD and GNAD participants similarly had to include at least six women each and were otherwise geographically and ethnically diverse. Although having fewer delegates, their numbers were relatively proportional because at the time the Nigerian population was approximately 140 million people, as compared to Ghana's 21 million and Cameroon's 17.5 million.

The workshop was structured in such a way that Gallaudet University would pay for most of the costs associated with the program, including room and meals for all participants, workshop materials, and other associated expenses. Participants also received a small stipend equivalent to approximately $4 (US) a day, or slightly less than $20 if they participated for the entire week, as a concession toward lost work time and other unreimbursed costs. In a region where about half the population lives on less than $2 a day, $20 was a significant stipend. Participants were expected to cover their own transportation costs to the venue in Jos, Nigeria, which we had selected for its temperate climate and central location in Nigeria. (The location was chosen during the period when the training was expected to focus solely on Nigeria.) The out-of-pocket expenditure on travel expected of program participants was intended to ensure their commitment to program goals.

COMPLICATIONS

The idea to add Cameroonians and Ghanaians to the training project was proposed around June 2005, after planning had been under way for six months. Tinat had been in communication with the leaders of GNAD, and they had articulated a desire to participate in the program. At the same time, a deaf Cameroonian leader was visiting Gallaudet University and also expressed interest, and so the program was widened to include these two neighboring countries. It was anticipated that having deaf leaders from all three countries attend the training program together would foster relationships that would pay off in the long-term by increasing trust and cooperation across West Africa fostering Tinat's ideal of DEAF-SAME. The GNAD and NNAD presidents also believed that such cooperation would result in greater clout and perhaps a seat on the board of the World Federation of the Deaf (WFD), which at that point had rarely had deaf Africans on its board. (As of this writing, only one person from sub-Saharan Africa is on the WFD board.) Because the team from Cameroon ultimately did not come due to transportation issues, and because problems occurred mostly with the Nigerian contingent, I devote the remainder of the chapter to discussing the Nigerian team.

The Nigerians became notorious for the extent of their bickering, both among each other and with the team leaders. First, many of them were upset that they had to spend money for transportation to Jos since they expected the university to cover this expense (an expectation fostered by previous experiences of aid to deaf Africans). Second, many of the Nigerians were highly educated, including Deaf lawyers, teachers, university graduates with bachelor's and master's degrees, and a variety of other professionals. Because of this and their wide exposure to international events and organizations including the WFD, they felt that they already possessed leadership skills and so were more combative and challenging to each other. Third, disputes broke out among the Nigerians on the basis of religion, ethnicity, educational qualifications, and even regional affiliation, and it took all the skills of the program leaders to get the participants back on track.

Parallel with this development among program participants was agitation outside. Not everyone who applied for participation in the program was accepted, and some of those who were declined began a campaign of misinformation with allegations of mismanagement and nepotism. One deaf Muslim who had previously served as an NNAD officer alleged that only "beggars," "Christians," "students," and other such "nuisances" were invited to participate, rather than the "category of Deaf people who formed the bulk that really controls deaf Nigerians" such as past national presidents of NNAD and traditional chiefs or "deaf elders of thought."[4] This emphasis on "deaf elders" is important because in West Africa, elders are considered the repositories of wisdom and the accumulated knowledge of the community.[5]

REFLECTIONS ON A COMPLICATED ENDEAVOR

The uproar among Deaf Nigerians in the program was contrary to the expectations of the US- and UK-based team leaders. As mentioned earlier, as a group we represented a wide diversity of Nigerian origin; we hoped that if we could model our ability to work together as a team, this would provide an example for the participants. We tried to demonstrate respectful communication even in disagreement, and in consultation with NNAD leaders at the time we developed criteria that we believed to be neutral and fair. These standards were specifically set so

---

[4] Chief Zubairu Dugu, personal communication, December 31, 2005.
[5] See for instance, Issahaku and Neysmith (2013), 188: "In traditional African societies old age is a time of honor and care since age is regarded as a marker of wisdom, experience and long years of dedicated service to society. It is . . . also considered a key credential for election to rulership."

that young Deaf leaders would have an equal chance of being selected as older and more experienced Deaf people. Moreover, we wanted to ensure that women were not marginalized and that all areas of the countries were represented equally. Unfortunately, religious strictures and the gap in educational attainment in the Muslim northern part of both Ghana and Nigeria meant that fewer women from that region were qualified for selection to attend the training, and that these who were deemed suitable were mostly younger and more secular. This resulted in the workshop being attacked as an elitist establishment, an expatriates' power trip, and a colonialist imposition without input from locals, even though it had been requested and mostly planned by the leaders of the NNAD and GNAD.

As team leaders based in the United Kingdom and United States, we had assimilated these countries' ostensible values of secularism, respect for and tolerance of ethnic diversity, individualism, differentiation between the personal and the political (or the organizational), belief in the capability of everyone to contribute something, and other such Western values. Simultaneously, we tried to remain aware and were careful to avoid imposing our languages, mannerisms, attitudes, and expectations on program participants. For example, the workshop was conducted entirely in the variant of West African Sign Language (including Ghanaian Sign Language and Nigerian Sign Language which were very similar) that was understood by all these present. Occasionally, team leaders unconsciously slipped into American Sign Language (ASL) or British Sign Language (BSL) but when that happened we called each other's attention to the problem and immediately reversed course and repeated the statement in West African Sign Language. Program participants were encouraged to ignore these lapses and to stick with GSL or NSL.

We also encouraged attendees to bring up problems and issues they were currently confronting within their national organizations, and these were then discussed and solutions brainstormed by workshop participants. We made it clear that we did not have ready answers for every problem and that part of their responsibility as leaders was to develop solutions to their issues using the tools and analytic methods that they had learned over the course of the workshop.

Because of our values and background, we expected that as participants incorporated the leadership principles we taught and developed trust among each other, rifts between participants and among specific groups would be healed or at least that the attendees would develop greater tolerance and empathy for each other. In contrast, however, conflicts that had developed among NNAD members and leadership following Tinat's election became even more visible. Although Tinat had championed DEAF-SAME as a guiding principle of the leadership training workshop, it became glaringly apparent over the course of the week that there were too many regional, ethnic, sectarian, and gender differences to be resolved by a single leadership training. Nigeria had undergone a civil war between north and south from 1967 to 1970 largely along these lines, and although the country ostensibly reconciled, Nigeria still had many unresolved issues that periodically erupted in ethnic conflict. This was the context in which NNAD members valiantly strove to ignore their differences, but these disagreements simmered just under the surface and could emerge with minimal provocation. For example, one Christian woman from the south made a comment to a Muslim woman from the north about the difference in educational attainment between northern and southern Nigeria. The resulting dispute lasted the length of the workshop and drew in other members of their respective state and regional delegations as well as the team leaders before it was finally (inconclusively) settled.

Deaf people in Nigeria do not live in isolation from their larger communities— the values that underpin these societies are reflected within their deaf populations. For example, one foundational value is respect for elders, and we trainers adhered to that ingrained custom. At the same time, we promoted and supported the development of young leaders, a stance that might eventually strip Deaf elders of their power and upend the order of things in the community. Some of the older attendees felt disrespected and patronized by the younger ones who wanted to approach issues, such as the structure of the NNAD, differently than had been done in the past.

Ethnic issues were another serious flashpoint. Because of past and continuing government policies, certain ethnic groups and regions were favored over others in terms of political benefits, infrastructure development, educational attainment, and wealth accumulation. The result was enduring suspicion among the three main ethnic groups (Hausa, Ibo, and Yoruba), as well as a complicated national political and economic framework supposedly set up to encourage equality and minimize discrimination but which actually resulted in even more mistrust. These national trends were reflected in Deaf communities as well. In southern Nigeria, every state had at least one school for the Deaf and usually a few private and mission schools as well. In the north, I could not find more than six schools for the Deaf altogether, including some that had closed, in an area that geographically was larger than southern Nigeria (see, for instance, Eleweke 2002, Ajavon 2006, and 1994). This disparity was further complicated by religious differences because northern Nigeria is primarily Muslim, and many Muslims did not want to send their children to schools founded by Christian missionaries.[6]

All four of us trainers came from relatively comfortable backgrounds in the United States and United Kingdom. We all had stable careers with comfortable incomes and owned our own homes, cars, and other accoutrements of a middle-class life in our respective countries. Although we initially hailed from Nigeria, we had all spent so much time living elsewhere that it was challenging to re-assimilate the values that underpinned life in West Africa. Although we four trainers to some extent still retained some West African values and assumed DEAF-SAME with workshop participants, they viewed us as "other" because of our differences in status, our role as experts, and our advocacy of new ideas. Youth leadership, for example, is a Western idea that needed to be approached with more finesse.

Because we were used to separation of the personal from the organizational, it was hard to relate to the battle for control of NNAD, which was really a struggle for the resources that a national organization can command from the government, from its members, and from international organizations, including such perks as travel abroad, development contracts, and monthly stipends. Indeed, despite his idealistic goals, Tinat had been facing a lot of tension and a fractious coalition of

---

[6] My Muslim parents, who lived in northern Nigeria, had to send me to a Christian boarding school for the Deaf in southern Nigeria since there was nothing suitable in the north when I was growing up. The schools in northern Nigeria would not accept me, and so my parents made the decision to send me hundreds of miles away from home in order to get an education. For many families who could not afford the transportation and schooling fees, however, this was not an option.

deaf individuals. In a precarious political economic context, control of Deaf organizations was one avenue by which educated Deaf people could guarantee continued access to resources.

Our insistence on accountability, strategic planning, democracy, inclusion, and other such value-laden concepts threatened the old order of the NNAD, where elders ruled and power was divided along ethnic and sectarian lines. Part of the pushback Tinat faced was because of his relative youth and his introduction of ideas that minimized the importance of ethnicity and emphasized a "national" Deaf movement. Indeed, fierce resistance should have been expected from these whose power base was undermined.

Conclusion

As I write this, the leadership training program was concluded almost a decade ago and enough time has passed that we can evaluate its impact. Unfortunately, the leaders of NNAD continue to bicker. It is instructive to read the welcome statement on the organization's home page (www.nnadeaf.org), which was last updated in 2011:

> We enjoin members to therefore, eschew misconceptions about religion or tribe—we as a Community are neither Christians nor Moslems neither Ibo nor Hausa nor Yoruba. We are brothers and sisters bound by a common goal and purpose of achieving freedom and equal opportunity for ourselves through our collective advocacy efforts. Let us not join issues with ourselves, rather let us join issues with the society that has erected barriers to the actualization of our goal of equal opportunity for all Deaf Nigerians. . . . Let's put aside suspicion and distrust and support one another in our journey. Let's come together to lay a foundation for the coming future generation of Deaf boys and girls. Let's come together to define our values that will guide us as a Community—Values of Unity, Respect for one another, Honesty, Transparency and Sincerity, Respect for the Rule of Law and so on.

This statement could almost have come directly from Tinat, as it emphasizes DEAF-SAME in the way that he did a decade ago. However, on the website there is no mention of Tinat's pioneering efforts or the restructuring and leadership trainings that happened since 2000. Recent (2014) communication with members of the Nigerian Deaf community and current and former NNAD officers suggest that the organization is still struggling to find its way, much as it was in 2005. However, there are positive seeds in this statement, which was an address to the members by the newly elected (2011) leadership of NNAD. This group was religiously, ethnically, economically, and regionally diverse, and it included several women. The takeaway from this is that change must reflect the larger society in which the Deaf community is based. The concept of DEAF-SAME as a unifier does not work when so many of the underlying realities of the society in which the Deaf community is based militate against it, as they do in Nigeria.

References

Aina, 'G. 2006. "Report on Leadership Training in Nigeria: December 18–23 2005," Gallaudet University, unpublished.

_____. 2005. "Leadership Literacy Development among Deaf and Hard of Hearing People in Cameroon, Ghana, and Nigeria," Gallaudet University, unpublished.

Ajavon, P. A. 2006. *An Overview of Deaf Education in Nigeria.* Deaf Child Worldwide. Accessed October 19, 2014. http://www.ndcs.org.uk/document.rm?id=2875 .

Eleweke, C. J. 2002. "A Review of Issues in Deaf Education under Nigeria's 6-3-3-4 Education System." *Journal of Deaf Studies and Deaf Education* 7 (1): 74–82.

Harris, R., H. M. Holmes, and D. M. Mertens. 2009. "Research Ethics in Sign Language Communities." *Journal of Deaf Studies and Deaf Education* 9 (2): 104–31.

Issahaku, P. A., and S. Neysmith. 2013. "Policy Implications of Population Ageing in West Africa."*International Journal of Sociology and Social Policy* 33 (3/4): 186–202.

Jackson, J. T. 2007. *The Globalizers: Development Workers in Action.* Baltimore: Johns Hopkins University Press.

Nigeria National Association of the Deaf. n.d. Accessed September 7, 2014. http://www.nnadeaf.org.

Ojile, E.. 1994. "Education of the Deaf in Nigeria: An Historical Perspective," in *The Deaf Way: Perspectives from the International Conference on Deaf Culture,* edited by C. J. Erting. Washington, DC: Gallaudet University Press.

Wilson, A., and N. Kakiri. 2007, July. "Improving Development Assistance to Deaf People in Developing Countries: Lessons Learned with the Kenyan Deaf Community." Paper presented at the Fifteenth World Congress of the World Federation of the Deaf, Madrid, Spain.

14 | Sign Language Recognition: Tensions between Specificity and Universalism in International Deaf Discourses

Maartje De Meulder

When deaf people from different countries discuss their national sign language(s) being "recognized," they often assume they have a shared image in their minds of how they can understand the concept, what it could or should entail, and why it is important. This international discourse is linked to a specific sign in International Sign (IS) for RECOGNITION. Similarly, when the World Federation of the Deaf (WFD) urges their members to have their national sign languages "recognized," a cross-national understanding among their members of what this means is implied, although the practical implementation of this will need to be achieved through national legislation.

Also, the UN Convention on the Rights of Persons with Disabilities (UNCRPD) urges ratifying states to "*recognize* and promote" the use of sign languages (Article 21e) and "*recognize* and support" the specific cultural and linguistic identity of deaf people, including sign languages and deaf culture (Article 30.4) (my emphasis). The inclusion of the concept of *recognition* in an international convention such as the UNCRPD again points to the cross-national use of the concept, although its interpretation and implementation is left to the discretion of ratifying states, and again determined by national contexts.

Sign language recognition is one of the major concepts used in international deaf political discourse. However, to date the meaning of the concept has not warranted much critical academic reflection. When it is used, by deaf political organizations and individual deaf people alike, it is implied to mean both the international deaf political demand for recognition (and the internationally oriented aspirations behind this demand) as well as the specific national implementations of this universal idea. This is the very tension between universalism and specificity inherent in the topic of sign language recognition.

To illustrate this, I first use the example of Danish Sign Language, which was recognized on May 13, 2014, while writing this chapter.[1] In this specific case, the recognition meant that a law amendment was passed stipulating that a Danish Sign Language Council would be established as part of the Danish Language Council.[2] This effectively meant that Danish Sign Language received status as a language in Denmark, on an equal par with Danish.

On the Internet, the pride, relief, and hope of Danish deaf people were tangible that day. The past few years Denmark has lost much of its former appeal among deaf people. It became associated with cochlear implants (ninety-nine percent of deaf children receive one), closure of deaf schools, shrinking numbers of deaf teachers, and auditory-verbal therapy (e.g., Niemelä 2011). Denmark became an illustration of how things can change for the worse. Recognition of Danish Sign Language seemed a far-fetched dream. There were also legal challenges. Because Denmark does not have any language legislation or any statutory documents stating official language policy for any language, including Danish, it was hard for the Danish Deaf Association to find a way to legally recognize Danish Sign Language. Its eventual recognition, although not granting any substantial rights to the language nor its users, was thus an important—although mainly symbolic—step for Denmark.

During the final voting of the law proposal in parliament, which was live streamed, one could see the members of parliament looking up at the public gallery with wonderment. They had not seen this before: a gallery full of people applauding with waving hands, hugging, and congratulating each other. The achievement immediately became part of Danish collective deaf consciousness and history. In the evening, the president of the Danish Deaf Association gave a speech in Copenhagen, which was again live streamed and broadcasted in all the major deaf clubs, where deaf people had gathered to celebrate. The recognition also gained international attention, the news was shared on Facebook and Twitter, and deaf people from other countries congratulated Denmark. People from the Netherlands and Canada hoped those countries would be next, while deaf people in the United States stated that Denmark was doing much better than they were regarding recognition and respect for sign language.

In this chapter I introduce the difference between implicit and explicit recognition, sketch when and how explicit legal recognition became a topic on the deaf political agenda, and explore what the concept means in international deaf discourses and how this foregrounds tensions between universalism and specificity in international deaf discourses. I also ask what opportunities and threats are inherent in formulating recognition of sign languages as a transnational concept.

RESEARCH METHODOLOGY AND POSITIONING THE RESEARCHER

My research explores the questions of what it does and could mean to legally recognize Sign Language Peoples' (SLPs) languages, cultures, and identities

---

[1] http://deaf.dk/breaking-news-uk-version

[2] Language councils are scientific institutions that set out guidelines and give advice on the use of a specific language or languages.

and explores SLPs' aspirations for this recognition and the main barriers encountered when trying to achieve it.

The concept of SLP and the ideas, which it embodies, are beginning to gain acceptance following its emergence in Deaf Studies literature (Batterbury, Ladd, and Gulliver 2007). The concept represents the notion that sign-language-using deaf people are collectivities and need to be recognized as culturo-linguistic minorities requiring legal protection akin to what is granted to other linguistic and cultural minorities. This chapter focuses specifically on sign language recognition and on the rights that deaf people, as sign-language-using collectivities, want to achieve. Therefore, I will use "SLPs" or "SLP" in the remainder of this chapter instead of "deaf people," unless in some cases where the use of SLPs is not appropriate. The SLPs concept also foregrounds relevant similarities between SLPs' aspirations and those of other language and cultural groups, for example, indigenous people. The concept further highlights some differences between SLPs and persons with disabilities (De Meulder 2014) and between SLPs and deaf people who do not use sign language. These differences can be relevant when developing legislation specifically aimed at SLPs, of which sign language recognition legislation is an example.

Prior to my research, I worked as an advocate for the Flemish deaf association for five years and was also very closely involved with the recognition of Flemish Sign Language (VGT). This position, combined with a broad international network and my knowledge of International Sign (IS) and active/passive knowledge of other sign languages, enabled me to witness, participate in, and reflect on the international SLP discourse on sign language recognition.

My research is global in scope because information about legislation and sign language recognition is collected from as many countries as possible, but it specifically focuses on the development of sign language legislation in Finland and Scotland. In March 2015 the Finnish Parliament approved the Sign Language Act and in May 2015, the Scottish Parliament is still discussing the British Sign Language (Scotland) Bill (De Meulder 2015a). I collect data through semi-structured interviews with people involved in the recognition processes (academics, activists, politicians); participant observation; informal conversations at SLPs' (political) conferences, meetings, marches, political activities, and social media; and analysis of official documents, which shape language policy on a macro level (government memoranda, policy statements, and recognition legislation itself).

IMPLICIT AND EXPLICIT RECOGNITION

On the international political timeline as used by the WFD and the European Union of the Deaf (EUD) and in international SLP discourse, Finland is often mentioned as the first country in the world to "officially recognize" its sign language (in this case in its constitution, in 1995). Uganda constitutionally recognized its sign language in the same year but generally receives less attention. Further in 1995, Slovakia passed the "Law on the Sign Language of the Deaf" and Lithuania passed an act proclaiming 1996 as the Year of the Disabled, which led to the recognition of sign language as the official language of deaf people (Timmermans 2005; Reagan 2010).[3]

It is interesting that the timeline's "year zero" is 1995. Indeed, some countries mentioned sign language in legislation prior to then. The Swedish government, for example, passed a parliamentary bill on the national budget in 1981. The appendix to this bill mentions that resources will be allocated to make "sign language" a language of instruction (Bagga-Gupta 2010). This indirectly meant that Swedish Sign Language was recognized as a language of instruction and as the first language of deaf people, although it received no legal protection (Hedberg 2014). Another example is the Danish Education Act (1991), which considers Danish Sign Language as the primary language of deaf children and the recommended primary language for their instruction (Timmermans 2005). Before the Danish deaf community celebrated the recognition of Danish Sign Language in May 2014, it thus already was implicitly mentioned in legislation. Similarly, the United Kingdom has several acts referring to sign language or sign language interpreters in general as well as British Sign Language (BSL) in particular (Wheatley and Pabsch 2012): for example, the Police and Criminal Evidence Act (PACE 1984), the Broadcasting Act 1996, the Mental Capacity Act 2005 and the Disability Discrimination Act (DDA 1995 and 2005) all mention BSL. However, BSL as a language in itself or the BSL community as a culturo-linguistic minority are not yet legally recognized (BDA 2014).

This kind of recognition is called "implicit recognition" here, although "indirect recognition" is used too by e.g. Murray (2015). This legislation directly or indirectly refers to sign language or signers: for example it entitles deaf people to the use of interpreting services, accepts the use of sign language in certain judicial situations, or enables its use in the education of deaf children. It can also imply that the law or policy does not directly mention sign language but nevertheless implicitly includes it, such as in judicial situations where it is often stated that the proceedings must be conducted in a language that the acquitted understands. But it does not *explicitly* state that sign language is a language and/or the language of a specific culturo-linguistic community.

The line between implicit and explicit recognition is often blurred and the exact difference between the two is not the main focus of this chapter, nor is it especially relevant. What is important to understand, however, is that SLPs seem to demand *explicit* legal recognition, often in relation to already existing implicit recognition, where the explicit recognition can make implicit recognition work, make it stronger or supplement it. The Danish Education Act (1991) for example, has not been able to avoid that most deaf schools in Denmark closed and most deaf children in Denmark do not receive an education in sign language. The new "recognition law" passed in May 2014 will not avoid this either but is seen by the Danish SLP community as a first step towards a possible reversing of this situation by legally providing that Danish Sign Language is a language and should be recognized as such. The Finnish Deaf Association claimed that the 1995 constitutional recognition

---

[3] In 1991, Lithuania passed the Law on Social Integration of the Disabled, which stated that "sign language is the native language of the deaf" (Timmermans 2005; Reagan 2010; Wheatley and Pabsch 2012).

has not guaranteed linguistic rights into practice, i.e., has not made already exist-ing specific legislation (implicit recognition) work, which is why they successfully campaigned for language legislation (the Sign Language Act mentioned earlier in this chapter) to fill in the missing link between the constitution and special legisla-tion (Suomen viittomakielten kielipoliittinen ohjelma 2010).

Explicit Legal Recognition Becoming a Topic on SLPs' Political Agenda

As for any culturo-linguistic minority, the societal position of SLPs has always been intrinsically linked to the societal and legal position of their languages and cultures. SLP communities have thus always strived for a better positioning of their languages, especially from the end of the nineteenth century throughout the first part of the twentieth century onwards, when the educational discourse of "oralism" downplayed sign languages to the level of primitive and backward communication systems (Ladd 2003). It was only in the 1960s and 1970s that sign languages received academic linguistic recognition when modern scientific re-search (Tervoort 1953; Stokoe 1960) showed that sign languages possessed all the characteristics of languages. These research findings were initially received with mockery and disbelief, both by fellow hearing academics and by SLPs them-selves, who had internalized the oralist view of their languages. With time came a shift of consciousness in SLP communities, the acceptance and understand-ing of the status of their languages, in many cases also the naming of their lan-guages, and with it the desire to secure this status in law. This desire coincided with the growing external and internal identification of SLPs as culturo-linguistic minorities.

It is not exactly clear who put the topic of "sign language recognition" (mean-ing: explicit legal recognition) on the international "SLP political agenda." Nordic representatives claim the idea is a "Nordic invention." Indeed, many traces and personal influences point back to the Nordic countries and Finland was the first European country to constitutionally recognize its sign language.

The WFD first used the concept of recognition in a resolution passed by the World Congress held in Helsinki in 1987 (WFD 1993). Yerker Andersson from Swe-den (but living in the United States since 1955) had been the WFD's president for four years at that time, while Liisa Kauppinen from Finland had been the vice president (in 1987 she became the WFD's general secretary). Andersson initiated a major shift in policy goals, from accessibility issues to recognition of sign lan-guages[4] and during his term as WFD president (1983–1995) one of the strategic goals of the WFD was working with UNESCO to recognize sign languages as the legitimate languages of deaf people.

Other traces point to the United Kingdom. The British Deaf Association (BDA) Manifesto asked the British government as early as 1982 "to recognize BSL, to reflect this in its legislation, and to acknowledge that the British deaf community is

---

[4] Personal communication, John Bosco Conama, August 27, 2013.

a linguistic minority of British people." In 1985, the BDA initiated the establishment of the European Community Regional Secretariat (ECRS, now called European Union of the Deaf, EUD). Its first president was John Young from the United Kingdom and he remained in this position until 1990 when Knud Søndergaard from Denmark took over.

The European campaign for the recognition of sign languages originated in the ECRS meetings, which led to the adoption of the first European Parliament resolution on sign languages in 1988, reiterated in 1998 (Krausneker 2000). Article 2 of the 1988 resolution calls on the European Commission "to make a proposal to the Council concerning official recognition of the sign language used by deaf people in each Member State." In 1989, the concept of recognition was also used in the Statement on the Recognition of National Sign Languages of the Deaf passed by the Third European Congress on Sign Language Research in 1989 (Reagan 2010). For a more detailed account of the turn towards this linguistic human rights discourse, and the role of the WFD, EUD and national deaf associations, I refer to Murray (2015).

THE MEANING OF "SIGN LANGUAGE RECOGNITION" IN INTERNATIONAL DEAF DISCOURSES

Currently about thirty-one countries (of which the majority are European Union member states) have recognized their sign language(s) in legislation on language status and/or language rights (De Meulder 2015b).

The nature and scope of these recognition laws is very diverse. "Sign language recognition" as used in international SLP discourse is a very vague denominator including many different legal and even nonlegal measures, although there is increasing awareness of the fact that legislation is needed to make recognition work. The United Kingdom, for example, has recognized British Sign Language (BSL) "as a language in its own right" by means of a government declaration in 2003 (followed by Wales and Northern Ireland governments in 2004 and the Scottish government in 2011), but did not give BSL any legal protection (although at the moment of writing this chapter in May 2015, the Scottish Parliament is discussing a bill which might give BSL legal status in Scotland). Therefore, deaf people in the United Kingdom increasingly use the signs ACKNOWLEDGED or ACCEPTED when talking about BSL recognition, instead of the sign RECOGNIZED.

To get an analytical grip on this diversity, it is useful to offer some sort of categorization. In contrast to the recognition of most spoken languages, including minority languages, the recognition of sign languages rarely means that they receive national, official or minority status, or are included in the constitution or language legislation. Because of the dual category/definition of SLPs as both persons with a disability and members of culturolinguistic minority groups, there is a tendency among policy makers to categorize SLPs' issues only in disability legislation. Some states (e.g., Venezuela and Ecuador) have recognized their sign languages in sections of their constitutions pertaining to disability. This points to most policy makers' profound misunderstanding about the nature of SLPs' languages and cultures but equally to a certain inability of SLPs to communicate their demands in a way that policy makers understand.

FIVE CATEGORIES OF THE MOST COMMON TYPES OF EXPLICIT (LEGAL) RECOGNITION

Based on an analysis of current sign language recognition legislation, the follow-ing five categories of the most common types of explicit (legal) recognition can be discussed (for a more detailed discussion of these categories, see De Meulder 2015b).[5] The differences in types of recognition can be explained by various factors determined by national contexts. Some are linked to legislation itself (e.g., some countries do not have a constitution or language laws), while others are linked to a country's attitudes to linguistic and cultural diversity.

1. Constitutional recognition

2. Recognition by means of general language legislation

3. Recognition by means of a separate sign language law or act

4. Recognition by means of a separate sign language law or act including other means of communication

5. Recognition by means of legislation on the functioning of the national lan-guage council

The categories as listed here are not meant as hierarchies. Constitutional recogni-tion, for example, while often presented as the most prestigious form of recogni-tion, does not necessarily grant deaf people more rights than recognition by means of a separate sign language law. It can even be purely symbolic as has been demon-strated for Austria where deaf people lack any linguistic or other rights they can claim on the basis of this recognition (Krausneker 2008; Wilcox, Krausneker, and Armstrong 2012).

Currently, eleven countries worldwide have recognized their national sign languages at constitutional level: Finland (1995), Uganda (1995), South Africa (1996), Portugal (1997), Venezuela (1999), Austria (2005), New Zealand (2006), Ecuador (2008), Kenya (2010), Zimbabwe (2010), and Hungary (2011). In only one of these eleven countries (New Zealand) is the recognized sign language also an official language (in addition to te reo Māori), although Smiler and McKee (2007) points out there is still a huge gap between de facto and de jure recognition of New Zealand Sign Language.

Four countries recognized their sign language within general language leg-islation: Latvia (1999), Estonia (2007), Sweden (2009), and Iceland (2011). Other countries recognized their sign language through a specific sign language law (ex-amples include Slovakia in 1995, Lithuania in 1995, Uruguay in 2001, Slovenia in 2002, Belgium (Wallonia) in 2003, Brazil in 2006, Cyprus in 2006, Belgium (Flanders) in 2006, Bosnia and Herzegovina in 2009, Macedonia in 2009, and Catalonia (Spain) in 2010), sometimes also recognizing "other means of communication" (examples

---

[5] Some states may be missing from this overview due to barriers in accessing valid infor-mation about relevant legislation or changes in the situation of a country. Also, the time lag between submission and publication of this chapter will inevitably mean some information is not up to date by the time of publication. I welcome any feedback or additional information.

include Colombia in 1996, Spain in 2007, the Czech Republic in 2008, Hungary in 2009, and Poland in 2011). Norway and Denmark have recognized their national sign languages in legislation on the functioning of the language council in 2009 and 2014 respectively.

There are three other categories where the line between explicit and implicit recognition is not clear. Some states have mentioned their sign languages within other legislation, primarily disability or equality legislation (e.g., Germany in 2002, Mexico in 2005, and Chile in 2010) or educational legislation (e.g., Greece in 2002 and France in 2005). Others only have recognition by declaration or government decision (no legal recognition) (examples include Australia in 1991, Thailand in 1992, England in 2003, Wales in 2004, Northern Ireland in 2004, and Kosovo in 2010). American Sign Language (ASL) in the USA and ASL and Langue des Signes Québécoise (LSQ) in Canada are not yet recognized at the federal level but are mentioned in some state legislation. In Canada, some states have recognized ASL or LSQ in their legislation as a language of instruction. In the United States, several states have recognized ASL as a (foreign) language for educational purposes.[6] I have not included those three categories in the categories of explicit legal recognition and they are not included in the figure of thirty-one countries listed above.

ASPIRATIONS FOR RECOGNITION

What is it SLPs want to achieve with this recognition? Why do they feel recognition of their languages and cultures is so important? From how it is used in international SLP discourse, "recognition" seems to imply at least four aspirations. I list them here and state very briefly whether and how they are met by recognition legislation:

1. **Acquisition rights and educational linguistic rights**: the right of deaf children (and their parents) to acquire and learn sign language and the right of deaf children to receive an education in sign language. While this is one of the most important aspirations, it is also the one least often guaranteed in legislation (see also Murray 2015 and McKee and Manning 2015). *If* provided, those rights are often accompanied by opt-outs such as when parents demand it (e.g., Hungary) or only apply to those children who "need" it (e.g., Iceland).

2. **Linguistic rights**: SLPs' right to use sign language to receive information, services, and to communicate with public authorities. In some laws this also entails a positive obligation by states to promote and develop sign language. However, insofar as sign language recognition legislation provides language rights, they are often based on a norm-and-accommodation approach in which the state makes special accommodations for people who lack sufficient

---

[6] According to Reagan (2011) the recognition of ASL in the United States has largely affected hearing rather than deaf people because it is not concerned with language rights but with acceptance of ASL as a language fulfilling foreign language requirements.

proficiency in the dominant language, through the provision of interpreters in certain settings. While this approach may enable and facilitate communication and protect SLPs from discrimination, it does not give them substantial rights in terms of the recognition of their distinct cultural identities (Kymlicka and Patten 2003) and does not really promote the *use* of the language.

3. **Group rights**: increasingly, it is expected by SLPs that recognition of their languages and cultures also entails recognition of the fact that they are collectivities and as such are entitled to certain group rights to protect and develop their particular cultural characteristics (Emery 2006; Ladd 2007; Kusters et al. 2015). This is different from the second aspiration, which is merely about the right of individual deaf people to use sign language. Collective rights allow a collectivity to control matters relevant to their cultural survival and depend on a form of differential treatment of a group (Sanders 1991; Kymlicka 2002). For SLPs, group rights could entail the right to establish, maintain, and control their own educational institutions; the right to be protected from harmful interventions; the right to maintain and strengthen their distinct linguistic and cultural characteristics; the right to use, develop, and transmit to future generations their histories, languages, epistemologies, etc.; and the right to some sort of self-determination. It seems that the provision of those rights has been absent from most recognition legislation. Some laws, however, seem to have the potential to be used for claiming group rights. The Act on Hungarian Sign Language, for example, in its general provisions, Section 3(2), states: "The community of persons using the Hungarian Sign Language shall have the right to use, develop and preserve the Hungarian Sign Language, as well as to foster, extend and transmit deaf culture."

4. **Symbolical recognition**: the acknowledgment by states that sign languages exist and are valid languages. In some legislation this also entails the recognition that sign language is the first language of deaf people and that deaf people belong to a culturolinguistic minority group. While symbolical recognition may sound trivial, it is important for historical reasons, as a kind of redress for harms done in the past (and still ongoing).

While these aspirations seem to be internationally oriented, meeting them will be very much determined by national contexts. This brings us to the very tension between specificity and universalism.

Tensions between Specificity and Universalism

Because of their collective ethos, SLPs' desire for recognition is a common goal, and every time a sign language is recognized the achievement becomes part of the international collective SLP consciousness and history. This goal is nourished by and inspired at an international level through international conferences, meetings, social media, publications, etc., where sign language recognition is common on the agenda. At the moment of writing this chapter, the Second International Conference on the Linguistic Rights of the Deaf is taking place in Moscow, with presentations on sign language legislation, advocacy for official recognition of sign languages, and case presentations from different countries, such as Finland and Ukraine.[7]

One could argue that such settings capture "the global vision of a common Deaf political identity predicated on sign language" (Valentine and Skelton 2007, 135). Frustrated by the injustice and barriers experienced in their own countries, SLPs are increasingly developing alternative forms of political commitment and turn to an international human rights framework to address universal questions of linguistic justice and the right to have their sign languages recognized, something that Valentine and Skelton (2007) call "transborder activism." The WFD's involvement in the negotiations about the UNCRPD, and national associations of the deaf using this convention in their lobbying efforts, are examples of this (Batterbury 2012; De Meulder 2014).[8] The international struggle and aspirations for the recognition of sign languages also illustrate this.

The tension between specificity and universalism inherent to the concept of sign language recognition lies with the fact that, while the meaning of sign language recognition is determined and normatively inspired by internationally oriented aspirations and an international discourse, it has to be achieved, implemented, and understood through national legislation. When individual deaf people and deaf political organizations talk about recognition, they seem to refer first of all to the aspirations that guide the international agenda, not to the specifics of national recognition legislation.

Consequently, the risk for confusion and miscommunication is very much present. This risk increases because of the different languages of legislative instruments, different political and legal systems, and the fact that for international comparisons and at international gatherings, English or International Sign is used, which means nuances sometimes get lost in translation. Without enough clarification, we risk speaking past each other when we think we are speaking of the same thing.

Friedner and Kusters (2014) argue that major concepts used in international deaf discourse such as human rights, oppression, and empowerment are northern-situated concepts that engender ideas of deaf universalism and "are often uncritically adopted both as universal analytic concepts and as universal discourses." To a certain extent, this can be said of the concept of sign language recognition too. Still, this cross-national use and understanding (on a superficial level) of the concept also entails opportunities: it illustrates, inspires, and strengthens the collective ethos of deaf communities and seems to give them hope (even if the recognition is purely symbolic). Every time a sign language is recognized, this is welcomed as a collective feeling of accomplishment and deaf people in different countries cheer for each to have their sign languages recognized.

This collective feeling of accomplishment seems to happen regardless of the effective meaning and status of the recognition. To return to the Danish example,

---

[7] http://deaflinguisticconference2014.voginfo.ru/en/
[8] The UNCRPD brings along with it a host of tensions between national and transnational (see Michael Stein, this volume)

in social media, the message that Danish Sign Language was recognized and pictures of proud Danish deaf people in parliament received more attention than what the recognition effectively meant, how it was embedded in legislation, and how it was achieved. Deaf people like to make or see lists of recognized sign languages to keep score of how many countries have joined the club, although such lists only give a very superficial picture and are quickly outdated.

Deaf communities have the ability to and do support each other across borders to achieve successful recognition. This can make recognition legislation stronger. In the end, however, every country is different and there are limits for lobbying in support of each other. The strength of international collaboration seems to lie first of all in the formulation of collective and universalist aspirations that can fuel localized efforts in specific nations.

Conclusion

The international nature of the aspirations inspires another question with which I would like to end this chapter: what would an international convention on SLPs' rights look like? Comparisons could be made here with the Convention Concerning Indigenous and Tribal Peoples (ILO no. 169) and the United Nations Declaration on the Rights of Indigenous Peoples (2007). A SLP convention or declaration on the rights of SLPs would go beyond mere linguistic recognition and entail important aspects of cultural recognition as well, including group rights. The mere focus on sign language recognition, while immensely valuable, has often prevented us from seeing the full (legal) picture of recognition of SLPs. In the light of current medical and genetic intervention policies that are threatening the very existence of SLPs as part of human diversity (Emery and Ladd forthcoming), such a treaty could very well influence the further existence and health of future SLPs' communities.

Acknowledgments

I thank all the various people who have commented on earlier drafts of this chapter: Paddy Ladd, Verena Krausneker, Ritva Takkinen, and Annika Pabsch. Thanks go to Mette Sommer and Janne Boye Niemelä for information on the recognition of Danish Sign Language, to Paal Richard Peterson for information on the situation in Norway, and to Tommy Lyxell from the Swedish Language Council.

References

Bagga-Gupta, S. 2010. "Creating and (Re)negotiating Boundaries: Representations as Mediation in Visually Oriented Multilingual Swedish School Settings." *Language, Culture and Curriculum* 23 (3): 251–76.

Batterbury, S. 2012. "Language Justice for Sign Language Peoples: The UN Convention on the Rights of Persons with Disabilities."*Language Policy* 11 (3): 253–72.

———. 2014. "Legal Status for BSL and ISL." Discussion paper. Retrieved from http://www.bda.org.uk/news/155.

Batterbury, S., P. Ladd, and M. Gulliver. 2007. "Sign Language Peoples as Indigenous Minorities: Implications for Research and Policy."*Environment and Planning* 39:2899–915.

De Meulder, M. 2014. "The UNCRPD and Sign Language Peoples." In *UNCRPD Implementation in Europe—A Deaf Perspective. Article 29: Participation in Political and Public Life*," edited by A. Pabsch, 12–28. Brussels: European Union of the Deaf.

———. 2015a. "A Barking Dog That Never Bites? The British Sign Language (Scotland) Bill."*Sign Language Studies* 15 (4): 446–72.

———. 2015b. "The Legal Recognition of Sign Languages." *Sign Language Studies,* 15(4): 498–506.

Emery, S. 2006. "Citizenship and the Deaf Community." PhD diss., University of Central Lancashire.

Emery, S., and P. Ladd. Forthcoming. *Sleepwalking into Eugenics: Genetic Interventions and Disabled People*. Bristol: University of Bristol.

Friedner, M., and A. Kusters. 2014. "On the Possibilities and Limits of 'DEAF DEAF SAME': Tourism and Empowerment Camps in Adamorobe (Ghana), Bangalore, and Mumbai (India)."*Disability Studies Quarterly* 34 (3). http://dsq-sds.org/article/view/4246/3649.

Hedberg, T. 2014, May. "Sign Language as an Official Language in Sweden: How It Has Developed during the Past Twenty Years." Paper presented at MMX Days, Uppsala, Sweden.

Krausneker, V. 2000. "Sign Languages and the Minority Language Policy of the European Union." In *Bilingualism and Identity in Deaf Communities,* edited by M. Metzger, vol. 6, 142–58. Washington, DC: Gallaudet University Press.

———. 2003. "Has Something Changed? Sign Languages in Europe: The Case of Minorised Minority Languages." *Deaf Worlds* 19 (2): 33–46.

———. 2008, March. The Status of Sign Languages. European Aspirations. Presentation at the British Deaf Association, Annual General Meeting, Bristol.

Kusters, A., M. De Meulder, M. Friedner and S. D. Emery 2015. *On "Diversity" and "Inclusion": Exploring Paradigms for Achieving Sign Language Peoples' Rights*. MMG Working Paper 15-02. http://www.mmg.mpg.de/publications/working-papers/2015/wp-15-02.

Kymlicka, W. 2002. *Contemporary Political Philosophy: An Introduction.* Oxford: Oxford University Press.

Kymlicka, W., and A. Patten. 2003. "Language Rights and Political Theory." *Annual Review of Applied Linguistics* 23:3–21.

Ladd, P. 2003. *Understanding Deaf Culture: In Search of Deafhood*. Clevedon, UK: Multilingual Matters.

———. 2007. "Cultural Rights and Sign Language Peoples." Paper presented at the Tenth International Conference of the World Federation of the Deaf, July, Madrid, Spain.

McKee, R. and V. Manning. 2015. "Effects of Language Planning and Policy on Language Rights and the Vitality of New Zealand Sign Language." *Sign Language Studies* 15 (4): 473–97.

Murray, J. 2015. "Linguistic Human Rights Discourses in Deaf Community Activism." *Sign Language Studies* 15 (4): 379–410.

Niemelä, P. 2011. "Danish Sign Language as an Endangered Language?" Paper presented at the WFD Conference on Endangered Sign Languages, November, Ål, Norway.

Reagan, T. 2010. *Language Policy and Planning for Sign Languages.* Washington, DC: Gallaudet University Press.

———. 2011. "Ideological Barriers to American Sign Language: Unpacking Linguistic Resistance."*Sign Language Studies* 11 (4): 606–36.

Sanders, D. 1991. "Collective Rights."*Human Rights Quarterly* 13 (3): 368–86.

Smiler, K., and R. McKee 2007. "Perceptions of Maori Deaf Identity in New Zealand. *Journal of Deaf Studies and Deaf Education* 12(1): 93–11.

Stokoe, W. 1960. *Sign Language Structure: An Outline of the Visual Communication Systems of the American Deaf.* Buffalo, NY: Department of Anthropology and Linguistics, University of Buffalo.

Suomen viittomakielten kielipoliittinen ohjelma. 2014. [The Language Policy Programme for the National Sign Languages in Finland]. Helsinki: Kuurojen Liitto ry & Kotimaisten Kielten Tutkimuskeskus. Retrieved from http://www.kotus.fi/index.phtml?s=3834.

Tervoort, B. 1953. *Structurele analyse van visueel taalgebruik binnen een groep dove kinderen.* Amsterdam, the Netherlands: Noord-Hollandsche Uitgeverij.

Timmermans, N. 2005.*The Status of Sign Languages in Europe.* Strasbourg: Council of Europe Publishing.

Valentine, G., and T. Skelton. 2007. "The Right to Be Heard: Citizenship and Language." *Political Geography* 26:12–140.

Wheatley, M., and A. Pabsch. 2012. *Sign Language Legislation in the European Union*, 2nd ed. Brussels: European Union of the Deaf.

Wilcox, S., V. Krausneker, and D. Armstrong. 2012. "Language Policies and the Deaf Community." In *Cambridge Handbook of Language Policy*, edited by B. Spolsky, 374–95. Cambridge, UK: Cambridge University Press.

World Federation of the Deaf Scientific Commission on Sign Language. 1993. *Report on the Status of Sign Language.* Helsinki, Finland: World Federation of the Deaf.

15 | Implementing the Convention on the Rights of Persons with Disabilities: Supporting the Deaf Community in Chile through Legal Expertise

Michael Steven Stein

I am a deaf American lawyer who has visited Chile regularly since 2009, drawn by the opportunity to meet deaf people in another country.[1] In one sense, my story is but another example of the power of common experiences as deaf individuals to bring us together. Without that connection, I would never have traveled to Chile, much less gotten to know the country and its deaf community. Many other international deaf individuals and organizations have also visited Chile and talked of empowerment. However, our brief visits have not been enough to help deaf Chileans overcome the discrimination they encounter daily in all aspects of society. Although Chile signed the United Nations Convention on the Rights of Persons with Disabilities (CRPD) in 2008, sustained advocacy is required to translate the CRPD's general terms into specific legal provisions that result in the full inclusion of deaf people in Chilean society. Such advocacy requires familiarity with the political and legal system in Chile, a skill set that international deaf visitors and most deaf Chileans lack. My experience in Chile shows that deaf Chileans will achieve true equality only when they themselves possess the legal tools to advocate effectively for their human rights.

MY TRAVELS IN CHILE

I happened upon Chile through a friend from there who graduated from Gallaudet University and had stayed in the United States. I was working as a lawyer for the National Association of the Deaf (NAD) on a two-year fellowship for recent law

---

[1] In this article, I use the term *deaf* in the lowercase in its all-inclusive sense to include the full range of diversity in the universe of deaf people.

school graduates. My time at NAD was nearly up and I wanted to travel afterward to learn about the experiences of deaf people in other countries. When I asked my friend about Chile, he was thrilled. I plunged into studying Spanish and visited Chile in May 2009 for a week at his invitation.

When I visited, I was struck by how open and welcoming the deaf community was. They were patient with the limited Chilean Sign Language that I had learned during my few days there. And it was the first time I truly felt welcomed as a *deaf* person. In the United States, I found it difficult to fit into the deaf community because I was not the best signer. I also did not possess any of the status markers in the deaf community: I did not come from a deaf family, I did not go to a deaf school, and I did not grow up signing. But in Chile, none of that mattered. My lack of fluency in Chilean Sign Language was not because I had grown up oral—it was because I was new to Chile! That I was a deaf lawyer also helped; there were no deaf lawyers there. I liked Chile enough that I decided to go back in September 2009 for a year after I finished my fellowship at NAD.

During the first three months, I stayed with a deaf family in Santiago, where almost half of Chileans live and which has by far the largest deaf community. I visited the schools for the deaf where the methods ranged from total communication to bicultural-bilingual education to oral education. I visited associations for the deaf, including Asociación de Sordos de Chile (ASOCH), the oldest and largest deaf association in Chile. I also visited deaf associations that had splintered off from ASOCH over the years. I watched the associations play one another in soccer. I visited organizations that serve deaf people, including Proyecto Sol, a Catholic organization that provides tutoring for deaf students and support for their families. I had no other goal other than to get to know as much of the Chilean deaf community as possible.

After my initial time in Santiago, I traveled to the southern part of the country, and went as far south as Punta Arenas on the Magellan Strait that rounds the continental mainland. The cities were much smaller and the deaf associations smaller and more intimate. Deaf folks invited me to their houses and served *asado* (barbecue). In Coyhaique, in the heart of Patagonia where it is cold and rains constantly, the deaf association roasted lamb and taught me how to eat it: pull the meat and cut with a knife.

I also traveled the northern part of the country—the land of the Atacama Desert, with its lunar landscapes (and oddly enough, pink flamingos). I flew to Arica, which is on the border with Peru. I stayed there a week, and then took the bus several hours to the next city south and stayed there a week, and so on, all the way back to Santiago, and continuing south. A routine emerged. In each city, the deaf leaders who I had contacted ahead of time welcomed me and showed me their hometowns. I presented at deaf associations, giving a presentation on the human rights of deaf people and the disability laws of the United States and Chile. I showed the movie *Audism Unveiled*, which deaf Chileans identified strongly with. I visited the schools for the deaf and talked with students and teachers about how deaf people can do anything, even become a lawyer! I did this routine so often I felt like a traveling road show.

Chile became a second home, and in the years since, I have returned often. As a lecturer at the Rochester Institute of Technology (RIT), I was twice able to bring my students to Chile as part of a study-abroad program. Students took a semester-long course at RIT in which they learned about the deaf community in Chile and studied Chilean Sign Language. Then we traveled to Chile during intersessions and my students met the community that welcomed me during my travels. That we are all deaf brings us together.

Discrimination against Deaf People in Chile

During my time in Chile, I have heard stories of discrimination. Many deaf people cannot get driver's licenses. Although I visited some deaf schools where the teachers and students could communicate easily in Chilean Sign Language, I visited many other schools where the teachers and students could barely communicate with one another. At the high school level, deaf students are mainstreamed with interpreters only a few hours a week (if even that). Deaf students wishing to go on to university must apply annually for limited funds to pay for interpreter services; they may get the grant one year and not the next. Discrimination pervades the workplace. One deaf person told me that he worked for a department store for many years. Then one day, his boss summoned him and fired him for not being able to use the telephone. Another deaf individual told me that she went to university and got a degree in graphic design but no one would hire her because she was deaf. Her studies had all been for nothing. Deaf people have also been limited in other ways. I met a woman in southern Chile who told me her own parents took away her child because they did not think that a deaf person could be a good mother.

There was a large earthquake in 2010, one of the largest earthquakes in recorded history. Emergency alerts and broadcasts were not captioned. Deaf people told me afterward how they could not communicate with police officers and first aid responders. One deaf man had gestured to a police officer trying to ask if he should stay or leave his house, and the police officer had responded with a thumbs-up. Then the tsunamis came. Wave after wave pushed the deaf man and his son higher up in the house and onto the roof, where they waited for the waters to recede. In the weeks that followed, deaf people struggled to make sense of the chaos without any access to information.

And there has often seemed to be little that deaf Chileans can do to enforce what few legal rights they have under Chilean law. Many deaf Chileans are poorly educated and do not know their rights. Many are also unemployed and cannot afford the cost of a lawyer, and even if they could afford a lawyer, they would not be able to communicate (a consequence of both the lack of interpreters in Chile and a general unwillingness by lawyers to pay for interpreter services). Many lawyers are not familiar with deaf experiences and the communication needs of deaf individuals. In turn, many deaf individuals do not understand the general contours of the legal system and how to work with lawyers. And so for many deaf Chileans, the law seems beyond their reach.

The Limits of the Convention on the Rights of Persons with Disabilities and the Global Push for Inclusion of Deaf People

The CRPD has raised global awareness of the human rights of individuals with a disability. The treaty recognizes the broad right of individuals with disabilities to participate fully and independently in all facets of society including education, health care, employment, and recreation. For instance, Article 9 of the CRPD

recognizes and promotes sign language and Article 21 requires participating countries to ensure equal access to information through interpreters and other accessible means. (For a more complete discussion how the CRPD recognizes the human
rights of deaf people, see De Meulder 2014.)

Ratifying countries are obligated to amend their disability laws as necessary to
recognize the human rights of individuals with disabilities as spelled out in the CRPD.
This obligation has generated momentum that has resulted in revisions of national
laws around the globe. Chile is an example: it ratified the treaty in 2008 and amended
its disability law in 2010 with the explicit goal of complying with the CRPD. Chilean
bureaucrats and advocates continue to reference the CRPD as a reason to reconsider
government policies and increase access for individuals with a disability.[2]

However, the CRPD is not a self-executing file that countries can simply
"download" into their national legal codes. Article 4 states that ratifying countries
shall "adopt all appropriate legislative, administrative, and other measures for the
implementation of the rights recognized in the present Convention." This broad
wording, coupled with the general nature of the rights described in the CRPD,
gives countries considerable discretion in guaranteeing these rights.

Consequently, to implement the CRPD, countries must enact their own laws
that directly provide for equal access in concrete ways. For instance, if there is
a right to a sign language interpreter, it must be spelled out in sufficient detail:
when they must be provided, who provides them, and who pays for them (all
this assuming there are enough interpreters to meet demand). Otherwise, the de-
fault will be that deaf people must provide their own interpreters, as is the case
in most developing countries (and even in many developed countries). Countries
that provide for a right to interpreters have done so in differing ways. For instance,
the United States requires businesses to provide and pay for interpreters when
necessary for effective communication with deaf people, consistent with a civil
rights tradition that prohibits businesses from discriminating against people on
the basis of race, sex, or national origin (Stein and Teplin 2011). Other countries
with a more robust social welfare state such as Finland and Sweden have looked
to the government to pay for interpreter services (at least up to a certain number
of hours) (Timmermans 2005). Each country must tackle the bureaucratic details of
incorporating the CRPD and recognizing the human rights of individuals with a
disability in a manner consistent with its political and cultural traditions (also see
De Meulder, this volume).

Against this backdrop, generic talk of the human rights of deaf people and empowerment can only go so far in pushing for the inclusion of deaf people in society.
For instance, WFD leaders visited Chile in 2008 and talked about the human rights
of deaf people. The visit was memorable for deaf Chileans but, they asked me,
what was the next step? How could they advocate for themselves? Then in 2010,
while I was there, young deaf advocates from the Denmark-based Frontrunners
visited Chile for several weeks. They gave presentations on audism and deafhood.
They did workshops on deaf identity for young deaf Chileans between the ages
of eighteen and thirty. We all enjoyed the time together, but when Frontrunners
left, it was as if they had never come (also see Kusters, Toura-Jensen, Verhelst,

---

[2] For example, an executive agency cited the CRPD as a reason for implementing a regulation requiring captioning and interpreting on television (Decreto 32 2012).

and Vesterggaard, this volume). The same happened with the places that I visited during my road show—we got together, enjoyed the exchange, and then after I left, things went back to as they had been before. Our talk of deaf rights sounded good to everyone but it remained an abstract notion for most deaf Chileans, who lacked the legal expertise to translate the CRPD's guarantees into meaningful and enforceable rights. Incorporating the CRPD into the Chilean legal code requires a familiarity with the political and legal system in Chile that outsiders such as myself lack. For real change to happen, deaf Chileans must have access to the legal expertise necessary to navigate Chilean bureaucracy.

THE CHALLENGES OF DEAF ADVOCACY IN CHILE

The challenge in Chile—as in other countries around the world—is that many deaf individuals, due to the lack of accessible education and the lack of access to legal expertise, do not understand how the political and legal channels work, much less how to navigate them. There are few deaf people in Chile who can read and write well enough to master the complexities of legal language. Communication barriers and the differences in experiences between the political elite—dominated by hearing individuals who may have never met a deaf person before—and the deaf community make traversing the legal system even more challenging. For advocates to be effective in Chile, they need to know how to translate the needs of the deaf community into the language of the political and legal elite in Chile. However, there are no deaf lawyers in Chile and few people with strong connections to the deaf community who otherwise have the skill set necessary to maneuver the political and legal process there.

Further complicating the push for greater rights are divisions within the deaf community (also see Rashid, this volume). The deaf world is small in Chile, and it is even smaller among the "deaf elite," who are better educated and may possess the skills necessary to bridge the gap between the political elite and the deaf community. These deaf leaders are active within their associations during evenings and weekends; during the week they work to support their families. Some function entirely within the deaf world—they are teachers or psychologists who work with deaf students or they teach Chilean Sign Language—while others are part of the machinery that operates the hearing working world. Although they all share the same goal of greater inclusion of deaf people in Chile, they are deeply suspicious of one another. In Santiago, deaf associations break down largely along age and socioeconomic lines; deaf individuals pledge allegiance first to their local (urban) deaf association and then to the Chilean deaf community as a whole.[3]

The rivalry among deaf associations in Santiago is further intensified by a sense of ownership of the advocacy process. Some deaf leaders told me about their

---

[3] Outside of Santiago, there are fewer people, including deaf people. One result has been that there is usually only one deaf association per city, with deaf people from all ages and socioeconomic backgrounds coming together. In such cases, the best-educated deaf individuals have usually become the leaders of the associations, as was the case with Vianney Sierralta and the deaf association in Calama, discussed below.

grand plans to establish a nonprofit organization or to pursue a particular project that will benefit all deaf people in Chile. But—and they usually added—this idea was their "intellectual property" and they did not want to share it with anyone just yet, for fear that their ideas would be stolen and they would not get credit. This same jealousy led some individuals to refuse to participate in deaf advocacy efforts that they did not themselves organize. Also, when deaf individuals have obtained grants to fund their time on advocacy projects, others have complained that those individuals were merely profiteering. Deaf individuals are also suspicious of interpreters, particularly those who interpret on television; although these interpreters sometimes participate in advocacy efforts, deaf individuals have complained that the interpreters seek the attention for themselves.

Over the years, there has been talk of setting up a national confederation of deaf associations that could speak with one voice, but such efforts have never lasted. In January 2011, during the last serious effort, deaf leaders put aside their rivalries and hammered out a charter that thirteen presidents of deaf associations throughout Chile then signed. However, even this effort failed when the government agency charged with approving charters found several technical problems with the document that required revision and the re-affirmation by the various deaf associations. By this time, many months had passed and the deaf leaders had gone home and all momentum had been lost. Deaf leaders mistrust each other as before, and as of this writing, no further effort has been made to resurrect the confederation.

The result is a patchwork of advocacy efforts by deaf leaders who do not know what other deaf leaders are planning. One deaf association has an informal relationship with the government agency that provides services for individuals with a disability and has a member who works for the agency. That deaf association has also had some success focusing media attention on the lack of communication access for deaf people. Several deaf associations organize conferences but members of competing associations rarely attend. Yet another group of deaf individuals produces videos about deaf issues. Other deaf individuals have formed nonprofit organizations in the name of deaf advocacy but their efforts have not been public. These individuals work like ships passing in the night.

During my year in Chile, I tried to use my role as an outsider with a legal background to try to bring together leaders from rival deaf associations. It was a challenge. Some leaders would hesitate and maybe not come to the first meeting or two. Then they would start to come. I talked about the CRPD and the possible ways to translate it into Chilean law. The deaf leaders talked about what kind of laws they might want and listened to each other. They decided to form a group called Movimiento Sordo ("Deaf Movement"). We heard rumors about coming changes to the Chilean disability law and saw a draft of the proposed legislation. I pointed out some shortcomings such as the lack of clarity about who had to pay for the interpreters. The members of the new movement wanted to push for stronger legislation. We met with the government agency that provides services for individuals with a disability. However, the bill was already set to pass. Movimiento Sordo also did not last. After several months in Santiago, I traveled to the south and the north, and in my absence the meetings ceased. Although I urged the deaf leaders to meet without me—I was not Chilean and did not own the process—their suspicions of one another never completely went away and eventually overwhelmed the effort. With such a divided deaf elite, the deaf community was not able to speak with one voice that would carry weight with lawmakers.

The communication barriers that the CRPD was drafted to overcome further contributed to the problem. The communication barriers that have isolated deaf people generally have also significantly hampered their ability to participate in the political process. Deaf individuals were not a part of any larger disability movement in Chile and had few opportunities to meet directly with lawmakers after Chile ratified the CRPD. Apart from the meetings with Movimiento Sordo, in which government officials nodded politely, I am not aware of any other input from the deaf community during this time.

Against this background, Chile overhauled its disability law in 2010 with virtually no input from its deaf community. The result was Law No. 20,422, a statute that contains few provisions for deaf Chileans. Article 25 of the new law requires the government to implement regulations requiring captioning and interpreter services on television. Although the government had to write the regulations within six months of enacting the statute, it did not do so for more than two years. When the government finally wrote the regulation, it interpreted television programming very narrowly, excluding sports, music performances, foreign language programming, and shows for young children from the definition of what programming had to be accessible for deaf people. I do not know of any deaf individuals whom the government consulted in writing this regulation.

The second key provision of the new disability law is Article 26, which recognized Chilean Sign Language as the natural means of communication for deaf Chileans. Buried in the law was a requirement that the government form a commission to "define" Chilean Sign Language. When the deaf community learned of this provision, it interpreted it as a government effort to meddle with Chilean Sign Language. Deaf leaders organized protests in cities throughout the country and rallied around the cry of *"no hay nada que definir"* ("there is nothing to define"). The mass protests caught the attention of the government, which removed the section requiring the establishment of the commission. The deaf community celebrated this victory. However, the abrogation of this provision did not result in greater access to communication—recognizing sign language is one thing and mandating interpreters is another; deaf people remain as isolated as before.

The new disability law is notable for what it does *not* contain. Except with respect to court proceedings, there is no requirement that any entity actually provide interpreters or captioning or other accommodations for deaf individuals. There is no provision that requires hospitals or doctors to arrange for interpreter services to ensure meaningful access to medical care. There is no requirement that schools and universities provide interpreters. There is no requirement that employers provide accommodations for deaf employees; in fact employers can and continue to discriminate against deaf individuals in hiring. These weaknesses in the law are a result of the lack of involvement of deaf individuals in the political and legal process resulting in the law.

THE SEARCH FOR LEGAL EXPERTISE TO SERVE THE DEAF COMMUNITY IN CHILE

The Chilean experience demonstrates the importance of deaf participation in disability rights legislation. However, the very marginalization of the deaf community means that it lacks the political and cultural capital necessary to navigate the legal system to vindicate the human rights of deaf people in Chile. The participation of deaf people in the political process is a human right that the CRPD guarantees,[4] and one way to ensure this basic human right is to equip the deaf community with the skills necessary to participate in the process of implementing the CRPD. Empowering the deaf community in this fashion would fulfill Article 33 of the CRPD, which provides that "persons with disabilities and their representative organizations, shall be involved and participate fully in the monitoring" of the implementation of the CRPD.

Although the United States differs considerably from Chile in its legal system, its experience is instructive. In the United States, deaf people have voice in the political process because there are numerous disability rights organizations that have combined advocacy with the legal expertise required to translate broad notions of equal access into the legal language necessary to include deaf people in society. The NAD, where I was a fellow for two years, has a law and advocacy center that advocates for the equal rights of deaf individuals through both public policy and litigation. In this way, the NAD and other organizations by and for individuals with a disability can provide the legal knowledge to empower deaf individuals. Without such organizations, the risk is that able-bodied government officials will pass laws based on stereotypes such as the widely held belief that deaf people cannot drive. Even well-meaning legislators may wrongly presume to know what individuals with a disability need or they may enact laws that are so weak as to be unenforceable, as happened in Chile.

Given the lack of access to legal services for deaf people in Chile, I established the not-for-profit organization named Deaf We Can in 2010. The organization's mission is to equip the deaf community in Chile with the legal expertise needed to advocate effectively for communication access. Deaf We Can relies on donations to make grants to organizations in Chile that can push for deaf rights. I established this organization with the hope, perhaps naïve, that if deaf leaders could not come together on their own, providing legal expertise would be a way to unify the deaf elite in Chile. Deaf leaders could strategize with the lawyers, telling the lawyers what their needs were and debating the best strategy to move forward. The lawyers would analyze the options for the deaf leaders and then the community as a whole would move forward.

One ideal is to have deaf lawyers and advocates who can move back and forth between deaf experiences and the country's political and legal traditions. However, as I described earlier, there are presently no deaf lawyers in Chile. In the meantime, Deaf We Can has employed two strategies to equip the deaf community in Chile with legal expertise. One effort, working with outside (hearing) lawyers who do not know Chilean Sign Language and are unfamiliar with deaf culture, has had limited success. The other effort, awarding a deaf individual a scholarship to attend law school, is a much longer-term investment with a potentially large payoff. I describe these efforts in turn.

---

[4] Article 29 of the CRPD requires ratifying countries to "promote actively an environment in which persons with disabilities can effectively and fully participate in the conduct of public affairs, without discrimination and on an equal basis with others, and encourage their participation in public affairs."

Working with Outside Lawyers to Serve the Deaf Community

In an effort to provide the deaf community with access to legal services, Deaf We Can made a grant to Fundación Pro Bono, a legal services organization that coordinates the pro bono efforts of the sixty or so largest law firms in Santiago. Pro Bono focuses on social issues such as family law, bullying, and helping social organizations and small businesses. Pro Bono lawyers review requests for pro bono assistance and then post intriguing cases for the lawyers at the law firms to accept if interested. Through Pro Bono, deaf individuals have potentially unlimited access to the best lawyers in Chile.

Pro Bono agreed to hire a deaf advocate on a part-time basis to serve as a liaison between the deaf community and the lawyers. The deaf advocate's role was to educate the lawyers about deaf culture and to organize meetings in the deaf community that would help Pro Bono identify the needs of the community. The deaf advocate was the first deaf person many of the lawyers had ever met and having a deaf person in the office helped the lawyers better understand the community they would be serving. Through the deaf advocate, lawyers in the office even learned basic Chilean Sign Language.

Pro Bono also formed task forces to take on specific policy issues. One large law firm researched and drafted an analysis of the statute and regulations requiring captioning and interpreting services on television. Another large law firm studied driver's licenses in Chile. These law firms produced detailed analyses explaining the precise legal barriers on these issues. From the law firm that took on television captioning came the report that the statute was worded very broadly and that it would be very difficult to challenge the resulting regulation in court; reform must take place through political channels. Meanwhile, the law firm that studied driver's licenses discovered that while Chileans must take a hearing test to obtain a driver's license, a regulation specifically states that actually passing the hearing test is not necessary. Many municipalities are not aware of this regulation. Pro Bono successfully petitioned a government agency that oversees all municipalities to produce a report stating unequivocally that deaf people may obtain driver's licenses.

While Pro Bono was successful in providing legal expertise in identifying the precise legal barriers to greater access, it has not been able to unify the deaf community. Some deaf leaders have not taken Pro Bono seriously because the deaf advocate working for Pro Bono is a member of a rival deaf association. Pro Bono has also not allowed the deaf advocate to do much public outreach without explicit oversight. Although Pro Bono arranged for interpreters on some occasions to communicate with the deaf advocate, communication breakdowns occurred at other times. Such communication barriers have made such supervision difficult, and the result is that the deaf advocate was not able to do much outreach that would make the deaf community aware of the resources Pro Bono has to offer. Few deaf people have contacted Pro Bono for legal assistance with their cases, though Pro Bono did take on one case on behalf of a deaf individual. Pro Bono's experience shows that outside lawyers cannot meaningfully advocate for deaf rights with only marginal input from a divided deaf community.

Pro Bono also does not have the sense of ownership of the struggle for equality that only deaf individuals can have. Pro Bono is part of the institutional framework that it seeks to reform, and so has lacked the political will and sense of urgency that

deaf individuals long shut out from the mainstream have in pushing for a transformation of Chilean society that results in greater inclusion of deaf people. Deaf
individuals should be leading the fight, with Pro Bono (and other legal experts)
helping them make the case for equality in a language that lawmakers understand.

Training Deaf Leaders in the Law

Deaf We Can also awarded a scholarship to a deaf leader with exceptional promise
so she can attend law school. Vianney Sierralta is from Calama, a mining town in
the Atacama Desert in northern Chile. She went to university and got her degree
in special education. Since she was the best-educated and the one most fluent in
Spanish, she quickly became the leader of the deaf community in Calama.

When I visited Calama in 2010, she took me around to see the deaf community.
I also asked her if she wanted to see me make a video relay call. I needed to call
my bank in the United States. She sat next to me and watched. I connected to the
sign language interpreter and gave her the number of the bank to call. A customer
representative answered and I talked for a few minutes about my account. I finished the call and thanked the interpreter for her help with the call. Vianney saw
the whole thing. She started to cry. She *wanted* that for Chile's deaf people.

Two years later, when I was back in the United States, she e-mailed me and
asked if I knew of any scholarships to help her attend law school. Deaf We Can
agreed to give her a scholarship. In return, she had to commit time during and
after law school to deaf rights advocacy in Chile. She is now in her third year of
law school at the Universidad de Aconcagua in Calama and has earned excellent
marks that put her at or near the top of her class, attracting Chilean reporters looking for a feel-good story (Perra Espinosa 2014).

Although she has several years more to go before she becomes a lawyer, she
has the legal knowledge to disseminate information about Chilean law in a way
that is accessible to the deaf community. Pursuant to a grant from Skadden Arps,
the law firm that sponsored my fellowship at NAD, she directed the production of
fifteen videos in Chilean Sign Language about different areas of the law.[5] She has
a personal stake in deaf advocacy and the knowledge of the law to make projects
like this happen. She has also advised Pro Bono. Chile needs more people like her:
deaf leaders who *understand* the political and legal system.[6]

Looking Ahead in Chile

While the lack of unity among deaf Chileans and limited access to legal knowledge has slowed the realization of the promise of the CRPD, the signs of progress
are unmistakable. For all the shortcomings in the new disability law, television

---

[5] You can see the videos she produced by visiting http://www.leyesensenas.com.

[6] Vianney does not live in Santiago, and I see this as a hidden strength. She is not aligned
with any one of the deaf associations there. This means that while she is Chilean and has a
personal stake in achieving equality, she is enough of an outsider that she can move among
the deaf leaders in Santiago. She has even mediated disputes between them, all from the
desert of the north. She has been able to do this through e-mail, Skype conversations, and
the occasional visit to Santiago.

is increasingly accessible, and the government now offers a limited interpreter service through Skype to enable deaf people to make phone calls. These steps are small—vast swaths of Chilean society remain inaccessible—but they represent progress.

And most encouragingly, the movement is gathering steam as the deaf community learns how to use the legal system to advocate for significant change. I mentioned that the deaf community rallied to remove a legal provision requiring the establishment of a commission to "define" Chilean Sign Language. ASOCH, the largest deaf association in Chile, has contracted with a lawyer. ASOCH originally hired the lawyer to help revise its bylaws. The lawyer began attending meetings and learning Chilean Sign Language. Over time, he also began advising ASOCH on advocacy efforts. Vianney's graduation from law school in several years will be another big boost for the deaf community.

There may well be a snowball effect. As these advocacy efforts slowly but surely result in greater access to communication and ultimately better education, more deaf children will grow up to become lawyers and skilled advocates. They will provide the legal knowledge and political expertise that will power the deaf rights movement and result in greater inclusion in Chile.

LESSONS FROM THE CHILEAN EXPERIENCE

The Chilean experience demonstrates that ratification of the CRPD on the Rights of Persons with Disabilities is the easy part. The hard work is implementing the treaty, especially when it comes to the human rights of a deaf community without access to the political process or the legal expertise to advocate effectively for full inclusion in society. International deaf visitors can inspire, but what local deaf communities need most is ongoing advocacy to translate the promise of the CRPD into local policies that provide meaningfully for interpreter services, captioning, and other accommodations necessary for the full inclusion of deaf people in society.

The surest and most effective advocacy comes from the deaf community itself. Training more deaf lawyers is one approach; another, complementary approach is advocacy training that equips deaf individuals with a basic understanding of how to navigate political and legal channels to achieve more favorable laws and the enforcement of the rights contained therein. To this end, international organizations and dedicated individual advocates should provide or fund training specific to the country's political and legal environment (as opposed to hosting workshops on general concepts such as empowerment). Teaching deaf people how to navigate their country's bureaucracy and providing them with the resources to do so will result in the effective and sustained advocacy necessary to more fully realize the promise of the CRPD.

ACKNOWLEDGMENTS

I am grateful to Michele Friedner and Annelies Kusters for their careful stewardship of this article through the editing process. I also thank Jessica Cuculick, Elizabeth Lockwood, Jackie Pransky, and John Stanton for helpful comments on drafts.

REFERENCES

Decreto 32, February 4, 2012. "Aprueba Reglamento que Establece Normas para la Aplicación de Mecanismos de Comunicación Audiovisual que Posibiliten el Acceso a la Programación Televisiva para Personas con Discapacidad Auditiva" ["Approves Regulation that Establishes Rules for the Application of Means of Audiovisual Communication which Make Possible Access to Television Programming for Persons with Hearing Disabilities"]. http://www.leychile.cl/Navegar?idNorma=1037014.

De Meulder, Maartje. 2014. "The UNCRPD and Sign Language Peoples." In *UNCRPD Implementation in Europe—A Deaf Perspective. Article 29: Participation in Political and Public Life*, edited by Annika Pabsch, 12–28. Brussels: European Union of the Deaf.

Ley Número 20.422, February 10, 2010. "Establece Normas Sobre Igualdad de Oportunidades e Inclusión Social de Personas con Discapacidad" ["Establishes Rules about Equality of Opportunities and Social Inclusion of Persons with a Disability"]. http://www.leychile.cl/Navegar?idNorma=1010903&tipoVersion=0.

Ley Número 20.602, September 25, 2012, "Deroga el Inciso Sexto del Artículo Primero Transitorio de la Ley 20.422" ["Abrogates the Sixth Subsection of the First Transitory Article of Law 20,422"]. http://www.leychile.cl/Navegar?idNorma=1044075.

Perra Espinosa, Karen. 2014. "Loína será primera abogada en Chile con discapacidad auditiva" ["Person from Calama Will Be the First Lawyer in Chile with a Hearing Disability"], *La Estrella*, April 26. http://www.estrellaloa.cl/impresa/2014/04/26/full/5.

Stein, Michael S., and Emily Teplin Fox. 2011. "Rational Discrimination and Shared Compliance: Lessons from Title IV of the Americans with Disabilities Act." *Valparaiso University Law Review* 45:1110–15. Accessed April 12, 2015. http://scholar.valpo.edu/vulr/vol45/iss3/7.

Timmermans, Nina. 2005. "The Status of Sign Languages in Europe." *Council of Europe Publishing* 42:80–81. http://www.coe.int/t/e/social_cohesion/soc-sp/5720-0-ID2283-Langue%20signe_GB%20assemble.pdf.

Part 4

▊ NETWORKS

16 | A Deaf Diaspora? Imagining Deaf Worlds Across and Beyond Nations

Steven D. Emery

When I was invited to be part of a grant application at the University of Bristol to study a wide range of diaspora communities,[1] the notion that Deaf people make up a diaspora was strongly challenged. I was faced with many questions: In what ways are Deaf people a diaspora? Deaf people form communities that are traditionally understood to be a diaspora, but Deaf people themselves, how can that be so? Surely they are best understood as forming a linguistic minority group? Where or what is the historical homeland from which they have been expelled and seek to return? This experience challenged me to piece together an academic position paper to the group that outlined the extent to which Deaf people form a diaspora. It became apparent that the way in which Deaf communities make up a diaspora is mainly implicitly implied rather than explicitly theorized in the Deaf studies literature. The Deaf diaspora is thus currently putative and undertheorized. The aims of this chapter are not only to situate the Deaf diaspora within wider studies of diaspora but also to make the case that an exploration of it enhances our understanding of transnational Deaf lives and experiences.

Before continuing, I add two important caveats. Firstly, the chapter is best considered as an attempt at a concise and compact conceptualization of the Deaf diaspora; it is intended to encourage discussion and critique, to build on the perspective given, and invite writers to flesh out alternative perspectives. I welcome such input. Second, readers will notice a select number of diaspora authors cited, chosen mainly because they offer critiques and conceptualizations of the *wider* diaspora literature. Sociologist Brubaker's work is significantly cited: His conceptualization of a diaspora as constituting elements of homeland, boundary maintenance, and dispersal are highly relevant in a Deaf diaspora context and enables me

---

[1] I am indebted to Gabrielle Hogan-Brun for initially drawing the meeting to my attention that later brought about an invitation to become involved in the grant application.

to envision a succinct conceptualization. Brubaker has written on issues such as ethnicity, nationalism, and citizenship, which he sees not as categories and groups that people belong to but as processes and experiences that they undergo. He does the same with diaspora; hence it flows that homeland, boundary maintenance, and dispersal are not meant as categories that "make" the Deaf diaspora but assist us to understand these as *experiences* that are meaningful to the Deaf diaspora. With these caveats in mind, I now turn attention to the chapter structure and key points.

The notion that Deaf people make up a diaspora that transcends all nations is exciting. Once the Deaf diaspora is recognised transnationally, the notion can help us to understand the ways in which the diaspora expresses its *shared* experience (DEAF-SAME), the current process and journeys (routes) that it is taking, and what *homeland* means or can come to mean. Not all Deaf people will travel or seek to do so or have the means; therefore, the diaspora is as much imagined as it is experienced.

I set out the case for the Deaf diaspora in four parts. Firstly, I give a brief outline of the current literature on Deaf diaspora, closely followed by a general overview of key sections of the diaspora literature. This is necessary to engage with the mainstream academic literature because the concept of *diaspora* is contested. Scholars from several disciplines question whether the term can be meaningful any longer given that it is applied to a wide range of peoples, it is furnished with numerous adjectives, and checklists may no longer be possible to pin down what a diaspora should and should not include. In other words, it is insufficient to simply proclaim Deaf people as a diaspora. The third part will therefore offer a clear delineation of how Deaf people form a diaspora, which will be done by referring to Brubaker's (2005) categorization of diaspora as consisting of the three core aspects mentioned earlier. I draw attention to the Deaf diaspora as containing two different types: the traditional and the temporary. The fourth and final part will discuss the implications of the Deaf diaspora for Deaf and diaspora studies, describing the transnational and DEAF-SAME experiences that are part of the diaspora experience, and argue that there is a sense of loss that Deaf people experience in addition to what Allen (2008) has described as a yearning for homeland.

Previous Meanings of the Deaf Diaspora

Explicit reference to a Deaf diaspora starts with the theologian Ayers (2004), whose conceptualization of the Deaf diaspora draws mainly on the Deaf-World as a scattered people for whom religion can be the focus for bringing Deaf people back together. To Ayers, Deaf people can be reunited, or return to their homeland, guided by a religious narrative, which makes it hard to take Ayers's work seriously in an academic way, given it stands out as a reductionist text. It leaves the reader with the impression that diaspora theory is merely a subtext through which to promote an ideology strongly based on religion. This argument is not intended to dismiss Ayers's work because many parts of his book are relevant and insightful, for example, recognizing the variety of ways in which Deaf people are dispersed across the world and how we might think of the Deaf diaspora in waves across historical times.

The Deaf diaspora needs a broader analysis though, which is what the Deaf studies master's thesis by Allen (2008) seeks to do, and it is hoped that this chapter will become a close cousin of her dissertation, for there are many themes within her work that expand significantly on the arguments presented here. One of the important themes Allen addresses is the transnational or global nature and experiences of the Deaf World, and her contention that this subject requires further research. Allen undertook an in-depth exploration of the grounded, real lived lives of Deaf people, and mainly identified the widespread *implicit* Deaf studies literature references that point to diaspora themes. Allen draws not only on scholarly work but also devotes a section to a wide range of "literary expressions for a deaf home" (95–106). She refers to the "physical homes" (Deaf clubs and schools) that come to be places where Deaf people congregate, of which more will be written later in this chapter, but is also careful to raise the problematic nature of calling these true Deaf homelands—because, for example, these were not all owned, run, managed, or led by Deaf people. Central to Allen's critique is that home does not only have to be a place; it can also be a yearning, which is central to the thesis and one I agree with.

My main critique is that neither Ayers nor Allen adequately situate the Deaf diaspora in a concise way so that the world or mainstream academic disciplines can effectively understand and relate. Allen, for example, makes references to the experiences of the Jewish Diaspora (among others such as the Armenian), and how, in some instances, Deaf people share similar experiences, a comparison which does not do justice to the more adverse experiences of these peoples. While that is clearly not Allen's intention, the wider risk is that the Deaf diaspora will not be taken seriously until it is subject to critique within the wider range of diaspora theory. This risk can be seen when, in her conclusion, Allen makes reference to the online encyclopaedia Wikipedia, suggesting the Deaf diaspora is situated amongst many diasporas on a Wikipedia-created chart (Allen 2008, 145). Hence the Deaf diaspora, she argues, should share a column with "Armenian-Americans, Arab-Americans, Cuban-Americans, Greek-Americans, Irish-Americans, Jewish Americans, Mexican Americans, Muslim-Americans, and Taiwanese-Americans" (Allen 2008, 145). Her attempt to fit the Deaf diaspora to this table raises more questions than answers, for all these people share or shared a geographical homeland, with more clearly defined boundaries, unlike the Deaf diaspora: the only uniting factor is the aspect of dispersal. Further critiques of Allen will be outlined in the chapter, as I turn to mainstream academic literature on diaspora.

Imagining and Experiencing Communities Across and Beyond Nations

There has been an exponential growth in studies of diaspora from a wide range of disciplines (for example, sociology, cultural studies, anthropology, postcolonial studies) since the 1980s (Brubaker 2005, Cho 2007, Bakewell 2008, Tsagarousianou 2004). In recent times diasporas have come to apply to a wider range of peoples or groups. According to Brubaker (2005), there are diasporas that are based upon transethnic and transborder linguistic categories (for example, Francophone and Anglophone), global religious categories (Muslim, Hindu, Catholic), putative or country-defined categories (Estonian, Iranian, Scottish, Lithuanian), and other putative diasporas (queer, Dixie, fundamentalist). Diaspora has come to mean experiences, ambitions, or adjectives, for example, and there are "Victim diasporas, Labour diasporas, Trade diasporas, and even . . . Imperial diasporas"

(Chariandry 2006). The proliferation is such that there are now concepts of diasporic networks, consciousness, imaginations, and culture (Brubaker 2005).

This expansion in definitions of diaspora has led authors from a wide range of disciplines to try to categorize diaspora; otherwise they fear it will become a meaningless concept, for "if everyone is a diasporic, then no one is distinctively so" (Brubaker 2005, 3). The most recognized scholars who have attempted to categorize the concept are Safran (1991) and Cohen (1996), but others have suggested that categorizing and attempting to redefine the term create a list that risks excluding peoples or narrowing its meanings (Tsagarousianou 2004; Cho 2007). This has led Brubaker (2005) to argue that the term has itself become a diaspora. In a much cited quote it has become a "promiscuously capacious category" (Tölölyan 1996, 8). Authors have therefore begun to refrain from identifying exclusive diasporas through specifications, because there is little consensus about what it means anyway (Vertovec 1997; Tsagarousianou 2004; Cho 2007). For these reasons Brubaker critiques the literature on diaspora but suggests three core aspects that are broadly common to all diasporas.

The present chapter jumps into this fray and could arguably reflect an increased tendency in the Deaf studies literature to replicate what Tölölyan, in a similar context, describes as a "theory driven revolution in the humanities and social sciences" (Tölölyan 1996, 27). In recent years we have seen concepts of audism (Humphries 1975, in Bauman 2004), Deafhood (Ladd 2003), Deaf gain (Bauman and Murray 2014), Deaf-space (Gulliver 2009), and Deaf citizenship (Emery 2011), among others. If this chapter is a continuation of a trend, it is possibly because bringing together Deaf and diaspora assists scholars and lay Deaf people to illustrate the complex nature of the everyday life experiences of Deaf people, and part of that complexity is their growing transnational nature. This chapter could therefore be said to be a contribution to the growing resistance or disruption to the hegemonic curative perspectives of defining Deaf people throughout social policy and in the medical literature as a broken people in need of fixing. In addition, I demonstrate that theorizing the Deaf diaspora is a suitable concept to frame transnational Deaf connections and experiences, as well as contribute to a "theory-driven revolution" in Deaf studies.

Brubaker's Three Core Aspects

Here I come to the three core aspects Brubaker (2005) uses to define and delineate the definition of a diaspora: homeland, boundary maintenance, and dispersal. I discuss Deaf experiences through these core aspects, beginning with dispersal.

Dispersal

Ultimately Deaf people are and have always been a *dispersed* people because they are known to be present in all countries of the world and are therefore ultimately dispersed across nations (Rayman 2009). Brubaker (2005, 5) suggests the fact of dispersal is the most widely accepted criteria of diaspora, and while it tends to be "forced," there is also a broader understanding that such a dispersal "crosses state borders," although it may also occur within a state. It is well illustrated in the literature that 90 percent of deaf children are born to hearing parents, for example, and that these children are largely brought together to be educated within mainstream schools, often disconnected from any of the homelands described earlier. This argument does not suggest that Deaf people reject attempts to be citizens of their nation or societies, as Murray (2007) has highlighted through the concept of coequality (see later). Deaf people's identities also intersect (see Ruiz et al., this volume), an area that has been subject of far less research, as they often find common cause with others with similar experiences (e.g., black and Asian Deaf people; gay, lesbian, bisexual, and transgendered Deaf people; disabled Deaf people; Deaf-blind people; Jewish Deaf people) or identify themselves as having intersectional identities; but I believe that we can also identify a common transnational cosmopolitan Deaf citizenship (Murray 2007).

Crucially, the lack of a clearly defined geographical homeland from which a people are dispersed is not unique. As Brubaker (2005) notes, citing Clifford (1994), centering diaspora on a homeland would arguably exclude the Jewish, African, Caribbean, and South Asian diasporas, which do not have an easily defined geographical home. It is, however, the queer diaspora with which the Deaf diaspora shares close similarities, for the queer diaspora does not have a geographical home as such; it refers mostly to searching and arriving, *coming* home, rather than emanating *from* a home (Fortier 2001). The family is normatively heterosexual (just as it is normatively "hearing" or "spoken" in the case of deaf children); hence when gays and lesbians leave that family they seek places and spaces where they meet other gays, lesbians, bisexual, transgender, and queer folk. One author has described Deaf ex-mainstreamers—that is, those who are dispersed across mainstream schools—as sojourners (Jones 1996), seeking a place of belonging and acceptance, as does Allen (2008), who uses the term *yearning* to describe a desire to return to or find a homeland. There is therefore a strong similarity in the sense that both the queer and Deaf diaspora experience horizontal, rather than vertical, socialization into the diaspora, that is, in places other than the family home.

Homeland

Brubaker conceptualizes *homeland* as "the orientation to a real or imagined 'homeland' as an authoritative source of value, identity and loyalty" (2005, 5). This is something with which the Deaf diaspora can identify. For the Deaf diaspora the key emphasis is "space(s)," which are not necessarily fixed with predefined boundaries but can be fluid and uncertain. I will distinguish these spaces loosely as traditional and temporary. By traditional, I mean established and institutional spaces, and by temporary I mean spaces that Deaf people themselves create and that may not be permanent. I believe that such a distinction is important because the established spaces of the traditional diaspora, the schools and clubs, were overwhelmingly run by and subject to the control of non-Deaf people, such as missionaries, philanthropists, or charities. Deaf people did not own nor manage the old Deaf schools. Deaf children may have resided in many residential schools but they were rarely instructed in sign language by Deaf teachers. Ladd (2003) suggests parallels with colonialism while other scholars have suggested that this process coincided in the late eighteenth and nineteenth centuries with the rise of the nation-state and suppression of minority languages (Baynton 1996;

Monaghan 2003). Deaf people did, however, occupy spaces within the Deaf school by which sign languages developed.[2] These traditional spaces have been and still are subject to intrusion and control; for example, through oral-only means of instruction or the use of artificial sign systems (e.g., Sign Supported English or cued speech). This process, which Ladd describes as colonialism—the taking over of the Deaf homeland by missionaries, hearing educators, and the modern medical profession—has been fiercely resisted by Deaf people since the late nineteenth century until the unsuccessful resistance died down between around 1910 and 1960 (Gulliver, this volume; Ladd 2003).

With Deaf clubs and schools increasingly closing down (at least in the global North), scholars have increasingly come to study different kinds of homeland, existing in different kinds of spaces outside the realm of these traditional places. While not all of these spaces are new (see, for example, Desloges 1779 and Gulliver, this volume, for a discussion of the existence of a Parisian Deaf community previous to the existence of a Deaf school), as clubs and schools close, Deaf people are increasingly coming to find "home" within these temporary spaces, which are increasingly studied by geographers, sociologists, and anthropologists. The temporary spaces include gathering in pubs (O'Brien 2005), malls, cafés, and night clubs; in public transport such as on trains (Kusters 2010); at employment training courses or workplaces (Friedner 2013); at conferences within universities or colleges; at family gatherings, local community events, and village gatherings (Kusters 2015); or simply around brightly lit places. They gather for caravans, motorcycling, rambling, raves, or football events. Again, I term these spaces "temporary" for the sake of distinguishing these from the traditional occupied spaces.

These temporary spaces of the diaspora constitute a vital part of what Deaf people deem to be "homeland." The temporary homeland, where Deaf people congregate or gather in a multitude of places, becomes Deaf space, or "Deaf bubbles" as Gulliver and Kitzel (2014) have defined these spaces. Allen (2008, 116) also argued something along these lines:

> The Deaf homeland doesn't have to be a place; instead it's a yearning to be and actual being with people who hold the same beliefs, the place where the cultural practices of the minority become the norm. These "cultural practices" reinforce a sense of agency, "a sense of belonging and autonomy (Findley, 2005 p. 29). Instead the place is no longer important, but instead, what is important is the space created through cultural agency. Through yearning, a temporary home appears.

It is possible to understand *home* as a multitude of physical entities in order to situate the Deaf experience more succinctly. As I will argue later in the chapter, yearning remains a strong aspect of the Deaf diaspora, but it can be more effectively and realistically identified as part of the sense of loss that the diaspora experiences, or fears.

The spaces, or bubbles, are also evident at a transnational level, as is discussed elaborately in the "Events" section of this book. Examples include the World Federation for the Deaf conferences (Haualand et al., this volume), youth camps

---

[2] We can go as far back as the 1789 French Revolution to see how these spaces developed; see Gulliver 2009 for a description.

(Merricks, this volume), the Deaf Olympics (Haualand et al., this volume), the biennial International Deaf Academics conferences, and arts festivals (Schmitt, this volume). Neither are these limited to the post–World War Two periods: for example, there were the international Paris Banquets of the early 1800s, where Deaf people would gather to celebrate and discuss issues relating to sign language and Deaf culture (see Gulliver, this volume, and also Murray 2007 for other examples).

BOUNDARY MAINTENANCE

It follows that while the traditional spaces are fixed by the bricks and mortar of the school or club, the temporary spaces are more fluid and not necessarily separated by walls, doors, windows, and architecture. For Brubaker the concept of boundary *maintenance* becomes important, as temporary spaces need to be preserved through maintaining "a distinctive identity" (6) and involve "deliberate resistance to assimilation." A unique feature of the Deaf diaspora is their constant state of flux, negotiation, and maintenance, because there are no fixed geographical spaces. Deaf people may have been resident in, and socialized regularly in, their traditional homelands (the club and school) but they also sought to create national boundaries that they could then come to geographically maintain. Indeed, the term the *Deaf Nation* is a nineteenth-century construct (Lane 1984; Gulliver, this volume) and some Deaf people during this time (mostly unsuccessfully) advanced the case for taking over and settling into geographical terrain (Flournoy et al. 1858; Carbin 1996; Murphy 1972). These aspirations may continue to the present day, in Jamaica and Ireland, for example (Lawrence 2013), and while most are unsuccessful, they are based on a powerful ideology that dispersed Deaf people should be able to live in close vicinity of other Deaf or signing people.

This brings us immediately to two instances in which the Deaf diaspora is unique, for there *are* permanently lived places which one could consider geographical homelands. First, there are the villages where there is a relatively high prevalence of deafness, leading to the use of sign language by hearing people within the larger village location (Kusters 2014). The second are the family homes, where 4.4% of deaf children are born to Deaf families where the use of sign language in the home is the norm (Toohey 2010). I argue that these are essential parts of the Deaf diaspora, along with the more recognized traditional and temporary spaces already discussed, because even if they may not fit precisely within the category of traditional or temporary, they are part of a transnational consciousness. They stir up the yearning (or longing) of which Allen writes and point to possibilities and hopes, even if recent research has found these are not the kind of places where Deaf people are free from restrictions (for example, in Adamorobe Deaf people are legally banned from marrying each other; see Kusters 2014).

Therefore, when conceptualizing Deaf people as a diaspora, as *experienced* and lived through homeland, boundary maintenance, and dispersal, this chapter draws upon cultural studies to identify that the Deaf diaspora is chiefly one that consists of a series of routes; and although there are roots, they always have been tentative.[3]

---

[3] The idea of using "routes and roots" is taken from Vertovec's use of the term in a diaspora context, but the original use of the term belongs to Gilroy 1993, who argued the roots of the black diaspora could not be explored without the routes or the movements of its people.

AN IMAGINED TRANSNATIONAL CONSCIOUSNESS WITH A COMMON
TRANSNATIONAL EXPERIENCE

Having defined the Deaf diaspora in terms of homeland, boundary maintenance, and dispersal, it is now time to explore issues of transnational imagined and experienced Deaf worlds. The Deaf diaspora consists of 70 million people[4] scattered across the world, and I argue that just as *nations* are bound through being imagined as a community (see Anderson 1983 for an exploration of communities as imagined), the transnational international *Deaf diaspora* also has an imagined aspect, just like the utopian imaginations of the Deaf nation. The fact the majority are unlikely to cross these national or even local boundaries (for example, they may simply not want to do so, or, more likely, not have the means to because 80 percent live in the global South and may not earn the kind of wages of the global North) does not mean that they do not do so at all, as we have seen in the section on homeland. When they coalesce into an international gathering, the *imagined* transnational community becomes truly *experienced*. It is worth expanding on what that translation from imagined to experienced looks like in practice.

During the Deaflympics, for example, there was evidence of Deaf people overcoming financial barriers to travel to these games (Haualand 2007). Breivik et al.'s (2002) and Haualand's (2007) research encapsulates how that transnational community is expressed across not only space but also place, not only in the imagination but also in experience. In a description of these visual-spatial encounters across space-time, Haualand (2007, 40) writes of the Rome 2001 Deaflympics:

> The games were a chance for making the imagined Deaf community into a temporarily very visible one. They provided an opportunity to articulate imagined cultural differences between Deaf and hearing/non-signing people. This in turn allowed the members of this community to establish space "in between" their own imagined community and the people beyond this imagined community—in this case—hearing Romans.

Citing Bhabha (1994, 1–2), Breivik et al. (2002, 23) states that this interaction became "terrain for elaborating strategies of selfhood . . . and innovative sites of collaboration, and contestation," where "members of the Deaf community were able to collectively spell out the differences between themselves and nonsigning people." One is reminded of Hall's (1990) contention that it is by their very difference that diasporas emerge. This Deaf space becomes what Cho (2007) in a different context has described as a longing for something, and Allen's identifying this in a Deaf diaspora context as a yearning. A transnational consciousness becomes a part of the Deaf experience.

As Ladd (2003, this volume) has suggested, this imagining can constitute a model for a world cosmopolitan citizenship, where part of Deaf people realizing their Deafhood—that is, what it means to be Deaf in the world—is recognition that they are part of an international transnational citizenship. However, the Deaf

---

[4] This figure is from the World Federation of the Deaf, http://wfdeaf.org/human-rights (accessed 9 Dec 2014).

diaspora is not only expressed through these positive representations of a transnational community, but also by a sense of loss.

Discussion: What the Diaspora Concept Can Contribute to Deaf and Diaspora Studies

The Deaf diaspora is therefore unlike any other, not just because of the modality of its (visual) language and uniqueness of its culture but precisely because of the nature of its network of homeland spaces across the world. There is one final, but crucial, aspect of the Deaf diaspora that requires exploring: the sense of *loss* that comes from being constantly disconnected from or even excluded from Deaf homelands. Diaspora theory can be a useful adjunction, because this loss is not medical-centric but sociopolitical, and the theory helps to understand how this diaspora shares with other diasporas that feeling or experience of a sense of loss. The Deaf diaspora cannot be understood without the sense of loss that comes from its people not being part of a permanent Deaf homeland, in addition to a feeling of social exclusion from majority society (Emery 2011). To consider a sense of loss as part of the Deaf diaspora experience therefore in some way challenges Murray's concept of co-equality, which relates to Deaf people holding their place in a larger society, where they are able to be successful and productive, capable workers, family members, and citizens in a larger society but without being submerged in it; they are also members of a sign-language-using community. Loss, however, is crucial to diaspora experience. Vertovec (1997) writes of the duality of the experience of diaspora: it has negatives in terms of the discrimination experienced, but positives in terms of identifying with historical, cultural, and political heritage. Vertovec goes on to suggest this duality can be the development of a consciousness that is simultaneous by its solidarity and connection.

The concept of loss, however, is not abstract but experienced. When Deaf people worry about the decline of Deaf clubs and schools, the reduction in their numbers via children implanted with cochlear implants, the increasing inability to have their language and culture fully recognized in spite of sign language recognition agreements, and, crucially, with genetic interventions becoming serious political issues where the end of the community is feared, a sense of loss is real within the diaspora. Then one realizes that loss has always been present. This fear of loss is best exemplified in the current period by the threats posed by genetic interventions (Emery and Ladd, forthcoming), where there is a real concern that a "black hole" will gradually overshadow the landscape of the Deaf diaspora and through which all homelands risk being sucked out of existence.

Summary

In three core areas of homeland, boundary maintenance, and dispersal, the Deaf diaspora is both imagined and experienced. The argument posed in this chapter is that the Deaf diaspora has two different types: the traditional and the temporary. In an academic context, the Deaf diaspora encourages sociologists, anthropologists, social scientists, geographers, and Deaf and diaspora theorists to recognize the unique features that make up the Deaf diaspora. The concept is not meant to stretch the meaning of *diaspora*.

By recognizing the transnational experiences of Deaf people, gathering in transnational spaces, whether they journey to these traditional or temporary spaces, they come to experience DEAF-SAME. There is at least one example of the term *diaspora* being considered in this context: the UK city of Brighton holds an annual Deaf Diaspora Day.[5] The Deaf diaspora concept stands in the tradition of concepts such as Deafhood and Deaf gain, for it values and cherishes what brings Deaf people together, transnationally, and not what keeps them apart, globally. Diaspora peoples usually experience a sense of loss, of their homeland, for example, and the Deaf diaspora is no different. Just as crucial to the experience of crossing these boundaries is the yearning, or a longing, to connect or reconnect. In all these respects, therefore, the concept of Deaf diaspora has the potential to add to theorization about this transnational dimension, where any sense of loss is just but the flip side of a strong sense of yearning, for Deaf people know that there are abundant places across the world to find home.

ACKNOWLEDGMENTS

This paper was originally created as a position paper on the Deaf diaspora with Paddy Ladd and Mike Gulliver, and I thank both for their input, which has evolved into this article. I also thank Annelies Kusters and Michele Friedner for offering their support and encouragement to write and complete this chapter, as well as drawing my attention to Allen's important thesis and Murray's concept of co-equality. Responsibility for the contents, however, is entirely mine.

REFERENCES

Allen, S. 2008. "A Deaf Diaspora: Underlying Cultural Yearnings for a Deaf Home." Master's thesis, Gallaudet University.
Anderson, B. 1983. *Imagined Communities: Reflections on the Origin and Spread of Nationalism*. London: Verso.
Ayers, B. 2004. *Deaf Diaspora: The Third Wave of Deaf Ministry*. New York: Universe.
Bakewell, O. 2008. "In Search of the Diasporas within Africa."*African Diaspora: A Journal of Transnational Africa in a Global World* 1 (1): 5–27.
Batterbury, S. C. E., M. Gulliver, and P. Ladd. 2007. "Sign Language Peoples as Indigenous Minorities: Implications for Research and Policy." *Environment and Planning A* 39:2899–915.
Bauman, H.-D. 2004. "Audism: Exploring the Metaphysics of Oppression."*Journal of Deaf Studies and Deaf Education* 9 (2): 239–46.
Bauman, H.-D., and J. Murray. 2009. "Reframing: From Hearing Loss to Deaf Gain."*Deaf Studies Digital Journal*. Accessed May 14, 2015. http://dsdj.gallaudet.edu/index .php?issue=1&section_id=2&entry_id=19.
———. 2014. *Deaf Gain: Raising the Stakes for Human Diversity*. Minneapolis: University of Minnesota Press.

---

[5] See www.deafdiaspora.org.uk. The year 2014 marked the fifth annual event in Brighton, UK, to celebrate sign language and Deaf culture. The website is regularly updated and was last accessed December 9, 2014.

Bauman, Z. 1998. *Globalization: The Human Consequences*. Cambridge, UK: Polity Press.

Baynton, D. C. 1996. *Forbidden Signs: American Culture and the Campaign against Sign Language*. Chicago: University of Chicago Press.

Bhabha, H. K. 1994. *The Location of Culture*. London: Routledge.

Breivik, J.-K., H. Haualand, and P. Solvang. 2002. "Rome—a Temporary Deaf City! Deaflympics 2001." Bergen University Research Foundation Working Paper 2-2002. Bergen: Stein Rokkan Centre for Social Studies.

Brubaker, R. 2005. "The 'Diaspora' Diaspora." *Ethnic and Racial Studies* 28 (1): 1–19.

Carbin, C. F. 1996. "Deaf Settlers in Western Canada." In *Deaf Heritage in Canada*, 235–36. Ontario, Canada: McGraw-Hill.

Chariandry, D. 2006. "Postcolonial Diasporas." *Postcolonial Text* 2 (1). Accessed June 4, 2014. http://www.postcolonial.org/index.php/pct/article/view/440/839.

Cho, L. 2007. "The Turn to Diaspora." *TOPIA: Canadian Journal of Cultural Studies* 17: 11–30.

Clifford, J. 1994. "Diasporas." *Cultural Anthropology* 9:302–38.

Cohen, R. 1996. "Diasporas and the Nation-State: From Victims to Challengers." *International Affairs* 72:507–20.

Desloges, P. 1779. *Observations d'un Sourd et Muèt, sur un cours élémentaire d'éducation des sourds et muets*. Paris: B. Morin.

Emery, S. D. 2011. *Citizenship and the Deaf Community*. Nijimen, the Netherlands: Ishara.

Flournoy, J. J., E. Booth, P. A. Emery, and H. M. Chamberlayne. 1858. "The Plans for a Community of Deaf Mutes." *American Annuls of the Deaf and Dumb* 10:40–160.

Fortier, A.-M. 2001. "'Coming Home': Queer Migrations and Multiple Evocations of Home." *European Journal of Cultural Studies* 4 (4): 405–24.

Friedner, M. 2013. "Producing 'Silent Brewmasters': Deaf Workers and Added Value in India's Coffee Cafés." *Anthropology of Work Review* 34 (1): 39–50.

Gilroy, P. 1993. *The Black Atlantic: Modernity and Double Consciousness*. London: Verso.

Gulliver, M. 2009. "DEAF Space, a History: The Production of DEAF Spaces Emergent, Autonomous, Located, and Disabled in Eighteenth- and Nineteenth-Century France." PhD thesis, University of Bristol.

Gulliver, M., and M. B. Kitzel. Forthcoming. "Deaf Geographies—an Introduction." In *The Sage Deaf Studies Encyclopedia*, ed. G. Gertz and P. Boudreault. Thousand Oaks, CA: Sage. Accessed December 9, 2014. http://www.academia.edu/7039348/Deaf_Geographies_an_introduction.

Hall, S. 1990. "Cultural identity and diaspora." In *Identity: Community, Culture, Difference*, edited by J. Rutherford, 222–37. London: Lawrence & Wishart.

Haualand, H. 2007. "The Two-Week Village: The Significance of Sacred Occasions for the Deaf Community." In *Disability in Local and Global Worlds*, edited by B. Ingstad and S. R. White, 33–55. Berkeley: University of California Press.

Humphries, T. 1975. "Audism: The Making of a Word." Unpublished essay.

Jones, J. 1996. "Bilingualism and Deaf Identity." In *Progress through Equality: New Perspectives in the Field of Mental Health and Deafness*. London: British Society of Mental Health and Deafness.

Kauppinen, L., and M. Jokinen. 2013. "Including Deaf Culture and Linguistic Rights." In *Human Rights and Disability Advocacy*, edited by M. Sabatello and M. Schulz, 131–45. Philadelphia: University of Pennsylvania Press.

Kenny, K. 2013. *Diaspora: A Very Short Introduction*. New York: Oxford University Press.

Kushalnagar, P., G. Mathur, C. J. Moreland, D. J. Napoli, W. Osterling, C. Padden, and C. Rathmann. 2010. "Infants and Children with Hearing Loss Need Early Language Access." *Journal of Clinical Ethics* 21 (2): 143–54.

Kusters, A. 2010. "Deaf on the Lifeline of Mumbai." *Sign Language Studies* 10 (1): 36–68.

———. 2014. "Deaf Gain and Shared Signing Communities." In *Deaf Gain: Raising the Stakes for Human Diversity*, edited by H.-D. Bauman and J. Murray, 285–305. Minneapolis: University of Minnesota Press.

_____. 2015. *Deaf Space in Adamorobe: An Ethnographic Study in a Village in Ghana*. Washington, DC: Gallaudet University Press.

Ladd, P. 2003. *Understanding Deaf Culture: In Search of Deafhood*. Clevedon, UK: Multilingual Matters.

Lane, H. 1984. *When the Mind Hears*. London: Penguin.

Lawrence, S. 2013. "The Development of Deaf Villages: Deaf Villages in Ireland and Jamaica Provide Sanctuary for Deaf Visitors." *SLFirst Magazine*, November 10. Accessed June 4, 2014. http://slfirst.co.uk/community/deaf-life/the-development-of-deaf-villages.

Monaghan, L. 2003. "A World's Eye View: Deaf Cultures in Global Perspective." In *Many Ways to Be Deaf: International Variation in Deaf Communities*, edited by L. Monaghan, C. Schmaling, K. Nakamura, and G. H. Turner, 1–24. Washington, DC: Gallaudet University Press.

Moores, D. 2001. *Educating the Deaf: Psychology, Principles, and Practices*, 5th ed. Boston: Houghton Mifflin.

Murphy, F. R. 1972. "Commonwealth of the Deaf Once Proposed." *Deaf American* 24 (6): 6–7.

Murray, J. 2007. "'One Touch of Nature Makes the Whole World Kin': The Transnational Lives of Deaf Americans, 1870–1924." PhD diss., University of Iowa.

O'Brien, D. 2005. "What's the Sign for 'Pint'? An Investigation into the Validity of Two Different Models to Describe Bristol's Current Deaf Pub Culture." MSc diss., University of Bristol.

Rayman, J. 2009. "Why Doesn't Everyone Here Speak Sign Language? Questions of Language Policy, Ideology, and Economics." *Current Issues in Language Planning* 10 (3): 342–54.

Safran, W. 1991. "Diasporas in Modern Societies: Myths of Homeland and Return."*Diaspora* 1:83–99.

Tölölyan, K. 1991. "Nation State and Its Others: In Lieu of a Preface."*Diaspora: Journal of Transnational Affairs* 1 (1): 4–5.

_____. 1996. "(Re)thinking Diasporas: Stateless Power in the Transnational Moment." *Diaspora* 5 (1): 3–36.

Toohey, E. N. 2010. "Phonological Development in Hearing Children of Deaf Parents." Honors Scholar Thesis, University of Connecticut. Accessed June 4, 2014. http://digitalcommons.uconn.edu/srhonors_theses/153.

Tsagarousianou, R. 2004. "Rethinking the Concept of Diaspora: Mobility, Connectivity, and Communication in a Globalised World."*Westminster Papers in Communication and Culture* 1:52–65.

Vertovec, S. 1997. "Three Meanings of 'Diaspora,' Exemplified among South Asian Religions." *Diaspora: A Journal of Transnational Studies* 6 (3): 277–99.

17 | SAME-SAME but Different: Tourism and the Deaf Global Circuit in Cambodia

Erin Moriarty Harrelson

Cambodia is a popular destination for tourists, including deaf tourists. Since 2000, there has been an explosive growth of North Atlantic–based organizations (e.g., Deaf Nation, Discovering Deaf Worlds, and Global Reach Out) that facilitate deaf leisure tourism, study tours, and educational exchanges with the intent to empower deaf people in developing countries through informal social interactions, as well as formal programming such as team-building activities, leadership enrichment, and workshops. In this chapter I illustrate how many of these encounters are shaped by a moral geography where Deaf people in the North Atlantic believe they have a responsibility to empower deaf people in developing countries by helping them find their Deaf identity and their potential as Deaf people through formal training and personal example. For the purposes of this chapter, I define *moral geography* as an ideological categorization of the world that associates certain people, things, and practices with specific sites and spaces (Cresswell 2005).

The primary sites of these encounters in Cambodia are three nongovernmental organizations (NGOs) working with deaf people: Deaf Development Programme, Epic Arts, and Krousar Thmey. These NGOs have become "destinations" in their own right, obligatory stops on the Deaf global circuit as Deaf tourists make their way to Angkor Wat. What I term *the Deaf global circuit* is the purposeful quest for Deaf spaces, encompassing locations, primarily in the (exoticized) global South, where deaf people live and work, such as deaf clubs in northern Vietnam (Audrey C. Cooper, personal communication), cafes staffed by deaf people in Cambodia and Vietnam (Cooper 2011), coffee shops and associations of the deaf in Nepal (Hoffmann-Dilloway 2011), signing villages (Friedner and Kusters 2014; Kusters 2015; Marsaja 2008), and NGOs working with deaf people in Cambodia. The deaf global circuit is perhaps best exemplified by Deaf Nation's *No Barriers with Joel Barish World Tour* and *Discovering Deaf Worlds 2007–2008 World Tour*, two sophisticated multimedia projects that feature deaf people in hundreds of businesses, deaf associations, schools, and nonprofit organizations throughout the world in videos, interviews, and newsletters. In addition, solo deaf and deaf-blind travelers have also produced blogs and online videos of their encounters with deaf people in the global South, and these are widely watched.

In this chapter, I argue that Cambodia occupies a unique place on the Deaf global circuit not only because of its popularity as a tourist destination but also because of how it is imagined as place where sign language and Deaf culture is still very new. Cambodia as a destination is more appealing to deaf travelers because of the presence of deaf expatriates from France, Germany, the United Kingdom, and the United States who function as magnets, attracting other deaf people to Cambodia; the availability of organized tours with deaf and hearing guides who use sign language; and increased publicity about deaf people in Cambodia.

Deaf expatriates in Cambodia have historically served as guides, facilitating contact with deaf Cambodians and bringing deaf tourists into deaf Cambodian spaces as part of their tourism experience. More recently, deaf tourists also have begun to find their way into local deaf spaces through contact with deaf Cambodians through Facebook and other social media. This chapter is primarily concerned with solo travelers and organized tours on the Deaf global circuit—those who specifically seek out deaf people and spaces, with the intent of giving a gift, through personal example, material objects, or money. Examining the discourses and practices of those traveling the Deaf global circuit helps illuminate possible political agendas behind these encounters and how the tourist's imagining of the suffering of distant others is inextricably connected to the affirmation of their own everyday privileges.

Fieldwork, Research Methods, and Positionality

To explore the Deaf global circuit in the Cambodian context, I draw on ethnographic research conducted with and among deaf people in Cambodia on four separate visits, varying in duration, in 2009, 2012, 2013, and 2014, for a total of fourteen months, as well as three years of online data collection on social media, especially Facebook and Instagram, as well as a survey of organizational websites. I also conducted an analysis of news articles and tour advertisements. The ethnographic research includes interviews in American Sign Language, British Sign Language, and Cambodian Sign Language (CSL) or combinations of such, with NGO administrators and staff, deaf volunteers, deaf Cambodians, visitors to Cambodia, their guides, and participant observation at various NGOs and other spaces where deaf people socialize and work.

I am a deaf anthropologist from the United States, fluent in American Sign Language (ASL), and I have made a concentrated effort to become fluent in Cambodian Sign Language.[1] As my ability to understand and converse in Cambodian Sign Language improved, I became more welcomed and accepted

---

[1] I use the designation *Cambodian Sign Language* as it is the convention established by the Cambodia Sign Language Documentation Project; however, in the early days of the project, it was called Khmer Sign Language.

in different, loosely overlapping social circles in a gradual process that was likely eased by my positionality as a signing deaf person. On my first day of participant observation at the Deaf Development Programme (DDP) Deaf Community Center, Chenda,[2] a deaf Cambodian staff member who later became a close friend, looked at me with a cocked head and narrowed eyes, then quickly signed, "deaf or hearing?" I responded with a smile, "deaf." A Deaf volunteer from Australia was standing nearby watching this conversation. A look of horror appeared on his face and he signed to Chenda, "I thought she was hearing too! But you should never ask that question. Always wait, observe, and figure it out." Smiling, I explained that people in the United States asked me this all the time too and asked jokingly, with a mock-exasperated look, why they thought I was hearing. Chenda said it was because of my posture and how I stood there, observing and taking in information, and mimicked me by crossing her arms and stiffening her back. The Deaf Australian volunteer then said it was the expressions on my face.

Throughout my fieldwork in Cambodia, I found that the identification of my hearing status was an important piece of information for both deaf and hearing Cambodian nationals and expatriates, probably because it served to position me so they knew how to interact with me, especially in terms of signed and spoken communication. Naturally, I was not only defined by my hearing status, as privileges as a white researcher from the North Atlantic remained present in my encounters with Cambodian nationals, both deaf and hearing. This will become clearer in my discussion of using a deaf guide and how I was constructed as a role model.

THE CAMBODIAN CONTEXT

Cambodia is a country indelibly associated in the popular imagination as suffering from a tragic legacy of genocide, haunting beauty, and desperate poverty. It remains one of the most aid-dependent countries in the world, receiving millions of dollars in foreign aid (Strangio 2014). Cambodia has been a site of humanitarian intervention since the early 1980s, after the fall of the Khmer Rouge (Strangio 2014; Widyono 2008). It became a "poster child for UN peacekeeping missions" and international cooperation, especially through humanitarian projects (Ear 2012). NGO activities cover almost every sector of social welfare and development. Human development indicators show that the majority of Cambodians live in the countryside in poor living conditions and people with disabilities are especially marginalized (Gartrell 2010; Mak and Nordtveit 2011).

According to newspaper articles and archived NGO documents, there was no Deaf community, nor was there a recognized sign language commonly used by groups of deaf people in Cambodia until 1997, when the first development workers began projects for people with disabilities (Disability Action Council 2003; Melamed n.d.). It is accurate to say that there is no documentation of a nationally recognized sign language; however, this does not mean that communication was not happening between deaf people or between deaf and hearing people.

---

[2] All names are pseudonyms and some locations or identifying characteristics have been changed.

From interviews and observations, it is clear that deaf people in Cambodia found ways to communicate through gestures and drawing. Many deaf people shared stories of using "home sign" with their families. During fieldwork in 2014–15, I observed encounters between members of a community outreach team and individual deaf people in villages who had neither received a formal education nor been exposed to Cambodian Sign Language (CSL). During these observations, I made connections between CSL signs currently in use and gestures that Cambodians use to communicate gender and familial hierarchy.

In contemporary Cambodia, three NGOs are the primary providers of services for deaf people in the country: Epic Arts, which provides arts instruction for deaf people and people with disabilities; Krousar Thmey, which provides formal schooling for deaf and blind children from preschool to grade 11; and the Maryknoll Deaf Development Program (DDP), which provides two years of basic literacy education, social services, and vocational training for deaf people who are aged sixteen years and older. DDP and Krousar Thmey are also engaged in a joint project to continue to develop and document CSL.

As Cambodia politically stabilized after the remaining vestiges of the Khmer Rouge either died or assimilated into society, it became a viable tourist destination and these NGOs became stops on the deaf global circuit. For many deaf visitors to Cambodia, spaces where deaf people gathered became destinations in their own right, along with the temples of Angkor Wat, the golden spires of the Royal Palace, the decaying buildings of Toul Sleng Genocide Museum, and the killing fields.

The Deaf Global Circuit

There has been a proliferation of for-profit and nonprofit organizations that organize or promote contact with deaf people in developing countries through tourism, capacity-building projects, humanitarian assistance, and study tours (often labeled as an "exchange"), primarily in countries in the global South. For example, several organizations, such as Discovering Deaf Worlds (DDW), Global Reach Out, and Global Connection, provide tours that offer opportunities for voluntourism—the combination of travel and "seeing" with volunteer work (Mostafanezhad 2013). DDW has changed its focus since the completion of its world tour, which I mentioned in the introduction, and, like Global Reach Out and Global Deaf Connection, it now organizes "empowerment" and "capacity building" workshops phasing out the provision of a tourism experience for its participants from the global North. Several authors noted that these exchanges are more often than not one-sided exchanges (Friedner 2008; Friedner and Kusters 2014; Kusters, Toura-Jensen, Verhelst, and Vestergaard, this volume).

Other deaf-owned organizations function as leisure travel agencies, arranging tours in sign language for deaf people, such as Hands On Travel (HOT), owned by a US-born deaf person based in Italy; Wesemann Travels, owned by a Dutch deaf person based in the Netherlands; and Cambodia Deaf Tours (CDT), also operated by a US-born deaf person living in Cambodia. These organizations offer sightseeing tours in sign language in Asia, Africa, Europe, and South America, often also organizing group tours for Deaf clubs, youth groups, and schools for the deaf.

These organizations all have slightly different, sometimes overlapping, objectives but a common denominator is their facilitation of encounters between deaf people in the global North and South. There is often interest in seeing residential schools and other imagined deaf spaces, such as cafes and NGOs working with deaf people, and these become stops on the deaf global circuit.

DISCOURSES AND PRACTICES ON GUIDING

Expatriate and local deaf people, especially those enmeshed in international social networks, become hosts to deaf visitors. Before the boom in deaf-owned tour companies, exemplified by the far-reaching success of HOT and CDT, this activity was informal and uncompensated. However, as the deaf tourism business expanded and more deaf tourists started coming through Cambodia, deaf Cambodians have themselves become interested in becoming guides, leading to some tension. This tension is the result of competing desires and beliefs, such as the belief in showing deaf visitors to Cambodia the sights as a friendly, welcoming gesture, reinforced by the assumption of affinity between deaf people, and the desire for economic opportunities.

Tourists, both exchange program participants and solo, have had a definite impact on deaf people in Cambodia. For example, during my 2013 visit, I observed new discourses of "guiding" and receiving payment from other deaf visitors. These discourses and practices included a deaf man's purchase of a tuk-tuk, a three-wheeled motorized vehicle used as a taxi, with a monetary gift from a visitor from another country with the intent of establishing himself as a tour guide, deaf NGO employees taking time off from work to travel to Siem Reap as a part of a tour group, and multiple offers, from many different individuals in different cities, to guide me through Cambodia if I paid for hotel rooms and transportation.

The ASL sign for "guide" was always used to describe these experiences. One deaf man spoke of how he brought tourists to see a deaf artisan workshop in Siem Reap but was rebuffed by the hearing manager of this workshop. He spoke proudly of how he was able to convince the manager to admit tourists through apologies and pleading. The concept of "guiding" and tourism spread through the deaf network in Cambodia after CDT began recruiting local deaf people to work with them. These discourses seemed especially salient during my fieldwork in the fall of 2013, perhaps because of the sheer volume of deaf people visiting Cambodia through tours organized by CDT.

Sitting in the grass with a large group of deaf people, a deaf Cambodian recounted a story about how he had guided a deaf man from the United States to his house, climbed a tree to pick coconuts and chopped the head off of a chicken while being videotaped. Gleefully, he explained how the man had given him money for this video performance. Another person in the group reprimanded him for asking money for it, saying, "We should have a good heart and guide other deaf people for free. We should welcome them and show them that Cambodians have a good heart." However, this same person who had reprimanded the other person for earning money later asked me if I would join her to go to Sihanoukville, a beach town on the coast of Cambodia, and pay for the hotel room. Like Kusters (2015) in Adamorobe, I noticed an increasingly transactional aspect to some of my relationships, especially with those who regularly interacted with deaf visitors on the deaf global circuit.

During fieldwork in 2013, it seemed as if suddenly, everyone was a guide. I took one man up on his offer to guide me. As our first stop, he took me to his home, a traditional wooden structure, about ten feet high, atop sturdy logs plunged into a clearing of hard earth deep in the rice fields. There, he told me I could film him and he would sign his story. He explained who he was, his family's history, and then showed me the still where his sister made palm wine, the chickens, and the tree that he had climbed for one of the multimedia projects I discuss earlier in this chapter. Later, we rode to the far reaches of the province and I was delighted to see the Gulf of Thailand. In all, it was a fun day but I was left wondering about what "guiding" meant to him especially as his home was a stop on the tour.

Tourism is an important economic opportunity. Guides receive direct cash payments for guiding services and/or indirect benefits such as a free hotel room at a popular tourist destination and the opportunity to travel; most importantly, gifts from abroad can allow for large purchases such as a tuk-tuk. There is also tension between tourist agencies and local NGOs as deaf Cambodian people take leave from their regular jobs, authorized or unauthorized, to act as guides or support staff for larger tour groups, such as those led by CDT.

Some deaf people in Cambodia have recognized that guiding foreigners through their country is an opportunity to earn money, and have developed various repertoires, some which include stops on the Deaf global circuit, such as meals with a large group of deaf people, a visit to DDP or Krousar Thmey, and deaf individuals have developed "authentic" personal narratives illustrating dark moments in Cambodian history, such as stories of hiding during bombing runs in the 1970s or stories of trading drawings for rice with Vietnamese soldiers after the fall of the Khmer Rouge.

THE PORTRAYAL OF DEAF FOREIGNERS IN CAMBODIA

In this section I give three examples of how deaf foreigners are portrayed or portray themselves in Cambodia: first, an example of how a deaf volunteer portrays herself as a benefactor by gifting clothes; second, how a deaf foreigner is seen as "taking away opportunities from Cambodians;" and third, how deaf foreigners regard themselves as role models. These examples show us the complicated roles that foreigners play in everyday deaf lives as well as the various ways moral geographies are mapped in Cambodia.

VIGNETTE 1: ANNIKE

As I looked up from my laptop, Annike, a young, deaf, solo backpacker traveling through Southeast Asia, stepped into the relatively cooler shadows of the Epic Arts café, a popular stop for backpackers and tourists on the deaf global circuit. Annike kicked off her flip-flops, causing the elephants on her loose harem pants to undulate with every step. She joined me at my table and, smiling, explained that she had a bag of clothing that she wanted to get rid of to lighten her load for the next leg of her trip. I stared at Annike, wondering somewhat unkindly why anyone would want her sweaty cast-offs and if she realized her clothes were possibly made in Phnom Penh, home to Cambodia's thriving garment sector.

Annike announced in a combination of gestures and International Sign (IS) to the assorted deaf people hanging out at the café that she wanted to give them clothes.[3] She instructed us to meet her at the riverside at 5 p.m. Noticing the glances between them and the slight furrowing of their eyebrows, but possibly misinterpreting their reaction as a lack of comprehension, Annike signed with more emphasis, "Free clothes. I give to you!" She pointed in the direction of the riverside, tapped her watch, and made the gesture for "five," then slipped her flip-flops back on and walked out into the heat of the afternoon, leaving behind deaf Cambodians smirking in the dimness of the café.

At 5 p.m., I found the group at their regular meeting place, the steps of a now-defunct nightclub on the riverside. I noticed a stir as Annike rode up on her bicycle with a bag of clothing. She dismounted from her bicycle and started pulling out various items of well-worn clothing from a white, plastic bag. She gave a pink t-shirt to Maly, who, with a slight, almost imperceptible roll of eyes, held it up at arm's length with a small smile that didn't quite spread to her eyes. Annike dug through the bag, holding up different items of clothing but nobody stepped forward to accept her gifts. As she offered various items to the deaf men who remained seated on the steps, they shook their heads. Ultimately, she decided to leave the remainder of the clothing at the café. Later, I learned that Peou, a hearing man with Down syndrome and a café regular, was the only one who took any of the donated clothing.

VIGNETTE 2: FOREIGNERS TAKING AWAY OPPORTUNITIES

When I returned to Phnom Penh in 2014, I sought out more information on visitors to Cambodia and how DDP and Krousar Thmey function as stops on the deaf global circuit. Over sweet, iced coffees at the Ueda Cafe, a few doors down from DDP, Justin Smith, deputy director of DDP (a deaf man from the United Kingdom), explained that visits from deaf tourists are disruptive because there are so many visitors, which takes time away from daily administrative tasks. These visitors also require education regarding the realities of the situation in Cambodia for deaf people.

Smith, describing a recent visit by a deaf man from New Zealand, explained, "I saw a man enter the building, breezing past the guard and go into the room

---

[3] International Sign is the controversial designation for the signed communication used by signers in contact situations such as international academic or political conferences, world sporting events (e.g., Deaflympics), and traveling. As such, this could be considered an "elite" communication system available only to those embedded within global networks or with the means to travel. International Sign is understood as a continuum: on the one end, there is the standardized version of IS that is used during international conferences and events, and on the other end, an ad hoc form of mutual communication between two deaf people who use different sign languages as they work towards understanding each other (e.g., Green, this volume; Crasborn and Hiddings, this volume). In this particular situation, Annike is using the elite version of IS.

where our students eat their lunches. I approached him to ask him if I could help him. He whirled around and asked with a particularly unpleasant expression, 'Who are you?' I said, 'The deputy director!' He then said to me, 'Why are you the director? You should let a deaf Cambodian be the director!'"

This is an example of how deaf visitors to Cambodia assume that deaf people in Cambodia need protection from other deaf Westerners. This man thought that Smith, being a deaf man from the United Kingdom who has lived and worked in Cambodia for many years, was taking an opportunity away from a deaf Cambodian person, not realizing that opportunities for education and training for deaf people are still very limited because of societal barriers and limited resources. This man from New Zealand understood Cambodia as a place where deaf people did not have the agency to advocate on their own behalf. He assumed a position of moral superiority, chastising another deaf foreigner for being in a leadership position of an organization working with deaf people in Cambodia.

Vignette 3: Role Models

In an interview, Hervé Roqueplan, director of Krousar Thmey and a hearing man originally from France, described a similar experience with a visitor from Australia. Roqueplan said:

> About a month or so ago, a deaf teacher, who I think was from Australia but I'm not sure, contacted us. This person wrote, "Oh, I am sorry for the last minute notice but I will show up in Cambodia next week and can I come see your school?" We explained to him that the school is not a tourist destination. It doesn't matter if you are a teacher. People just don't understand, deaf, not deaf, it is a school. Even if you are Deaf or not deaf, it doesn't matter. It does not matter which country you are from. You don't just show up at a school and say, I would like to see your school because I am a Deaf teacher, and as such, I have the right to visit. We draw the line. No, you cannot visit. At that time, we had received several requests of the same type. . . . It was funny because the guy apologized for the last minute request but when we said no, he got really upset and sent us an angry email, saying, "I have a Master's degree, I have two or three diplomas, I am a role model (for the deaf students). It is too bad you won't accept me as a visitor." For us, deaf, not deaf, it doesn't matter. Education for our students is our priority. Providing a safe environment for our students is a priority. . . . This is not entertainment. It is not an exhibit for people to gawk at, oh look! Cambodian deaf children!

What Roqueplan described is a phenomenon I have observed, as have other anthropologists (Cooper 2012, personal communication), of deaf visitors, specifically those visiting a "developing" country, assuming they are role models for the deaf people there and it is their moral responsibility to visit schools and other deaf spaces to either inspire by the virtue of being there or to give a workshop on deaf empowerment.

In other words, deaf tourists in Cambodia, and other countries in the global South, imagine they are giving the gift of deaf pride and empowerment to other deaf people simply through their presence. Visitors also might be put in this position even when they are not assuming such a role themselves, such as myself: hearing government officials in Cambodia and NGO administrators often referred to me as a role model and an inspiration for deaf Cambodians, based on my academic credentials, which I was very uncomfortable with.

MORAL GEOGRAPHY

The three vignettes I described, as well as the examples I have given of the perspectives of deaf Cambodians, illustrate the various moral geographies present in Cambodia. These vignettes show that tourists imagine Cambodia as a place lacking in resources, material and social. Deaf visitors imagine their gifts of used clothing and inspirational examples will make a difference in the lives of deaf people. Deaf tourists and other visitors imagine Cambodia as an anachronism, a place where deaf people are disempowered due to the very recent emergence of Cambodian Sign Language and the limited opportunities for a formal education. The North Atlantic geospatial imagination creates a moral geography where deaf people and organizations in the North Atlantic are responsible for the social and material improvement of deaf people in the global South.

Deaf tourists expect to be warmly welcomed by deaf-centric organizations working with deaf people. In vignettes 2 and 3, deaf tourists clearly feel some form of ownership of DDP and Krousar Thmey. For example, in vignette 2, the tourist did not have an appointment nor was there an event open to the public. This man walked into DDP, a site where people work, study, and receive social services, fully expecting that as a deaf organization, it would welcome him without reservation and reacted angrily when the deputy director of DDP challenged his presence. This tourist clearly felt he had every right to be there.

A similar scenario plays out in vignette 3. In this vignette, the deaf tourist though that, based on an e-mail, without an introduction or background check, he would be welcomed on a campus that serves deaf children. The director of Krousar Thmey also challenged him, a challenge that also sparked an angry reaction. In vignettes 2 and 3, these tourists behaved in a way that shows they imagined a form of affinity based on being deaf, an affinity that possibly sparked feelings of obligation and concern for the material and social development of deaf people in Cambodia. The Deaf global circuit is superimposed upon a moral geography of progress, which encompasses many things, including a country's supposed development or underdevelopment, in terms of the documentation and recognition of national sign language(s), the presence of an organized Deaf community and/or a national Deaf association, and a legal framework that provides rights and protection to deaf people.

As an instance of how people from the global North map the moral geography of deaf people and sign language, a 2008 publication from DDW painted a vignette of the life of a deaf person in Cambodia that conflates the possession of a recognized, formal language with everyday communication and understanding. A situation of (assumed) extreme poverty is made even more dire by the lack of a national, recognized, sign language, and by extension, a Deaf identity.

Imagine yourself, whatever age you are—be it 10, 30, or 50 years old—never fully developing a language to express yourself, never completely understanding the life and people around you. . . . Imagine living in total isolation, unable to effectively communicate, never meeting someone else like you to connect with.

What is your identity? Your family sees you as a burden and your government does not support you. You are pushed aside as an annoyance your entire life. Imagine this life with the added stress of poverty. Your belongings can fit in a plastic garbage bag, your tap water is contaminated, city power outages happen twice a day, your family earns enough to eat two or three meals a day, maybe, and your public bus for transportation is a pick-up truck or a moped with a trailer. (Discovering Deaf Worlds 2008)

For deaf people from the North Atlantic, the situation of deaf people in the global South has special poignancy because of a widespread certainty that deaf people, especially in developing countries, are isolated because they have not received a formal education nor do they have access to a nationally recognized signed language. Deaf people in developing countries without a nationally recognized sign language or a deaf association are constructed as materially deprived others (Friedner and Kusters 2014).

In a video produced for his campaign to become the president of the World Federation of the Deaf (WFD), one of the candidates referenced his experience working with deaf people in Cambodia (Allen n.d.). He pointed to this experience as a qualification for the presidency because the WFD has in recent years shifted its focus to be more inclusive of deaf people in the global South. According to the statement that accompanies the video, "For the first time ever, Deaf Cambodians who had no education were given basic training in reading, writing, mathematics, general knowledge, current affairs of the world, and Deaf Human Rights, Consequently, small Deaf groups were forming and developing. Although, the Deaf Community of Cambodia has a long way to go" (n.d.). In a more extreme form of this sentiment, a deaf expatriate I met in Cambodia in 2012, said "Cambodia is in the stone age."

This narrative relies on a teleological trajectory of progress that includes awareness of Deaf human rights, drawing a correlation between the training provided by deaf people based in the North Atlantic and the perceived development of a Deaf consciousness, which then promoted deaf Cambodians to begin to seek out other deaf Cambodians. North Atlantic development projects for deaf people in underdeveloped countries formulate prescriptive principles targeted not only at the relief of suffering, but at the moral and material improvement of distant subjects through the development of a Deaf community, sign language documentation projects, and movements for the legal recognition of a national sign language.

The assumption of a universal desire for a Deaf identity and membership in a national Deaf community provides a moral basis for intervention to help "develop" deaf communities where there is a perception that they do not exist. For some deaf people, this is a call to "do something" by participating in organized "exchanges" or if they are solo travelers, by giving a presentation about human rights or some other area of expertise, an expertise often assumed by the virtue of being a deaf person from a country with a politically organized Deaf community. For example, during a conversation with Annike, the tourist I discussed in vignette 1, about her experiences traveling alone, I asked her if she sought out other deaf people during her travels. In response, she said, "I avoid deaf locals if I can. They are very poor, always want money and steal things. I only like being with them if I have something to teach them."

In all of these vignettes, as well intentioned as the charitable impulse is, it objectifies and removes agency from the deaf people who are the recipients of these charitable efforts. Many individuals and groups operate under the assumption that empowerment and skills transfer (such as ASL) can happen over a six-day tour or during a one-hour workshop. What is often missing from offers of classes and workshops is an analysis of the gifts being given, in the form of material goods or intangible knowledge, and whether these gifts truly benefit the recipients.

In contrast to the disempowered deaf Cambodian imagined by deaf visitors, deaf Cambodians themselves have recognized tourism and transnational encounters as opportunities to increase economic and social capital. Many of the deaf Cambodians I encountered during my fieldwork use ASL signs and International Sign to communicate with foreigners, which they had learned during their schooling at Krousar Thmey or from earlier interactions with other deaf foreigners traveling trough Cambodia or their own travels abroad. Recently, I attended a wedding with my hearing partner who had just arrived in Cambodia and only knew a few CSL signs. A friend who also acted as a tour guide in his spare time outside of his full-time job sat next to us and as each new dish arrived at our table, he explained each dish, its ingredients and cultural significance in a mixture of ASL signs, CSL, and International Sign. When my partner held up his beer can, examining the tiny print on its side to determine if it was made in Cambodia, my friend also expounded on beer, holding up his own can, explaining that it was made in Cambodia and had a higher alcohol content. In this way, he revealed a moral geography of sharing knowledge about Cambodia and its products.

The moral geography of sharing native knowledge of Cambodia with visitors is a geography shared among many deaf people in Cambodia who regularly interact with foreigners. Often, if a deaf Cambodian noticed that I had a puzzled look on my face while looking at something, he or she would stop to explain to me what was happening. On one such occasion, I was in the back of a tuk-tuk stopped at a traffic light downtown Phnom Penh. The tuk-tuk driver, himself deaf, peered at me in the mirrors, noticed that I was intent on two policemen who had just forced a motorcyclist to pull over. He turned around to explain that the motorcyclist had run a red light and they were writing him a ticket. This tuk-tuk driver, who I used often, would also look at me in the mirror while in transit and explain a particular landmark.

As deaf people from the global North travel, they carry with them geospatially situated discourses about identity and language. Deaf people in certain parts of the world are imagined as vulnerable, disempowered, or dispossessed. A geography of inequality, as deaf tourists on the global circuit imagine it, inspires altruistic giving and feelings of protective obligation based on the assumption of deaf universalism. In this case, however, deaf universalism promotes essentialist ideologies and practices regarding deaf people and language, replicating the system of ideological dominance by a moral agenda to "save the other," in this case, the deaf other, who is SAME SAME BUT DIFFERENT.

CONCLUSION: SAME SAME BUT DIFFERENT

Weaving through the chaotic traffic in Phnom Penh in the back of a tuk-tuk provided ample opportunities for me to observe street life. After I had been in Phnom Penh for several weeks in 2013, I could not help but notice the ubiquitousness of t-shirts emblazoned with the phrase, "Same Same but Different." Various sizes and colors of these shirts were stacked in teetering piles in stalls in the portion of Russian Market that primarily caters to tourists; however, tourists and Cambodians alike wore these t-shirts. Puzzling over the meaning of the seemingly contradictory phrase "Same Same but Different," I asked Justin Smith, deputy director of DDP and long-time Phnom Penh resident, what it meant. He explained that it means exactly what it says—something that is the same, but not quite. On the surface, this appeared to be a contradiction but the more I thought about it, the more I realized its usefulness as an analytical tool to interrogate the deaf global circuit.

"Same Same but Different" encapsulates Deaf universalism in the sense that deaf people in the global North imagine deaf people in developing countries to be the same as them but different because of their circumstances of poverty (material and social). Based on a sense of deaf sameness, deaf tourists seek out deaf people and spaces on the Deaf global circuit; however, certain ideologies regarding deaf people in the global South creates a dynamic where deaf tourists from the global North imagine themselves as saviors, bringing gifts of clothing and knowledge, exposing deaf people in developing countries to role models and discourses of empowerment that will "help them move forward." Deaf tourists travel the Deaf global circuit, expecting to be welcomed into deaf spaces such as NGOs and schools, based on their identification as culturally deaf people and feel upset, angry, or confused when they are not welcomed with open arms.

Deaf Cambodians, on the other hand, experience tensions between being hospitable to foreign guests and "guiding" them for free, and the economic opportunities that the presence of deaf foreign travelers creates. Deaf tour guides make use of the presence of those tourists as source of income or an opportunity to do business, again based on a *sameness*: sameness as deaf people due to which they are able to communicate in sign language. However, the role they take as tour guides is motivated by a number of *differences* in backgrounds too. Examples of such differences are having money for travel versus earning money by leading travelers around and being a first-time visitor to Cambodia versus having an intimate knowledge of the country and being aware of appropriate behavior for the local milieu.

In many cases, deaf tourists from the global North and deaf Cambodians both identify a commonality based on being deaf but this commonality does not always translate into wholesale acceptance of "gifts" (in the form of ideas or material objects) by deaf Cambodians. Deaf people in Cambodia may request and accept certain gifts that benefit their ability to earn money for themselves and their families, such as the gift of a tuk-tuk, but they will put aside gifts they find useless, such as used clothing. Deaf people in Cambodia are giving gifts as well, by sharing their country and worldview with visitors from the global North.

REFERENCES

Allen, C. n.d. "Colin Allen President Nominee for the World Federation of the Deaf." Accessed November 22, 2014. http://www.colinallen.info/global-work-cambodia.html.
Central Intelligence Agency. n.d. "The World Factbook: Cambodia." Accessed May 25, 2013. http://www.cia.gov/library/publications/the-world-factbook/geos/cb.html.
Cooper, A. C. 2011. "Overcoming the Backwards Body: How State Institutions, Language and Embodiment Shape Deaf Education in Contemporary Southern Vietnam." PhD diss., American University.
Cresswell, T. 2005. "Moral Geographies." In *Cultural Geography: A Critical Dictionary of Key Concepts*, edited by D. Atkinson, P. Jackson, D. Sibley, and N. Washbourne, 128–34. London: I. B. Tauris.
Disability Action Council. 2003. "The Development of Cambodian (Khmer) Sign Language: History on the Development of Cambodian (Khmer) Sign Language." Accessed September 18, 2009. http://www.dac.org.kh/highlighted-activities/kslc.htm.
Discovering Deaf Worlds. 2008. *Discovering Deaf Worlds April Newsletter* 1 (9): 1–6. Accessed May 25, 2013. http://issuu.com/discoveringdeafworlds/docs/ddwapril08-2-.
Ear, S. 2012. *Aid Dependence in Cambodia: How Foreign Assistance Undermines Democracy.* New York: Columbia University.
Friedner, M. 2008. "On Flat and Round Worlds: Deaf Communities in Bangalore." *Economic and Political Weekly* 43 (38): 17–21.
Friedner, M., and A. Kusters. 2014. "On the Possibilities and Limits of 'DEAF DEAF SAME': Tourism and empowerment camps in Adamorobe (Ghana), Bangalore, and Mumbai (India)." *Disability Studies Quarterly* 34 (3). Accessed November 22, 2014. http://dsq-sds.org/article/view/4246/3649.
Gartrell, A. 2010. "'A Frog in a Well': The Exclusion of Disabled People from Work in Cambodia." *Disability and Society* 25 (3): 289–301.
Hoffman-Dilloway, E. 2011. "Lending a Hand: Competence through Cooperation in Nepal's Deaf Associations."*Language in Society* 40:285–306.
Kusters, A. 2015. *Deaf Space in Adamorobe: An Ethnographic Study in a Village in Ghana.* Washington, DC: Gallaudet University Press.
Leve, L., and L. Karim. 2001. "Introduction: Privatizing the State: Ethnography of Development, Transnational Capital, and NGOs." *PoLAR: Political and Legal Anthropology Review* 24 (1): 53–58.
Mak, M., and B. Nordtveit. 2011. "'Reasonable Accommodations' or Education for All? The Case of Children Living with Disabilities in Cambodia." *Journal of Disability Policy Studies* 22 (1): 55–64.
Marsaja, I. G. 2008. *Desa Kolok: A Deaf Village and Its Sign Language in Bali, Indonesia.* Nijmegen, the Netherlands: Ishara Press.
Melamed, S. n.d. "Cambodia's Deaf Wait for Words of Their Own."*Cambodia Daily*. Accessed June 7, 2013. http://www.parish-without-borders.net/ddp/resources/sign%20lang%20 article.htm.
Mostafanezhad, M. 2013. "The Geography of Compassion in Volunteer Tourism." *Tourism Geographies: An International Journal of Tourism Space, Place and Environment* 15 (2): 318–37.
Strangio, S. 2014. *Hun Sen's Cambodia.* Bangkok, Thailand: Silkworm Books.
Widyono, B. 2008. *Dancing in Shadows: Sihanouk, the Khmer Rouge, and the United Nations in Cambodia.* New York: Rowman & Littlefield.

18 | The Role of Regional, National, and Transnational Influences in the Creation of Strong Deaf Activist Networks in Uruguay

Elizabeth M. Lockwood

I believe the community has gained achievements from frequent contact with one another, access and sharing of information, collaboration, agreement, and working together toward goals. The Deaf community also has always worked as a team, with both Deaf and hearing persons. (Teresa, leader)

Despite ubiquitous barriers, the Deaf community in Uruguay has mobilized to gain greater access to majority society and as a result has created significant programs, policies, and laws for deaf persons in the Latin American and the Caribbean region. Moreover, the Uruguayan Deaf community has achieved more objectives than other national disability groups and thus the impressive development of the community is not simply a result of effective national disability legislation but rather the combination of a supportive social structure and continual advocacy efforts from within the Deaf community. Uruguay has less disability legislation than other culturally, politically, and economically similar nations such as Costa Rica and Argentina, as well as differently structured nations such as the Dominican Republic and Honduras. Yet at the same time, Uruguay boasts more deaf-focused laws and decrees than any of these countries (Allen 2008). Furthermore, deaf-related legislation and policies in Uruguay are not modeled after foreign systems but rather are the first of their kind in the region (Michailakis 1997).

Although it makes up less than one percent of the national population and is one of the smaller disability groups, the Uruguayan Deaf community has advocated and achieved several deaf-focused programs, policies, and laws. Achievements include, among others, the following:

- the official recognition of bilingual education (Lengua de Señas Uruguaya [LSU] and Spanish) in the primary deaf school in Montevideo in 1993;

- the implementation of full-time interpreters at two Montevideo secondary schools: Liceo 32, Guayabos (middle school) in 1996 and Instituto Alfredo Vazquez Acevedo (IAVA, high school) in 1999;

- the addition of relay operators by Administración Nacional de Telecomunicaciones (National Telecommunications Administration, ANTEL) in 1999;

- the recognition of LSU as an official language of Deaf Uruguayans and of Uruguay (along with Spanish) in national legislation in 2001 (ley no. 17.378, 2001);

- the enactment of a 75 percent discount on text messages from ANCEL, ANTEL's cellular phone service, in 2005;

- the State provision of sign language interpreters at the Universidad de la República (National University) and Universidad del Trabajo del Uruguay (Technical University of Uruguay, UTU) in Montevideo in 2007 (Cursos en UTU 2008; Lima and Gallardo 2007);

- the provision of full-time interpreters at employment competitions in 2007;

- the creation of the first accessible (through LSU and Spanish subtitles) national film in 2008;

- and a State-sponsored program to teach State employees LSU in 2009.

To understand the development of the Uruguayan Deaf community, this chapter explores the process of how the Deaf community in Uruguay builds and engages in strategic intragroup networks without utilizing strong transnational linkages.

NETWORKS AND THE DEAF COMMUNITY IN URUGUAY

I define *networks* as relationships between two entities, such as an individual or groups and another individual, group, organization, or government entity (Emibayer and Goodwin 1994). *Transnational networks* are linkages among Deaf communities, organizations, and advocates across national borders while *intragroup networks* are connections within and among organizations and advocates in the Uruguayan Deaf community. *Deaf community* does not refer to communities of a geographic place but rather Deaf collective life in which Deaf individuals share a common language, experiences, and interactions (Ladd 2003). In this case, because I focus on the Deaf community in Uruguay's capital Montevideo, *Uruguayan Deaf community* refers to the Deaf community in Montevideo unless otherwise noted. As defined by Deaf leaders during my fieldwork, the Uruguayan Deaf community also includes certain hearing individuals, including children of Deaf adults (CODAS) and hearing parents and siblings of Deaf persons.

Networks between groups are considered strategic elements in gaining resources and self-representation in grassroots and social movements (Stanley 2006; Tarrow 1998) because they can create a space for negotiation between and across stakeholders, such as Deaf organizations and governments. From this negotiation comes the possibility of change, including the creation of Deaf-centered programs, policies, and laws. Studies indicate that grassroots organizations, such as local indigenous peoples' groups, recognize the value in creating networks with supporters from wider circles and acknowledge that inadequate attempts to build alliances create common barriers in group sustainability (Dey and Westendorff 1996). Specifically, intragroup and transnational networks, such as local grassroots organizations and cross-border coalitions, are important in grassroots activism and social movements (Tarrow 1998; Yashar 2007). Even with an increased focus on networks and social movements in recent years, this is greatly understudied. Even less prevalent are studies on the effects of intragroup and transnational networks and the relationship with Deaf activism. Thus, the connection between building and utilizing networks in Deaf movements and consequent achievements are important to investigate.

This chapter is based on a case study of the Deaf community in Montevideo. Montevideo was chosen because approximately one third of the national population resides and works in the capital city. Furthermore, the majority of Deaf organizations are based in Montevideo and most Deaf activism takes place in this centralized location. In 2008 and 2009, I conducted research with the Deaf community to gain insight into the development of the community's collective action. Previously in 2001 and 2002, as a Fulbright scholar, I carried out preliminary research in Uruguay on the deaf educational system and effects on employment opportunities for Deaf adults. From this I possessed fluency in LSU and Spanish and had maintained relationships with the community.

The research draws on an identity-based grassroots development and social movement framework to provide insight into the development of the Uruguayan Deaf community. Qualitative data was gathered over a twelve-month period as an Inter-American Foundation Grassroots Development fellow through in-depth interviews with fourteen community leaders (individuals who held leadership roles in Deaf organizations) and twelve community members (individuals active in Deaf organizations, but not in leadership roles), extensive participant observation, and document analysis (print and online newspaper articles, conference brochures, and Deaf organization documents).

I interviewed community leaders to gain insight about their leadership roles and direct involvement in the process and sustainability of community collective action. In addition, a subsample of community members was interviewed to complement the leaders' perspectives and to provide ground-level viewpoints. Each participant was interviewed approximately one to three times for one to two hours each. All names of research participants have been changed for confidentiality. All interviews were privately videotaped in LSU or in spoken Spanish: almost all participants were Deaf LSU users, but in a few cases spoken Spanish was used with hearing people (considered members of the Deaf community). All participants were between the ages of eighteen and sixty-four, and age and gender were evenly distributed between both leader and member groups.

It is important to note that I am an outsider on two levels, hearing and North American, and this was discussed with the community and considered throughout the research. Because of my outsider status, at times I was provided with certain information that individuals would not have shared with other members of the community. Although an outsider, mutual respect was established, the community appeared to view me as an ally in their development, and I continually strove to overcome power imbalances by ensuring that the research was collaborative and participatory in nature. Initially and throughout my fieldwork, I discussed research themes with the community and received valuable feedback. Specifically, in 2009 I presented the research findings at the VI Latin American Meeting of the Deaf (VI Encuentro Latinoamericano de Sordos) in Bogotá to regional Deaf leaders and afterward to the Deaf community in Montevideo. In both cases, Deaf leaders and members expressed that they recognized the research findings as valid.

DEAF PEOPLE IN URUGUAY AND MONTEVIDEO

There are approximately 3.3 million people living in Uruguay (CIA 2014). A report from the Instituto Nacional de Estadística (National Institute of Statistics) estimates that 30,193 deaf and hard-of-hearing persons reside in Uruguay ("La lengua," 2001), although some community members estimate that the number is closer to 38,000. The precise number of sign language users is difficult to ascertain, although the main concentration of signers resides in metropolitan areas (Administración Nacional De Educación Pública and Consejo Directivo Central 2008). The Uruguayan Association of the Deaf, ASUR (Asociación de Sordos del Uruguay) estimates that 10,000 Uruguayans use LSU, 1500 are active in the Montevideo Deaf community (through schools, organizations, and Deaf events), and approximately 120 people are paying members of ASUR.

There are four Montevideo-based Deaf organizations, all of which are places of social interaction, information sharing, education, and advocacy for the Deaf community, although the national Deaf association always has been and continues to be integral for the community. Deaf Uruguayans began organizing in Montevideo in 1902 and by 1928 officially established the first national Deaf association. The original name, Asociación de Sordomudos del Uruguay (Uruguayan Association of the Deaf-mute), was used until 1997 when *mudo* (mute) was dropped and officially changed to Asociación de Sordos del Uruguay (Uruguayan Association of the Deaf, ASUR). Initially the association permitted only Deaf men as members, with the first Deaf woman becoming a member in 1947. The other important Deaf-focused organizations are described later.

In 1983 Organización Deportiva de Sordos del Uruguay (Uruguayan Sports Organization for the Deaf, ODSU) formed when ASUR shifted in focus toward Deaf culture and away from athletics (although ASUR did and still provides sports activities). In 2001 ODSU became a full member of the International Committee of Sports for the Deaf. Centro de Investigación y Desarrollo para la Persona Sorda (Center for Research and Development for the Deaf, CINDE) began organizing inside ASUR in 1988 and was officially established in 1991. CINDE provides LSU courses, interpreter training (for five years), and a LSU teacher program. In 1994 hearing parents of Deaf children formed Asociación de Padres y Amigos de Sordos del Uruguay (Uruguayan Association of Parents and Friends of the Deaf, APASU) to advocate for the rights of Deaf children and adults in Uruguay. APASU leaders trained at CINDE and became certified interpreters and consequently actively involved with the Deaf community.

THE URUGUAYAN DEAF COMMUNITY AND TRANSNATIONAL CONNECTIONS

Historically the Uruguayan Deaf community sought out transnational connections. ASUR is affiliated with World Federation of the Deaf (WFD) and Uruguay was the first South American country to become a member of WFD in 1955. However, almost all cross-border linkages transpired in South America with little exposure to the global North, which is not surprising because some global Deaf leaders consider Latin American and Caribbean Deaf communities to be among the most overlooked regions in terms of projects and funding (Piñedo 2007). In Uruguay, most transnational Deaf exchanges occurred during the early part of the twentieth century for social reasons, such as Deaf athletic tournaments, in particular with Argentina and other Southern Cone nations (Chile, Brazil, and Paraguay). An example of an early transnational meeting occurred in 1912 when Deaf Argentines visited Deaf Uruguayans in Montevideo and shared information about the creation of the first Deaf association in Argentina. This exchange was the impetus for Deaf Uruguayans to create the first Deaf association in Uruguay, established sixteen years later, with the knowledge that "if Argentines can do it, then we can do it" (leader interviews). These transnational encounters were thus inspirational for Uruguayans.

In contrast to Deaf communities in many other countries, since the 1990s only infrequent cross-border exchanges have occurred. The Deaf community in Uruguay is not opposed to transnational linkages, but rather these relationships take a back seat to local networks through which the community creates visible, successful, and sustainable policy changes. Furthermore, despite having a relatively large middle class, most Uruguayans have little discretionary income to spend on international travel. Consequently, a strong sentiment exists within the community to develop its own path with a focus on intragroup networks building upon a sense of DEAF SAME within the community, as a Deaf leader indicates:

> Uruguay has developed on its own path. We haven't asked for help from other nations. We respect other nations' differences, but haven't copied their ways. We have interacted with Argentina and Brazil, but our path of development has been different and on our own. (Felipe, leader)

To be clear, there have been regional connections in Latin America and the Caribbean, and these are underexamined. At the 2009 regional conference VI Encuentro Latinoamericano de Sordos conference, José Antonio Leal, a Deaf leader from Colombia, presented on the process of strengthening Deaf communities. He encouraged Latin American Deaf communities to actively foster intragroup networks within their respective nations in order to function as a collective unit, which is necessary, he argued, to successfully obtain community goals. Leal encouraged regional solidarity, yet also the importance of unified national Deaf communities, citing Federación Nacional de Sordos de Colombia (FENASCOL), Colombia's national federation of the Deaf, as a model for success. The conference created the space for instances of DEAF SAME to emerge among Deaf communities in Latin America and the Caribbean and consequently influenced respective Deaf community development. One such example is that in 2010 the Deaf community in Uruguay formed its own national federation of the Deaf, FENASUR, consequently creating a more cohesive Deaf community throughout the country.

In recent years, leadership roles and community identity have shifted in Uruguay and, as a result, earlier influential cross-border exchanges have less importance within the community. This recent lack of transnational networking does not seem to hinder the community, because its path of development functions well for its needs. On the contrary, by and large the community positively views itself as distinct from other Deaf communities by its creation of an effective path of development from within the nation. Perhaps, as Keck and Sikkink (1998) suggest, there is no need to turn to global sources since local grassroots action works effectively. As a consequence, a sense of pride or DEAF SAME appears when the community discusses its path.

> Some Deaf people gather information from Deaf communities in other countries, but really our path has been on our own and we haven't had any help from any other countries. Our path has been solitary. Yes, people from other nations may have provided information many years ago, but now we are actually making things happen. Before it was all talk, now we have action. (Gabriel, member)

REASONS FOR URUGUAY'S INWARD FOCUS

The Deaf community's inward focus is not specific to Deaf networks in Uruguay but is a pattern found throughout the country. Perhaps some of the Deaf community's resistance in networking with Argentina and Brazil arises from pervasive unilateralism from both Argentina and Brazil through Mercosur (Mercado Común del Sur, Southern Common Market), the trade bloc in South America (Phillips 2004). These actions have forced Uruguay to act independently and focus instead on State-run services, creating the largest viable social policy framework in the region. Moreover, Uruguayans at times feel overshadowed as a small nation nestled between much larger neighbors, as expressed by poet and scholar Hugo Achugar: "Uruguay is a small country and a border country. It is difficult to be small. It is worse being small and to know the border is close. But even worse is to know you are a small border nation in between two giants, which perhaps still make you feel diminutive" (1992, 13, author's translation). An additional challenge in cross-border networking is the extremely high cost of travel within and outside the region.

Similarly, Uruguay attempts to rely less on global markets compared to its South American counterparts because it is such a small nation and therefore more

easily affected by both positive and negative global economic changes. A Deaf
leader expresses this inward focus:

> Uruguay is considered a Third World country and we don't have large
> factories or a large economy, but we do produce a lot of food that the
> world will need one day. In many countries the land is dwindling and ur-
> banization is growing, but here we still have our land for free range cattle
> and produce so we will be important one day in the future. (Felipe)

Since the 1960s Uruguay has applied import substitution industrialization policies, protectionist measures, and stimulus of internal production. These policies
closed export centers and created employment for the middle and working classes
in protected markets. This lessened the need for employers to absorb contribution
costs, but instead passed them on to consumers with more expensive products
(Huber 1995). This national economic policy and related burden of living in a high-
cost economy is reflected in the Deaf community in that it relies inwardly on the
nation rather than looking to or depending on outward global assistance.

DEAF INTRAGROUP NETWORKING IN URUGUAY

Uruguayan citizens have strong voting power, which makes it difficult for
the government to privatize State-run entities since invariably voters block the
change (Stein et al. 2006). This too affects the Deaf community because once a
State-funded policy exists it likely remains, thus creating stability. An example
includes the policy to fund full-time interpreters at the national (and free) university in Montevideo, Universidad de la República, which started as a short-term
initiative but has continued and improved.

   The Deaf community engages in intragroup networking to aid in its process of
development toward group goals. Key intragroup dynamics include organization,
collaboration, cohesiveness, communication, and collective identity; these characteristics can assist in the emergence, efficacy, and sustainability of community
activism. On the other hand, with the absence of strong intragroup networks, a
community is more likely to fracture and consequently lose power and control to
paternalistic organizations (Bettencourt, Dillmann, and Wollman 1996). Therefore
the challenge lies in the ability to sustain these networks:

> One of the reasons that the Deaf community has been so successful is
> because ASUR, CINDE, and APASU have worked together to get rights
> passed and the government has respected that. (Jorge, leader)

> The community has gained rights from groups inside the Deaf commu-
> nity, which work well together and have been fighting to obtain rights for
> many years. (Francisco, member)

Deaf community protests are also collaboratively organized and evoke a
sense of DEAF SAME within the community. In turn this creates a strong collective

Figure 1. Uruguayan Deaf community protest in Montevideo in September 2008.

identity among community members and provides the space for a new generation of leaders. In 2006, leaders and members from ASUR, CINDE, and APASU jointly organized the community's premier public protest. These team efforts continued in 2007 and 2008. The lead banner of the 2008 march exemplified the interconnected spirit, by exhibiting all three associations side by side.

The names were strategically placed to equally acknowledge all three organizations and to convey a united Deaf community rather than giving priority to one group, which can cause factions within a movement (Stanley 2006).

Two months following the 2008 protest, Deaf and hearing allies in the community collaborated to organize the first national Deaf community conference: Primer Encuentro de la Comunidad Sorda: Construyendo vínculos en la sociedad (First Deaf Community Conference: Creating Linkages within Society). The conference title and objectives reflect the community's values and efforts to further advocate for access into hearing society. Occasionally, as in the case of this conference, even deaf persons not actively involved in the community collaborated in Deaf community development, benefiting both parties.

Intragroup collaboration is also evident between ODSU and ASUR even though both provide athletic activities to Deaf and hard-of-hearing Uruguayans. Competition between the two groups is mitigated because ODSU focuses on major national and regional athletic activities and ASUR centers on cultural and social activities with smaller scale athletic activities (ASUR also rents out its athletic facilities to the public). Community members prefer having a choice in their athletic activities and most frequent both locations. As in this situation, rather than competing for a small pool of resources, each Deaf organization recognizes and uses its strength to gain a wider range of resources. This cogent process allows space for the community to more easily complete and follow through with proposals and projects rather than waste resources and energy on competition:

> APASU has been really important in the process of working to gain rights. ASUR and CINDE also have assisted by training and employing Deaf LSU professors who travel to different departments to teach Deaf and hearing people and then connect them to Montevideo. In my opinion, CINDE is very active in starting projects, but hits barriers and APASU finds solutions to carry them out. (Gabriel, member)

As indicated, no particular organization is considered more effective than another in gaining access and shares in the advocacy process, thus providing a fruitful and empowering environment.

Perhaps intragroup connections are fostered and sustained more easily because of Montevideo's small geographic size of 74.9 square miles (Instituto Nacional de Estadística 2012) and the close proximity of Deaf organizations within the city limits. Moreover, the three main organizations for certain periods of time have shared physical spaces, thereby creating a fluid, accessible, and cohesive working environment among the community. Prior to 2008, APASU gathered within ASUR until moving into its own building on the other side of the city. CINDE, too, began organizing within ASUR in the late 1980s and later moved across from the deaf school. But in 2001, CINDE returned to ASUR and henceforth has rented classroom space. Close proximity between the organizations creates a space for frequent information exchange; easy collaboration among leaders, members, allies, instructors, interpreters, and students; and fosters DEAF SAME in the community. Overlapping contact also provides students with invaluable exposure to the Deaf community and ample opportunities to develop fluency in LSU.

A positive outcome from frequent interaction between organizations is that Deaf and hearing allies cooperate to advocate for common goals. Hearing parents of deaf children, CODAS, siblings, and some hearing teachers at the deaf primary school have provided assistance in realizing Deaf-related projects, policies, and laws. These valuable allies also provide additional resources to the community. Deaf and hearing persons from CINDE join forces and areas of skill are recognized and utilized. Classes are often taught in Deaf-hearing and Deaf-Deaf teams, creating a positive bicultural atmosphere. Deaf and hearing allies also join forces to develop LSU outreach programs aimed at Deaf and hearing individuals outside of Montevideo to increase the interconnectedness of the national Deaf community. The community exemplifies Ladd's (2003) argument that Deaf communities must collaborate with hearing allies to successfully gain rights:

> Deaf people in Uruguay need to work with hearing allies and without this collaboration they won't gain achievements. An example of when

collaboration works is when APASU works with the Deaf community and speaks out in support in certain situations for the benefit of the community. (Sebastián, member)

Good collaboration takes place among Deaf and hearing allies as long as respect for equality is present between the groups. If Deaf people feel discriminated against or devalued by hearing persons in the community, such as being left out of decision-making processes, tension invariably emerges between groups. To prevent such roadblocks, open and frequent channels of communication between Deaf and hearing individuals are encouraged. Strategies such as this are an example of effective networking that contributes to a unified movement.

Solidarity within the community leads to the creation of proposals and projects that Deaf community leaders use to lobby the government. Along with intergroup cohesion, effective coordination with allies in the government is arguably an integral attribute in the development of the Deaf community from which it gains access to valuable resources and information:

In the past Deaf people were not accepted by society, but now acceptance is increasing from the Deaf law (Law 17.378) being enforced. The Frente Amplio (Broad Front political party) has helped the Deaf community by increasing access to job competitions and by accepting LSU, our language. These changes occurred from discussions between politicians and the Deaf community. (Viviana, member)

As a group from CINDE we went to Intendencia (City Hall) and explained why Deaf people need separate employment exams with interpreters. We discovered this situation because a Deaf person who was scheduled to take the employment exam discovered that there was no interpreter and asked CINDE for our assistance. So we contacted Intendencia, scheduled an appointment, and went to discuss the issue. Now other organizations, such as Banco República, have summoned us to discuss how to resolve the same issue. (María Laura, leader)

Uruguay's long tradition of social welfare policies assists in creating the space to build strong networks with (and within) the State. Indeed, Uruguay's fluid political system provides an avenue for advocacy, dialogue, and change to take place. Additionally, strategic advocacy with key allies in the government also greatly contribute to these examples and other State-funded initiatives for Deaf Uruguayans. The process of building these alliances and gaining Deaf rights in society have contributed to a sense of Deaf community empowerment and the emergence of DEAF SAME, as expressed here:

The Deaf community has developed differently than other grassroots movements in Uruguay. We have been constantly fighting to have equal rights and are now becoming empowered. ASUR has been very important in fighting for Deaf rights. Proposals are written and revised at ASUR and then taken to the government in which hearing allies work with the Deaf for equality. It was much worse for the Deaf community in the past and little by little we are getting somewhere. (Alejandra, leader)

CONCLUSION

The Deaf community in Uruguay applies Leal's push for engagement in intragroup networks to achieve community objectives. Particularly effective strategies appear to be the active utilization of strong alliances and collaboration between the main Montevideo-based Deaf organizations to push for change. There is an emphasis on each organization's strengths and consequently little competition for resources. Moreover, Deaf and hearing allies within the community as well as active connections with allies in the national government add to the strong development of the community. The Deaf community strongly engages in intragroup activities, yet it also includes and incorporates allies from outside the group to create a broader and stronger movement. These findings thus show that the study of (different kinds of) networks is an understudied but an important topic for Deaf studies.

The strategic utilization of networks within the Uruguayan Deaf community and subsequent development may be unique due to the particular political economy in Uruguay. Yet, lessons learned from this community can be applied as a model for other Deaf communities. Transnational connections, often considered integral for the success of a social movement, have only been a minor factor in the Deaf movement in Uruguay. Although transnational connections, particularly from the region, assisted the community in its early formation, less influence is evident in recent years. This lack of consistent cross-border exchange does not appear to have thwarted community development, but rather pushed the community to focus inward on sustainable national policies. The Deaf community is not opposed to transnational connections; however, it wears a badge of pride in charting its own course of development. This has resulted in a sense of Uruguayan nationalism within the Deaf community. This case provides the perspective that transnational linkages should not always be privileged over intragroup or regional networks.

REFERENCES

Achugar, H. 1992. *La balsa de la Medusa: Ensayos sobre identidad, cultura y fin de siglo en Uruguay.* Montevideo, Uruguay: Ediciones Trilcce.

Administración Nacional De Educación Pública and Consejo Directivo Central. 2008. *Documentos de la Comisión de Políticas lingüísticas en la Educación Pública, Montevideo,* Montevideo: Administración Nacional De Educación Pública and Consejo Directivo Central.

Allen, C. 2008. *Global Education Pre-planning Project on the Human Rights of Deaf People.* Helsinki, Finland: World Federation of the Deaf and Swedish National Association of the Deaf.

Bettencourt, A., G. Dillmann, and N. Wollman. 1996. "The Intragroup Dynamics of Maintaining a Successful Grassroots Organization: A Case Study."*Journal of Social Issues* 52 (1): 169–86.

Calvo, C. 2003. "Demanda y Uso de Banco de Datos sobre Discapacidad." Presentation at the XVIII Meeting of the Latin American Network of Central Banks and Finance Ministries, Washington D.C., April 9.

CIA. 2014. *The World Factbook: Uruguay.* Accessed April 17, 2015. https://www.cia.gov/library/publications/the-world-factbook/geos/uy.html.

"Cursos en UTU para sordos." March 4, 2008. Montevideo, Uruguay: Sociedad Uruguay.

Dey, K., and D. Westendorff. 1996. "Getting Down to Ground Level: A Community Perspective on Social Development." *Development in Practice* 6 (3): 265–69.

Emibayer, M., and J. Goodwin. 1994. "Network Analysis, Culture, and the Problem of Agency." *American Journal of Sociology* 99 (6): 1411–54.

Huber, E. 1995. "Options for Social Policy in Latin America: Neoliberal versus Social Democratic Models." In *Welfare States in Transition: National Adaptations in Global Economies*, edited by G. Esping-Anderson, 141–91. London: Sage.

Instituto Nacional de Estadística. 2012. *Censos 2011: Contame que te cuento.* Accessed April 17, 2015. http://www.ine.gub.uy/censos2011/index.html.

Keck, M. E., and K. Sikkink. 1998. *Activists beyond Borders: Advocacy Networks in International Politics.* Ithaca, NY: Cornell University Press.

"La lengua de señas uruguaya es casi oficial." May 20, 2001. *El Observador.*

Ladd, P. 2003. *Understanding Deaf Culture: In Search of Deafhood.* Clevedon, UK: Multilingual Matters.

Leal, J. A. 2009. "El Proceso de Fortalecimiento de la Comunidad Sorda en el Marco de La Convención de la ONU y el Desarrollo Inclusivo." Paper presented at the Sixth Encuentro Latinoamericano de Sordos, Bogotá, July 10, 2009.

Ley No. 16.095. 1989. "Personas Discapacitadas." Accessed April 17, 2015. http://www.parlamento.gub.uy/leyes/AccesoTextoLey.asp?Ley=16095&Anchor=.

Ley No. 17.378. 2001. "Reconocese a Todos Los Efectos a La Lengua de Señas Uruguaya Como La Lengua Natural de Las Personas Sordas y de Sus Comunidades en Todo El Territorio de la República." Accessed April 17, 2015. http://www.parlamento.gub.uy/leyes/AccesoTextoLey.asp?Ley=17378&Anchor=.

Lima, M. E., and M. Gallardo. 2007, April 9. "Los sordos podrán ir a la universidad en este 2007 Educación, La Udelar financiará intérpreters por 10 años." Montevideo, Uruguay: El País. Accessed April 17, 2015. http://historico.elpais.com.uy/07/04/09/pciuda_273962.asp.

Michailakis, D. 1997. "Government Action on Disability Policy: A Global Policy." Accessed April 17, 2015. http://www.independentliving.org/standardrules/UN_Answers/UN.pdf.

Phillips, N. 2004. *The Southern Cone Model: The political Economy of Regional Capitalist Development in Latin America.* London: Routledge.

Piñedo, F. 2007. "Commission on Developing Countries: Introduction." Paper presented at the Fifteenth World Congress of the World Federation of the Deaf, Madrid, July 16, 2007.

Stanley, K. 2006. "Partnership in the Irish Deaf Community." In *The Deaf Way II Reader: Perspectives from the Second International Conference on Deaf Culture,* edited by H. Goodstein, 38–41. Washington, DC: Gallaudet University Press.

Stein, E., T. Mariano, K. Echebarría, E. Lora, and M. Payne. 2006. "Direct Democracy and Resistance to Privatization: The Case of Uruguay." In *The Politics of Policies: Economic and Social Progress in Latin America 2006 Report.* Cambridge, MA: InterAmerican

Development Bank, David Rockefeller Center for Latin American Studies, Harvard University.

Tarrow, S. 1998. *Power in Movement: Social Movements and Contentious Politics.* Cambridge, UK: Cambridge University Press.

Woliver, L. R. 1996. "Mobilizing and Sustaining Grassroots Dissent." *Journal of Social Issues* 52 (1): 139–51.

Yashar, D. 2007. "Resistance and Identity Politics in an Age of Globalization." *Annals, AAPSS* 610:160–81.

19 International Deaf Space in Social Media: The Deaf Experience in the United States

Christopher A. N. Kurz and Jess Cuculick

My smartphone is my DEAF-SPACE. *. . . . I go there . . . for Deaf people.*

—A Deaf American during an interview

Most descriptions of *Deaf space* define the term as physical spaces where Deaf people meet and share experiences through visual communication (Gulliver 2009; Solvang and Haualand 2014; Valentine and Skelton 2008, 2009). Places in which Deaf spaces were established could be, but were not limited to, schools, clubs, organizations, conferences, congresses, sports, religious sites, and Deaf community events. In this chapter, we document how Deaf space also can be created in nonphysical spaces such as social network sites (SNS). Physical encounters are not required for creating Deaf spaces. People have turned to social media to enhance interaction opportunities in schools, businesses, communities, and society in general (Hanna, Rohm, and Crittenden 2011). Social media has become an Internet-based movement where people utilize community-based websites and share information with others. For some, social media has transformed the way people live (Correa, Hinsley, and de Zuniga 2010). Hanna, Rohm, and Crittenden (2011, 269) went as far as to describe social media sites, such as Facebook, Twitter, and Instagram, as a part of an emerging ecosystem rather than just a platform.

The implications of social media for the Deaf community are enormous. Unlike the teletypewriter (TTY) and videophones, the Internet allows Deaf people to build and/or maintain digital communities, nonphysical spaces called *digital Deaf spaces*. The Internet made possible the formation of multiple Deaf geographies: Deaf clubs and Deaf communities can be created, maintained, and influenced by their members' online participation (Valentine and Skelton 2008). Digital Deaf spaces are readily accessible anywhere and anytime as long as there is an (preferably speedy) Internet connection. Deaf people use the Internet as an alternative way to access Deaf-related information, through both sign language and text, without physically being in the same place at the same time (Valentine and Skelton 2008). Cuculick (2014) found that Deaf college students used social media, specifically Facebook, for many purposes including keeping abreast of Deaf sporting events (internationally and nationally) and sharing information about such events. Finding these connections, through friends, friends of friends, followers, and following posts, has expanded Deaf individuals' repertoires of Deaf networks (Cuculick 2014). The use of social media has made interaction with Deaf people from all over the world possible.

This chapter focuses on the experience of Deaf social media users from the United States, as they connect with fellow Deaf Americans and with Deaf international contacts. We explore in what ways social media allow Deaf people in the United States to construct Deaf spaces. Because we are Deaf and use social media ourselves, we have an insider perspective on social media. Cuculick, who is fluent in American Sign Language (ASL), interviewed seven Deaf participants in ASL for thirty to sixty minutes. Videos were then transcribed into written English. There were three male and four female adult participants; five of them worked at a higher education institution and two were from the local Deaf community. Participants were between thirty and sixty-five years old. All were Caucasian, were college educated, and have traveled abroad. All participants used Facebook for international interactions with Deaf people from other countries.

The four themes that emerged in the interviews were (1) maintaining Deaf contacts and connections through online communication, (2) the use of multiple written and signed languages, (3) access to information and transmission of information, and (4) globalization of personal space.

Maintaining Deaf Contacts and Connections through Online Communication

All participants used social media to connect with their families and friends, but they primarily used SNS to connect with Deaf friends, including their international contacts. A participant discussed how Deaf spaces and communication are important for Deaf-to-Deaf interaction:

> Sign language demands space and social media with video feeds allow the formation of Deaf space. Communication is important for Deaf people, and social media provides space for them. (Ashley)[1]

Social media has provided Deaf people the ability to interact even when they cannot meet each other in person:

> I have a Deaf friend in a Middle East country. She cannot see her Deaf fiancé in person due to the tribal cultural rules, but she uses social media

---

[1] All personal names are pseudonyms.

to communicate face-to-face with him, which is permissible. I found this fascinating as social media allows visual communication, as sign language is visual. (Ashley)

Six of the seven participants admitted that they would not maintain contact with any international friends without social media. Here is an example:

Before social media, I had no international friends. (Mackenzie)

We met and became friends at international conferences, but if not for social media, I would not maintain with any one of them. (Jordan)

Participants noted the intimacy that social media offered for interacting with their international contacts:

I feel more personal with international Deaf individuals through their video feeds. Through video feeds, I feel as if I am in present with the speaker. (Hayden)

We felt a sense of connection. We have common grounds. . . . Same culture, same Deaf culture, SAME, STAY-STRONG. Same challenges, same experience. . . . Human nature that. (Kris)

Nearly all of the participants read or watch news feeds of their international Deaf contacts:

I enjoy being up to date with international current events, including Deaf current events. (Ashley)

I enjoy learning international Deaf jokes, sign languages, and Deaf experiences in different countries. (Riley)

Another participant used SNS contact information and message to arrange an international tour for Deaf senior citizens:

I saw about the people from Signs Restaurant [in Canada] where they hire Deaf waiters/waitresses. I contacted them through Facebook and talked to them. I have arranged a tour for a group of Deaf senior citizens in my town to visit and dine at the restaurant and then to Deaf agency or club in the town. (Adrian)

In the same vein, five participants made travel arrangements with their international Deaf contacts:

My husband and I made plans with his golfing friends and their spouses for upcoming international golf tournaments. (Mackenzie)

My partner and I have contacted a Deaf friend from Cambodia to arrange travel plans through Facebook Messenger. (Hayden)

> I used Facebook Messenger with Deaf Chilean friends to plan my next trip to Chile. (Riley)

Participants thus felt that social media made it possible to interact easily with their local and international Deaf contacts. They also felt connected when they watched their contacts' video feeds. They learned new information about Deaf international experiences and Deaf narratives (e.g., jokes, stories) in text and/or sign form.

THE USE OF MULTIPLE WRITTEN AND SIGNED LANGUAGES

Participants reported that while international Deaf connections can be maintained through SNS, they depend on language knowledge in both written and signed languages to access information, and they also use SNS to learn new sign languages. For example, these two participants demonstrate how they use SNS to learn new signs:

> I use Facebook to learn the International Signs. Deaf people in Europe created v-logs in International Signs and I watched them in my FB feeds and learned how to use the International Signs. (Ashley)

> In Facebook, I observe their sign languages because I am an ASL teacher. I study different sign languages. I do not make comments, but I just observed their signs. (Adrian)

A participant compared language access through two different online platforms, e-mail and SNS, and shows how SNS is more enabling than email:

> [With] e-mail there is the barrier of language; face to face there is not that much of a barrier. Facebook is a mix of both; typed (written) and visual . . . more of a middle ground. E-mail I think is the most difficult due to translating or not fluent with the language itself. PERIOD. (Kris)

However, language choice between signed and written languages can also have limitations or tensions as well. Participants discuss how they use translate features built into SNS to help make written communication easier. Three participants used a feature called Facebook Translate, which translates post updates and comments on Facebook from one language to the preferred language, such as from Spanish to English. The Facebook Translate feature works with written languages but not signed languages. A participant discussed how she set up a Facebook page for a weeklong retreat with participants from multiple countries. However, the differences in written language used among the countries prevented the successful use of the Facebook page:

> A lot of language translation. . . . For instance, at [the retreat] which takes place one week in England, five countries meet there and network. I set up a Facebook page after and people used it for a while before they stopped

using it. All of the people use different languages and it needs to be translated; we still try but sometimes the translation is a little off. (Kris)

Deaf people thus have figured out ways to use social media to their benefit, in both
written and signed languages, but particularly the latter, which gives them access
to information.

ACCESS TO INFORMATION AND TRANSMISSION OF INFORMATION

Some participants said that they felt that social media would benefit Deaf international individuals by providing visual access to information that has been traditionally in print. One participant remarked that a couple of Deaf Africans learned
about the concept of audism by watching Deaf people from the United States v-log
[video blog] feeds and making comments about them:

> Deaf people type on Facebook using English and make v-logs using ASL. . . .
> They go back and forth. . . . I see Deaf people learning a lot through the Inter-
> net, Facebook . . . word expression, meaning. . . . You know the word *audism*.
> I know some Deaf people in South Africa who never heard of it because our
> [American] books aren't sold over there. Now, on v-logs you can explain the
> meaning and the word can pop up on the screen while you sign. You can
> self-analyze. . . . Deaf people . . . learn from it. They see a key word and can
> learn the meaning. It's an educational tool. (Ashley)

Deaf people have access to information that is regulated and owned by the Deaf
community, regardless of what type of space:

> Social media with video feeds empowers Deaf people, so it is like Deaf-
> gain for Deaf people. We should take advantage of social media to spread
> knowledge and form collaboration for personal gain, community gain
> and international gain. (Jordan)

> Ownership—hearing people use their primary language to write books
> and blogs; Deaf use their primary language to create v-logs. I believe that
> we Deaf people should own that space. (Ashley)

According to Ashley and Jordan, Deaf people can create and own Deaf spaces in
terms of language use as they use signed languages to transmit information across
SNS and other online platforms. Participants discussed the existence of a certain
digital Deaf space that requires fluency in a particular sign language such as ASL
or International Sign, and they emphasized the importance for users to put some
effort into respecting the sign language space:

> Facebook . . . has Deaf space, but I called it ASL space, not just Deaf. ASL
> space has a lot of what anthropologists call the emic concept—insider
> group knowledge. Emic users—or Deaf sign language speakers—create

and post video clips talking about different things. There are people who complain that we are excluding hard of hearing or hearing people for not including captions. I know there are international video posts that are captioned, but some International Sign video posts do not have captions. People think we are excluding those who do not understand International Sign. I mean, what does this tell us about Deaf space in social media? How often do we see hearing space that is not accessible to us? We would say "Oh, well!" On the other hand, Deaf-to-Deaf, complaints about access— BLAH! So much to work to include captions. I just want to record myself signing and then fire it away in Facebook. Anyway we do have Deaf space, but ASL space is for those who use ASL. (Ashley)

Similarly, one participant talked about something he called "International Signs space":

[There] is what I call International Signs space. It does not have to be related to academics—it can be sports like Deaflympics that use the International Signs; WFD uses the International Signs as the communication of politics. They gather—and only those who know the International Signs are members of that Deaf International signs space. It does not require a membership card, but those who understand the International Signs can participate actively for exchange information. We do not intend to exclude specific groups—we are trying to create our own space. Those who want to join our space have to work hard to learn the International Signs. Otherwise, they exclude themselves from the space. Attitude! (Jordan)

In these sign language spaces, one has to be fluent in the used sign languages to understand their contents. Ashley comments on how hearing people do not make their digital spaces accessible to the Deaf community, yet ask that the digital Deaf spaces are made accessible for hearing people. Ashley and Jordan describe ASL space and International Sign space as precious spaces in which a particular language is used and where people do not want to be required to make their discourses accessible to people who do not know these languages.

Some participants observed that social media has become a tool for sharing information about Deaf community action and legislation. Participants stressed that SNS has provided them with the opportunity to do something when issues in the Deaf community require some sort of action. No longer does one need to meet at a Deaf club for community action, because Deaf people use social media to learn and communicate about plans for collective action. According to Whyte and Esposito (2011), *community accountability* is defined as when a community has an opinion regarding to a situation and then takes action upon that situation. We like this definition, although it was developed in relation to Deaf survivors of domestic violence and sexual assault, and we feel that it applies to community-based issues more broadly. Whyte and Esposito stressed that the Deaf community is tight-knit and sectarian and that any issue that affects the Deaf community would require

Deaf people to get involved collectively. Here, community accountability involves educating the Deaf community about an issue and how to respond collectively to that issue:

> On Facebook all the time, there are posts about movements, concerns, advocacy, lawsuits—or to fight for new laws. Activities are posted and people join or share their comments. I see it all the time. Almost every day. (Kris)

One participant emphasized that the Deaf community should take advantage of social media for knowledge diffusion and community collective action, and felt that the Deaf community underutilized the SNS space. However, another participant disagreed and said that the Deaf club has reacted to technology progress by changing its distribution method for club and community information; in response, however, this participant was concerned about Deaf people who do not have a computer or do not have access to the Internet:

> I would say about 40 percent [from this participant's experience] of the Deaf club members do not have computers. Ten percent of the Deaf club members do not have computers and do not have access to the Internet. It is like they are back to square one. We need to do something about them while the Internet is growing. (Adrian)

One example of community action that was very successful through the use of SNS was the information sharing and activism around the memorial service for Nelson Mandela in South Africa in 2013, which included a person impersonating a sign language interpreter. This participant spread the word about the travesty by communicating about this event with local media outlets:

> Deaf people used social media to collect actual information about the South African interpreter and communicate them to their Deaf communities and to national and local media companies and newspapers. (Ashley)

Another participant mentioned that Deaf social media users awaiting court rulings or new legislations on Deaf-related issues would publicize outcomes and promote community involvement in dialogue and demand for changes.

One participant believed the Deaf community in the United States and international Deaf communities could learn from each other when it comes to legislation and litigation:

> They [the National Association for the Deaf] advocated permitting Deaf people [to] drive commercial trucks. New celebrations. They posted about that. . . . It's a long time coming. It's a life struggle. I hope that people from other countries monitor our progress. Again, I don't like to say that we are the leader, but quite often we are the leader for Deaf rights. Certainly not

in all areas in terms of Deaf rights, but some for sure. So I hope that helps them to be inspired to lobby for Deaf rights in their country (better rights, better education) to see what is possible. (Kris)

This participant went on to discuss lessons learned from other countries:

We learned from them too. Deaf education from several countries is supposed to be very good. Like what are their requirements for sign languages, medical care, which we certainly learned from them. (Kris)

Deaf-related information was not the only topic that was shared with other countries; topics also involved non-Deaf current events. For example, with recent media attention in fall 2014 on Ebola in Africa and confusion about what Ebola is, a participant benefitted from watching a Deaf African's video explaining his experience with Ebola:

He started to explain about his country and what was happening there. It seemed to alleviate some fears and concerns. It was shared through people. (Kris)

Although social media tools are advantageous for the Deaf community, it is important for the community to provide information through sign language and/or text.

Globalization of Personal Space

Balisacan (2008, 67) provided a concept of how personal space has changed with the advent of SNS and resulted in "technological globalization." He stated that "the delimitation of the right to privacy has undergone a contextual shift from the contained, domestic context of old to the diffused, information civilization context of today" (Balisacan 2007, 67).

As an expansion of Balisacan's discussion of technological globalization, we define the globalization of personal space as a change in the imaginary boundary surrounding a person. This boundary is now expandable as the person makes decisions about being public and reachable in social media. Participants reported that their personal space became globalized as they connected to their international friends through SNS:

When a Deaf speaker at a Deaf school or a Deaf club has something to say to me, the speaker would stand up and point at me with "you!" and the people in the room would look at me. Now in social media, a Deaf speaker can easily say the same thing on the feed and everyone who is on my list and the Deaf speaker's list would look at me. It is like my personal boundary has grown from the small ground up to the larger digital world. (Ashley)

Ashley and Jordan discussed how in such a globalized context accountability for one's own actions is inevitable:

> My personal space is no longer hidden. I became visible when I participate in social media. I have to become more accountable with what I share in social media, because it is a digital space where everyone can see me, my thoughts, and my life. (Ashley)

> When I started Facebook, I screened friend requests carefully based on personal relationships. But I realized that it was not what I wanted and I decided to accept all friend requests, no matter what. There are many international Deaf people whom I met once or twice, but we become Facebook friends. I would not post any messages that are inappropriate on my Facebook. (Jordan)

Some participants felt that social media removed international boundaries or at least made it easier to cross such boundaries: "Deaf people [in the United States] do not feel there is a boundary between the United States and international countries" (Ashley).

One participant reported that the United States is isolated in nature with two large oceans on each end but felt that social media allowed Deaf individuals learn more about Deaf people and communities beyond the ocean: "I showed my Deaf international friends' video feed to my class, so they can learn more about the . . . sign language and some issues in the Deaf community in that country" (Mackenzie).

A participant recognized the significant reduction of time response when a person from Asia responded to a v-log feed within a few minutes of posting. She noted that this would never happen twenty years ago and is an example of space-time compression.

Social media was also used to keep up to date with international Deaf organizations: "I followed events leading up to upcoming conferences, such as Deaf Academics and the World Federation of the Deaf" (Jordan).

At the same time, some participants felt that because of (1) language barriers, (2) elitism within the Deaf community, and (3) difference in academic proficiencies that international boundaries were clearly in place. Indeed, Riley reveals such elitism: "I only interact with those who are able to communicate intelligibly. I do not interact with those who did not have education, because we do not have much to talk about" (Riley).

The purpose of social media is to make connections by providing tools for users to move out of their physical comfort zone and share their thoughts, experiences, and the like. For some users, their level of engagement becomes global. Self-control regulates their decisions to go local, regional, national, or international.

DISCUSSION AND IMPLICATIONS

The participants recognized the power of social media. Deaf participants use it to interact with other Deaf people, to have a connection, and to learn new information about the Deaf World and the world in general. The findings show the significance of social media for maintaining connections not only with Deaf individuals from the United States but also with international Deaf connections, hence reinforcing the notion of international digital Deaf space. SNS, such as Facebook, Twitter, and Instagram, allow Deaf people to connect with one another, regardless of geographical limitations, although we do not know the intensity of such connections and how those outside our very small and well-educated study sample experience them. Social media has given well-educated Deaf people the opportunity to create and maintain communities online, using their shared experiences. There is an interactional overlap between SNS and Deaf spaces: Deaf people create spaces in the SNS realm and move in and out of that realm.

Deaf people often use their smart phones when they are the only Deaf people in the physical space. For example, when Deaf people are waiting in an area full of nonsigners, they may use a smartphone to seek out interaction with other Deaf people via the use of Glide, Facebook, or another type of social media. Some may choose to e-mail or text. A participant commented: "My smartphone is my DEAF space. I go there every time I see hearing people talking to each other in the room" (Ashley). This quote shows the power of smartphones as Deaf spaces for Deaf people who are in mainstreamed environments. We thus argue that Deaf spaces permit Deaf people to interact within physical and nonphysical spheres and that the presence or use of sign language is not necessarily prerequisite for Deaf space to emerge, as our data show that Deaf people also use text for communication on SNS. The critical point here is that a Deaf space is defined by the action by a Deaf person in seeking a DEAF+SAME space, whether that is through written or signed languages. Deaf people are encouraged to establish community-based dialogue about the creation, ownership, and participation of Deaf spaces in SNS in relation to language accessibility, community accountability, and technology access that were raised in this study.

REFERENCES

Alexa. 2014. "Top Sites in United States." Accessed June 10, 2014. http://www.alexa.com/topsites/countries/US.

Balisacan, R. H. C. 2008. "Claiming Personal Space in a Globalized World: Contextual and Paradigm Shifts in the Delimitation of the Right to Privacy."*Philippine Law Journal* 82:67–87.

Correa, T., A. M. Hinsley, and H. G. de Zuniga. 2010. "Who Interacts on the Web? The Intersection of Users' Personality and Social Media Use." *Computers in Human Behavior* 28 (2): 247–53.

Cuculick, J. 2014. "Facebooking among Deaf College Students: Deaf-gain and Funds of Knowledge." PhD diss., University of Rochester.

Facebook. 2014. "About Facebook." Accessed November 11, 2014. https://docs.google.com/document/d/11Q65oQeSPfBXioSBwWWtmLByKX3Wb2A9NrWKVIwmQ0k/edit.

Friedner, M. I., and A. Kusters. 2014. "On the Possibilities and Limits of 'DEAF DEAF SAME': Tourism and Empowerment Camps in Adamorobe (Ghana), Bangalore, and Mumbai (India)."*Disability Studies Quarterly* 34 (3). http://dsq-sds.org/article/view/4246/3649.

Gulliver, M. S. 2009. "DEAF Space, a History: The Production of DEAF Spaces Emergent, Autonomous, Located, and Disabled in Eighteenth- and Nineteenth-Century France." PhD dissertation, University of Bristol, Bristol, UK.

————. n.d. "deaf Space." Available at http://mikegulliver.com/research/ (accessed November 1, 2014).

Hanna, R., A. Rohm, and V. L. Crittenden. 2011. "We're All Connected: The Power of the Social Media Ecosystem." *Business Horizons* 54 (3): 265–73.

Holcomb, T. K. 1997. "Development of Deaf Bicultural Identity."*American Annals of the Deaf* 142 (2): 89–93.

Murray, J. J. 2007. "'One Touch of Nature Makes the Whole World Kin': The Transnational Lives of Deaf Americans, 1870–1924." PhD diss., University of Iowa.

Padden, C., and T. Humphries. 2006. *Inside Deaf Culture*. Cambridge, MA: Harvard University Press.

Pew Research Internet Project. 2013. "Social Media Update 2013." Accessed June 10, 2014. http://www.pewinternet.org/2013/12/30/social-media-update-2013.

Solvang, P. K., and H. Haualand. 2014. "Accessibility and Diversity: Deaf Space in Action." *Scandinavian Journal of Disability Research* 16 (1): 1–13.

Valentine, G., and T. Skelton. 2008. "Changing Spaces: The Role of the Internet in Shaping Deaf Geographies."*Social and Cultural Geography* 9 (5): 469–85.

————. 2009. "'An Umbilical Cord to the World': The Role of the Internet in D/deaf people's Information and Communication Practices."*Information, Communication and Society* 12 (1): 44–65.

Whyte, A. K., and E. Esposito. 2011, Fall. "Deaf Community Accountability Model." *Voice: A Journal of the Battered Women's Movement* 24–29. https://www.academia.edu/11849938/Deaf_Community_Accountability_Model.

Part 5

∎ Visions

20 Deaf International Development Practitioners and Researchers Working Effectively in Deaf Communities

Arlinda S. Boland, Amy T. Wilson,
and Rowena E. Winiarczyk

One afternoon at Gallaudet University, as the three of us shared our stories about working overseas, Rowena and Arlinda talked about gathering data in Deaf communities. Upon meeting Deaf people, they both had discovered an instantaneous "Deaf connection" where people insisted, "You Deaf. Me Deaf. Same-same." To the delight of both, this initial Deaf bond facilitated the cooperation of and collaboration with Deaf stakeholders and made data collection a breeze. Yet, within a short period of time, Rowena and Arlinda both felt that the DEAF DEAF SAME phenomena caused Deaf stakeholders to relate a bit too familiarly.

Amy, a hearing researcher, shared a story about how she had just finished two years living in a South American country, working with Deaf communities, when she felt she was finally prepared to host a young Deaf American woman who planned to volunteer at the local Deaf association in her neighborhood. It had taken Amy more than a year and a half to feel comfortable using the spoken language and signing the native sign language, to learn the hearing and Deaf cultures, and for the Deaf community to learn to trust her. The second evening after her arrival in the country, Amy brought her new Deaf protégé to a Deaf association meeting and then did not see her again for a week! Amy exaggerated when she told that story, but her point was that she was shocked at how easily the Deaf community embraced the Deaf American visitor, who was quickly swept into the local Deaf community, while the community had been much slower in trusting Amy, a hearing person.

Amy also shared how when she worked overseas in countries that use American Sign Language (ASL) or a local sign language heavily influenced by ASL, Deaf adults were excited to meet a hearing person who could communicate with them and with hearing people in their community. Very often during her work, Deaf people and their friends and family ask her to interpret despite the fact she has no interpreter training and easily admits her lack of interpreting skills and unease at the requests. Additionally, although Amy requested the presence of professional interpreters to communicate with Deaf stakeholders during her work, cooperating agencies and the Deaf stakeholders decided she knew "enough sign" to do trainings or gather information for evaluation or research on her own.

Through our work and research in the field of international development, we encountered numerous situations, such as these examples, where the swift connection because of DEAF DEAF SAME (or, in Amy's case, a shared sign language), if left unexamined, could interfere with the data we collect, the validity of our findings, and the effectiveness of our collaborative efforts. The three of us were happy to have the opportunity to write this chapter to examine how we work overseas in Deaf communities and to consider the DEAF DEAF SAME phenomena by sharing our experiences. Rowena and Arlinda have been especially interested in examining the roles and responsibilities of the Deaf development worker conducting evaluations and research and have found it productive to discuss these things with Amy. Our casual conversations have led us to reflect on how we might have responded differently in circumstances such as where we were not sure if "being Deaf" and/or fluency of sign language did or did not affect the outcomes of the work. In this chapter we share dilemmas we faced when doing development work in Deaf communities outside of our own cultures and countries.

OUR BACKGROUNDS

The three authors of this chapter met through Gallaudet's international development graduate program. Arlinda and Rowena graduated with master's degrees in international development, and Amy was their professor and advisor. Arlinda, a Deaf woman whose native language is ASL, comes from a fourth-generation Deaf family. Her life is centered in American Deaf culture and she is a member of the Deaf community in the Washington, DC metropolitan area. Arlinda interned with Mobility International USA (MIUSA), assisting them with various projects designed and managed by disability organizations in South America and Africa. She also has traveled extensively and in 2013 completed research for her master's thesis with Amy as her advisor. Arlinda currently works as project manager for the Deaf Community Development project under Deaf Development Programme in Cambodia.

Rowena is also Deaf and was raised in the Deaf grassroots[1] community in Ottawa, Canada, with ASL as her native language. She currently works in Gallaudet University's office of Research Support and International Affairs, and her international work includes project coordination, advocacy, and research and evaluation in several countries including Panama, Malaysia, Vietnam, Chile, and Argentina.

---

[1] The middle-class and working-class Deaf community.

Rowena assisted a nongovernmental organization (NGO) in securing a grant for a project in Nepal and gathered data about persons with disabilities in China and Tibet to ensure their inclusion in educational programs. Amy was Rowena's thesis advisor as well, and since she graduated in 2010, the two of them have collaborated on several projects.

Amy is hearing and developed Gallaudet's master's degree in international development in 2007 after living overseas in developing countries and noting the poor assistance deaf people received from American development assistance and faith-based organizations. Amy teaches students how to implement policies and practices inclusive of deaf persons within (federal, NGO, and faith-based) development assistance organizations and include Deaf people in programs and projects overseas. She conducts research and teaches through a transformative lens in which the political, social, and development issues of being Deaf are continually considered as graduates work with Deaf people in attaining their human rights. Amy advises international development organizations and agencies about the inclusiveness of their programs and their effectiveness in collaborating with various Deaf and disability communities.

INTERNATIONAL DEVELOPMENT WORK AND RESEARCH

Our work in international development focuses on serving Deaf people in economically poor countries by implementing long-term sustainable solutions to barriers they face in areas such as education, employment, social services, or access to their native sign language in courts, hospitals, and schools. The work is as diverse as the needs of Deaf people around the world. We have helped design and evaluate projects and programs targeted for Deaf populations, carried out national and local research ascertaining the needs of the Deaf community, sought funding for nongovernmental organizations of and for Deaf people, and led trainings on capacity building, Deaf awareness, and training of trainers on various topics.

We have frequently been unsettled when seeing development work overseas intended to benefit Deaf people. Both short- and long-term development assistance, such as Deaf education programs or the development of sign language materials, are often managed by well-meaning, but untrained hearing northerners who communicate poorly in sign language. When local Deaf people are uninvolved (other than as beneficiaries), "assistance" projects can morph into charity projects in which empowerment fades, leading to dependency on foreigners and projects that crumble and die. Charity has its time and place, such as during natural disasters or famine. However, we believe that true sustainable development work does not come from the assumption that Deaf people should be pitied, cared for or seen as having a problem needing to be fixed but as people who, once acquiring the necessary knowledge and material resources, are capable of leading full, independent lives.

A significant amount of development work leaves Deaf beneficiaries unsatisfied because assistance has been designed and managed by foreigners with little input from the Deaf community (Wilson 2005; Wilson and Kakiri 2010; Wilson and Winiarczyk 2014; Friedner and Kusters 2014; VanGilder, this volume). In a West

African country,[2] Amy observed how the Deaf association hesitated to set their annual goals without the blessing of the American donor and would adjust the goals if told. In another setting, local Deaf leaders in South America shared with Amy that they (or other Deaf people) were not included in the design phase of a project designed to work with Deaf children.

When Amy was evaluating a school for Deaf children in Eastern Europe for the United States Agency of International Development (USAID), Amy asked that all of the stakeholders contribute to the design of the evaluation and interview protocol and be interviewed to gather data about the effectiveness of the Deaf education program. Amy included the principal of the school, the hearing and deaf teachers, the teachers' aides, parents, and deaf graduates of the school as stakeholders. The administrators were hesitant to cooperate as they believed that they and the hearing teachers were the sole experts. The administrators were confused as to why Amy included Deaf teacher aides, Deaf parents, and Deaf community members. In this example, inequalities were brought to light that would have remained hidden if Deaf people had not been included in the survey and interviews. Amy and her team learned that school meetings were not interpreted and Deaf parents were not given an interpreter when communicating with teachers about their Deaf child.

We work in a human rights framework: all stakeholders own the research; it is not left in only the hands of those in power. All parties, not just those in management or budgetary positions, own the reports we generate. The parents of the Deaf children, for example, could become change agents and use the data to advocate for their children's rights to a quality education. Sustainable development of projects and programs occurs when administrators, teachers, parents, and the Deaf community all possess the same knowledge and work toward the same goals. Therefore, we always include Deaf participants in our development projects, reviews, evaluations, trainings, and other work that is for or about them.

Unfortunately we know of very few academically trained development practitioners from the global North, hearing or deaf, who work in Deaf communities. There is also scarce literature exploring the activities of hearing or Deaf development practitioners who are involved in Deaf communities and working in the global South. Therefore, our overseas research focus has gravitated toward discovering best practices for those working in government, nongovernmental, and faith-based organizations to include Deaf people in the design, implementation, monitoring, and evaluation of projects and programs to best meet the needs of Deaf communities.

Discussions by academics concerning the participation of Deaf people in research studies about Deaf people (Baker-Shenk and Kyle 1990; Harris, Holmes, and Mertens 2009; Pollard 1992; Singleton et al. 2014) resemble our conversations about the inclusion of Deaf people in the design and evaluation of development assistance projects. At times, during research studies, Deaf people felt pitied or felt as if they were the "token Deaf person" used by the hearing scientific community (Baker-Shenk and Kyle 1990: Harris et al. 2009; Pollard 1992; Singleton et al. 2014). Although some researchers involved Deaf people by having them film, conduct, or transcribe interviews, they were not included in the critical tasks of analyzing

---

[2] We avoid specifically naming many of the countries as this would jeopardize the confidentiality we have promised participants.

the data or making meaning from it. Some Deaf researchers believe research should be "Deaf led," whereas others write that collaboration would suffice if the Deaf people were included in all aspects of the study (Ladd 2003; Hochgesang et al. 2010; Ladd and Lane 2013; Singleton, Jones, and Hanumantha 2014). We contribute to these bodies of research by discussing benefits and challenges of DEAF DEAF SAME connections in research.

Benefits of deaf deaf same Encountered by Deaf Researchers

It would seem that employing a Deaf development practitioner to work within a signing Deaf community would be advantageous for many reasons. The feelings of DEAF DEAF SAME create bonds because Deaf people around the world share similar experiences of negotiating their position in hearing societies. The Deaf stakeholders might be more comfortable with another Deaf person, even a researcher or worker from a different country. Even if the Deaf development practitioner is not specifically doing capacity-building or advocacy training, just their presence in the Deaf community and the connection of DEAF DEAF SAME could encourage Deaf people in economically poor countries to advocate for their rights. Indeed, deaf people may regard this foreign deaf person as a role model and see that it is possible for Deaf people to improve their position in society as well as change negative attitudes and stigma toward deaf people. Indeed, Deaf people are more likely to stimulate the process of including Deaf people in the development assistance or research process so that they would be able to gain ownership of their work or simply share their voices.

The Deaf development practitioner may find it easy to communicate during interactions with Deaf members of the community. When possible, Arlinda and Rowena learned the local sign languages to ensure ease of communication and to be part of the local deaf communities as they worked alongside them. When embarking on research in an African country, Arlinda started to learn the local sign language two months prior. In addition, when Arlinda started her research, there was a local deaf school in the area that had previously used ASL to teach deaf children. Local deaf people still remembered ASL so it was used as a bridge for her to learn the local sign language. Moreover, she went to several local deaf associations to introduce herself and to explain her research to local deaf members as well as to network with other Deaf community members.

Rowena attended a sign language class prior to conducting a needs assessment in a Deaf community in Southeast Asia to improve her communication during casual settings and she also worked with a well-respected hearing research facilitator who facilitated communication between Rowena and the research participants during research activities. Rowena's other research activities in Southeast Asia and South America were framed within a strict timeline, which meant she did not have time to learn the local sign language. Therefore, she worked with a local deaf interpreter, who interpreted between ASL and the country's native sign language, and a spoken language. Rowena collaborated with those interpreters a few months prior to implementing research activities so they were familiar with Rowena's signing style and research questions. This process of working with interpreters was lengthy and challenging but effective in the terms of communicating with research participants. This also allowed hearing research participants to recognize the necessity of having both deaf and hearing interpreters onboard (also see Green, this volume). At the first research meeting, the communication flow was a bit challenging but with time it improved dramatically. The Deaf interpreter also was able to gain employment and experience through this opportunity.

The social stratification in many communities worldwide means Deaf people must overcome numerous obstacles to achieve their goals. Deaf development practitioners, because of their own lived personal experience, may be less inclined to overlook the participation of Deaf people who do not actively participate in the Deaf community. For example, Rowena and Arlinda's parents, all deaf, grew up in a generation without social media technologies, when Deaf people could not easily communicate with one another. Deaf people would often select a date, a time, and a place to meet weekly, such as at a Deaf association or Deaf sport meeting, to catch up on the latest news, share information, and advocate for their community's needs.

Rowena and Arlinda's knowledge of their parents' histories affects their work overseas. They know that today in many developing countries, Deaf people often rely on schedules rather than technology to meet one another. They know that today in some countries, just as it had been in the United States and Canada, some deaf children and adults remain isolated because of their distant proximity to urban areas and may have limited or no contact with the closest Deaf community. Deaf people may not come to local deaf events because they are unaware of these events. Deaf people or their families may not be aware of the services and education designed to work with Deaf children and/or adults, and some parents may keep their Deaf children at home.

Rowena and Arlinda also found that having connections in the global Deaf community is advantageous to network before, during, and after their work in another country. Arlinda knew some people in the United States who had connections to Deaf people in Africa. This social networking based on the feelings of DEAF DEAF SAME allowed Arlinda to develop connections with African Deaf people through mutual friends even before she arrived in the country. The hearing research organization where Arlinda interned in Africa was only aware of one local deaf association. By networking with local deaf people in the country, Arlinda discovered there were additional deaf associations. Similarly, in Southeast Asia, Rowena learned that Deaf women were not active participants of their Deaf association's board because of household and/or work-related obligations. Rowena's ability to communicate with Deaf leaders allowed her to use the social network of deaf women in one Deaf community to participate in a needs assessment.

CHALLENGES OF DEAF DEAF SAME ENCOUNTERED BY DEAF RESEARCHERS

Deaf development practitioners working in Deaf communities in other countries experiencing the feelings of DEAF DEAF SAME may find their research is at risk of being compromised. The influence of allowing "sameness" to unconsciously creep in may affect how they ask questions or how they analyze and interpret the data. As development practitioners who do research with Deaf communities, we want participants to respond to questions as honestly and as accurately as possible. We wondered if *how* Deaf practitioners questioned deaf people interfered with the integrity of their data. Did the feelings of DEAF DEAF SAME influence questioning techniques when a Deaf practitioner offers examples or clarifications that are too leading based on his/her own life experiences?

During an interview in South America, a man talked about his challenge of finding a job. Hypothetically speaking, Rowena, based on her own personal experience, could have thought he meant that it is a challenge because he is Deaf. However, this man could have meant that he has difficulties finding a job because of the economic situation in his country (and it could have nothing to do with him being deaf). In a case like this, with more conversation, Rowena would need to determine if she had understood the man's response through her own Deaf experience or through that man's native Deaf experience The feelings of DEAF DEAF SAME could lead development practitioners to unintentionally impose their (Western) Deaf perceptions and presumptions onto the Deaf communities in the global South without attempting to understand local dynamics as well as cultural and religious traditions (VanGilder, this volume).

Another example is a group interview in Southeast Asia, in which Rowena observed a few rural Deaf participants asking for clarification to questions such as "What kind of challenges do you face?" The Deaf participants were given (suggestive) examples of challenges based on the Deaf practitioner's experience, which created unnatural or triggered responses to the question. The participants' challenges may be different from the Deaf practitioner's experiences. Instead of suggesting a challenge from his or her home context, the Deaf practitioner should be prepared to give out examples unique to the Deaf participants' situation. Hence, after spending two months in Africa, Arlinda changed her previously prepared interview questions to be more specific, reflecting the feedback she received and observations she made about local deaf peoples' context and the availability of social services.

This is reminiscent of Friedner and Kusters's (2014) discussion of an American/Indian Deaf youth camp in which American delegates did not allow the Indian delegates to come up with problems that reflected their experiences nor did they factor in the difference between American and Indian cultures. In the end, the Indians delegates "parroted" the problems from the American delegates. These situations are good examples of bringing bias into the field and affecting the quality of data collection (and interventions).

Another challenge related to DEAF DEAF SAME was that Arlinda and Rowena were invited to social events by their Deaf research participants; while they valued these networking opportunities, they also felt that it was important for the community to be aware of the possibility of them sharing information from these social events in reports or published articles. Deaf participants could tell them if they preferred them not to document any observations from these settings. This is an important consideration in terms of confidentiality and anonymity because local deaf communities tend to be closely knit and it may be easy for local deaf people to identify who was part of the research process.

DEAF DEAF SAME: EXPECTATIONS AND ASSUMPTIONS BY RESEARCH PARTICIPANTS

During their research and development work, Arlinda and Rowena found that the local Deaf communities assumed that northerners possess a wealth of information and material resources, which they were expected to share. We wondered if these requests occurred because of DEAF DEAF SAME: perhaps the research participants felt safe or at ease with us and so they made these assumptions and expectations?

We also considered the role of our relatively privileged backgrounds (with regard to citizenship and education) in comparison to their own, and the practitioner and participant power-differential (which also could be true for a hearing researcher).

For instance, in recruiting participants in Africa for research focusing on deaf people's experience in accessing HIV/AIDS services, Arlinda faced the challenge of how and when to respond to requests for information about Gallaudet University. The local Deaf community assumed Arlinda could answer their questions about the Nippon Foundation's World Deaf Leadership scholarship program because she was a graduate student at Gallaudet University. They expressed disappointment that Arlinda was unable to answer their questions because she was not familiar with the application process (including reasons why applications were rejected) arguing that YOU DEAF ME DEAF, WE SAME should lead to sharing such information.

In addition, when Arlinda attended several deaf events, she was pulled aside and privately asked for information about HIV/AIDS and repeatedly asked to give presentations about HIV/AIDS at a local deaf school even though she stated many times that she was not an expert on the topic and was there to ask about their experiences with and access to HIV/AIDS services. In another instance, Arlinda was conducting an interview with one Deaf participant and when she was done, the Deaf participant took out a brown bag filled with bottles of pills. The participant asked Arlinda to explain what each medicine did and how to take the pills properly. Assumptions of the Deaf participants put Arlinda in the roles of social worker, doctor, and health worker rather than as a researcher. When Arlinda explained that the focus of her research was about Deaf people's experience of accessing HIV/AIDS services, they were befuddled.

IS IT REALLY ALL ABOUT DEAF DEAF SAME?

Yet, is it DEAF DEAF SAME that leads Deaf participants to respond to Deaf development practitioners differently than they would to a hearing development practitioner who can sign? For instance, although Amy is hearing, she reports that because she is able to use a common sign language with Deaf participants, she too is asked for information about Deaf people in the United States, or for health or legal information, or to give gifts. In these cases, DEAF DEAF SAME is not as important as "language same," and the fact that the researcher is hearing loses significance. It may be important not whether Amy is deaf or hearing but that the research participants can communicate with her in sign language.

Ladd (2003, 104) wrote that research about Deaf people should be centered in the sign language community because it represents a "collectivist culture in which participants are bound to one another through common cultural traditions, beliefs, actions and responsibilities—both personal and communal." We agree with Ladd that it is valuable to include local deaf communities, but to exclude hearing researchers who sign well and work and/or live in Deaf communities may be an error. For instance, when Amy and a Deaf male colleague were interviewing deaf people about their experiences of an advocacy training program, one deaf female participant said she preferred that Amy interview her as she was more comfortable being interviewed by a hearing foreign woman than a local Deaf man. As mentioned previously, we do need to be cognizant that when hearing and Deaf practitioners work together, there has traditionally been a power imbalance. Awareness of this is important to ensure that both hearing and deaf practitioners are equal in their work. By working together, they could contribute valuable insights that might not be possible separately.

Conclusion

We have addressed the challenges of DEAF DEAF SAME in the process of doing research. We have examined the feelings of "sameness" that enables Deaf development practitioners to connect with local deaf communities. The discussion of our experiences in conducting research studies may help Deaf development practitioners to be cautious when doing research using the feelings of DEAF DEAF SAME, by being conscious of the subtle differences in cultures, power differentials between the researcher and interviewees, and the temptation to fall into the delusion of "we are DEAF DEAF SAME." Moreover, we stress the importance of including all stakeholders (both deaf and hearing) in the research study, and we point out that it is important to assure that hearing researchers and/or sign language interpreters possess maximum signing language skills to facilitate effective communication. We also stress the importance of using a human rights framework when doing research with Deaf communities. In addition, it is important to include Deaf interpreters in the research process because deaf interpreters are fluent in local sign languages, and this could lead to an opportunity for deaf interpreters to become both valued in the community and gainfully employed. Of course, the existence of deaf interpreters helps to facilitate communication for all parties involved while conducting research.

Finally, although we know we are not experts on the situation of Deaf people in economically less developed countries, we do believe that when we conduct research, evaluate programs, and seek out information about local contexts, our training at Gallaudet, our personal experiences, and our connections in the global Deaf community do increase our ability to obtain information and knowledge. The three of us look forward to the day when there are more educated Deaf development practitioners and researchers working in Deaf communities overseas.

References

Baker-Shenk, C., and J. Kyle. 1990. "Research with Deaf People: Issues and Conflicts." *Disability, Handicap and Society* 5:65–75.

Batterbury, S. C. E., P. Ladd, and M. Gulliver. 2007. "Sign Language Peoples as Indigenous Minorities: Implications for Research and Policy."*Environment and Planning A* 39 (12): 2899–915.

Friedner, M., and A. Kusters. 2014. "On the Possibilities and Limits of 'DEAF DEAF SAME': Tourism and Empowerment Camps in Adamorobe (Ghana), Bangalore, and Mumbai (India)."*Disability Studies Quarterly* 34 (3). http://dsq-sds.org/article/view/4246/3649.

Harris, R., H. Holmes, and D. Mertens. 2009. "Research Ethics in Sign Language Communities." *Sign Language Studies* 9 (2): 104–31.

Hochgesang, J. A., Pascual Villanueva, G. Mathur, and D. Lillo-Martin. 2010. "Building a Database while Considering Research Ethics in Sign Language Communities."

In *Proceedings of the Fourth Workshop on the Representation and Processing of Sign Languages: Corpora and Sign Language Technologies*, 112–16. LREC, Malta. Accessed June 23, 2015. http://www.juliehochgesang.com/?page_id=557.

Kusters, A. 2012. "Being a Deaf White Anthropologist in Adamorobe: Some Ethical and Methodological Issues." In *Village Sign Languages: Anthropological and Linguistic Insights*, edited by U. Zeshan and C. De Vos, 27–52. Nijmegen, the Netherlands: Ishara Press.

Ladd, P. 2003. *Understanding Deaf Culture: In Search of Deafhood*. Clevedon, UK: Multilingual Matters.

Ladd, P., and H. Lane. 2013. "Deaf Ethnicity, Deafhood, and Their Relationship."*Sign Language Studies* 13 (4): 565–79.

Mertens, D. 2007. "Transformative Paradigm: Mixed Methods and Social Justice."*Journal of Mixed Methods Research* 1 (3): 212–25.

Pollard R. 1992. "Cross-Cultural Ethics in the Conduct of Deafness Research." *Rehabilitation Psychology* 37:87–101.

Singleton, J., G. Jones, and S. Hanumantha. 2014. "Toward Ethical Research Practice with Deaf Participants." *Journal of Empirical Research on Human Research Ethics* 9 (3): 59–66.

Wilson, A. 2005. "Studying the Effectiveness of International Development Assistance from American Organizations to Deaf Communities." *American Annals of the Deaf* 150:292–304.

Wilson, A., and N. Kakiri. 2010. "Best Practice for Collaborating with Deaf Communities in Developing Countries." In *Deaf around the World: The Impact of Language*, edited by D. Napoli and G. Mathur, 271–86. New York: Oxford University Press.

Wilson, A., and R. Winiarczyk. 2014. "Mixed Methods Research Strategies with Deaf People." *Journal of Mixed Methods Research* 8:266–77.

21 Changing the World (or Not): Reflecting on Interactions in the Global South during the Frontrunners Program

*Annelies Kusters, Outi Toura-Jensen,
Filip Verhelst, and Ole Vestergaard*

This chapter is based upon a conversation with Outi Toura-Jensen, Filip Ver-helst, and Ole Vestergaard, deaf teachers in the well-known and influential Den-mark-based Frontrunners program (http://frontrunners.dk), an international deaf youth leadership training program (though its focus has recently changed and it is now a deaf international education program). The idea for Frontrunners came from a think tank in which Danish deaf youth participated and the initial goal of the program was to educate deaf participants to be leaders, lobbyists and activists in order to create a better world for deaf people (hence the name "Frontrunners"). The slogan during its early iterations was "Wanna change the world?!"

Each Frontrunners program lasts nine months, from September to May each year, accepts deaf youth between the ages of eighteen and thirty from all over the world, and is taught in International Sign (IS). The first program was conducted in 2005–2006, and annual groups are named Frontrunners 1, Frontrunners 2, and so on. At the time of the interview (September 2013), the program was in its ninth iteration (Frontrunners 9). Frontrunners takes place in Castberggård (http://www.cbg.dk), an institution for deaf students located in a remote rural area in Denmark. The program includes two classroom components (module 1, from September to December, and module 3, from the middle of February to the middle of May) and an applied component (module 2, from the middle of December to the middle of February). In the classroom (modules 1 and 3), participants learn about deaf-related themes and concepts (such as Deafhood, audism, deaf history, deaf art), (signed) language and communication, bilingualism, media, leadership, team-work, project management, and social entrepreneurship (see http://frontrunners.dk/curriculum/). In the applied component (module 2), participants are expected to devise a short (one- or two-month-long) project to put theory into practice in either their home country or a foreign country.

The Frontrunners program is international in five different aspects, which makes it interesting to consider in the framework of this book. First, the participants come to Denmark from all over the world. Most come from European countries, but deaf youth from the USA, Canada, Australia, and countries in the global South such as Ghana, Mongolia, India, South Korea, Hong Kong, and Chile have participated. Second, during modules 1 and 3, one or more educational trips are organized, often to another European country such as Germany or Belgium. Third, during module 2, participants often visit other countries to do an internship in which they apply the theories they have learned. Fourth, about once a week, a deaf guest lecturer visits the Frontrunners classroom and teaches for one or two days. Over the first nine years, ninety-five different deaf guest lecturers from a range of (mainly European) countries have visited the course. Fifth, the three permanent deaf staff are from different international backgrounds: Ole, a Danish man in his fifties, initiated the program and has experience as an administrator and teacher in Castberggård; Filip, a Belgian former teacher in his thirties, participated in Frontrunners 1; and Outi, a Finnish woman in her thirties, is an education specialist.

The number of participants in the Frontrunners course differs every year and has ranged between nine and nineteen participants. Only the classroom/residential components (modules 1 and 3) are included in the fee of around 8600 euros; thus participants themselves decide how much to spend in module 2. A number of participants obtain sponsorship. In their application, potential participants must include a video in which they explain who they are and why they would like to attend Frontrunners, and an online interview is conducted. When evaluating the applications, the teachers look for motivation, signs of ability to learn and reflect, and signs of capability to operate in a team. A maximum of two people from the same country are accepted in each group. Each Frontrunners group had its own website (http://frontrunners.dk/) on which participants posted pictures and movies in International Sign about what they have learned and experienced.

The Frontrunners course has grown into a place where deaf people can learn what it means to be deaf and to look at themselves in a group context, while leaving everything else aside. This is a particularly powerful space of opportunity for deaf youth in the current (European) climate, with the closing of deaf schools and diminishing popularity of deaf clubs: it is increasingly difficult to find places where deaf people gather frequently in a structured environment. Metaphors the teachers used to describe the Frontrunners program included "a mirror," "an energy center," and an "an injection." Hence, throughout the years, particularly during and after Frontrunners 5, the program aim has shifted and the curriculum has broadened. The emphasis on leadership did not disappear but has lightened, and there is a growing focus on sign language work in the curriculum. The slogan "wanna change the world?!" has been discarded, because (particularly in the first years of the program) it put a lot of pressure on former Frontrunners. As Ole commented: "the name [Frontrunners] was an aim, and now it's just a name to us."

Parallel to this shift was a shift in the backgrounds of international deaf guest speakers: in the beginning, people with high status were invited, such as Markku Jokinen, the then president of the World Federation of the Deaf (WFD). Now, guest lecturers have more practical experience working directly with people on the ground and they are closer in age to Frontrunners. Former Frontrunners are invited as guest teachers also, to reflect on whether the theories they were taught earlier have worked for them. From Frontrunners 11 onwards (2015–2016), a new shift is planned: the program is now called a deaf international education program rather than a leadership program; Frontrunners can get European Credit Transfer and Accumulation System (ECTS) credits when they attend, and can opt for choosing only the first module (focused on culture) or third module (focused on language) (see http://frontrunners.dk/curriculum/). The new slogan is "We exist, we believe, we do."

In module 2, the Frontrunners participants are responsible for developing a project and making contact with stakeholders in the country they want to visit. During the past few years, the majority of the participants have gone to a southern country, alone or with a few other Frontrunners. Some have traveled to countries such as Nepal, India, Chile, and Ghana, where they organized "awareness programs" in which the concepts taught in the Frontrunners course are transmitted, such as leadership, human rights, audism, Deafhood, and empowerment. Others have organized theater training, volunteered in deaf youth associations, or made documentaries. Just like the general curriculum, the aim of the projects in module 2 has shifted over time, for reasons discussed in this chapter. A turning point for Frontrunners took place in its sixth year, when a five-week stay in Ghana was part of the curriculum. This trip was not organized again, for reasons that are discussed here.

The conversation in this chapter focused on the teachers' experience of the program over the years; their perspectives on what to teach, how to teach, how to mentor and guide deaf youth on their journey to "discover themselves" within international contexts, and the dilemmas the teachers face in their pedagogical practices in their international class groups with regard to module 2 and the study visits abroad, particularly the one in Ghana. Annelies Kusters, who asked the questions and organized this text, is a Belgian deaf anthropologist.[1] She has a long-standing relationship with this program as a visiting lecturer (including preparing the Frontrunners 6 group for the group stay in Ghana), is married to an Indian participant of Frontrunners 3, and has observed parts and consequences of a number of Frontrunners' module 2 projects in Mumbai between 2009 and 2013. The conversation, which lasted two hours, was held in Castberggård in September 2013, conducted in International Sign, video-recorded, and translated into English.

DEAF-SAME WITHIN FRONTRUNNERS GROUPS

> *Outi:* When a group comes to us, there are so many reasons within the group for why they come to us. The desire for change, the desire to look within, feeling oppressed, feeling a lack of confidence. A desire for experience. So many different experiences, but I see something come up in them that gives them some confidence and a breath of relief. They see and experience DEAF-SAME. . . . They are relieved to see that even though there are so many differences among us, there's something that's the same. . . . They feel how much they have in common. Then with time, they get a little

---

[1] Thanks to Kirk VanGilder for his suggestion to structure the text in this way.

fed up and see how different they are culturally, and then disputes come up. . . . And then in the third module, the message went forth, of acceptance . . . . They could see that there were some things DEAF-SAME, and some things that were very different. Culture, views of the world, experiences of the world. Values, philosophies—many things that are different.

Potential differences include having attended a deaf school versus having been mainstreamed, and differences in language use and communication.

Outi: An Indian man brought up the topic of interpreters. It was about how interpreters can engage and then disengage. The Scandinavians in the group were very convinced that when an interpreter is there, they could fit in with hearing people but if there was no interpreter, it was such a different experience, of being separated from hearing people. The Indian man disagreed, saying that the interpreter came in between and separated the deaf people into a different group. This became such a controversy. People wouldn't accept this point. This topic stayed around for a long time. At the end, the Indian person said, "Ok, this is my opinion and that's all. This is my culture that I grew up in and a different environment. Deaf and hearing people in India communicate with each other through gesture with ease, and Scandinavia is very different. But if you would come to my country, you must understand the experience and culture of that place." . . . And then, over time, I could see that if the topic of interpreters came up, people knew clearly where this person stood and that their experience was different. . . . That's one of the points where DEAF-SAME doesn't work.

Entering the Global South during Module 2

Outi: What's interesting is that we never say "you have to go and give lectures." We never say that. . . . Because it was in the curriculum, people thought they had to go in and change the world. They got the idea that they have to change the world in just one or two months. [smiles] But maybe it was the wrong wording in the curriculum, the wrong message we gave, it could have been misleading.

The teachers think the focus on the Global South was caused by a combination of guest lectures and current global trends.

Filip: There has been so much discussion about how to go into developing countries and how to do this or that. In Frontrunners 2, Colin Allen [now WFD president, previously active as development worker] came for a week or three days to teach.
Ole: That really blew up.

Filip: Yes, yes. . . . He came for teaching, and then he came to teach again in Frontrunners 3, and this was repeated for Frontrunners 4. This way of thinking was passed on and on. . . .

Ole: The people that come to give talks—they are inspirational. . . .

Filip: Since nine or ten years ago, many deaf organisations went over to different places, such as Nepal. . . . Swedish people and others went over there. People from Denmark were active in Uganda. Finland went over to Albania. To encourage development and change. There have been individuals who have come here to give talks and they say that . . . they have experienced clashes of culture. The group watches eagerly and they want the same thing. . . . There are different points that all come together that sort of become the prevailing philosophy that is given over to the Frontrunners. It's not only what we tell them. There's a prevailing mindset already out there. . . .

Ole: A trend—it's a trend that is followed.

ENCOUNTERING AND RESPONDING TO CULTURAL DIFFERENCES IN THE GLOBAL SOUTH

Frontrunners teachers became gradually aware of problems related to the transfer of Western concepts to different contexts in the Global South.

Outi: Two years ago, a Frontrunner was from [Asian country] and for module 2 that person wanted to go back and work in [the same Asian country]. I thought that was really good, that this person would know the location, culture, and all of that and be able to adjust what was taught to suit this specific country. . . . After learning these strongly Western theories, that person went over there and started to teach and things were jarring. During a workshop in [this Asian country], people said, look here, what you are saying is very Western and very European and it doesn't suit us here. That really surprised the Frontrunner and took them aback. From this we can see that even when you know a certain place and culture, and when you hope that what you've taught takes in different views . . . [and] that we've given them the ability to see from different perspectives and decide about what can be taken to a certain location and taught or not, the person may still . . . not be aware of this.

In former conversations with the Frontrunners, Annelies shared observations in Mumbai with the teachers. She had observed parts and consequences of several Frontrunners projects in Mumbai between 2009 and 2013. For example, two Frontrunners gave lectures on leadership in International Sign that were not understood: both the sign language and the concepts were too foreign for the audience to readily comprehend. Other Frontrunners came to film a documentary about "deaf life in Mumbai" by visiting three deaf associations they visited once, where they gave a lecture to elicit perspectives rather than observing and hence got a skewed image of deaf life in Mumbai. Other Frontrunners introduced the concept of audism in deaf schools, which led to tensions between teachers and students in these schools. In addition, some Frontrunners were inspired by the (western) philosophy of age limits for youth clubs and imposed an age limit (eighteen to thirty) on an existing all-ages club for the deaf in Mumbai in order to turn it into a youth club. This led to tensions between deaf youth and older deaf people. As a result of Annelies's and two Indian people's observations in Mumbai, anecdotes and stories from Frontrunners themselves such as the abovementioned participant from the Asian country, and the Ghana project during Frontrunners 6, the aims of module 2 (as envisaged by the teachers) became more modest. Today the teachers encourage the participants to plan a visit to another country using the principles of exchange, observation, and learning about another culture, rather than giving lectures about the concepts they have learned in Frontrunners.

> *Outi:* The participants of the group go out, and it does not matter where, it could be their home location. They have got the tools to closely examine, to see if the theories work, or there are some sharp differences, or it's more like they sit back and look at things, decide what they can use from the theories we have given them to suit whichever location. Or they go to a very different location where they are not from, not to offer them those theories but to see what the deaf community is like there and what the different values and philosophies are there, and don't bring things from here with them, but more step away from that and see the varying factors in the deaf community there. We can't give them the matching theories for each situation. It's more like seeing that there are so many varying factors in the deaf communities. . . . When we teach, there are some things that are DEAF-SAME, but once they're out in the field, it's surprising to see that it's not all DEAF-SAME. We want them to observe more. To learn from what's there. . . . *Ole:* A Frontrunner who came here asked if Frontrunners have to so intensely try to empower. And I said no, no, it's about what *you* want to do. This person wanted to do art in Japan with a famous deaf artist and asked if they can meet with and learn about how the artist worked. And I thought, this is a good idea. But they said that others [such as previous Frontrunners] had told them that you had to try to intensely empower.

Preparing Frontrunners for Stays in the Global South

When preparing the Frontrunners for module 2, the teachers are aware of their own strongly Western background. None of the teachers have been active in development work or long-term stays in the Global South.

> *Outi:* I can't give guidance on how to teach over there. I can only hope that they can themselves understand the different perspectives and decide. And I thought that this would be possible, but it wasn't. Things unfolded and it didn't work out [in the case of the Frontrunner from the

Asian country]. . . . And we [the teachers] didn't know what to do. We said, hmm, and tried to take a step back and look at things with some objectivity. . . . It has to be more self-reflection and critical thinking from us whether they are really ready for what they want to do. . . . It's more about pushing them to examine whether their thinking is a good match to the location they're going to and guiding them into a suitable direction.

This is one of the areas in which the guest teachers are seen as crucial:

Outi: I think that my vision about the best way to nurture thinking about module 2 is to recruit teachers who themselves have experience and who know more. . . . Our teaching philosophy is not to try to show that we know everything. It's more about nurturing, bringing in people with a wealth of knowledge. Using people . . . who have looked more deeply into other cultures and countries. . . . They can relate all kinds of things and our hope is that the Frontrunners will take advantage of this knowledge. My job is to ask what each Frontrunners' clear ambition is and then to bring information in.

The teachers discussed the need for a balance between steering the participants on the one hand, and leaving things up to them as much as possible on the other hand:

Outi: We caution them to be aware that they have a big responsibility. To go into a different culture that they do not know and they are only one person. Can you really give a speech? Can you match the local culture? Do you know if the local people need this topic that you are talking about? . . .
Ole: In truth, for me, when I work with the group, preparing module 2, . . . once they have made contact and made an agreement on how to go forward, . . . if both parties have agreed then I take a step back. I think the important thing is that both parties agree. I think the host location can say, mmm, no, I don't like this and I don't want this. . . . For example, one girl wanted to go to Africa last year. She made plans and I asked her if she had made contact. She said she had. I asked if the involved people in the host country were aware of the program that she planned to carry out. She said no, only she knew the details. I asked, how do you know then that the people there want the program you are planning? There needs to be contact and mutual agreement. That's important to me. In reality, sometimes the people in the host country may take a look and say "no, we do not like this and we do not want this. That's not a good idea and changes need to be made." And maybe after changes are made, they will welcome the Frontrunner. But it's impossible for us to go over and see. . . .
Filip: If I mentor them, I always say, one, don't set your sights big. Set them small. Choose a small project. Many think grandiosely, and I don't

encourage that. . . . And second, I need to remind many that they need self-reflection and they need to think about ethical questions. When looking back, they have to be honest and admit a mistake. . . . We need to . . . emphasize more the need to adjust to the other culture. . . . Looking back, there should have been more thought about ethical issues. More thought about what it means to be a Westerner going over somewhere to sort of help or save the world. That's not what it should be like. Maybe before that was okay, but not now. Maybe our philosophies have changed.

Ole: Also, we need to be more aware. People tell us things [such as about Frontrunners projects in Mumbai] and we have just been getting on with things here unaware and then when we learn of certain things, we're blown away. We look at each other and say, is this the way it really is? And then we realize yes, that's how it is, and try to think of what we should do about it. But what to change, how—maybe we should make more contact with people in the host countries, making sure that their needs are a close match with what the person will come and do there. That's one thing. Another thing is changing module 2, but module 2 doesn't need to be paid for. It is free. How do I force people not to go over to these places? That's an example of the difficulties of the framework.

Follow-up and Feedback after Travels to the Global South

During module 3, an important element is reflection on the projects in module 2:

Outi: When they come back to us, they have had various experiences of learning from wherever they have been. Individual ability to think and to reflect is very different from person to person. That risk is always going to be there: they go over and then they come back, and we see whether they have in fact been able to take advantage of everything they could, or there's the risk that things haven't really worked out as well as we hoped. . . . I noticed that there have been clashes, so I ask them to be honest towards us. What were they frustrated with. Maybe the group together can sit down and analyze where the frustration comes from. . . . Once it's looked at from different angles, I think they will be better able to look at themselves and address where the frustration comes from. Maybe they don't know the country and culture, they had too little time there, they brought too much of their own background over with them when they should have set it aside, stayed open, and tried to learn as much as possible from where they were.

The teachers note that a challenge is that all the reflection comes from the Frontrunners themselves and not from the people in the places where they have done projects.

Filip: There have been previous experiences where things have really failed. And I say, that's okay, failure is okay. That's an experience in itself, a new experience. And then there have been people who have felt good about what they did. But has it been good for the people around, who are affected by the project? I have no idea. . . .

Outi: We really don't have anyone looking in from the other side, we don't have that contact. . . . We'd like more contact with people looking in from the other side. . . . Do the accounts match up or are there many differences? . . . I think it's taken us a long time to realize we need to have contact with people in other countries. It's been a while. And now we're stopping ourselves and saying, wait. Trying to make changes in the Frontrunners program. From Frontrunners 6, changes were being made.

FRONTRUNNERS 6 TRIP TO GHANA

An important turning point during Frontrunners 6 was the five-week trip to Ghana during module 1 (see http://fr6.frontrunners.dk), as part of the curriculum (and thus the module 1 fee for Frontrunners 6 was higher than the other years). The Frontrunners 6 group consisted of thirteen people. Outi and Filip both went to Ghana along with the group: Filip stayed for the first two and a half weeks and Outi stayed the full five weeks. Before going over with the group, Outi visited Ghana to plan the program. During the trip, Frontrunners 6 organized activities such as theater and dance in a large deaf school in the town of Mampong and gave lectures on human rights and social justice. Deaf Ghanaians in turn gave lectures about deaf organizations and deaf life in Ghana. The decision to go to Ghana was motivated by the history of Danish people from the Danish Deaf Association (DDL) and the Danish Youth Deaf Association (DDU) working in Ghana to strengthen its national and youth deaf associations. There were thus existing contacts and a network between deaf Ghanaians and Danish deaf people. Outi narrates the aim of the trip as follows:

> *Outi:* The aim was a desire to see how the deaf communities were different. . . . When we went there, it was with the aim of an exchange.

She emphasizes that the Frontrunners took away a lot from it:

> *Outi:* Frontrunners 6 went to Ghana and had a very positive awakening there. [They observed that] there was no real separation between deaf and hard of hearing people in Ghana. Deaf and hard of hearing people mixed together effortlessly. They asked the deaf association, GNAD [the Ghanaian National Association of the Deaf], if there were structural differences between deaf and hard of hearing people. They said no, we all use sign language so there are the same aims for everyone. This was an awakening for the Frontrunners. Ghana was ahead in this way. . . . Here in

Europe, deaf and hard of hearing are more separate, still. It's more focused on the amount of hearing you have. In Ghana it was more about the shared language. The Frontrunners were openmouthed about this difference. . . . It was surprising and different for them—the forms, the differences in the deaf communities, the philosophies, everything.

However, Outi experienced a sharp disconnect between the aim of exchange and the reality during the stay in Ghana:

> *Outi:* The Frontrunners got satisfaction and experience but the local people didn't get much. Just another white group that came and went. I found that interesting. The idea of an exchange wasn't 100 percent fulfilled. The schoolkids were inspired by the experience of theater and dance, yes, but that wasn't something sustainable. . . . We worked with teachers and staff who said in a negative way that people kept on coming and coming. What did the people here at the school gain? People gave things, but of what value was it? The people went hooray and they went back home to their countries with a feeling that they had achieved change but for the local people, everything felt the same. Nothing had been achieved. . . . Where was the genuine exchange? . . . I felt I saw who takes most advantage of these opportunities of this sort of project: the Frontrunners. . . . Every year there would be a different group in Ghana and the locals would feel that it was the same thing over and over, every year. For the Frontrunners it would be exciting and new, but not for the locals. It would always return to the same spot, a sort of regression.

The teachers realized that even when the aim is exchange (rather than empowerment), there may be a clash in expectations. The relationship developed during this one-time encounter did not have a chance to develop into something sustainable over the years.

> *Outi:* What eats at me is that the Ghanaians asked when the Frontrunners would be back. "From now on, will there be no more? What do we get from it?" I saw two big differing perspectives. Just the other day, someone from Ghana got in touch with me on Facebook and asked when the Frontrunners would be back again and was a bit like, "what's up with that, what happened?" I felt uneasy. . . . Yes, experience is good, but I could see two very different perspectives here that didn't meet in the middle.

Talking about the Ghana project led us back to module 2, in which individual projects are undertaken without the security of the group. Filip stressed the advantages of going as a group rather than as an individual, while Outi pointed out the disadvantages of going as a group, based on a comment of a Ghanaian man.

Filip: The positive thing is that when a Frontrunners group goes out, they have meetings most evenings. These meetings, they're more about not thinking that you're above the other people. It's about everyone being on the same level. An example, they went over [to the deaf school in Mampong] and in the mornings everyone queued. If someone was late, the teacher would smack them and tell them to go. Many Frontrunners felt that this was wrong. But they needed to hush up and leave things alone. This was their [Ghanaian] culture. . . . You can't meddle with it. At the evening meetings, there would be potential and space for us teachers [i.e., Outi and Filip] to manage things a little, or for them. To see things from different perspectives. . . . In this way, a group is better. But is a group of people going over a good idea?

Outi: A Ghanaian man, Robert Sampana, had been [to the Rochester Institute of Technology] to study and then he came back to Ghana. He worked in the GNAD. The Frontrunners were there and he said to them: "You come here to do volunteer work. But you aren't truly doing volunteer work." The Frontrunners said, "no, we are volunteering." He said "no, you are in a group and you are safe within your own culture in the group. You haven't gone out on your own into this country and culture. You should be on your own, you should dismantle the group. . . . The Frontrunners were taken aback and surprised and didn't agree, but I could see that his point was real. They are safe within the group and their sameness in front of any differences that come to them.

The Thin Line between Interventions That Are "Okay" and "Not Okay"

Following the discussion of the Ghana trip, a distinction was made between module 2 projects in Europe and in the global South.

Ole: Suppose they want a project in Italy—that's okay. If they want a project in Turkey . . . that's okay, that's possible. We need to understand the spectrum of what [kinds of projects in what locations] are okay and what's not okay. That's hard.

Outi: An example . . . one year ago, a Frontrunner, a girl from [South American country] . . . was active in the [South American country] deaf youth association, and she wanted to do a project in [South Europe]. . . . She asked their youth association to give her work and at the same time she wanted to see the structure and goals of her own country's deaf youth association and compare it to [South European country's] and see what they had in common, compare all the points. This person said that this experience was advantageous and the [South European country's] deaf youth association said that she really helped them with her work. . . . They were able to learn a bit from her about how things were done in [her South American country], and she learned a lot about the [South European country's] way and their differences. . . . Both got something out of it. I think it worked well. . . . In Ghana, that didn't happen. It was more the Frontrunners who got something out of it, but the Ghanaians did not. . . . The [South American country's] girl—it was two-way. There has been talk about [the South European country's] group going to [the South American country], to see how they do things there and at the association there and so forth, . . . so that it would be a true exchange. . . .

Filip: It's important to have crossover [i.e., learning through exchange, by visiting each other's countries and/or philosophies] . . .

Outi: But is crossover a bit of a Western concept? It's us Westerners who have the money to travel. For example, the Frontrunners who went to Ghana—do the Ghanaians have the money to come over to Europe? Mmmm . . . so how is crossover possible? . . . But my point is "crossover," what does it mean? "Equal crossover?" Would it benefit them to come here? . . . Do what the Frontrunners did there, have a look around and then go back? Would they be able to bring something back with them that they could then develop, take advantage of, show others?

OTHER STUDY TRIPS AND THE DIFFERENCE WITH THE GHANA TRIP

The Ghana trip was not only compared with the individual projects in module 2 but also with other study trips that were undertaken in the past, for a few days to a week, during modules 1 and 3. These trips were mostly to Copenhagen, but also to Berlin and Brussels. In Berlin, for example, the Frontrunners visited a deaf politician, a sign language business, a deaf café, a deaf psychologist, and other deaf-related entities.

Ole: [points at Filip] When you went to Berlin [with the Frontrunners], was it a good idea or a bad idea? Frontrunners in Berlin, observing and taking advantage of that experience. What did they bring? How did both sides benefit? Is it more equal in Berlin? . . .

Outi: The people in Berlin were happier that we came. They talked to us, us being there wasn't a problem for them. I feel that it was a problem for the Ghanaians. It was a problem that they are fed up with white people going there all the time without any lasting development coming from it. And us Frontrunners being a part of that. . . . I feel uneasy with that.

CONCLUSION

At the time of writing, Frontrunners is in its tenth iteration. On one weekend in November 2014, all former Frontrunners were invited to a reunion in Castberggård. The fact that the program has continued to exist for ten years is indicative of the popularity of (and the need for) this international learning environment. The fact that such a program can exist at all is based on commonalities between deaf participants, teachers, and guest teachers from different countries (DEAF-SAME) and the possibility of communication in International Sign. The program is a beacon not only for the participants but also for many deaf youth who are aware of its existence and who aspire to attend, or who are inspired by Frontrunners groups' websites. Their active presence on the Internet through v-logs in International Sign is one of the strengths of the program. It is an international deaf space, both physical and virtual, that is famous for its opportunities for learning, study, and reflection. It differs from places such as Gallaudet University or the former deaf studies program in Bristol because of its use of International Sign rather than a national sign language, the fact that the threshold (and the fee) to attend is lower, and the frequency with which deaf guest teachers are invited.

During the conversation, the teachers highlighted what happens when people from diverse backgrounds come together in the context of an international class-room in Castberggård. The participants are together in the classroom and during meals, and some of them share rooms. They are constantly confronted with and forced to manage their commonalities and differences. When they went out to the global South, in the frame of the group trip to Ghana and the individual module 2 projects, observers, participants, and teachers experienced a number of discon-nects in expectations and disconnects with the experience of "gaining something" (or not). These trips to the global South were contrasted with study trips and module 2 projects in Europe.

The teachers attempt to make the Frontrunners aware of the importance of exchange during their pedagogical practices: creating opportunity for learning and discussion in a nurturing environment where they bring in guest teachers, stimulate ethical consciousness, and steer reflection. They also wish to have more feedback and contacts with people in the host countries in the future. At the same time, the questions that the teachers have raised about whether real exchange is possible, whether real crossover is possible, and about the limits of DEAF-SAME in international contexts are very real.

According to the teachers, the ten-year anniversary of the Frontrunners pro-gram would not have been possible without the enthusiasm and bravery of the participants to jump into the unknown and test their limits. The teachers have the special privilege to observe the participants' inner journeys and their physical journeys to other deaf people and their cultures. There have been bumps on the road, but they have been open and honest about their efforts and mistakes. Because of their honesty and that of collaborators and observers during module 2, it has been possible to improve the teaching philosophy, psychology, and contents of the program and, most importantly, to expand understanding of the similarities and differences among deaf people. The participants in Frontrunners have shown that one should not be afraid of mistakes, because only through trying one can learn and improve. The teachers want to hold onto this in the future, also in the light of the changes in the curriculum from Frontrunners 11 onwards, which is why they agreed to work together on this article: to encourage open dialogue among deaf people in international encounters, while they observe, define, and name phenom-ena that are little known.

22 | "My Deaf Is Not Your Deaf": Realizing Intersectional Realities at Gallaudet University

Elena Ruiz-Williams, Meredith Burke,
Vee Yee Chong, and Noppawan Chainarong

In December 2012, we, as students in the Gallaudet University master's program in Deaf studies, hosted a film screening and campus presentation titled "Beyond Deaf-Hearing: Communities and Intersectionalities." In our presentation, we showed the audience an image visually and textually representative of us: a black and white stock photograph of small pile of wooden sticks strewn atop a white surface, many intersecting each other, some paralleling each other, and some apart from the others. In the spaces of those sticks, we had placed words that described our identities:

hearing family	oral	working class	middle class
residential school	Queer	Deaf family	professional class
mainstreamed	Christian	Lesbian	Brown
Deaf	Gay	cis	multiracial-multiethnic
literate	Catholic	straight	secular
Person of Color	Asian	Latin@	college educated
Thai	Chicano	Xican@	
Chinese-Malayisan	hearing	cholo	Deaf Wimmin of Color
body normative	woman	white	Waardenburg syndrome
Jewish	feminist	Cerebral Palsy	nonconforming body
man	Disabled	able bodied	US-ian
first generation	international	immigrant family	Spanish speaking
Barrio	language loss	Hebrew	English speaking
speaking abled	ASL user	native signer	

By using that image in the context of our presentation, we felt that we had shattered a dominant, Deaf studies binary of Deaf-hearing that defined *Deaf* only in opposition to *hearing*, with the category *Deaf* containing narrow cultural paradigms that deny multiplicity. *Deaf* could no longer erase all other differentials; *Deaf* was a source of connection but not a totalizing one. By presenting ourselves as multifaceted, we moved toward multiple representations, away from DEAF SAME. Our main theoretical vehicle was *intersectionality*. By utilizing this concept, we paid homage not only to scholar Kimberlé Crenshaw, who coined it, but also to other Black women (Sojourner Truth, the founders of the Combahee River Collective, Patricia Hill Collins, bell hooks, Angela Y. Davis, and many more) throughout US history who made the inextricable intersection racism and sexism known.

Crenshaw utilized the concept of intersectionality in the context of recognizing and comprehending structures of power and dominance in society, a crucial foundation for understanding the workings of social groups and identity (1989, 1991). Crenshaw's work shifted gears toward recognizing the multidimensionality of groups and identities, instead of seeing them in terms of categorical, mutually exclusive social experiences. This is especially important in discussing identity and group experiences because binary or simplified terms of *privileged* and *not privileged* did not work for understanding these experiences. More privileged versus less privileged neglects the reality of those who experience more than one kind of social marginalization, and this neglect furthers the marginalization of multiply marginalized people or those with multiple experiences of marginalization. In Crenshaw's and others' works, we saw fundamental reflections of our struggles in our graduate program, at our university, and in the larger Deaf-signing community.

In this essay, we present the theoretical foundations of our experiences at Gallaudet: we unpack, critique, and interrogate what *Deaf* means on experiential, community, and academic levels for people who have multiple, intersecting, and overlapping experiences along different axes of experience. In particular, we carve out a space for DeafBlind, DeafDisabled, and Hard of Hearing signing people's experiences to come to the fore rather than be erased by a presumptuous, singular, and essentialist term, *Deaf*. We emphasize that sighted and able-privileged[1] Deaf, signing people are not the sole members of (local and international) Signing communities, and we believe that by using only *Deaf*, we exclude the physical, cultural, and linguistic experiences of others. To represent all of these realities, we use the acronym DDBDDHH to include Deaf, DeafBlind, DeafDisabled, and Hard of Hearing peoples. A first step toward intersectional inclusivity is to name different experiences rather than continue to erase multiple realities that exist in signing communities. In utilizing and drawing attention to the acronmyn DDBDDHH (in contrast to *Deaf*), we are able to start being more exacting in our naming of multiple experiences across different axes of identity and group experiences.[2]

---

[1] Though *able-bodied* is the most widely used term to denote privileges of ability, we use *able-privileged* to emphasize that not all privileges of ability are embodied or visible. We thank our former classmate, Ian Smith, for this insight and terminology.

[2] We recognize that we do not include oral, nonsigning Deaf, DeafBlind, DeafDisabled, or Hard of Hearing persons in this acronym. We are referring to the specific context of those who have varying biophysical experiences yet who feel cultural and linguistic membership and affinity among sign language users.

Representing deaf intersectional realities was part of our individual and collective journey in recognizing what was lacking and erased in our study program and wider community. Though we were utilizing theories of intersectionality by the time of our campus-wide presentation, it had been a long road to feeling liberated and connected to this theory. Earlier in the program, we had felt personally shunned by much of what we read and watched for our courses, and often our longing to reveal our own personal experiences was shut down in the classroom and in daily discourses outside of classes.

To provide a specific example: those of us in our cohort who identified as Deaf People of Color (DPOC, also including DBPOC, DDPOC, and HHPOC) often noticed that cultural appropriations of the experiences of Peoples of Color were rife in Deaf studies materials. Namely, several authors and resources have heavily drawn upon analogic examples to hearing US Black, Black-African, and North American Indigenous populations to prove the case of the structural oppression of Deaf persons, conveniently erasing the realities of DDBDDHH POC (as well as POC in general). For two examples of this analogic exploitation, see Harlan Lane's *The Mask of Benevolence* and Paddy Ladd's *Understanding Deaf Culture: In Search of Deafhood* to identify how two white men, one hearing and one Deaf, buttressed their theoretical constructions by relying on appropriating experiences that are not their own, decontextualizing histories of European colonialism that endure to the present day, presuming that racialized oppressions share the same structures and processes as phonocentrism and audism, and rendering the intersections of DDDBDDHH-POC invisible. In such works, the hierarchy of realizing experiences only based on audism becomes clear: intersectional realities are ignored.

When DPOC students in our cohort attempted to bring this analysis to classes and community discourses, they were dismissed or faulted as being too negative and critical. Our attempts to bring to light the experiences of what Patricia Hill Collins (2000) has framed as "both/and" were not taken seriously, which led us to feel alienated, not accepted, and defenseless. Additionally, a complex issue started to surface and resurface among the DPOC students regarding nationalities: those who were born and/or raised in the United States had specific, politicized perspectives that were not always shared by the international DPOC students, who had alternate perspectives about race and racial dynamics. This complexity informed the DPOC students about how nationality provided another axis of difference. The commonalities and differences among the DPOC students foregrounded the importance of doing away with frameworks where race, ethnicity, and nationality were transcended to examine only a Deaf-based axis of identity and experience. Needless to say, as we integrated intersectionality in our discussions and analyses, the trajectory of our graduate studies drastically changed.

Intersectionality, our theoretical vehicle, rescued us from the restrictions we continued to grapple with. Intersectionality can be understood as a camera lens approach to the world because identities are contextual, complex, both deeply rooted and emerging, layered, and intermeshed. A camera lens moves across the landscape of our experiences, zooming in, zooming out, panning, becoming still, rapidly moving forward, slowly recollecting the past. This metaphor helps us realize that fixed and static representations are inaccurate and that hierarchies of identities and experiences have no place. This approach allowed for consideration of the vast array of diverse experiences we as individuals had in our cohort, despite us not seeing such realities on the pages of most the books we read or in many of frames of the films we watched.

Ultimately, we started learning not only how to take the reins on our own camera lens but also how to follow each other's lens of experiences, which is where our academic learning was heightened by personal and collective processes of realizing and honoring our multiple experiences. We continued to dismantle the restrictive category *Deaf* as meaning white, cisgender, from the United States or developed Western countries, sighted, and able privileged, realizing that there could not be an authentic, totalizing DEAF-SAME framework. We four came together because our intensive class discussions and continued exchange of personal information had created strong bonds among us. However, this was not without some struggle: barriers of language fluency in American Sign Language (ASL) and English existed, not all of us were white, not all of us were Deaf, able-privileged people,[3] and not all of us were US citizens. These differences created a landscape of power differentials and it required strenuous work to connect with one another. The spaces we shared for classes became contested sites of race, gender, nationality, disability, language, and education; encounters where power, privilege, oppression, and disenfranchisement were clearly visible. But without the foundation of both personal relationships and a shared, collective investment in forms of social change, we doubt that we would have arrived at the points where we are today. We have kept in touch since graduation to sustain and continue the lines of exchange and learning that we initiated in fall 2011. This demonstrates the importance of personalizing the academic, of ensuring that academic inquiry and theory is not made abstract and removed from the personal authenticity of lived realities and relationships.

To convey our experiences in Gallaudet's Deaf studies master's program, we provide brief autoethnographies, or condensed analytical pieces based on our lived experiences. In those autoethnogprahies, we present reflexive narratives that demonstrate our personal and collective transformations. We wrote these pieces individually in spaces ranging from northern California and Ohio to Thailand and Malaysia. We utilized video calls and YouTube messages to communicate with a shared language modality: sign language. We read through each others' drafts and offered suggestions for changes, engaging in a new layer of collaboration and collective academic work, reflecting our values of intersectional approaches and understandings. Through these collaborations, we developed spontaneous transnational spaces that were oriented toward connective and transformative work.

Vee Yee

I am Vee Yee, Deaf since birth and from Malaysia. I learned about Gallaudet University in 2002 when I attended the Deaf Way II conference. I spent every cent I had in my bank, and my parents sponsored the rest of the conference cost. At the time, I was only eighteen years old and I was shocked that there was such a thing as a university for the Deaf. I started digging for information related to Deaf people around the world. I even started thinking that I would not be an actual Deaf person if I did not go to Gallaudet University: I could not get Gallaudet out of my

---

[3] An alternate phrase for this is *Deaf abled*.

mind. Such thought was rooted in me and brought me back to the United States, when I finally attended Gallaudet for my second master's degree, after receiving a master's in linguistics at the University of Malaya.

I understood that it would be impossible for me to study at Gallaudet as my family's finances were limited. I searched for a scholarship for many years to attend Gallaudet, even when I was pursuing my bachelor's and master's degrees at the local university. After all that time, I came across the World Deaf Leadership scholarship, initiated by the Nippon Foundation and Gallaudet University in the 1990s. I applied and won the scholarship, and Gallaudet accepted me. I chose Deaf studies so that I could better understand Deaf people, and I also wanted to advance the Deaf community in Malaysia.

I did not have any confidence that I would be experiencing "sameness" in the United States, or that any of the Deaf students would support me merely because we had the sameness of being Deaf. Upon my arrival in summer 2011, my mind was totally frozen, and I could not think speedily like I did usually in Malaysia. I do not believe that it was cultural shock, because it was not my first time being in the United States. Soon, I made a few hearing friends who were classmates in ASL classes at Gallaudet, and they helped me acquire some ASL signs to prepare myself for graduate classes in the fall.

When graduate classes started, I thought my classmates would be around my age. Surprisingly, I was wrong. I met Jenny, a Deaf person in her fifties, who told me that she would be in the same class with me. Soon after, I finally met the Deaf studies cohort during the program orientation. For an ice-breaking activity, I was paired with Joel, a student of Mexican descent who identified as a Chicano. We both talked about ourselves but I could not understand him because my ASL was still not strong and I was not very familiar with his background. I struggled to understand him: I had never learned about Mexican, Mexican American, or Chicano cultures. As part of the activity, I was supposed to introduce Joel to my classmates and explain his background. But I did not do it well. I was still very confused.

After we had taken more courses together as a cohort, I learned more about my classmates. I felt lost in classes during the first year as I struggled to understand, and I felt that I was not able to bring any issues from Malaysia into the classroom discussion. Over time, I slowly acquired more advanced ASL skills and started sharing the issues that Deaf people encountered in Malaysia.

In Malaysia, I was very active in the Deaf community, yet never really discussed any heated issues in the community in my classes. It impressed me how much I was learning and I began to think that I actually could not say that these folks in the classroom are the same as me; they are very different from me. Sometimes I felt like they looked down at me. I was wrong because I assumed that every Deaf person is the same. We had all grown up in different environments and therefore we received different degrees of exposure.

My experiences at Gallaudet in classroom discussions and my social life have shaped who I am now. The classroom discussions made me think about many issues about identity. I became more aware about the developments of Deaf community, for example, sign language teaching, human rights, society accessibility, and multiple identities. Through the classroom discussions, I developed my own identities, new opinions, understandings, and views about myself and Deaf people in Malaysia. I also became an openly gay man after I arrived at Gallaudet

University when a good friend said it was okay to embrace who I am and then gave me a warm hug.

It was really awkward to be in my hometown again after two years of being a different person in the United States. I was confused about whether I should go back to my old image or if I should continue with my new identities. Before Gallaudet, I was a passive Deaf person. I used to accept what I received without further comments or questions. In the United States, based on the experience and exposure I received from friends, classmates, roommates, and professors, I developed myself further and made the decision that I should keep my new identities. I am proud of myself for finally being an openly Deaf and gay man.

MEREDITH

I am a white, DeafDisabled, queer woman. I was born one month early with Rh incompatibility, which lead to my deafness and cerebral palsy. I grew up in a very supportive and educated family, who encouraged me to catch my dreams regardless of my DeafDisability status. I went to Gallaudet as an undergraduate student. I entered with a proud identity of being Deaf and thought that I would be more accepted at Gallaudet than in hearing society because I use ASL as my primary language. I also envisioned that my peers at Gallaudet would be more understanding of my cerebral palsy (CP) because I identified myself as "Deaf first." I believed in DEAF-SAME: that nothing else mattered, such as race, sexial orientation, class, gender, and disabilty, and that my peers and professors would approach me with that attitude. Eventually I realized that was not going to happen. I was excluded while I tried to introduce myself or try to talk to someone, my CP-ASL was not understandable at first, and I was forever aware of that at Gallaudet University. My peers pretended to understand me by nodding their heads. I did not have friends at first, I ate alone often in the cafeteria, and I felt totally isolated, as if I was alone in the mainstream, except that I was among Deaf-abled people. After a long conversation with my mother, when I almost decided not to return to Gallaudet, I gave another semester a chance. I joined a sorority, which gave me self-confidence to meet new people, and I became a well-known person on campus. If I had not joined the sorority, would I have become a well-known person on campus? The answer is simply no. I was that marginalized on my own campus.

I majored in Deaf studies, after changing from Deaf education to psychology to Deaf studies with a minor in psychology. The main reason I decided to major in Deaf studies was to learn more about my identity, as a Deaf person, and I wanted to become a strong advocate for Deaf people. Yet as I took a few courses during my last year as an undergraduate, I felt something was wrong. I took a course called "Dynamics of Oppression," which discussed different forms of oppression, including ableism. Although we did not discuss it in depth, I saw and felt something that gave me awareness of what Deaf able-privileged, sighted, and able-minded are doing to DeafDisabled, DeafBlind people. They do the exact same thing that they feel hearing people do to them: denying their experiences of oppression and even carrying out this oppression. Based on those realizations, in my bachelor's thesis I analyzed how Gallaudet oppresses students with disabilities. Sadly, my work on the topic was constantly overlooked.

After graduating with my bachelor's degree, I enrolled in graduate school in Deaf cultural studies. My first semester experience was a difficult one. At the beginning of my cohort's journey together, the question of Deaf people being labeled disabled and the issue of disability in defining Deaf people was a common topic in our classes. Those class discussions became heated, with different opinions being shared. During one discussion, I fought back tears: most of my classmates were Deaf sighted and able-privileged people who resisted the disabled label and were critical of any author who wrote about being disabled in society, because of their own able privileges, privileges that I did not have. Eventually, they turned to me and asked which I was: Deaf or disabled first? Despite what I felt inside, I told them "Deaf-first." I continued to put aside my true feelings for the rest of the semester.

We took a course titled "Enforcing Normalcy" the following semester, which discussed how society enforces normalcy in people with disabilities and Deaf people. I was relieved, because it was a course that really opened discussions of what I was trying to express the semester before. In one of our weekly assignments, our professor asked us to respond to the question, "Why should we be Deaf if we don't have to be?" which had us think about genetic engineering and how Deaf people and disabled people did not have to exist. Most of us resisted answering the question. In response, I said to our professor, "And you as a white, hearing, abled, man asking me that question was wrong. That question should not have been asked." My professor was speechless, but I expressed how I felt violated by such a question as a DeafDisabled person. Because he was an able-bodied and hearing person with many privileges, he had the guts to ask that question? It felt as if he was asking me, "Why be disabled if you did not have to be?" My classmates witnessed my emotional reaction and started to realize that it is possible to think of disability in a positive way. I finally felt that my cohort started to understand and remember DeafDisabled and DeafBlind experiences.

Toward the end of my graduate program, I obtained an adjunct job teaching undergraduate Disability courses online for my department and had given my first professional presentation about my thesis for a Deaf studies conference in Utah. A few well-known Deaf activists wanted to know my perspective about what it means to be Deaf *and* to have a disability. At the end of my program, some awareness was happening in Deaf studies about DeafDisability, but I still strongly feel that we DeafDisabled people still have long and difficult battles against oppression within our own signing communities and among hearing, able-privileged communities, too.

Noppawan

I come from a Deaf signing family in Thailand. In Thailand, most deaf children come from hearing families. Usually, those who are from Deaf families are not able to get an education because hearing people look down on Deaf families and (mistakenly) believe that being a part of a Deaf family means bad karma in the Buddhist religion. In spite of this, my family sent me to the nearby Deaf school for my education. I did not have any siblings, and when I attended school, I was the only student from a Deaf family, which made me feel different from my peers.

I did not dare reveal that my family was Deaf because I was the only one at school who had this background. In fact, I thought I was the only child in all of Bangkok who had Deaf parents. I never met any other Deaf family in Thailand. Years later, I found out that an English teacher of mine had a Deaf family, and I was shocked that I did not know at the time. In 1999, I participated in an exchange program in which I went to Japan for two and a half weeks. In Japan, I saw for the first time many Deaf families who all communicated with each other, with no one being left out. A number of those family members explained that there were many more Deaf families all over the world.

I had first learned about Gallaudet when a woman who volunteered at my school told us about the university. She explained to us that Gallaudet was special because it had a Deaf community, Deaf education, Deaf access services, and welcomed Deaf people from all over the world. She explained to me that the Deaf people there were like Thai Deaf people—friendly and sweethearts—and that there was access to communication everywhere.

I was able to gain government support to attend Gallaudet: out of thirty-five people who took the examination, only two people passed. I spent two years studying ASL and English at the English Language Institute at Gallaudet and then a year as a special graduate student in education classes to develop an understanding of graduate-level work. I eventually decided to apply for the Deaf studies graduate program because Thailand had no Deaf studies program and Deaf education training programs in Thailand rarely made any connections to Deaf culture and cultural awareness about Deaf people. I felt that I needed to gain more knowledge and understanding about Deaf culture, identity, community, education, language, and the meaning of being Deaf.

When I entered the gates of Gallaudet University, I felt strange noticing that people of color formed separate groups. I had never seen so many white or Black Deaf people. However, I soon noticed that many Gallaudet students made prejudgments about international students—many of them would judge us based on our appearances, and I could not understand why so many of them looked down on international Deaf students. I had not experienced something like that with other Deaf people. I only had experiences of discrimination with hearing people before that. I remembered how I used to dream about what life in the United States was like, expecting people to be friendly and have open minds, but reality was not like that. I often saw international Deaf students try to communicate with Gallaudet students from the United States, but those students did not want to waste time on communication struggles or misunderstandings in ASL or in English. It was clear that because many of them did not have to learn ASL or English as their second or third or fourth languages, they did not have to work so hard to communicate with us, like we international Deaf students had to. I could also tell that they had never really thought about our experiences.

My classmates and I all had very different cultural backgrounds and experiences of struggle. I found out that there were different Deaf cultures all over the world, different identities, languages, and backgrounds, but yet we were learning in class that we were all human and that Deaf people are all the same. Some teachers and some students did not recognize different experiences among Deaf people. Our classmates struggled to share their experiences with each other, but over time we discussed more and learned a lot. We made incredible impacts on each other's learning about disability, race, gender, language, and international identities. I learned that my experience of being Deaf is different than others and that we are not the same. I started to share my negative experiences with other students at Gallaudet and chose to start being upfront with people. Those discussions helped me better understand my experiences with white Deaf students when I first arrived at Gallaudet.

ELENA

Throughout my childhood and adolescence in Sacramento, California, I had gravitated toward living life "hearing," opting to use largely spoken English with some supplemented Signed English via a sole interpreter at school and with my mother, the lone signer in my family. I had little to no socialization with other Deaf peers and adults. Though my Deaf identity formation did not happen in my early life, I became self-determined as a Xicanx[4] in high school, politicizing my Salvadoran ancestry. In college, I began coming to terms with my bisexuality, which I later politicized as a Queer identity. Later, as an adult, I would further politicize myself as a multiracial/multiethnic lightskinned/often-white-presenting Person of Color, reconciling the complexity of being mixed with a Salvadoran-born father and Euro-Hispanic mother.

Though my adolescence and early adulthood were marked with crucial identity formations, negotiations, and evolutions, I still operated with shame and fear regarding my Deaf identity. In retrospect, I think this was a consequence of having being raised in an environment that was predominantly hearing. But at twenty-three years old, I applied to work as a teacher at a prominent school for the Deaf in northern California. And what a leap it was: within the period of a few months, I had made drastic changes to my life—I went from being surrounded totally by hearing family members, friends, and work spaces to total cultural and linguistic immersion in a Deaf school context.

By the time I attended Gallaudet, I was seeking cultural and community validation and subscribed to a narrow set of identity politics and a narrow paradigm of what it meant to be Deaf—no doubt, the renowned residential Deaf school where I worked strongly influenced this mentality. But I needed to become *really* Deaf. In that period of my life, to be Deaf meant to have L1, or native/near-native, fluency in ASL; to have a vast, wide network of Deaf friends, colleagues, and family members; to have minimal interaction with hearing people; and to have exacting knowledge of the history and cultural features of Deaf people in the United States and beyond. I had already taken the first step of abandoning my hearing aid, inadvertently closing off relationships with nonsigners in my life, and of course, heading to Gallaudet.

At the time, I did not have the consciousness to discern that how I was framing "Deaf" meant to be sighted and to be able privileged. It also meant that racial and ethnic identity had to be secondary to Deaf identity. It also meant that discussing other identities to the same extent as Deaf identity was detractory and

---

[4] With the intention of gender inclusivity and fluidity, "x" is used in place of the gendered binary in the Spanish language. This applies to the term Latinx as well.

inappropriate. And this meant that my Queer Xicanx identities and my Person of Color identity were dismissed and sidelined. I operated under the premise that identities had to be ranked and made permanently separate. I internalized the construct of identity hierarchies, without even knowing I was ranking my own and others' life experiences.

I had arrived at Gallaudet for fall semester 2010, spending a year under the education department before changing to cultural studies in fall 2011. While excited to jump into theory-heavy and intensive discussions, I had only started scratching at recognizing the impact audism had in my life to date; and much later, I started realizing how I abandoned my path toward becoming a politicized Person of Color to become "really Deaf." As a result, I had lost even more of the little Spanish I had managed to relearn later in my life and had become out of touch with both hearing and Signing Ch/Xicanx and Latinx community members. It was incredibly difficult to realize that the very critiques about essentialism and hierarchized identities I was making of the canonical works in my program I was truly making of myself and my own process. Rather than openly accept the extent of my pain, trauma, and internalized behaviors and thoughts, I became increasingly combative in my thoughts, class discussions, and my academic work. I ferociously argued for the recognition of multiple intersections and tore down most of the outdated, exclusionary works I was expected to read and write on. Despite my impassioned efforts toward academic intersectionality, I started withdrawing from creating deeper relationships with my classmates, escaping further self-analysis and connections with others. This program made for perhaps the most emotionally intense years of my twenties, given what it had me touch on after years of denial.

What brought me "back" to my cohort, to the process of academic and personal unpacking? In the fall semester of my last year in the program I and a few other classmates had opted to be a part of a weekend training program provided by the department of counseling on campus. As often happened, I had found myself yet again sparring with a white Deaf cis, heterosexual, male participant. I slipped back into the pursuit of "winning" the argument, of defending intersectional realities. During a tense break from the activities Noppawan turned to me and said: "You forget about us. You forget about us international Deaf people—you talk about Deaf People of Color but you do not remember us when you want to talk about us." I was floored. In spite of all my academic efforts, I forgot the true roots of intersectional work: personal relationships, nurturing connections, and building bridges. Months later, I left with a beginning understanding that intersectionality had to go beyond the academic and started to undertake the very real personal work of integrating intersectionality into my worldview and my personal connections.

Conclusion

In our shared two years at Gallaudet's Deaf studies master's program, we underwent individual and collective unpacking processes that took place on academic grounds, certainly not without resistance and some chagrin from many faculty and staff, who were accustomed to single-issue academics and politics and insistent on seeking out universalisms rather than multiple experiences, truths, and realities. Indeed, our unpacking often began in the classroom, with addressing the omissions of multiply marginalized people who have endured decades of Deaf studies, of the experiential appropriations that cut several of us at our core, and the resistance of many on campus about moving away from the restrictive Deaf-hearing binary. We had difficult conversations and experiences; these revolved around serious disagreements about language use in how to define collective Deaf experiences, the historical and current realities of white Deaf privilege, and neocolonial actions of language and culture committed by Deaf-signing people from Western developed countries (such as the United Kingdom, Nordic countries, Germany, and so forth) to people from developing countries. The hypocrisy of single-issue topics, concepts, published works, identity, and politics had instigated our realizations that multiply marginalized representations must be brought to the forefront.

Eventually, our unpacking led us to addressing the relationships we had with ourselves and with each other: making the academic the personal. Such processes made for many experiences of struggle, but not without some crucial personal and shared growth. For instance, Vee Yee went from feeling uncertain of his potential contributions at Gallaudet and his master's program to feeling freer in expressing his multiple identities as a Chinese-Malaysian gay Deaf man. Additionally, Vee Yee had opportunities to critique and rework his former perspectives on DEAF-SAME after realizing the complex nuances of multiple social factors and identities. Meredith spent her years at Gallaudet embarking on a continuous journey, shedding single-model frameworks of Deaf identity to a reclaimed, politicized DeafDisabled identity. Her journey culminated in a graduate thesis titled "Ableism in the Deaf Community and the Field of Deaf Studies: Through the Eyes of a DeafDisabled Person," which explores intersectional experiences of DeafDisability (Burke 2014). Noppawan came to understand and better analyze her prior and transformed perspectives of the United States DDBDDHH community, positioning herself in such contexts as a Deaf International Asian woman, arriving at deeper understandings of the experiences of discrimination she had faced during her time in the United States. Elena ended up deconstructing and opting out of essentialist and hierarchized frameworks of a singular Deaf identity, both reconciling and highlighting her multiple identities, seeking out spaces and opportunities to centralize other DDBDDHH people's multiplicities, and, as Noppawan had reminded her, cultivating and maintaining meaningful relationships (Spectra Speaks 2013).

Our personal experiences offer experiential text as to why essentialist, universalist, singular, hierarchized frameworks of identity and group dynamics no longer have places in the future of Deaf studies. Additionally, our collaborative efforts during and beyond graduate school demonstrate bridge building across national, cultural, linguistic, racial, ethnic, and disability lines. Though at first glance, this assertion may seem contrary to our position on DEAF-SAME being mythical, we point out that our connections were borne out of intensive, personalized work conducted through dialogue and relationship building and that our differences are highlighted rather than minimized. These differences inform our connections.

We recognize we are not the first set of DDBDDHH individuals who discuss and utilize the concept of intersectionality within the signing community; after our graduate program, some of us later learned that there had been a number of other DDBDDHH writers and activists with multiply marginalized identities who had been utilizing the concept for some time. Despite others before us having engaged in intersectional thought, writing, and work, we question why we had not been exposed to their work in our graduate program. We do recognize that there was a section devoted to "intersections" in *Open Your Eyes* (2008), which discussed the intersections of race, gender, and sexuality and the Deaf experience, and while this section was an important step toward intersectionality in Deaf studies, we feel that it is possible for us to go even further with recording, writing about, and expounding intersectional realities. For instance, we believe that the intersection of gender and DDBDDHH people can include the intersections of race, disabilities, and class, or that sexuality can include the intersections of gender, race, disabilities, nationality, class, and numerous social experiences. In acknowledging what has been written and discussed before us, it remains our hope that this chapter offers a call to academic action for us to integrate, centralize, and honor the multiple in our work, and in the process to realize the importance of building bridges with one another so that our work is not solely cerebral but also connective and transformative. In completing this work, we state that we look forward to such paradigm shifts in the new generation of scholarly pursuits in *our* field of Deaf studies.

References

Bauman, H-D. L. 2008. *Open Your Eyes: Deaf Studies Talking.* Minneapolis: University of Minnesota Press.

Burke, M. L. 2014. "Ableism in the Deaf Community and the Field of Deaf Studies: Through the Eyes of a DeafDisabled Person." MA thesis, Galladuet University.

Crenshaw, K. 1989. "Demarginalizing the Intersection of Race and Sex: A Black Feminist Critique of Antidiscrimination Doctrine, Feminist Theory, and Antiracist Politics." *University of Chicago Legal Forum* 140:139–67.

———. 1991. "Mapping the Margins: Intersectionality, Identity Politics, and Violence against Women of Color." *Stanford Law Review* 43 (6): 1241–99.

Hill Collins, P. 2000. *Black Feminist Thought: Knowledge, Consciousness, and the Politics of Empowerment,* 2nd ed. New York: Routledge.

Ladd, P. 2003. *Understanding Deaf Culture: In Search of Deafhood.* Clevedon, UK: Multilingual Matters.

Lane, H. 1999. *The Mask of Benevolence: Disabling the Deaf Community.* San Diego, CA: Dawn-Sign Press.

Spectra Speaks. 2013. "Straight Allies, White Anti-racists, Male Feminists (and Other Labels That Mean Nothing To Me)." *Spectra Speaks: Our Voices, Our Stories, Our Revolution* (blog), May 29. Accessed April 20, 2015. http://www.spectraspeaks.com/2013/05/afrofeminism-labels-politically-correct-straight-allies-white-antiracissts-male-feminists.

23 | Global Deafhood: Exploring Myths and Realities

Paddy Ladd

I am honored to contribute to this important book, which has implications beyond Deaf studies itself and asks questions of great significance for Deaf people in every country in the world. In this chapter I tease out some of those implications and indicate their importance not only on the individual level of personal identity but on the collective level as well. Implications for the latter include how Sign Language Peoples (SLPs)[1] in each country prioritize activities and policy development necessary for advancing the health of their communities, and how these relate to transnational organizations such as the World Federation of the Deaf (WFD). I examine Deaf differences and commonalities through the lens of the Deafhood concept to help illustrate how existing tensions between both might be resolved.

During the past ten years, the Deafhood concept has spread rapidly around the world and has been embraced by a wide range of Deaf people on a number of different levels. Perhaps above all, the concept stressed that it is long overdue that the world listen to Deaf people, their experiences, stories, beliefs, and values and that these should be researched by Deaf people keen to give voice to the *full range of Deaf experiences.* The Deafhood concept asked these fundamental questions: What does it mean to be a Deaf person, an individual living as a member of the world's Sign Language Peoples, occupying local, regional, national, and international dimensions, spaces, and places? Do we have common ways of thinking, of being in the world? What are Deaf cultures and how have these been affected by oppression? Can this oppression usefully be understood as "colonialism"? Can the diversity of our thinking and being, when better understood, contribute to a greater sense of global Deaf unity? Deafhood courses and study groups have been

---

[1] In developing the term *Sign Language Peoples* (Batterbury, Ladd, and Gulliver 2007) I sought not only to diminish the power of medicalized perspectives of our existence but to emphasize parallels with indigenous peoples and their use of the First Peoples concept. In this context, the emphasis on *peoples* as those who have shared past, present, and aspirations for the future makes the concept a different one that the term *Sign Language Persons* proposed by Jokinen (2001), which is used to include all persons who sign, whether Deaf or hearing.

created in the United States, Belgium, Ireland, and elsewhere and have begun to tackle some of these questions. The term itself has resonated so strongly with some people that individuals around the world have marketed shirts and other paraphernalia, and some have even tattooed it on their bodies.

Deafhood theory emphasizes that all discourses, both Deaf and hearing, are historically situated; thus the perspectives we find in this book have emerged as responses to previous Deaf discourses. Whatever our differences, we should rejoice in the fact that we have reached the stage in our histories where ideas of Deaf globalism—that is, that Deaf people share profound global commonalities—can both be celebrated and challenged. As I hope to show, the tensions between commonality and diversity stem from our multicultural status, which is inherent in our membership of SLPs, on both national and international levels.

Another important dimension of Deafhood theory lies in recognizing that Deaf cultures are minority cultures and in understanding how similar tensions can be found in other minority cultures and oppressed groups such as African American, Native American and other indigenous peoples, and diasporic communities. Evidence suggests that these tensions are an inescapable part of life for minority peoples and that internal conflicts are a direct consequence of the nature of oppression itself. Further, because these minority studies are fairly new academic disciplines, they have not yet progressed to the point where cross-minority study is a reality. This means that few people are able to see beyond their own situation to understand the parallels in their experiences and thus be in a better position to challenge oppression. In illustrating some of these parallels, I hope to make suggestions for the development of an overarching framework that can accommodate these different perspectives, take the heat out of some of the internal tensions found in Deaf communities, and help us all to envisage a global Deafhood that fully embraces and celebrates its diversity.

CELEBRATING DEAF COMMONALITIES

Let us begin by a brief celebration of some of our commonalities, particularly the skills required by Deaf people to manifest and develop the unique powers of International Sign (IS). In doing so we can appreciate Deaf ingenuity in developing these skills initially through interregional contact, as small communities made contact with others in the same country and adjusted to the fact that they used different signs (which we now call dialects). This pattern of development continues across the world today. We should celebrate how IS can now be used for academic and political conferences and how this uniquely flexible tool enables Deaf people from one country to be welcomed (in theory) into the lives of another culture in ways that most hearing people are unable to achieve. We should celebrate being able to say to young Deaf children and their hearing parents (at the present mainly in more wealthy countries, but as the century advances, we hope to others also): "There is a whole planet out there waiting for you when you grow up—and this is your birthright as a Deaf child."

There are also other domains we can examine in search of those commonalities. One is education. In most of the world's Deaf communities, the passionate desire to bring Deaf children together means that Deaf education is a major priority for

Deaf discourses across the world. But we can go further and examine how Deaf adults educate Deaf children in different countries. Indeed, the very first example of international Deaf contact recorded is the encounter between the French Deaf teacher Laurent Clerc and the English Deaf children at the London School (see Gulliver, this volume).

Research by myself (forthcoming) and others such as Goncalves (cf. Ladd and Goncalves 2011) and Kusters (2014) suggests that Deaf educators in the United Kingdom, United States, Brazil, and Belgium have developed remarkably similar Deafhood pedagogies, which utilize more than eighty different values, skills, and strategies across six key stages of Deaf children's development, based on a philosophy I term *cultural holism*. The key issue is that these pedagogies have been developed *with minimal contact between each country*. If similar pedagogies can be found in other countries, and that there has been minimal contact in those cases, we may be on the verge of being able to identify something quite remarkable—a global commonality in how we see ourselves and "perform" ourselves when we attempt to communicate our views of the world to the next generations.

In celebrating these and other Deaf qualities and achievements, and having only recently emerged from intense and extensive oralist oppression (which among numerous other negative effects has seriously damaged our self-image and confidence), we have understandably let our enthusiasm carry us further than we are capable of explaining when we express ideas or beliefs in DEAF-ALL-SAME. We urgently require sociological and cultural studies of every Deaf community in the world to understand what our commonalities and differences might be. We also require more studies of transnational Deaf contact, such as those collected for this book.

ESSENTIALISM, INTERSECTIONALITY, AND THE DEAFHOOD CONCEPT

One of the most important criticisms of Western-derived concepts such as the use of the d/D ascription, Deaf culture, and Deafhood is similar to that presented in other minority studies—the dangers of falling into the trap of "essentialism." Critics point out that a key factor of oppression was that the oppressed Other was largely undifferentiated, in other words that Black people, indigenous peoples, women, and so on were "all the same." As a consequence, perspectives that sought to identify commonalities, even if they were developed within oppressed groups, have risked being labelled *essentialist*.

Writers such as the African American feminist bell hooks (1981) challenged the way Black Studies was developing, noting that it was being developed primarily from the perspective of university-educated Black males and downplayed the perspectives of Black women and working-class and rural Black people. A parallel development can be found in India in the development of Subaltern Studies, which highlighted the important contributions made by grassroots Indian people to the decolonization process (Guha 1982). A similar challenge was issued to feminism and how its development was based on the ideas and values of white middle-class women (hooks 1981).

These challenges are important because they give voice to sectors of oppressed communities that were being in effect doubly oppressed—externally and internally.

In so doing they aided the construction of more accurate models of the cultural lives of those peoples. This work has in recent years led to the development of the term *intersectionality* as a tool to unpack the relationships between various sectors and identities within their communities.

Intersectionality emphasizes the fact that human beings have multiple identities, that some of these identities carry more social, cultural, and economic capital than others, and that less powerful identities are usually overlooked. Intersectionality theory also holds that the classical conceptualizations of oppression within society, such as racism, sexism, homophobia, transphobia, and belief-based bigotry, do not act independently of one another. Instead, these forms of oppression interrelate, creating a system of oppression that reflects the intersection of multiple forms of discrimination (Knudsen 2008, 61).

Intersectionality is a most welcome development, and it will be interesting to see how it is developed in future Deaf discourses in relation to the Deafhood concept. It is useful to remind ourselves that the Deafhood concept was designed to identify both Deaf commonalities and Deaf diversity. In my book (Ladd 2003) I sought, on the one hand, to identify UK Deaf cultural traditions and to locate values and beliefs that had been passed down through many generations of lives centered around the Deaf clubs. On the other hand, I also sought to identify areas of conflict within those cultures (because conflict observation is a good tool for bringing to the surface underlying cultural values and attitudes). I utilized Gramsci's analysis of class (1992) to describe "grassroots" Deaf people as "subalterns" and those who carried out the policies of the hearing professionals who controlled Deaf clubs as "elite subaltern," or members of the "comprador" class. In so doing, I explored how the sectors defined their "Deafhoods" differently, how these differences were reflected in the cultural values they each adopted, and how these related to the political situations in which UK Deaf culture was embedded. But above all, with the Deafhood concept I stressed the importance of understanding how these communities sought to maintain unity within diversity and which cultural values and beliefs underpinned those efforts. Further, the concept emphasized that similar dynamics played out in other Deaf communities around the world, even though their specific circumstances varied.

In prioritizing the search for overarching commonalities and cultural threads maintained down the generations, Deafhood theory has been criticized as essentialist and for "perpetuating binary opposition" (Fernandez and Myers 2010, 19). However, without identifying cultural traditions, it is impossible to evaluate Deaf cultural changes—one needs to understand the central threads around which a culture coheres. Thus I advocated "strategic essentialism" as a necessary first step for Deaf cultural studies, in much the same way that indigenous minorities stressed the importance of first gathering together their histories and cultural knowledge and later moving to relate these threads to changes that had been imposed on their cultures. Kusters and De Meulder (2013) use the term *open-ended essentialism* to help distinguish this from the forms of *close-ended essentialism* found in some Deaf cultural discourses.

So by attempting to identify global Deaf commonalities and global Deafhoods, we run the risk of being labelled essentialist. Yet many of us feel very deeply, at a gut level, that there is something powerful that occurs when those of us who have had the good fortune to belong to a Deaf community meet others across the world.

It cannot simply be dismissed by saying, "That's because you all understand each other's suffering, poor dears."

Romanticizing Deaf Globalism: Some Caveats

How should we then evaluate the inclination of large numbers of Deaf people to say DEAF-ALL-SAME? The romantic idea that when we meet another Deaf person we automatically engage in affirmative commonality can be challenged by considering certain Deaf situations. I remember my surprise on first arriving at Gallaudet in 1985 to find that most people looked at me oddly when I tried to greet them. After a while it became clear that being Deaf was taken for granted and that people behaved just as other humans do, forming groups and subgroups, and this was especially visible in the refectory and the student union building, where such groups sat at their own tables. Moreover, foreign Deaf students repeatedly stated that they felt excluded, and as a consequence formed their own social groups (see Ruiz et al., this volume). Similar situations have been reported by foreign Deaf people who have migrated to London.

Clearly there is a need for many more anthropological and sociological studies to explore the cultural dynamics that exist both within Deaf communities and in contact between different communities. We should also show greater respect for deaf communities in the Global South by researching how commonality-diversity tensions play out in different cultures (across class, gender, and religious lines, for example).

We require a greater understanding of the cultural dynamics within Deaf communities, and their shared values, beliefs, and norms, before we can interpret the positive valence given to transnational contact and the bond that is said to exist when Deaf individuals from different countries meet. Of course it is far too early to tell, and before we can respond to such questions about Deaf commonalities, we first need to consider relationships between Western Deaf communities and the rest of the world.

Western Deaf Relationships with the DeafWorld

As chapters in this book have shown, Western Deaf communities have a history of intervention in other Deaf cultures that while undoubtedly having had positive effects nevertheless also had important negative effects that we need to understand more clearly.

In 1990 I met Western hearing (but signing) persons working in a far Eastern country trying to encourage local Deaf people to promote and develop their own local sign language. They had become the subject of criticism from members of the World Federation of the Deaf (WFD) because "they were not Deaf." Western Deaf agencies then took over the project and appeared to be far more oppressive of the local Deaf people than the hearing people had been. Wrigley (1996, chapter 4) provides an extensive critique of these kinds of oppressive situations and even labels them "colonialist." Since then, the WFD has made great progress in involving non-Western countries as equal partners in the global Deaf project. However, many more studies are required to understand whether these interventions are based on false ideas of Deaf-sameness or whether they are simply reproducing Western colonialist attitudes.

Deafhood theory, in seeking to understand the effects of oppression on national Deaf communities, can also help us to understand how such ethnocentricity has developed alongside positive transnational Deaf bonds and how these might be related to ideas about global Deafhood. To do so, I utilize a key aspect of Deafhood theory, the concept of minority cultures.

DEAFHOOD, MINORITY CULTURES, AND MULTICULTURALISM

There has still been very little research on Deaf cultures, and consequently there is minimal reference to the other parts of our multicultural identities—the cultural information we have imbibed from the majority cultures we grew up in and how this has influenced our Deaf cultural values and beliefs. Although writers such as Mindess (2001) and Padden and Humphries (1988) have tried to advance our understanding by stressing, for example, that their work describes American Deaf culture, they have not attempted to extensively examine the American nature of that experience, and the same problem applies to discussion of the rest of the world's Deaf cultures. The cultural significance of our membership of those majority cultures is therefore denied or downplayed, and the consequences of this for international Deaf contact are thereby also often ignored.

So we have first to accept the existence of a crucial difference between people who are enculturated into a single majority culture and those who are members of minority cultures. The former are only required to understand one culture; the latter are required to understand both that culture and the culture of their own minority. If the two cultures are unequal in power and "cultural capital," minority culture members face pressures and struggles that the majority never have to experience. This will be explored in greater depth later.

We as Deaf people therefore have to accept that our thoughts and beliefs are also shaped by our being American, English, Thai, Egyptian, Nepalese, Indian, Columbian, and so on.[2] This requires us to understand what it is that we have imbibed, which is a huge task even for hearing people, whose conscious understanding of their own culture is so minimal and yet who still expect us to understand and explain our Deaf cultures to them. People are beginning to realize that the best way to begin to understand their own culture is to have meaningful contact with other cultures. Even so, there are few academic courses that focus on one of the most important challenges facing humanity in the twenty-first century. It can be argued that cultural study poses a threat to the ruling sectors of societies because it automatically questions the norms and values they have established in order to unify their country under their system of rule—and this applies not only in Europe and America, but in the rest of the world also.[3]

---

[2] Indeed we need to go further than this, and understand, for example that we are also enculturated by the region of the country we come from and majority societies' attitudes to gender, class, and so on. This is beyond the scope of this chapter.

[3] In this respect we should note that anthropology historically played a key role in the colonization process by "proving" the superiority of Western cultures while actually shying away from examining them.

The positive news, the potential gain for us in being forced to explain ourselves to hearing people, is that this challenge has been issued during an era of globalization when we are finally able to have frequent contact with other Deaf cultures. Because of the unique plasticity of International Sign, in theory we are able to make deeper and more meaningful contact with those cultures and thus make swifter progress in drawing the kind of comparisons that the world needs.

Minority Cultures and Bipolar Pressures

Before tackling international dimensions we need to begin in a single country, with some simple examples from the United States. In selecting these examples, no criticism of the United States is intended—Deaf racism in Europe has its own sad stories to tell—but rather that American history offers more clear-cut examples that help us grasp the points being made.

For 150 years, white American Deaf citizens were faced in effect with the following questions: When you look at African American and Native American Deaf people, do you see them through American eyes or Deaf eyes? Do you see the commonalities or the differences? Do you comply with the views of the hearing white majority or do you resist them? If the answer had been "Deaf eyes," then commonality would have been sought and fought for. As is now known, the answer was in fact the former: Gallaudet refused to accept Deaf students from those minorities until the 1950s, and, more pertinently, they were excluded from the National Association of the Deaf until the mid-1960s. Similar patterns of Deaf racism can be found all over the world but have rarely been researched. Conversely, informal Deaf discourses suggest that in some countries at some time periods "Deaf eyes" did prevail to some extent, notably in Northern Ireland during the "Troubles" and in the Balkans during the recent conflict. I am sure we would all welcome learning of other examples. But we should also be careful not to fall into the trap of thinking that compliance and resistance are the only possible responses to oppression. Responses can operate along a continuum and involve a huge number of individual and collective situations, decisions, and strategies.

Another dimension of influence that we need to be aware of is the extent to which some nations enculturate their children more overtly (as in Japan and the United States, and other countries with highly nationalistic cultures, and in countries that strictly segregate Deaf children and adults by gender). Similarly we need to understand that other cultures may claim to be less prescriptive, more laissez faire, in their cultural attitudes, but that gives us greater difficulties in identifying their influence on their Deaf communities, precisely because it is less overt and therefore harder to identify.

Deafhood theory stresses that an understanding of all these issues is crucial to our development and that each Deaf person will define and explain their deafness and Deafhood in a multiplicity of ways. At the same time, it stresses the importance of understanding how we have been damaged by those majority cultures, not only as individuals but as communities, and to strive to recognize our commonalities and our unique biological qualities. Understanding ourselves in this way, as conveyed in Deafhood courses, has initially focused on the national level. But the international dimension has been present as well, since the IS and Deaf transnationalism have been significant for our peoples since the nineteenth century (see Gulliver, this volume), and thus Deafhood theory asks us to view and envision the entire globe through those Deaf eyes.

Although responses to oppression operate along a continuum, minority cultures are nevertheless continually forced into "double-bind" patterns (cf. Ladd 2003), where oppression creates numerous situations where we must choose between two options or paths, and no matter which we choose, we lose out in a significant way. These are also termed "no win" or "lose-lose" situations. As the Afro-Caribbean writer Pryce (1979) stresses, this means that minority cultural lives are conducted under conditions of endless pressure, wherein many situations and decision-making processes become highly volatile, resulting in "horizontal violence" that fails to recognize that these situations were created by oppression itself.

DOUBLE-BIND DILEMMAS

Classic examples from minority studies include Willis's (1977) study of white working-class "lads," who, in resisting the middle-class values of education to retain their working-class cultural status, fulfill the prophecies of low expectations in the job market. African American teenagers, especially males, who focus on their studies are accused of being "white" and face potential rejection from their peers if they continue to do so (Cook and Ludwig 1998). This kind of pejorative labelling, using terms such as "Uncle Tom," "Oreo" (Black on the outside, white on the inside), and, in Native American communities, "Apple" (red on the outside, white on the inside), is widespread and indicates the scale of double-bind dilemmas for some minorities. Malcolm et al. (1976) also describe how the intersections of race and gender can force minority women to choose between the competing pressures of two kinds of oppression.

Double binds within Deaf communities include the use of the sign THINK-HEARING in the USA, the tensions which exist around Deaf-hearing friendship and marriage, the dilemma of placing one's child in a Deaf school of lower educational attainment versus a culturally isolated "better" education in mainstream schools, and many more. In Western countries with indigenous populations, the double-bind dilemma crosses racial boundaries. In Alaska, for instance, an Inuit Deaf child may be faced with the choice of remaining within their own culture and being isolated there because of communication issues, or of moving to a white Deaf school elsewhere in the USA and losing touch with their own cultural identity, without even the guarantee of acceptance by the Deaf community. These are just some of the more obvious examples of double binds. The more we examine Deaf communities, the more cases we find.

DEAF AFRICAN AMERICAN DOUBLE-BIND SITUATIONS

As with the Alaskan example, Deaf people who are themselves members of cultural minorities experience especially complex sets of situations. The African American situation reveals ongoing tensions in relation to primary allegiances, as expressed in the YOU FIRST WHICH? debates that arose during the Deaf Resurgence of the 1980s. Once African American Deaf people began to finally take their places within US society, many were dismayed and even angered to be asked that particular question by white Deaf people, not least because the ancestors of those same people had clearly prioritized "white" above "Deaf." Further, as Aramburo (1992) and other studies have shown, many felt that being Black was their primary identity, in part because their blackness was visible, thus exposing them to daily oppression as African Americans.

There is not space here to unpack the numerous ramifications and subtleties of these double binds, but one story related to me by an African American Deaf person working at Gallaudet is particularly helpful in understanding the complexity of these issues. Arriving late to a meeting on campus, she took the only available seat next to a white Deaf person and noted how, as so often before, the white person moved her chair slightly away from her. At the appropriate moment in the meeting, she stood up and signed her comments. The white Deaf person's response was "Oh, you're Deaf," signed in such a way as to mean "That's alright then." Her unspoken reply was "Too late, missy, you've given yourself away."

This example is complex because although it might suggest that the white person's expression of Deaf commonality was laudable, the rejection of her colleague's Black identity and by implication her Black family members and friends, both Deaf and hearing, was nevertheless very hurtful. As our conversation continued she pointed out to me another dimension of Black-Deaf tension: the Deaf nationalist rejection of music and how this clashed with many Southern Black Deaf people's love of music, which is part of their own cultural heritage.

There is another complex intersectional dimension to these tensions: it is said that African Americans from the northern states who attended mixed residential schools often see their primary identity as Deaf, not least because they were not able to communicate with their families and access their cultural heritage. In turn, some of these people have experienced criticism from other hearing (and Deaf) African Americans for "not being Black enough."

Similar internal and external conflicts can be found in the United Kingdom among Asian and Afro-Caribbean Deaf people, and across the world. In India, for example, Deaf intersectionalities between identities situated in religion, caste, language, and gender are especially complex, and doubtless there are many more examples waiting to be formally identified.

These kind of double-bind situations are therefore particularly challenging for "minorities within minorities," who are already suffering double oppression, and one of the most important lessons we can learn from these examples is that there are no easy solutions to be had. Deafhood theory, by highlighting the need to study and learn from other minority cultural experiences, thus helps us to appreciate these kinds of tensions between commonality and diversity and serves as an all-embracing lens that can aid the process of understanding and reconciliation.

Exploring and Manifesting Deaf Globalism

Having briefly reviewed Deaf differences and diversity, we return to Deaf commonalities. Almost all Deaf communities are highly concerned with developing unity, which is why internal division and dissent can be so painful (cf. Stein and Rashid, both in this volume). This applies also to other minority cultures. These pressures to achieve unity are increased by questions around minority representation. In majority cultures it is virtually a truism that countries are politically divided, and such divisions can often be close to 50:50 in terms of "left"/"right" voting. Yet, these same societies demand of minorities that they operate differently from these human norms and speak with a single voice. The pressures of these demands are one of the reasons that disagreements within minorities become so heated and often discouraged.

It is thus all the more remarkable that over the past sixty years, the WFD has managed to develop policies endorsed by its 132 member countries and eight regional secretariats, all while operating on a shoestring budget. One should also note the importance of International Sign in making these developments possible (although see Haualand et al. and Green, both in this volume), while acknowledging that important debates continue to take place around whether IS's vocabulary is "too Western." Closer study of WFD policies would enable us to identify numerous global Deaf commonalities, chief among which is the belief in the need to improve the quality of life for every Deaf person in the world. To locate other commonalities, one can examine some of the processes by which international Deaf decision making is conducted, in light of what we have learned about multicultural identity and intersectionality. At the global level, this plays out in terms of national characteristics and how they are accommodated, or sublimated to, a sense of Deaf globalism.

To begin with a more light-hearted example, one can note the culture shock experienced by a Deaf American running a course in Italy and finding that Italian culture's idea of timekeeping was very different from his own.[4] Another example is often quoted by North European Deaf, who become aware of the extent to which their hearing cultures prioritize privacy when encountering Latin American and other Deaf countries, who become offended when the former request "time out."[5]

Discussions with UK Deaf colleagues illustrated the challenges of organizing at a pan-European level. These organizational differences spanned a formal-informal range from Southern to Northern Europe, exhibiting the same cultural differences as experienced by hearing people from those countries. My colleagues described how these difficulties took some time to overcome and how the main strategy by which they eventually attained unity was to become aware of the extent that their hearing cultural identities were influencing their approach to the work, and from there work toward "Deaf ways" of resolving these challenges. They needed constant reference to their shared identity and sharpen their focus on improving the quality of life for their Deaf constituents back home. Investigating these kinds of dynamics seems to be crucial in understanding how Deaf globalism can be better understood.

---

[4] These kinds of cultural clashes have been noted in other minority cultures, for example, when African Americans have traveled to Africa expecting to find a form of brother/sisterhood, only to be brought up short by the limitations of their own cultural conditioning as Americans.

[5] Since one difference between Western Deaf and hearing families that is often remarked on is the extent to which the former require less "time out" than the latter, it is instructive to note that this example also applies to their own Latin-American experiences, albeit on a lesser scale than for those from hearing families.

Deafhood theory suggests that these kinds of problem-solving strategies can be seen as attempts to refer to a sense of "global Deafhood"—that is, prioritizing Deaf kinship over hearing cultural influences. But many more studies of the kind found in this book are required to unpack this further. For now, it seems appropriate to end with a brief examination of some further aspects of international Deaf experiences.

When we meet Deaf people from a country whose sign language we do not know, we cannot fall back on the spoken or written language of our countries of origin, which can be said to reside to some extent in our "hearing selves." Instead, we have to make a conscious effort to move into a deeper Deaf self, one in which visuality is key.

As Crasborn and Hiddinga (this volume) have discussed, this process is guided by what we might call a "deep structure" of Deafhood—first the linguistic commonalities that underpin most of the world's sign languages: signing space, directionality, and facial expression. These, together with the temporary borrowing of signs from each other's vocabularies (itself a marker of cross-national respect), the use of mime, and the spontaneous creation of more visual signs, are augmented by the use of visual Deaf humor, underpinned by the potential sense of comradeship that arises from shared oppression.

To attend international Deaf gatherings of several thousand people and experience the processes that enable thousands of new contacts and innumerable friendships to be made (see Haualand et al., this volume) is to experience an enlarged sense of global Deaf selfhood. The contrast between the size of this self and the minimal, atomistic hearing-impaired selves propagated by medical model adherents is truly profound, and one wishes that the latter could be compelled to witness such spectacles.

Of course, many Deaf people have not yet had the opportunity to experience en masse cross-national contact, and as Green (this volume) has shown, there are many variables at play in cross-national contact that must make us wary of romanticizing these experiences. However, I would like to flag one set of dynamics that deserves further exploration. I have repeatedly been told by informants that some countries (such as the United Kingdom, USA, and Japan) appear to be less willing to "enlarge" their Deaf selves in this way—that in international gatherings Deaf people from these countries tend to stick together and to some extent avoid extensive contact with other countries. As the emerging expression has it—they seem more American/British than Deaf. I am not criticizing these situations, but merely noting how the plurality of our identities still requires more sophisticated framing. One can, for example, hypothesize that Deaf Americans' and Deaf Britons' concept of their Deafhood places minimal emphasis on internationalism. By contrast, as implied in the quote above, certain other countries may be experiencing their Deafhood as global in aspiration.

Deafhood theory points out that these different perspectives and dualities, as with the double binds, cannot be easily resolved. However, at the end of the day, it suggests that global Deafhood might be best framed as valorizing *the process of searching for global Deaf commonalities while identifying and respecting Deaf diversity* and invites us all to walk hand in hand through the coming century to explore all these dimensions of our remarkable existence.

REFERENCES

Aramburo, A. 1992. "Sociolinguistic Aspects of the Black Deaf Community." In *Conference Proceedings: Empowerment and Black Deaf Persons.* Washington, DC: Gallaudet University.

Batterbury, S. C. E., P. Ladd, and M. Gulliver. 2007. "Sign Language Peoples as Indigenous Minorities: Implications for Research and Policy."*Environment and Planning A* 39 (12): 2899–915.

Cook, P. J., and J. Ludwig. 1998. "The Burden of 'Acting White': Do Black Adolescents Disparage Academic Achievement?" In *The Black-White Test Score Gap,* 375–400. Washington, DC: Brookings Institution Press.

Fernandez, J., and S. Myers. 2010. "Inclusive Deaf Studies: Barriers and Pathways."*Journal of Deaf Studies and Deaf Education* 15 (1): 17–29.

Gramsci, A. 1992. *Prison Notebooks.* New York: Columbia University Press.

Guha, R. 1982. "On Some Aspects of the Historiography of Colonial India." In *Subaltern Studies I,* edited by R. Guha. Delhi, India: Oxford University Press.

hooks, b. 1981. *Ain't I a Woman? Black Women and Feminism.* Boston: South End Press.

Jokinen, M. 2001. "'The Sign Language Person': A Term to Describe Us and Our Future More Clearly?" In *Looking Forward: EUD in the Third Millenium: The Deaf Citizen in the Twenty-First Century: Proceedings of a Conference to Celebrate Fifteen Years of the European Union of the Deaf,* edited by L. Leeson, 50–63. London: Douglas McLean.

Knudsen, S. V. 2008. "Intersectionality: A Theoretical Inspiration in the Analysis of Minority Cultures and Identities in Textbooks." In *Caught in the Web or Lost in the Textbook?* edited by B. Aamotsbakken, M. Horsley, and S. V. Knudsen, 53, 61–76. Jouve, France: IARTEM.

Kusters, M. 2014. "Dove leerkrachten als motor voor verandering? Een etnografisch onderzoek naar de beleving van dove leerkrachten in Vlaanderen." MA thesis, KULeuven.

Kusters, A., and M. De Meulder. 2013. "Understanding Deafhood: In Search of Its Meanings."*American Annals of the Deaf* 258 (5): 428–38.

Ladd, P. 2003. *Understanding Deaf Culture: In Search of Deafhood.* Clevedon, UK: Multilingual Matters.

Ladd, P., and J. Goncalves. 2011. *Culturas surdas eo desenvolvimento de pedagogias surdas: Cultura Surda na Contemporaneidade: negociações, intercorrências e provocações,* 295–329. Canoas: ULBRA.

Malcom, S. M., P. Q. Hall, and J. W. Brown. 1976. *The Double Bind: The Price of Being a Minority Woman in Science.* Washington, DC: American Association for the Advancement of Science.

Mindess, A. 2001. *Reading between the Signs: Intercultural Communication for Sign Language Interpreters.* Yarmouth, ME: Intercultural Press.

Padden, C., and T. Humphries. 1988. *Deaf in America: Voices from a Culture.* Cambridge, MA: Harvard University Press.

Pryce, K. 1979. *Endless Pressure: A Study of West Indian Lifestyles in Britain.* Harmondsworth, UK: Penguin.

Willis, P. E. 1977. *Learning to Labor: How Working Class Kids Get Working Class Jobs.* New York: Columbia University Press.

Wrigley, O. 1996. *The Politics of Deafness.* Washington DC : Gallaudet University Press.

Young, K. 2012. *The Grey Album: On the Blackness of Blackness.* Minneapolis, MN: Grey Wolf Press.

Afterword:
It's a Small World?

Michele Friedner and Annelies Kusters

Paddy Ladd, who wrote the last chapter of this book, jokingly chided us for using the phrase "it's a small world" in our title, as he argued that the DEAF-WORLD is actually very big, in that deaf people actively seek to make connections with diverse deaf people around the world. Rather than judging whether the DEAF-WORLD is small or big, we see the idea of "it's a small world" as being productive to think with but we do want to problematize the idea of a *singular* DEAF-WORLD. The chapters in this book have shown that deaf worlds can be experienced as big (expansive, and crossing spaces) precisely because they are experienced as small (connected) at the same time.

When we think of the phrase "it's a small world," it is difficult (for some of us) not to think about the song and Walt Disney ride with the same name. Originally designed for the 1964 New York World's Fair UNICEF pavilion, the ride features dancing dolls dressed in brightly colored "native" costumes singing, "It's a small world after all" in different languages. The installation and ride are now main features at Walt Disney parks around the world. The ride gives visitors the experience of moving through the countries of the world, experiencing the vastness of the world's cultures, while at the same time hearing the same song repeatedly in different languages. The ride promotes the message that there is sameness across difference.

Perhaps in the spirit of the Disney experience, in 2011 Joel Barish of DeafNation made a video called "We Are Deaf," featuring deaf people from around the world signing "I am deaf."[1] The video featured deaf people, many of them wearing "native" dress standing amidst iconic architecture or natural features in their countries, signing "I am deaf" in their national sign languages or International Sign. A dizzying array of deaf people populate the video, their signs different but not so different as to be incommensurable or incomprehensible. After all, the people in the video are only signing "I am deaf." The video went viral

---

[1] See https://www.youtube.com/watch?v=BfiIMGDkzHg

and was enthusiastically received in deaf worlds, specifically those with access to social media. Perhaps the video was embraced so easily because it affirmed deaf peoples' experience of belonging to an international community, and at the same time diversity was presented in a colorful, attractive, and "authentic" way. Those watching it could understand the signs and feel connected. In the space created in and through the video, the simple words "I am deaf" offered entry into a deaf small world.

However, it is interesting to consider what might have happened if instead of or in addition to signing "I am deaf," those on the screen signed something else too. What if a man from Cambodia talked about what happened to his family under the Khmer Rouge? What if a woman from Uruguay talked about her country's desire to remain independent from world superpowers? What if a deaf Nigerian woman had talked about the complicated gender politics in her country? And what if they had discussed these things in their national sign languages? These conversation topics would have shown how deaf people are often embedded in local and national contexts and how deaf people around the world often have specific concerns and aspirations. It is interesting to consider what kinds of comprehension and commensuration might have taken place. Of course, it matters whether those viewing the video (or engaging in encounters) are willing to engage and attempt to understand, and it also matters if there are shared contextual factors as well as shared language repertoires.

Our point is that once we move beyond "I am deaf" *as a starting point*, it is possible that significant differences will emerge. More important, our argument is that we—academics and members of deaf worlds—must move beyond "I am deaf" *as an end point* and allow the ways that deaf people are different to emerge. Similarly, we need to be aware of how differences play a role in establishing what kinds of encounters and relationships are possible. We hope this book has made a needed intervention into providing a new lens as well as a new conceptual and analytical vocabulary for people who are both experiencing and analyzing international deaf encounters. But what to do with the statement "It's a small world?" Perhaps it is a hopeful statement in the same way that DEAF-SAME is a hopeful claim. We could write another song or coin another phrase such as "it's both a small and big world," but that would not be as catchy or enticing as "It's a small world."

Contributors

'Gbenga Aina is a deaf Nigerian lawyer and director of the Office of Diversity and Equity for Students at Gallaudet University with oversight of the Keeping the Promise black and Latino student retention program, LGBTQA Resource Center, and multicultural student programs.

Arlinda S. Boland is a deaf American woman and a graduate of Gallaudet University's master's program in international development. Her thesis focused on the accessibility of HIV/AIDS services to deaf people in the Kwa-Zulu Natal region, South Africa. She is currently working as a development officer in Cambodia.

Jan-Kåre Breivik is professor of community work at Bergen University College. He is a hearing Norwegian anthropologist writing about minority issues such as deafness, homelessness, disability, ethnicity, and gender.

Meredith Burke is a DeafDisabled woman from the United States who received her master's degree in deaf studies with a concentration in cultural studies from Gallaudet University. She currently teaches disability studies as a contract instructor at Gallaudet University.

Noppawan Chainarong is a deaf woman from Bangkok, Thailand, who received her master's degree in deaf studies with a concentration in cultural studies from Gallaudet University. She currently works at the English Language Institute, Office of the Basic Education Commission, Ministry of Education, Thailand.

Vee Yee Chong is a deaf Chinese man from Malaysia who received his master's degree in deaf studies with a concentration in cultural studies from Gallaudet University. As a PhD student in social science at the University of Malaya, Kuala Lumpur, his current research focuses on deaf identity and culture.

Audrey C. Cooper is a lecturer in the Department of Anthropology at American University, Washington, DC. She is a hearing anthropologist from the United States whose research focuses on deaf education and deaf social change movements in Việt Nam.

Onno Crasborn is an associate professor of linguistics at Radboud University, Nijmegen, the Netherlands. He is a hearing Dutch linguist who has been working on the linguistics of the Sign Language of the Netherlands since 1995.

Jess Cuculick is an assistant professor in the Liberal Studies Department at Rochester Institute of Technology in Rochester, New York. She is a deaf American who teaches sociology. Her research focuses on social media, deaf education, and public health.

Maartje De Meulder is a Belgian deaf PhD researcher at the University of Jyväskylä in Finland. Her current research mainly focuses on the development of sign language recognition legislation in Finland and Scotland.

Steven D. Emery is a deaf political activist who has undertaken several work roles with the UK Deaf community, including development work, counseling, advice work and academic research. His PhD thesis was on citizenship and the deaf community and he has also undertaken research around genetics and group rights.

Michele Friedner is an assistant professor of health and rehabilitation sciences at Stony Brook University. She is a deaf American medical anthropologist who studies deaf peoples' social, moral, political, and economic practices in urban India.

E. Mara Green is a postdoctoral researcher at the University of California San Diego. She is a hearing American linguistic anthropologist who has conducted long-term research in Nepal with deaf signers.

Mike Gulliver is currently a research associate in religion and Deaf history at the University of Bristol. He is a hearing British historian and geographer whose historical research focuses on "Deaf space" in France and the United Kingdom.

Hilde Haualand is a Norwegian deaf social anthropologist who focuses on disability and Deaf social and cultural themes. She is currently a postdoctoral researcher at the Faculty of Teacher and Interpreter Education at Sør-Trøndelag University College.

Anja Hiddinga is an assistant professor at the Department of Social and Behavioral Sciences at the University of Amsterdam in the Netherlands. She is a hearing social scientist interested in the sociology and anthropology of health, disease, normality, and disability.

Deniz İlkbaşaran is a hearing Turkish scholar who studies the cultural heritage and communicative practices of deaf people in Turkey and designs multilingual interactive learning environments for deaf people.

Christopher A. N. Kurz is a Deaf associate professor at Rochester Institute of Technology in Rochester, New York. His current research focuses on deaf studies, mathematics and science education, and technology in education.

Annelies Kusters is a postdoctoral researcher at the Max Planck Institute for the Study of Religious and Ethnic Diversity in Göttingen, Germany. She is a Belgian deaf ethnographer whose interests are deaf studies, anthropology, human geography, and sociolinguistics. She has conducted research in Surinam, Ghana, and India.

Paddy Ladd is a former reader at the (now defunct) Centre for Deaf Studies, Bristol, England. He coined the "Deafhood" concept and in his current writing he focuses on Deafhood pedagogies.

Elizabeth M. Lockwood is CBM's representative at the United Nations. She is a hearing American ethnographer who is interested in deaf peoples' social and political movements.

Philippa Merricks, a British deaf woman, currently works for Deafway, a UK-based deaf organization with projects in the United Kingdom, Nepal, Uganda, and the Philippines, and has worked in various international deaf events and organizations including the European Union of the Deaf Youth.

Rezenet Tsegay Moges is an archaeological graphics director at SRS Inc. She is a Deaf Eritrean-American linguistic anthropologist who focused on Eritrean Sign Language for her master's degree in anthropology.

Erin Moriarty Harrelson is a deaf researcher from the United States and a PhD candidate in the Department of Anthropology at American University. She recently returned from fieldwork in Cambodia where she was the 2014–2015 Fulbright-National Geographic Digital Storytelling Fellow. Her research interests include Deaf subjectivities, tourism, international development projects, and NGOs.

Khadijat Rashid is a professor in the business and international development programs at Gallaudet University. She is a deaf American of Nigerian origin who has worked with development projects for the deaf communities in South Africa, Nigeria, Ghana, and Thailand.

Elena Ruiz-Williams is a multiracial/multiethnic Xicanx Deaf teacher, writer, and activist in the United States. She received a master's degree in Deaf cultural studies from Gallaudet University.

Pierre Schmitt is a PhD candidate in social anthropology and ethnology at the School for Advanced Studies in Social Sciences (EHESS) in Paris. He is a hearing French anthropologist whose work focuses on sign language artistic practices and networks at local and international levels.

Per Koren Solvang is a Norwegian hearing sociologist and disability studies scholar. He is currently professor of rehabilitation at Oslo and Akershus University College of Applied Sciences.

Michael Steven Stein is a deaf American attorney and partner with the firm Stein & Vargas, LLP, a law firm that advocates for the rights of people with disabilities. He is also executive director of Deaf We Can, a 501(c)(3) organization that helps deaf people advocate for their own legal rights.

Outi Toura-Jensen, a deaf Finnish woman with a master's degree in education, teaches in the Denmark-based Frontrunners program, an international deaf education program.

Kirk VanGilder is an assistant professor of religion at Gallaudet University. He is a Deaf American theologian whose research draws upon experiences in short-term missions with Deaf people in Zimbabwe, Kenya, and Turkey.

Filip Verhelst, a deaf Belgian man, teaches in the Denmark-based Frontrunners program, an international education program.

Ole Vestergaard, a deaf Danish man, teaches in the Denmark-based Frontrunners program.

Amy T. Wilson is a professor in the Department of Education at Gallaudet University. She developed Gallaudet's master's degree program in international development and is its program director. She is a hearing American researcher studying how to improve development assistance to Deaf communities in economically poor countries. As of November 1st, 2015, she will be leaving Gallaudet to become the director of international programs for deaf projects in economically poor countries with the Mill Neck Foundation.

Rowena E. Winiarczyk, a Canadian deaf woman, is a graduate of Gallaudet University's master's program in international development. She coordinates the research and global projects at Gallaudet University's Office of Research Support and International Affairs and has international development experience in Panama, Slovakia, Chile, Argentina, Malaysia, and Việt Nam.

Mark Zaurov is a Russian-born Israeli German Deaf Jew. Currently, he is a PhD candidate at the University of Hamburg. His scope of research includes the Deaf Holocaust and Deaf Jews in the arts, sciences, and politics.

Index

Figures, notes, and tables are indicated by "f," "n," and "t" following the page numbers.